KU-572-916

The New Small Business Guide

THE
NEW SMALL BUSINESS
GUIDE

COLIN BARROW

BBC Books

First published in conjunction with the BBC Television series
Business Club which was produced by John Twitchin.

The author would like to thank the National Westminster Bank
for permission to reproduce their business checklist; Chris Miller
for the use of her local authority survey data; and Derry Young
for assistance with researching, and with collating and typing up
the manuscript.

Cover illustration: John Montgomery

Published by BBC Books,
A division of BBC Enterprises Ltd
Woodlands, 80 Wood Lane, London W12 0TT

First published 1982
Second edition 1984; third edition 1989

© Colin Barrow 1982, 1984, 1989

ISBN 0 563 21476 7

Typeset in 10/11 pt Century Schoolbook
by Ace Filmsetting Ltd, Frome, Somerset

Printed and bound in Great Britain by
Redwood Burn Ltd, Trowbridge, Wiltshire

Cover printed by Fletchers of Norwich

CONTENTS

SECTION 8   Training for Business   279

THE NEED FOR INFORMATION

Starting a new business is no longer a spectator sport. Nearly three million people are now working for themselves, with a record 200,000 new recruits in 1988. But to launch a small business or expand an existing one successfully is not a simple task. Good ideas, hard work, enthusiasm, skills and knowledge about your product and how to make it, though essential, are not enough. Evidence for this is the substantial volume of business failures and liquidations. In 1982, when the first edition of this guide was published, firms were folding at a record rate and that upward trend has continued largely uninterrupted. Various estimates put the number of business 'deaths' last year at around 180,000, with most of the failures occurring within the first few years. These facts have made it increasingly clear that small businesses need special help, particularly in their formative period. For example, owners and managers often need help in acquiring business skills in such areas as basic book-keeping and accounting. Most failing businesses simply do not know their financial position. The order book is very often full when the cash runs out. Then they need information with which to make realistic market assessments of the size and possibilities of their chosen market. Over-optimism about the size and ease with which a market can be reached is an all too common mistake.

Owners and managers also need to know what sorts of finance are available and how to put themselves in the best possible position to raise it. Surprisingly, there is no shortage of funds. Problems lie, rather, in the business proposition itself, or, more often, in the way in which the proposition is made to the financier. This calls for a 'business plan', a statement of business purpose, with the consequences spelt out in financial terms. For example, you must describe what you want your business to do, who its customers will be, how much they will spend, who will supply you, how much their supplies will cost. Then you must translate those plans and projections into cash; how much your business will need, how much you already have; how much you expect 'outsiders' to put in. For most people this calls for new knowledge. They have never prepared a business plan before, and they do not know how to start. Very often the same is true of the bank manager they are talking to, so they too may need help or education in this important area.

This plan will also help them to escape the 'pneumonia' of small businesses – underestimation of the amount of start-up capital they will need. It is difficult, if not impossible, to go back to a bank and ask for another 30% of funding six months after opening the doors, and retain any credibility at all. And yet this is what happens. New businesses consistently underestimate how much they will need to finance growth. Both end up struggling where they need not have struggled, or failing where there was no 'market' reason for failure. Inventors and technologists have special problems of communication and security when they try to translate their ideas into businesses. All too often their inventions have been left for other countries to exploit, or else they feel unhappy about discussing ideas, believing that a patent is their only protection. But more often than not they simply do not know who to talk to, little realising that sophisticated help is often close at hand. Thus a path from the laboratory to the marketplace has to be illuminated so that small firms and inventors can see a clear route. New technologies have to be made available to new business. The microcomputer that has revolutionised big business has now begun to knock on the doors of smaller businesses. For this reason these firms have to know how to exploit this technology and so remain competitive – or they may join the ranks of the failures.

New and revived business opportunities are springing up to meet the needs and aspirations of would-be 'entrepreneurs'. Franchising, workers' co-operatives and management buy-outs are just three such areas. These have grown from relative obscurity in the late 1970s to being major business opportunities in the 1980s and 1990s. Grants and incentives to start up in rural areas, or in declining city areas are also a new feature of the small business scene.

There is inevitably a spate of paperwork, red tape and legislation surrounding every business venture. The registrations for VAT, pensions for the self-employed and employees' rights very often deter people either from launching into business or expanding in it. They believe, incorrectly, that it is possible to stand still and survive. They also over-estimate the problems and under-estimate the skills of the army of inexpensive professional advisers on hand to educate the novice.

All this implies that in order to keep out of the failure statistics it is vital for the owner or manager of a new or small business to be better informed.

There are now thousands of organisations and even more publications that can provide the much-needed information for small business. Many of these organisations have only recently come into being. For example in 1979 there were only six active enterprise agencies, in 1982 there were about 100, in 1984 200, and this edition lists nearly 300. There has been a parallel growth in other organisations, some shaping their policies to recognise the needs of small ventures, and others being wholly new activities. So 'entrepreneurs' have plenty of help to turn to and evidence is beginning to emerge that those that take this advice improve their chances of survival significantly. They very often do not know where that help is, or just how much it can do for them. This book is a guide to these organisations and their services, and the important directories, books and periodicals that will provide up-to-date information on each main topic. Enough information is generally included to allow a choice of service, organisation, or of publications to find and read. The decision to include or exclude an entry is based on two criteria. Does the organisation (or directory) provide either a service or information of specific help to a new or small business? Would the entry simply extend the reader's choice without necessarily extending the possible reward?

This is a reference book and is not intended to be read in its entirety. The reader will need to use the contents page to focus attention on the areas of greatest interest (or importance) to him or her. The index lists organisations, books and publications and the topics referred to in the main text, complementing the contents page and extending the cross referencing provided in the text. The glossary explains any technical words in the text.

Colin Barrow
January 1989

SOURCES OF DIRECT HELP AND ADVICE

Each year over 600,000 people used the services of a small business advisory organisation. Most were simple telephone enquiries but others involved face to face counselling sessions – perhaps to help raise money or to cope with an in-depth tax problem. There are now several hundrd organisations specifically concerned with providing help, advice and resources (including finance) for small businesses and those starting them. For the most part, these services are provided free or at a very low cost. In order to give a better understanding of their nature and purpose it will help to look at them in six groups: National Agencies, Local Enterprise Agencies, Local Councils, Property Services, Enterprise Zones and Business Associations.

NATIONAL AGENCIES

Although all the agencies and advisory services have their roots in the local community, the direct initiative for starting them often came from a central body. These bodies are in the forefront of these initiatives.

Small Firms Service

This service, which is provided by the Department of Employment, is an information and counselling service to help owners and managers of small businesses with their plans and problems. It is also an advisory service to those thinking of starting their own business. The service operates through a nationwide network of 13 Small Firms Centres backed up by over 200 Area Counselling Offices throughout Great Britain.

The service can help with almost any type of business enquiry and will provide information on such topics as raising finance, Government grants, sources of supply, industrial training, exporting, planning, industrial relations, new technology and marketing. It can also put you in touch with the right people in Government departments, local authorities, chambers of commerce, the professions or any other body that can help in solving your problems. As well as answering enquiries over the telephone the Small Firms Centre can arrange for a meeting with a Small Firms Business Counsellor who is himself an experienced businessman and who can offer impartial and confidential advice and guidance. Such meetings can either be at a local area counselling office or at the client's own premises. However, the decisions you make on the basis of the advice given are your responsibility and yours alone. The information service is free. For counselling, the first three sessions are free; if further counselling is required a modest charge of about £30.00 is made for the fourth and subsequent sessions. To contact your regional Small Firms Centre dial 100 and ask the operator for Freefone Enterprise, or you can telephone direct or walk in and talk to them.

Small Firms Centres
Birmingham: 9th Floor, Alpha Tower, Suffolk Street, Queensway, Birmingham B1 1TT (021 643 3844)
Bristol: 6th Floor, The Pithay, Bristol BS1 2NB (0272 294546)
Cambridge: Carlyle House, Carlyle Road, Cambridge CB4 3DN (0223 63312)
Cardiff: 16 St David's House, Wood Street, Cardiff CF1 1ER (0222 396116)
Glasgow: 120 Bothwell Street, Glasgow G2 6NR (041 248 6014)
Leeds: 1 Park Row, City Square, Leeds LS1 5NR (0532 445151)
Liverpool: Graeme House, Derby Square, Liverpool L2 7UJ (051 236 5756)
London: Ebury Bridge House, 2–18 Ebury Bridge Road, London SW1W 8QD (01 730 8451)
Manchester: 26/28 Deansgate, Manchester M3 1RH (061 832 5282)
Newcastle: 15th Floor, Cale Cross House, 156 Pilgrim Street, Newcastle-upon-Tyne NE1 6PZ (091 232 5353)
Nottingham:Severns House, 20 Middle Pavement, Nottingham NG1 7DW (0602 481184)
Reading: Abbey Hall, Abbey Square, Reading RG1 3BE (0734 591733)
Stevenage: Business & Technology Centre, Bessemer Drive, Stevenage, Herts SG1 2DX (0438 743377)

The Enterprise Initiative
This is the name given by the Department of Trade and Industry (DTI) to its comprehensive package of self help launched in January 1988. In part it is a repackaging of long established services, for example the manufacturing advisory service is relaunched in much the same form as 'The Manufacturing Initiative'. Others, such as the Business Planning and Financial Information Systems, are completely new.

To be eligible you must be an independent firm with fewer than 500 employees.

The entry point for all the following services is by contacting your local DTI Regional Office, or other contact points in Scotland and Wales as listed at the end of this section. They will

16

then ask you to complete a short application form after which they can arrange for a free visit by an Enterprise Counsellor. He will spend up to two days with you, at your convenience. During his stay he will examine your business and offer you impartial, confidential advice and then recommend how the Enterprise Initiative can help you. This could consist of an offer of financial support for between 5 and 15 man days of specialised consultancy in a number of key management functions.

The DTI will then put you in touch with the body managing the Initiative on their behalf, for example the Institute of Marketing, the Design Council, the Production Engineering Research Association or 3i's. They will use their expertise to make sure you are teamed up with the specialist who has the right background for your firm. This consultant will work with you to draw up the terms of reference for your particular project. The DTI will pay half the cost of between 5 and 15 man days of consultancy. In assisted areas and Urban Programme areas, they will pay two thirds. You pay the rest. (The boundaries of these areas change from time to time, but your local DTI office, listed later, can advise you as to the current situation.

The Marketing Initiative
Whether your market is at home or abroad this initiative can help you to review your marketing strategy. Specialists can help you to identify the most profitable part of your market; help you find out how your customer needs and demands are changing; look at your pricing, distribution and after sales service – and your competition. The Marketing Initiative is intended to leave you with a comprehensive marketing plan.

The Design Initiative
Managed by the Design Council, this Initiative offers expert advice on design from product concept to corporate image. They can help with:
■ Product innovation and feasibility studies
■ Design for efficient production
■ Mechanical and electrical engineering design
■ Selection and use of materials
■ Industrial design and styling
■ Product safety and ergonomic considerations
■ Packaging and point of sale material
■ Corporate identity

The Quality Initiative
Managed by the Production Engineering Research Association (PERA) and in the North West by Salford University Business Services Ltd, this Initiative offers expert advice on introducing an

appropriate quality management system and so keep both standards and output at satisfactory and profitable levels.

The Manufacturing Initiative
Also managed by PERA, this initiative seeks to reduce stock, and so release valuable cash, by the effective introduction of modern manufacturing methods and systems.

The Business Planning Initiative
Managed by Investors in Industry, this Initiative was launched in April 1988 to provide expert advice on the development of business plans. This process involves a review of business objectives and competitive strategies.

Financial and Information Systems Initiative
Also managed by Investors in Industry, this Initiative provides expert advice on improving existing budgeting and financial control systems or designing and introducing new ones. It will also include a review of accounting records, the use of data services and any computer and software needs.

The DTI plan to support around a thousand consultancies every month under these six Initiatives. Having taken any one you will still be able to benefit from one other at a later stage.

These other 'Initiatives' essentially describe support provided in ways other than pure consultancy for enterprise – many have been in existence in one form or another for some time.

The Regional Initiative
This is the title given to the revised Regional Aid Programme to be provided from April 1988. Under this programme independent firms with fewer than 25 employees located in Development Areas may apply for:

- Investment grants of 15% of the cost of fixed assets up to a maximum grant of £15,000
- Innovation grants of 50% of the agreed project cost up to a maximum grant of £25,000

The Export Initiative
This covers the services provided by the British Overseas Trade Board and the Exports Credit Guarantee Department, both described later in Section 5.

The Research and Technology Initiative
The solution to some problems may already exist, if only you knew where to look. Other problems may require research, often best achieved in collaboration with others. In either case this Initiative can help, either by providing information, putting you in touch with the right expert, or by funding up to half the agreed costs of a collaborative project.

The Business Education Initiative

These include:

■ The Teaching Company Scheme operated jointly with the Science & Engineering Research Council can provide financial help to universities and polytechnics to place bright young graduates in firms planning major operational changes. The firm makes a financial contribution and in return gains professional help, backed up by the resources of a major teaching institution

■ Regional Technology Centres have been established by the DTI to communicate about research & development work going on in higher education, that could be useful to firms developing new products and processes. The Centre acts as an information clearing house to enable firms to find out easily what is going on in their region.

Contact Points

DTI North East: (Cleveland, Durham, Northumberland, Tyne & Wear) Stanegate House, 2 Groat Market, Newcastle-upon-Tyne NE1 1YN (091 235 7292)

DTI North West (Liverpool): (Liverpool, Widnes/Runcorn, St Helens/ Wigan, Merseyside and Wirral/Chester) Graeme House, Derby Square, Liverpool L2 7UP (051 224 6300)

DTI North West (Manchester): (Cheshire, Cumbria, Lancashire, Greater Manchester and the High Peak District of Derbyshire) 75 Mosley Street, Manchester M2 3HR (061 838 5000)

DTI Yorkshire and Humberside: (North Yorkshire, South Yorkshire, West Yorkshire and Humberside) 4th Floor, Fairfax House, Merrion Street, Leeds LS2 8JU (0532 338300)

DTI East Midlands: (Nottinghamshire, Derbyshire (except the High Peak District), Leicestershire, Lincolnshire and Northamptonshire) Severns House, 20 Middle Pavement, Nottingham NG1 7DW (0602 596460)

DTI West Midlands: (Formerly West Midlands Metropolitan County, Hereford and Worcester, Shropshire, Staffordshire and Warwickshire) Ladywood House, Stephenson Street, Birmingham B2 4DT (021 631 6181)

DTI South East: Ebury Bridge House, 2–18 Ebury Bridge Road, London SW1 8QD (01 730 8451)

Cambridgeshire, Norfolk, Suffolk, Essex, Bedfordshire, Hertfordshire: (0223 461939)

Buckinghamshire, Oxfordshire, Berkshire, Hampshire, Isle of Wight: (0734 395600)

Sussex, Surrey and Kent: (0737 226900)

Greater London: (01 627 7800)

DTI South West: (Avon, Cornwall, Devon, Dorset, Gloucestershire, Somerset and Wiltshire) The Pithay, Bristol BS1 2PBN (0272 308400)

SCOTLAND

Highlands and Islands Development Board: Bridge House, 27 Bank Street, Inverness IV1 1QR (0463 234171)

Scottish Development Agency
Borders: 3 Market Street, Galashiels TD1 3AD (0896 3463)
Central: The Alpha Centre, Stirling Univeristy, Innovation Park, Stirling FK9 4NF (0786 70080)
Dumfries & Galloway: 16/18 Buccleuch Street, Dumfries DG1 2AH (0387 54444)
Fife: 441 High Street, Kirkcaldy KY1 2SX (0592 205171)
Grampian: 10 Queen's Road, Aberdeen AB1 6YT (0224 641791/645705)
Lothian: Rosebery House, Haymarket Terrace, Edinburgh EH12 5EZ (031 337 9595)
Strathclyde: 21 Bothwell Street, Glasgow G2 6NR (041 248 7806/7)
Tayside: The Nethergate Centre, Yeaman Shore, Dundee DD1 4BU (0382 29122)

WALES
Welsh Development Agency: Business Development Centre, Treforest Industrial Estate, Pontypridd, Mid Glamorgan CF37 5UT (0443 841777)

Rural Development Commission (RDC)

The Rural Development Commission was created in 1988 by bringing together into a single organisation the long-established Development Commission and its agency CoSIRA. The Commission's Business Service now provides the services previously provided by CoSIRA.

The Rural Development Commission exists to advise Government on all matters concerning the people and communities who live in the rural parts of England, and to use its resources to create or maintain stable and prosperous communities in villages and country towns. The Commission is therefore concerned with jobs and housing, communications and transport, and services and facilities from health and information to village halls and village shops. To achieve its objective the Commission works closely with Local Authorities, Community Councils and other bodies.

To assist job creation the Commission finances English Estates to build small factories and workshops in rural areas which are sold or rented to people who want to start up or expand their own businesses. In the designated Rural Development Areas nearly 2,000 of these small industrial units have been built and more are built each year.

The Rural Development Commission's Business Service, based at 31 offices all over rural England, provides business and technical advice and skill training to help small businesses to start up and prosper. Currently some 30,000 small rural businesses are in touch with the Business Service and many have enjoyed a friendly relationship with the Business Adviser for their county over a number of years.

In response to your enquiry a Business Adviser – the local representative – will arrange to meet you. Whether you are an established business or a new starter the Business Adviser will be able to answer or find the answers to many of the questions you may want to ask.

Technical and Professional Advice
The Business Adviser can arrange for one of their technical or professional advisers to give specialist help with difficult problems. Rural Development's team of professional and technical advisers have all worked in industry and have a wide range of skills and experience which is outlined below. Advice is normally given on a working visit to your factory or workshop.

Business Management Advice
Accountancy book-keeping, profit planning, cash flow forecasting, costing, applications for loans and overdraft facilities.
Marketing market research, product planning, pricing and distribution, advertising and sales, export, exhibitions.
Production management planning and control of production, buying and stock control, staff recruitment, employment legislation, statutory sick pay, supervisor training, use of microcomputers.

Technical Advice
Building and estimating, structural engineering, joinery, building conversions, thatching, dry stone walling.
Mechanical engineering electrical engineering, industrial safety, welding techniques, CNC machine tools, low-cost automation, jig and tool design, workshop layout, fibreglass lamination, thermoplastics, clay products technology and pottery, abrasive wheels, vehicle electrics.
Furniture making antique furniture restoration, upholstery, wood-working machinery, spraying and finishing, wheelwrighting.
Sawmill management timber technology, saw doctoring.
Farriery forgework.
Saddlery and leatherwork.
Engineering products and prototypes Rural Development's own workshops can undertake the design and production of jigs, press tools and special-purpose machinery for small firms. They will also develop prototypes. This service is particularly valuable to non-engineering businesses.

Finance
Rural Development normally expects the major part of funding for small businesses to be arranged with a bank, or other commercial lending source. However, Rural Development has its own limited loan fund which can be used in appropriate cases to finance part of the cost of the project, up to a maximum of £75,000. Repayment may be between 2 and 20 years according to

the type of loan. Management Accountants are available to assist with the preparation of a case to support an application for a loan.

Rural Development has agreements with major banks which provide favourable terms for client businesses and opportunities for joint lending by the Commission and the bank.

Grants

Grants are not generally available for rural businesses, however in certain circumstances the Commission does make grants to help a business start up or expand.

In Rural Development Areas* only, grants are available towards the cost of converting unused and redundant buildings into workshops, or into certain types of tourist facility, including the cost of installing or upgrading mains services.

In all areas grants may be available to help with the cost of taking a stand at a trade show or exhibition, or the cost of engaging a consultant to draft a marketing plan for your product.

From the Rural Transport Development Fund assistance may be available if you are starting a new bus service in a rural area.

Training

If you or one of your workers needs training or an extra skill, perhaps how to weld stainless steel, repair electronic ignition on a car, upholster an antique chair, or increase production from a spindle moulder, ask the Business Adviser. He can arrange either a visit from a technical adviser or one of our intensive 2–5 day courses. These courses are planned to give practical skills with the minimum waste of working time.

New Entrant Training Scheme (NETS) Rural Development provides longer periods of training for a limited number of young people, usually under 19 years of age. They must already be employed by a suitable firm. The training provided by Rural Development is a series of one-week sessions over a period of from 1–3 years. NETS training is available in most of the skills mentioned above.

* *Rural Development Areas.* In 1984 the Commission established its priority areas (the Rural Development Areas) following a review using criteria set by Government. These are considered to be the parts of rural England in greatest need of assistance and it is here that Rural Development concentrates the greatest part of its resources. There are 28 Rural Development Areas in the remoter parts of England covering generally the North, the East Coast, the Welsh borders and the West Country.

Other Services

Village shops   Advice is given on the purchase and management of a village shop. Residential weekend courses on Buying a Village Shop and on Professional Management for Small Shopkeepers are arranged at a number of centres.

Sales promotion   Rural Development arranges group stands at a series of national trade fairs and exhibitions on which you can exhibit your products at much lower costs than on an independent stand. Regular marketing seminars are arranged all over England which can help you to work out the best way of promoting and selling your product or service.

Rural transport   Rural Development's Transport Advisers can help with licensing, new laws and regulations, sources of financial assistance, route planning and registration, whether you operate or plan to operate a hire car, taxis, or buses serving country areas.

Tourism   In Rural Development Areas the Commission gives assistance to tourist and leisure enterprises, guest houses, bed-and-breakfasts and small hotels, as well as to restaurants, activity centres and tourist attractions. In addition to other financial and professional help, Tourist Advisers with wide experience of the trade can help you to start up or expand your business.

Who is Eligible?

If you live in the country or in a country town in England with less than 10,000 inhabitants the Business Service is available to help you to start up, run, or expand your business. Normally Rural Development helps manufacturing and service industries. Agriculture, horticulture and the professions are excluded but non-agricultural businesses on the farm are eligible for assistance. Any firm with less than 20 skilled employees can ask for Rural Development help.

If these conditions exclude you, ring the Small Firms Service (Freefone Enterprise) who work closely with Rural Development's Business Service.

Charges

No charge is made for the help and information given by the local Business Adviser. The fees for Technical and Business Management Advisers and Training Courses are modest.

For further information please get in touch with Rural Development's Business Adviser for your county.

County Offices
HEAD OFFICE
11 Cowley Street, London SW1P 3NA (01 276 6969)
or
141 Castle Street, Salisbury, Wiltshire SP1 3TP (0722 336255)

NORTH
Barnsley: 12 Churchfields Court, Barnsley, South Yorks S70 2JT (0226 204367)
Darlington: Morton Road, Yarm Road Industrial Estate, Darlington, Co Durham DL1 4PT (0325 487123)
Howden: 14 Market Place, Howden, Goole, North Humberside DN14 7BJ (0430 431138)
Morpeth: Northumberland Business Centre, Southgate, Morpeth, Northumberland NE61 2EH (0670 511221)
Penrith: Ullswater Road, Penrith, Cumbria CA11 7EH (0768 65752)
Preston: 15 Victoria Road, Fulwood, Preston, Lancashire PR2 4PS (0772 713038)
York: William House, Shipton Road, Skelton, York YO3 6XW (0904 646866/7)

EAST
Bingham: Chancel House, East Street, Bingham, Notts NG13 8DR (0949 39222/3)
Cambridge: 24 Brooklands Avenue, Cambridge CB2 2BU (0223 354505)
Hadleigh: 133 High Street, Hadleigh, Ipswich, Suffolk IP7 5EJ (0473 827893)
Northampton: Hunsbury Hill Centre, Harksome Hill, Northampton NN4 9QX (0604 765874)
Norwich: 13 Unthank Road, Norwich, Norfolk NR2 2PA (0603 624498)
Sleaford: Council Offices, Eastgate, Sleaford, Lincs NG34 7EB (0529 303241)

SOUTH EAST
Bedford: Agriculture House, 55 Goldington Road, Bedford MK40 3LU (0234 61381)
Braintree: 64a High Street, Braintree, Essex CM7 7JP (0376 47623)
Lewes: (Surrey & Sussex) Sussex House, 212 High Street, Lewes, Sussex BN7 2NH (0273 471399)
Maidstone: 8 Romney Place, Maidstone, Kent ME15 6LE (06223 65222)
Newport: 6/7 Town Lane, Newport, Isle of Wight, PO30 1JU (0983 528019)
Wallingford: (Oxford, Bucks & Berks) The Maltings, St John's Road, Wallingford, Oxford OX10 9BZ (0491 35523)
Winchester: Barton Farm, Andover Road, Winchester, Hants SO22 6AX (0962 880503)

SOUTH WEST
Bristol: (Avon) 209 Redland Road, Bristol, Avon BS6 6YU (0272 733433)
Dorchester: Wing D, Government Buildings, Prince of Wales Road, Dorchester, Dorset DT1 1QJ (0305 68558)
Exeter: 27 Victoria Park Road, Exeter, Devon EX2 4NT (0392 52616)
Salisbury: 141 Castle Street, Salisbury, Wiltshire SP1 3TP (0722 336255 ext 252)
Taunton: 1 The Crescent, Taunton, Somerset TA1 4EA (0823 276905)
Truro: 2nd Floor, Highshore House, New Bridge Street, Truro TR1 2AA (0872 73531)

·

WEST
Audlem: (Cheshire & Staffordshire) 6 Shropshire Street, Audlem,
Cheshire CW3 0DY (0270 812012)
Henley-In-Arden: (Warwickshire) Stanley House, 47a High Street,
Henley in Arden, Solihull, West Midlands B95 5AA (05642 4191)
Malvern: (Gloucester, Hereford & Worcester) 32 Church Street,
Malvern, Worcs WR14 2AZ (06845 64784/64506)
Telford: Strickland House, The Lawns, Park Street, Wellington, Telford,
Shropshire TF1 3BX (0952 47161)
Wirksworth: Ravenstor Road, Wirksworth, Derbyshire DE4 4FY (062 982
4848)

Action Resource Centre (ARC)

This was set up in 1973 by a group of businessmen to research
and demonstrate how business skills could best be used for the
community. They now concentrate on:

■ Bringing business skills and resources to community
development.

■ Bringing practical help from business to local needs through
its brokerage and matching service, and through its ten inner-
city based branches. Companies lend the skills of their
employees to community organisations, providing full-time and
part-time help in, for example, marketing and public relations,
building advice, management and administration, and project
development. ARC leads the development of secondment
practice, promoting secondment as a management training
tool, and providing workshops and consultancy for companies.
ARC's branches in Nottingham, Leicester, Manchester and
West Yorkshire can also offer advice and assistance to new
and established community businesses.

Branch Offices

Avon: c/o Sun Life Assurance Society plc, 5th Floor, St Lawrence
House, 29/31 Broad Street, Bristol BS1 2JE (0272 221144/290381)
Contact: Peter McGoldrick
Greater London: CAP House, 3rd Floor, 9/12 Long Lane, London EC1A
9HD (01 726 8987) *Contact: Veronica Chamberlain*
Greater Manchester: The Piazza, Piccadilly Plaza, Manchester M1 4AN
(061 236 3391) *Contact: Brian Barker*
Humberside: Hull Business Advice Centre, 24 Anlaby Road, Hull HU1
2PA (0482 27266) *Contact: Derek Bell*
Leicestershire: The Business Advice Centre, 30 New Walk, Leicester
LE1 6TF (0533 554464) *Contact: Caroline Eardley*
Merseyside: c/o Premier Brands UK Ltd, Pasture Road, Moreton,
Wirral, Merseyside L46 8SE (051 678 8888) *Contact: Peter Mitchell*
Northern Ireland: ARC House, Enterprise Centre, 103/107 York Street,
Belfast BT15 1AB (0232 328000) *Contact: Robin McConkey*
Nottinghamshire: 7th Floor, City House, Maid Marian Way,
Nottingham NG1 6BH (0602 470749/470839) *Contact: John Pike*

West Midlands: 160 Bishop Street, Birmingham B5 7EJ (021 666 6848)
Contact: George Garlick
West Yorkshire: c/o British Railways, Eastern Region, 1 Aire Street,
Room 101, Leeds LS1 4PR (0532 458123) *Contact: Gwyn Jones*

Ethnic Minority Enterprise – A Home Office Initiative

Ethnic minorities must be able to share the benefits of the enterprise culture which the Government is reviving. Some ethnic minority communities, however, are not attracted to existing business advice centres or enterprise agencies.

That is why the Home Office took the lead and helped to set up the business advice centres in areas with a high ethnic minority population. There are now 6 centres, in Deptford, Finsbury Park, Wandsworth, Tower Hamlets, Birmingham and Bristol. They are funded and managed jointly by the white and ethnic minority business communities, the Home Office and other Government Departments and the local authority. The Centres are open to all.

The Home Office also encourages and assists existing business advice or enterprise agencies who wish to develop their services to ethnic minorities. This has included grants for the employment of local authority staff, either with a council-run service or on detached duty in an enterprise agency, secondment of Home Office staff to an enterprise agency and a grant to Business in the Community for an outreach service to the Bangladeshi community from an enterprise agency in Tower Hamlets.

If you would like further information on the Home Office's work on ethnic minority business, please contact:
The Home Office, 50 Queen Anne's Gate, London SW1H 9AT (01 273 2737)

Contact addresses

Black Business in Birmingham (3Bs): 15 The Square, 111 Broad Street, Birmingham B15 1AS (021 631 2860) *Contact: K. Adjei*

Bristol Black Enterprise Association Ltd: 9 Lower Ashley Road, St Agnes, Bristol BS2 9QA (0272 559016/550935) *Contact: L. McDonald*

Deptford Enterprise Agency: 146 Deptford High Street, London SE8 3PQ (01 692 9204) *Contact: J. Greenland*

North London Business Development Agency: 35–37 Blackstock Road, Finsbury Park, London N4 2JF (01 359 7405/7) *Contact: E. H. Cotter*

Tower Hamlets Enterprise Outreach Service: c/o Business in the Community, 227a City Road, London EC1V 1LX (01 253 3716) *Contact: A. Barlas*

Wandsworth Enterprise Agency: 4th Floor, Woburn House, 155/159 Falcon Road, London SW11 2PD (01 924 2811) *Contact: A. Amponsah*

Task Force

An Initiative launched by the Department of Trade and Industry in 1986 and expanded in 1987 with funds of £14 million to:
■ Encourage and facilitate enterprise by local people through

the provision of enterprise training, financial and managerial assistance.

■ Provide more jobs for local people by identifying and removing impediments to their recruitment by local employers, and by encouraging local enterprise development.

■ Improve the employability of local people, including those about to enter the labour market, by training programmes aimed at specific employment opportunities or identified gaps in the labour market.

■ Support initiatives designed to improve the environment, the provision of community services and to reduce the level of crime where these can be linked to the reintegration of local people into local economic activity.

Task forces operate in the following 16 areas:

Chapeltown Harehills (Leeds): 158–160 Chapeltown Road, Leeds LS7 4EE (0532 626 202) *Contact: John Lister*

Coventry: R 415, Copthall House, Station Square, Coventry CV1 2PP (0203 24310) *Contact: Derek Player*

Doncaster: 2 Trafford Court, Trafford Way, Doncaster DN1 1PN (0302 329052) *Contact: David Wilkinson*

Handsworth: 227a Lozells Road, Handsworth, Birmingham B19 1RJ (021 523 3241/6211) *Contact: Mark Tovey*

Hartlepool: Suite 3, Municipal Buildings, Hartlepool TS24 7EQ (0429 860557) *Contact: Brian Pollard*

Highfields (Leicester): 23 Egginton Street, Highfields, Leicester LE5 5BD (0533 552248) *Contact: Bob Fenley*

Middlesbrough (North Central): 1st Floor, Bowmaker House, 132–134 Borough Road, Middlesbrough, Cleveland (0642 221162) *Contact: John Rundle*

Moss Side & Hulme: 7 Parisian Way, Moss Lane East, Moss Side, Manchester M15 5NQ (061 226 8899/3375) *Contact: Pat Shilliday*

North Kensington: 2 Acklam Road, London W10 5QZ (01 960 8455) *Contact: Colin Francis*

North Peckham: 2nd Floor, 72 Rye Lane, Peckham, London SE15 (01 358 9018/9019/9020) *Contact: Daniel Levy*

Nottingham: 2/4 Radford Road, Hyson Green, Nottingham NG7 5FS (0602 421565) *Contact: Ian Samways*

Preston: c/o 8th Floor, Victoria House, Ormskirk Road, Preston PR1 2DX (0772 201770 ext 18) *Contact: Howard Eastwood*

Rochdale: c/o Job Centre, Octagon House, Yorkshire Street, Rochdale DL16 1BW (0706 523623) *Contact: Mike Clarke*

St Pauls (Bristol): Bristol Inner City Project, 189a Newfoundland Road, St Pauls, Bristol BS2 9NY (0272 550205) *Contact: Barry Cornish*

Spitalfields: 3rd Floor, Cityside House, 40 Adler Street. London E1 (01 377 1866) *Contact: Ian Rosser*

Wolverhampton: c/o 50/54 Worcester Street, Wolverhampton WV2 4LL (0902 24005) *Contact: Fred Pickerill*

British Steel (Industry) Ltd

This company, a subsidiary of British Steel plc, aims to help businesses in Scotland, England and Wales, with the objective of helping to put back sound jobs in those areas where British Steel has discontinued or substantially reduced its activities.

In each of the areas British Steel Industry is associated with a local Business Opportunity Team, usually an Enterprise Agency but sometimes some other local organisation which exists to support businesses in the area. British Steel Industry itself will provide financial assistance, where such assistance is necessary for a project to proceed. Their assistance may be as a loan (unsecured up to £25,000) at below commercial rates of interest, but share capital will be considered in appropriate cases.

Their Accelerated Business Development Scheme is designed to unlock the growth potential possessed by established smaller businesses in the British Steel Industry Opportunity area. Under this scheme, companies who have been trading for over 3 years, with turnover of up to £3m, are eligible for a training and financial package.

British Steel Industry has also provided small industrial workshops in a number of its areas. These units range in size from a few hundred to a few thousand square feet, and are made available on a three-month rolling licence agreement with a minimum of formalities.

Contact points for further information

Head Office: British Steel (Industry) Ltd, Canterbury House, 2–6 Sydenham Road, Croydon CR9 2LJ (01 686 2311) *Contact: John Northcott*

SCOTLAND

British Steel Industry Regional Office: 41 Oswald Street, Glasgow G1 1PA (041 221 3372) *Contact: John Fairlie*

Cambuslang: Clyde Workshops, Fullarton Road, Tollcross, Glasgow G32 8YL (041 641 4972) *Contact: Stewart Morrison*

Garnock Valley: Garnock Valley Development Executive, 44 Main Street, Kilbirnie, Ayrshire KA25 7BY (0505 685455) *Contact: Bill Dunn*

Lanarkshire: LIFE Business Services, Lanarkshire Trade & Export Centre, 116 Cadzow Street, Hamilton ML3 6HP (0698 891515) *Contact: Peter Agneu*

NORTHERN

British Steel Industry Regional Office: Templetown, Knitsley Lane, Consett, Co. Durham BH8 7PG (0207 591000) *Contact: Laurie Haveron*

West Cumbria: Enterprise West Cumbria, Thirlmere Building, 50 Lakes Road, Derwent Howe, Workington, Cumbria CA14 3YP (0900 65656) *Contact: Tony Winterbottom*

Derwentside: Derwentside Industrial Development Agency, Berry Edge Road, Consett, Co. Durham DH8 5EU (0207 509124) *Contact: John Carney*

Hartlepool: Hartlepool Enterprise Agency, Suite 7, Municipal Buildings, Church Square, Hartlepool, Cleveland TS24 7ER (0429 221216) *Contact: Alan Humble*

Teesside: Cleveland Enterprise Agency, 4th Floor, Sun Alliance House, 16–26 Albert Road, Middlesbrough, Cleveland TS1 1PR (0642 222836) *Contact: David Bowles*

YORKSHIRE AND HUMBERSIDE

British Steel Industry Regional Office: 4–8 East Parade, Sheffield S1 2ET (0742 700933) *Contact: Vernon Smith*

South Humber: South Humber Business Advice Centre, 7 Market Place, Brigg, South Humberside DN20 8HA (0652 57637/8) *Contact: Derek Marshall*

Rotherham: Rotherham Enterprise Agency, All Saints Building, Corporation Street, Rotherham, South Yorks S60 1NX (0709 382121 ext 3463) *Contact: Ted Lunness*

Sheffield: Sheffield Business Venture, 61–69 Leavygreave Road, Sheffield, South Yorks S3 7RB (0742 755721) *Contact: Barrie Briggs*

EAST MIDLANDS

Corby: Corby Industrial Development Centre, 2nd Floor, Grosvenor House, George Street, Corby, Northants NN17 1TZ (0536 62571) *Contact: Ray Jackson*

WALES AND WEST MIDLANDS

Blaenau Gwent: Blaenau Gwent Business Advice Centre, Enterprise House, Rassau Industrial Estate, Ebbw Vale, Gwent NP3 5SD (0495 306770) *Contact: Jack Cater*

Deeside: Deeside Enterprise Trust, Park House, Deeside Industrial Park, Deeside, Clwyd CH5 2NZ (0244 815262/815783) *Contact: Peter Summers*

Dudley: Dudley Business Venture, 1st Floor, Stanton House, 10 Castle Street, Dudley, West Midlands DY1 1LQ (0384 231283)

South Glamorgan: Cardiff and Vale Enterprise, Enterprise House, 127 Bute Street, Cardiff CF1 5LE (0222 494411) *Contact: Peter Fortune*

West Glamorgan: West Glamorgan Enterprise Trust, 12a St Mary's Square, Swansea, West Glamorgan SA1 3LP (0792 475345) *Contact: George Atkins*

South Gwent: Newport Enterprise, Enterprise Way, Newport, Gwent NP9 2AQ (0633 54041) *Contact: G. Alan Prosper*

Llanelli: Llanelli Enterprise Co, 100 Trostre Road, Llanelli, Dyfed SA15 2EA (054 772122) *Contact: David Williams*

Merthyr: Merthyr–Aberdare Development Enterprise, The Enterprise Centre, Merthyr Tydfil, Mid Glamorgan CF48 4DR (0443 692233) *Contact: Jeff Pride*

MANAGED WORKSHOPS

Blaenau Gwent Workshops: Unit 22, Pond Road, Brynmawr, Gwent NP3 4BL (0495 311625) *Contact: Ray Davies*

Cardiff Workshops: Unit A, Lewis Road, East Moors, Cardiff CF1 5EG (0222 471122) *Contact: Graham Blackburn*

Clyde Workshops: Fullarton Road, Tollcross, Glasgow G32 8YL (041 641 4972) *Contact: Stewart Morrison*

Coatbridge Workshops: Coatbank Way, Coatbridge, Lanarkshire ML5 3AG (0236 23384) *Contact: Frances Sunderland*
Consett Workshops: Berry Edge Road, Consett, Co Durham DH8 5EU (0207 509124) *Contact: Eddie Hutchinson*
Corby Workshops: Central Works Site, Corby, Northants NN17 1YB (0536 404215) *Contact: George Deacon*
Hartlepool Workshops: Usworth Road Industrial Estate, Usworth Road, Hartlepool, Cleveland TS25 1PD (0429 265128/235648) *Contact: Barbara Elsdon*
Normanby Park Workshops: Normanby Road, Scunthorpe, South Humberside DN15 8QZ (0724 849457) *Contact: Alan Henderson*
Port Talbot Workshops: Addison Road, Port Talbot, West Glamorgan SA12 6HZ (0639 887171)

British Coal Enterprise

The National Coal Board set up British Coal Enterprise to increase job prospects and regenerate prosperity in coal mining areas. Help from British Coal Enterprise is not limited to British Coal employees but the projects which it supports must result in permanent jobs being created in mining areas. Each month Enterprise uses some £1.5m of its available £40m funding facility to invest in some 75 projects.

They can help almost anyone who has a proposal that will create real, new permanent jobs in mining areas. From a one-man operation, to big business – even international companies looking to expand and/or locate their operations in the coalfield areas of the UK.

The three major criteria are:
- New permanent jobs must be created
- The project must be located in an area associated with coal mining
- The project must be financially viable

British Coal Enterprise can help in five main ways:

Advice and Guidance

They know the coalfield areas, the advisers, the business people, the financiers, the government bodies and the local councils in and around them extremely well. Positive links have been forged with Enterprise Agencies and they have encouraged the establishment of Managed Workshops in all coalfield areas.

Finance

Enterprise financial help is usually provided in the form of a loan. The amount of loan would, normally, be geared to the job creating element of the project (usually based on a figure of up to £5,000 for each new job created) and would normally not exceed 25% of the total financial requirement of the project. Their loans can be arranged relatively quickly, at favourable rates of interest, with few formalities, and, for smaller loans, usually without security. In

30

addition to providing their own loans, they can help put you in touch with other sources, e.g., Department of Trade & Industry grants, local authorities, financial institutions, the private sector, the EEC and Enterprise Agencies.

Premises

They can help find suitable properties in coalfield areas for sale or rent – at competitive prices. In some coalfield areas, buildings no longer needed by the coal industry may be available, and they are also prepared to consider helping with the erection of new buildings in such coal mining areas for particular businesses. A number of ex-NCB premises and other buildings have been converted into Managed Workshops with great success, and this programme is continuing. A Managed Workshop provides smaller businesses and start-ups with workspace on an easy-in, easy-out basis at reasonable rentals and also provides on-site business advice, secretarial, reception, copying and other shared services.

Liaison with other forms and sources of help and advice

British Coal Enterprise also offers contacts with sources of other financial help, business advice, local expertise and government aid. By helping to cut through some of the red tape, Enterprise can save time, energy and money in relation to your business proposal.

Retraining

They can identify and co-ordinate retraining programmes for those ex-employees leaving coal mining and seeking work in new companies.

British Coal Enterprise have 7 Regional Offices who are responsible for activities in their localities:

Scotland: (Coalfield areas of Scotland) Suite 1, Alloa Business Centre, The Whins, Alloa FK10 3SA (0259 218021) *Contact: Jim Wells*

Western: (Coalfield areas of North West England, North Wales, Staffordshire, Shropshire and West Midlands (excluding Coventry)) Anderton House, Lowton, Warrington, Cheshire WA3 2AG (0942 672404) *Contact: John Dutton*

South Wales: Coal House, Ty Glas Avenue, Llanishen, Cardiff, South Glamorgan CF4 5YS (0222 761671) *Contact: Winsor Lewis*

South East: (Coalfield areas of Kent) 65 Burgate, Canterbury, Kent CT1 2HJ (0227 61477) *Contact: Randolph Pettigrew*

North East: (Coalfield areas of Northumberland, Tyne & Wear and Durham) Coal House, Team Valley, Gateshead, Tyne & Wear NE11 0JD (091 487 8822) *Contact: Bill Furness*

Yorkshire: (Coalfield areas of Yorkshire) Carcroft Enterprise Park, Station Road, Carcroft, Doncaster DN6 8DD (0302 727228) *Contact: Bob Iceton*

Midlands: (Nottinghamshire and the coalfield areas of Derbyshire, Leicestershire and Warwickshire) Huthwaite, Sutton-in-Ashfield, Nottinghamshire NG17 2NP (0623 554747) *Contact: Helen Lennox*

Enterprise House, Ashby Road, Coalville, Leicestershire LE6 2LA (0530 813143)

URBED (Urban and Economic Development) Ltd

3/7 Stamford Street, London SE1 9NT (01 928 9515)
This non-profit-making company was established in 1976 with a grant from one of the Sainsbury Charitable Trusts in order to 'find practical solutions to the problems of regenerating run-down areas and creating new work'.

It has carried out a series of research studies in a cross-section of inner city areas, which have enabled URBED to develop a unique understanding of local economies, the needs of small firms, and the problems of under-utilised resources in inner city areas.

Their services include the establishment of workshops, working communities, small enterprise centres, industrial associations, small business clubs and local enterprise trusts. Through research into demand, case studies of successful conversions, feasibility studies and promotion material, the company has encouraged the conversion of redundant buildings into premises for small firms and has become involved in property finance.

It provides consultancy services for a range of clients, including local and public authorities and government departments. URBED's training initiatives include: 'Assessing Your Prospects' (a weekend course) and 'Getting Going' (a 3-month course). Their New Enterprise Network (NET) meets on the last Tuesday of each month. It is intended for anyone who has recently set up a business and is looking for support.

URBED's regional offices are:

Birmingham: c/o Argent Centre, 60 Frederick Street, Birmingham B1 3HS (021 233 3829) *Contact: Peter White*

Bristol: c/o 35 King Street, Bristol BS1 4DZ (0272 268893/0225 891781) *Contact: Oliver Shirley*

Leeds: Design Centre, Studio 25, 46 The Calls, Leeds LS2 74Y (0532 420173) *Contact: Linda Houston*

Tourist Boards

The UK's four national tourist boards can offer financial assistance to tourist projects by way of capital grants, interest relief grants and loans for tourist facilities to be set up, improved or expanded. The Boards can offer advice as to the feasibility and likely viability of projects, but they will only fund projects for which outline planning has been granted. Any assistance given will normally fall in the range of 10–25% of capital costs and will not exceed 50%, up to a sum of not more than £200,000 of assistance.

The Boards act as agents for the European Investment Bank (EIB) and in that capacity can provide loans up to a maximum of £2.5m. Projects must fall in the Assisted Areas.

For information contact the appropriate Tourist Board, address given below:

English Tourist Board: Thames Tower, Blacks Road, Hammersmith, London W6 9E1 (01 846 9000)

Welsh Tourist Board: Brunel House, 2 Fitzalen Road, Cardiff CF2 1UY (0222 499909)

Scottish Tourist Board: 23 Ravelston Terrace, Edinburgh EH4 3EH (031 332 2433)

Northern Ireland Tourist Board: River House, 48 High Street, Belfast BT1 2DS (0232 231221)

Enterprise Boards

Most of these were created by the now abolished Metropolitan County Councils. For the most part they have survived, raising finance from private sector sources and directing it towards helping the larger new enterprise to develop.

Addresses, contacts and information on Enterprise Boards is available in a report published in March 1988 by the Centre for Local Economic Strategies, Heron House, Brazenose Street, Manchester M2 5DH (061 834 7036) Price £2.50.

Centre Points Outside England

The following agencies and organisations provide advisory services and assistance to new and small businesses outside England.

SCOTLAND

The Scottish Development Agency: Small Business Division, Rosebery House, Haymarket Terrace, Edinburgh EH12 5EZ (031 337 9595)

They provide a free confidential information and advice centre, and a national counselling service available on Freefone Enterprise. The SDA publishes a comprehensive range of booklets and can advise on: finance, Government aid, marketing, market research, exporting, diversification, training, industrial relations, and of course high technology.

The agency is also the largest provider of industrial space in Scotland – factories, workshops and industrial estates. Sizes range from a couple of hundred square feet, to many thousands. The SDA can make finance available for certain small industrial and service enterprises, and has a strong interest in the craft field.

Small Firms Information Centre: 120 Bothwell Street, Glasgow (041 248 6014, Freefone Enterprise)

Centres

Aberdeen: Aberdeen Office, Queen's Road, Aberdeen AB1 6YT (0224 641791)

Clydebank: Task Force Office, Erskine House, 1 North Avenue, Clydebank Business Park, Clydebank G81 9XX (041 952 0084)

Coatbridge: Project Office, 59 Main Street, Coatbridge ML5 3BA (0236 24371)

Dumfries: Business Development Centre, 16 Buccleuch Street, Dumfries DG1 5AH (0387 54444)

Dundee: Dundee Project Office, Nethergate Centre, Yeaman Shore, Dundee DD1 4BU (0382 29122)

Edinburgh: Small Business Division, Rosebery House, Haymarket Terrace, Edinburgh EH12 5EZ (031 337 9595)

Galashiels: Small Business Division, 3 Market Street, Galashiels TD1 3AD (0896 3463)

Glasgow: Area Property Office, Templeton Business Centre, Templeton Street, Glasgow G40 1DD (041 554 7787)

GEAR Information Centre, Parkhead Library, 64 Tollcross Road, Glasgow G31 4XA (041 556 7412)

Business Development Centre, 21 Bothwell Street, Glasgow G2 6NR (041 248 7806)

Hillington: Area Property Office, Seaforth Road North, Hillington, Glasgow G52 4SQ (041 882 6288)

Inverclyde: Project Office, 64/66 West Blackhall Street, Greenock PA15 1XG (0475 24533)

Kilmarnock: Area Property Office, Glencairn Industrial Estate, Kilmarnock HA1 4DQ (0563 26623)

Kirkcaldy: Area Property Office, 441 High Street, Kirkcaldy KY1 2SX (0592 205171)

London: 17/19 Cockspur Street, London SW1 (01 839 2117)

Motherwell: Project Office, 28 Brandon Parade, Motherwell ML1 1UJ (0698 54626)

Scottish Food Centre, Motherwell Foodpark, Bellshill Industrial Estate, Bellshill ML4 (0698 749911)

Newhouse: Area Property Office, Newhouse Industrial Estate, Rowantree Avenue, Motherwell ML1 5RX (0698 732637/732812)

Stirling: Business Development Centre, Unit 4, Scottish Metropolitan Alpha Centre, Stirling University Innovation Park, Stirling University (0324 70080)

Inverness: The Highlands and Islands Development Board: Bridge House, 20 Bank Street, Inverness, IV1 1QR (0463 234171) *Contact: Simon Armstrong*
Provides advice, assistance and counselling for new and existing businesses.

The Industry Department for Scotland: Alhambra House, 45 Waterloo Street, Glasgow G2 6AT (041 248 2855)
The key organisation for companies in Scotland to turn to for extra grant assistance for investment and innovation. Their publication, the *Investment and Innovation Handbook*, describes these services.

The Scottish Council: Development and Industry Department, 23 Chester Street, Edinburgh EH3 7ET (031 225 7911) *Contact: Hamish Morrison*
The Council are involved in a number of important initiatives to promote new and small businesses in Scotland.

WALES

Welsh Development Agency: Business Development Unit, Business Development Centre, Treforest Industrial Estate, Pontypridd, Mid Glamorgan CF35 5UT (0443 841777) *Contact: The local WDA office and/or the Business Development Unit*
The Business Development Unit offers a range of support programmes for small businesses. It has a team of advisers who have many years of experience of the private sector and small businesses. They are able to help companies identify their immediate and longer term requirements, provide up to date advice and information on a wide range of business matters including business planning, management accounting, training, premises, finance and grants. It also has a team of specialist advisers in the area of marketing and production. There is also a facility where individuals contemplating setting up in business can, in an open plan environment, license a range of plant and equipment in the areas of metal working, wood working, joinery, and garment manufacture in order to develop ideas and products before setting up on their own account. The Business Development Unit is also responsible for the Small Firms Service in Wales and its team of some 60 experienced business counsellors who give practical advice to enquirers. There is a range of courses available to those contemplating self employment as well as certain specialised courses for events both in the UK and overseas and is responsible for the administration of the funded consultancy element of the DTI's Enterprise Initiative.

WDA regional offices:

Bangor: Llys Garth, Garth Road, Bangor, Gwynedd LL57 2RT (0248 352606)

Bridgend: Bridgend Industrial Estate, Bridgend, Mid Glamorgan CF31 3SD (0656 56531)

Carmarthen: Cillefwr Industrial Estate, Johnstown, Carmarthen, Dyfed SA31 3RB (0267 235642)

Hirwaun: Hirwaun Industrial Estate, Near Aberdare, Mid Glamorgan CF44 9UU (0685 811268)

Newport: 1/2 Gold Tops, Newport, Gwent NP7 4YW (0633 50133)

Swansea: Swansea Industrial Estate, Fforestfach, Swansea, West Glamorgan SA5 4DL (0792 586715)

Treforest: Treforest Industrial Estate, Pontypridd, Mid Glamorgan CF37 5UT (0443 853131)

Wrexham: Wrexham Industrial Estate, Wrexham, Clwyd LL13 9UF (0978 61011)

NORTHERN IRELAND

The Local Enterprise Development Unit (LEDU): Lamont House, Purdy's Lane, Newtownbreda, Belfast BT8 4TB (Freefone LEDU) *Contact: George Mackey*

This Small Business Agency can help manufacturing, craft or service businesses which employ up to 50 people. Their Product Ideas Licensing Library can help you to find a start-up area, or their Research and Development Grant Scheme can help you to bring your own product to market. They maintain a register of private and public property and can provide technical advice on a wide range of matters.

Their business centre in Linenhall Street has been specially designed to hold trade shows, and are available for small businessmen to mount their own exhibition. They operate a counselling service and have Local Area Offices keen to assist. All can be contacted on the free phone number.

Area offices:

East: 17/19 Linenhall Street, Belfast BT2 8AA
North: 13 Ship Quay Street, Londonderry BT48 6DJ
South: 6-7 The Mall, Newry, Co Down BT34 1BX
West: 15 High Street, Omagh BT8 1BA

LOCAL ENTERPRISE AGENCIES

Local Enterprise Agencies or Trusts have been formed in about 350 places up and down the UK. Some have been in existence for a decade, but the great majority were formed in the last five years. They have in common the objectives of encouraging new and small businesses to start up in a particular area, and of helping businesses in their area to survive and prosper.

These agencies are usually run by a small staff (the largest has over 30 people, but the average is two or three) who can call on the wealth of expertise within the organisations sponsoring the agency. Many hundreds of organisations have sponsored one or more Enterprise Agency. Sponsors include: local government; chambers of commerce; universities, polytechnics and colleges; industrial and commercial companies, both large and not so large; banks and merchant banks; accountancy firms; newspapers and television companies; insurance companies; and building societies. Moreover, organisations such as HM Dockyards, the Port of London Authority and the General and Municipal Workers' Union have played significant roles in the launching of Local Enterprise Agencies.

The services provided by sponsoring bodies to the agencies include: financial support towards running costs; office and workshop space; secretarial and administrative services; management and commercial advice; training facilities and resources; literature production and dissemination (including the use of advertising media); desk or field research; board representation and help with forming and developing policy.

A rather smaller number of organisations second staff to help in the day-to-day running of the Enterprise Agency. These are very often specialists from banking or the property world, or experienced managers within big companies. There are even a few academics returning a step closer to the commercial world. These advisers are an important resource within the agency, but the sponsoring company is amply rewarded. For example, a secondee from a major clearing bank will see more new business proposals in a week at an Enterprise Agency than he may see in a year at a small local branch. At the end of his year's secondment he will be a seasoned campaigner and probably a better judge of a good proposal. Some organisations, such as BSC and ARC, who operate nationally, carry out much of their work through a local organisation similar to an Enterprise Agency in broad concept. Indeed, BSC Industry has converted some of its regional initiatives into Enterprise Trusts, taking local councils, chambers of commerce and others into partnership to ensure the continuity of their initiative.

The scope of activities of each agency varies considerably. Some have focused their attention on providing small workshops and office premises; others run business advice clinics to help people to find money and other resources. Courses on marketing, on exporting, book-keeping, tax and employing people are run by some agencies, usually through their links with local colleges. Still others run 'marriage bureaux', putting people with ideas in touch with people with resources.

If you are actively considering starting up a business or are experiencing problems with your existing business then you would certainly be well advised to contact your nearest Enterprise Agency. If they cannot help or answer your questions they will almost certainly know who can.

The following table is a guide to the agencies and their services.

KEY

EC Education and courses
BCL Business club link
FLG Funds/loans/grants
KPR Keep property register
MP Manage property
YE Youth Enterprise
MB Marriage bureau

ENGLAND

	EC	BCL	FLG	KPR	MP	YE	MB
ACCRINGTON: Hyndburn Enterprise Trust, 19 Avenue Parade, Accrington, Lancashire BB5 6PN (0254 390000) *Contact: Grant Seedhouse*	•	•			•	•	
ALDERSHOT: Blackwater Valley Enterprise Trust Ltd, The Old Town Hall, Gosvenor Road, Aldershot, Hants GU11 3DP (0252 319272) *Contact: Walter T. Oakey*	•	•			•	•	
ALNWICK: North Northumberland Enterprise Agency, Hill House, 39 Bondgate Within, Alnwick, Northumberland NE66 1SX (0665 605075) *Contact: Richard C. Morris*							
ALTON: East Hampshire Enterprise Ltd, c/o Bass Brewing (Alton) Ltd, Manor Park, Alton, Hants GU34 2PS (0420 87577) *Contact: Alex C. Addison*	•						
ASHFORD: Enterprise Ashford Ltd, Enterprise Centre, Old Railway Works, Newtown Road, Ashford, Kent TN24 0PD (0233 30307) *Contact: Alan Duncan*	•	•	•		•	•	
ASHTON UNDER LYNE: Tameside Business Advice Service, Charlestown Industrial Estate, Turner Street, Ashton-Under-Lyne OL6 8NS (061 339 8960) *Contact: Tom William Jackson*	•	•	•	•		•	
AYLESBURY: Aylesbury Vale Business Advice Scheme, 23a Walton Street, Aylesbury, Bucks HP20 1TZ (0296 394555) *Contact: Victor Nicholls*	•						

38

	EC	BCL	FLG	KPR	MP	YE	MB
BANBURY: North Oxfordshire Business Venture Ltd (NORBIS), 33a Crouch Street, Banbury, Oxon OX16 9PR (0295 679000) *Contact: John Trumper*	•						
BARNSLEY: Barnsley Enterprise Centre, 1 Pontefract Road, Barnsley S71 1AJ (0226 733291) *Contact: Valerie Fairbank*	•		•	•	•		
BARNSTAPLE: North Devon Enterprise Agency Ltd, Yelland Centre, West Yelland, Barnstaple EX31 3EZ (0271 861215) *Contact: Tony Jennings*				•	•	•	
BARROW-IN-FURNESS: Furness Business Initiative Ltd, 111 Duke Street, Barrow-In-Furness, Cumbria LA14 1XA (0229 22132) *Contact: Avril Willis*	•	•	•				
BASILDON: Basildon & District Local Enterprise Agency Ltd, 101a Keay House, 88 Town Square, Basildon, Essex SS14 1BN (0268 286977) *Contact: Brian Bazzard*	•	•					
BASINGSTOKE: Basingstoke & Andover Enterprise Centre, 9 New Street, Joices Yard, Basingstoke, Hampshire RG21 1DF (0256 54041) *Contact: Colin Close*	•		•			•	
BATH: Bath Enterprise Ltd, Green Park Station, Green Park Road, Bath BA1 1JB (0225 338383) *Contact: Robert Kelly*	•	•	•	•	•	•	•
BEDLINGTON STATION: South East Northumberland Enterprise Trust (SENET), School Road, Bedlington, Northumberland NE22 7JB (0670 828586) *Contact: Tom Dean*	•		•		•	•	
BIRKENHEAD: In Business Ltd, The Business Centre, Claughton Road, Birkenhead, Wirral L41 6EY (051 647 7574) *Contact: Denis Nork*	•		•		•		

	EC	BCL	FLG	KPR	MP	YE	MB
Cavendish Enterprise Centre Ltd, Brassey Street, Off Laird Street, Birkenhead, Wirral L41 8BY (051 653 4515) *Contact: Jack Edwards*	•			•	•	•	
BIRMINGHAM: Birmingham Venture Chamber of Commerce House, 75 Harborne Road, Birmingham B15 3DH (021 454 6171) *Contact: J. D. Bullivant*	•		•	•	•		•
3Bs Black Business in Birmingham, 15 The Square, 111 Broad Street, Birmingham B15 1AS (021 631 2860) *Contact: Kofi Adjei*			•	•			
BISHOP AUCKLAND: Wear Valley Enterprise Agency, St Helen Auckland Trading Estate, Bishop Auckland, Co. Durham DL14 9AL (0388 605061) *Contact: Peter Gawthrop*	•						
BLACKBURN: Blackburn & District Enterprise Trust, 14 Richmond Terrace, Blackburn, Lancs BB1 7BH (0254 664747/583862) *Contact: J. A. McKinstry*	•	•	•	•		•	
BLACKPOOL: Blackpool & Fylde Business Agency Ltd, 20 Queen Street, Blackpool, Lancs FY1 1PD (0253 294929) *Contact: John K. Perrins*			•				
BOLTON: Bolton Business Ventures Ltd, 46 Lower Bridgeman Street, Bolton BL2 1DG (0204 391400) *Contact Paul Davidson*	•	•	•		•	•	
BOOTLE: South Sefton Enterprise Agency Ltd, Beaver Enterprise Workspace, 58–60 Strand Road, Bootle, Merseyside L20 4BG (051 933 00240 *Contact: Peter Kennedy*		•	•				
BRADFORD: Bradford Enterprise Agency, Commerce House, Cheapside, Bradford, West Yorks BD1 4JZ (0274 734359) *Contact: J. Graham Fearnley*	•	•					

	EC	BCL	FLG	KPR	MP	YE	MB
BRADFORD ON AVON: West Wiltshire Enterprise, PO Box 15, Abbey Mills, Bradford on Avon, Wilts BA15 1YZ (02216 7843) *Contact: A. B. Zehetmayr*	•			•			
BRAINTREE: Braintree District Enterprise Agency Ltd, Town Hall Centre, Market Square, Braintree, Essex CM7 6YG (0376 43140) *Contact: Brian Holby*	•						
BRENTFORD: Enterprise Hounslow Ltd, 13 Boston Manor Road, Brentford, TW8 9DT (01 847 3269) *Contact: Tony Hazell*					•	•	
BRENTWOOD: Brentwood Enterprise Agency, 1–2 Severn Arches Road, Brentwood, Essex CM15 8AY (0277 213405) *Contact: Geoff Jennings*	•						
BRIDGWATER: Small Industries Group, 68–70 Friarn Street, Bridgwater, Somerset TA6 3LJ (0278 424456) *Contact: Fred Wedlake*			•	•	•		
BRIGHTON: Brighton & Hove Business Enterprise Agency Ltd, 23 Old Steine, Brighton BN1 1EL (0273 688882) *Contact: Michael Hogg*	•	•	•		•	•	
BRISTOL: Bristol & Avon Enterprise Agency (BRAVE), Canons Road, Bristol BS1 5UH	•	•	•	•		•	
New Work Trust Co Ltd, Avondale Workshops, Woodland Way, Kingswood, Bristol BS15 1QH	•				•		
The Coach House Small Business Centre, 2 Upper York Street, St Paul's, Bristol BS2 RH (0272 428022) *Contact: Barry Davies*	•				•		
Hartcliffe & Withywood Ventures Ltd, HMV Block, Hartcliffe School, Bishport Avenue, Hartcliffe, Bristol BS13 0RL (0272 784865) *Contact: Brian McInally*	•		•		•		

41

	EC	BCL	FLG	KPR	MP	YE	MB
BRIXTON: South London Business Initiative Ltd, 444 Brixton Road, Suite 113–114, Brixton Enterprise Centre, London sw9 8ej (01 274 4000 ex. 375) *Contact: Walter V. Baker*			•		•	•	
BROMLEY: Bromley Enterprise Agency Trust Ltd, 7 Palace Grove, Bromley, Kent br1 3ha (01 290 6568) *Contact: Ronnie W. Fenn*	•	•		•	•	•	
BURTON ON TRENT: Burton Enterprise Agency Ltd, Midland Railway Grain Warehouse, Derby Street, Burton on Trent de14 2jj (0283 37151/2) *Contact: F. D. Barrow*	•		•			•	
BURY: Bury Enterprise Centre, 12 Tithebarn Street, Bury, Lancashire bl9 0jr (061 797 5864) *Contact: D. Gough*	•	•		•		•	
BURY ST EDMUNDS: Mid-Anglian Enterprise Agency Ltd, 79 Whiting Street, Bury St Edmunds, Suffolk ip33 1nx (0284 60206) *Contact: Jeff Webb*	•	•	•		•	•	•
CAMBORNE: West Cornwall Enterprise Trust Ltd, Lloyds Bank Chambers, Market Square, Camborne, Cornwall tr14 8jt (0209 714914/715105) *Contact: Alex Bryce*	•	•	•				
CAMBRIDGE: Cambridge Enterprise Agency Ltd, 71a Lensfield Road, Cambridge cb2 1en (0223 323553) *Contact: Peter Manley*	•	•	•			•	•
CAMDEN: Camden Enterprise Ltd, 57 Pratt Street, Camden, London nw1 0dp (01 482 2128) *Contact: Allen Lever*	•		•		•	•	
CANNOCK: Cannock & Burntwood Enterprise Agency Ltd, c/o F. & V. Linford Ltd, PO Box 14, Park Road, Cannock, Staffs ws11 1jw (0543 466566)			•				

	EC	BCL	FLG	KPR	MP	YE	MB
CANTERBURY: East Kent Enterprise Agency, 45 North Lane, Canterbury, Kent CT2 7EF (0227 470234) *Contact: Rodney Jones*	•	•	•		•		•
CARLISLE: Business Initiatives Carlisle, Tower Buildings, Scotch Street, Carlisle, Cumbria CA3 8RB (0228 34129) *Contact: John Oliver*	•	•	•		•		
CHATHAM: Medway Enterprise Agency Ltd, Railway Street, Chatham, Kent ME4 4RR (0634 830301) *Contact: Guy Sibley*	•	•	•	•			
CHELMSFORD: Chelmsford Enterprise Agency Ltd, Unit AO3, Globe House, New Street, Chelmsford, Essex CM1 1PP (0245 490281) *Contact: John Antony Harris*			•	•	•		
Essex Business Centre, Chelmer Court, Church Street, Chelmsford, Essex CM1 1NH (0245 283030) *Contact: Roy McLarty*	•	•		•	•	•	
CHESTER: Chester Enterprise Agency, Hoole Bridge, Chester CH2 3NQ (0244 311474) *Contact: M. C. Talbot*	•	•	•	•	•	•	
CHESTERFIELD: North Derbyshire Enterprise Agency, 96 Saltergate, Chesterfield, Derbyshire S40 1LG (0246 207379/208743) *Contact: Michael Horner*	•	•		•			
CHESTER LE STREET: Chester Le Street and City of Durham Enterprise Agency (CDC), Mechanics Institute, Newcastle Road, Chester le Street, Co Durham DH3 3TS (091 3892648) *Contact: Ronald Batty*	•						
CHIPPENHAM: North Wiltshire Enterprise Agency, Pearl Assurance Building, New Road, Chippenham, Wilts SN15 1EJ (0249 659275) *Contact: Helen Norton*	•						•

	EC	BCL	FLG	KPR	MP	YE	MB
CLACTON-ON-SEA: Enterprise Tendring Ltd, 27a Pier Avenue, Clacton-on-Sea, Essex CO15 1QE (0255 421225) *Contact: Christine Curry*	•		•		•	•	
CLITHEROE: Ribble Valley Enterprise Agency Ltd, Bank House, 2 York Street, Clitheroe, Lancashire BB7 2DL (0200 22110) *Contact: R. D. Dewhurst*							
COLCHESTER: Colchester Business Enterprise Agency, Gate House, High Street, Colchester, Essex CO1 1UG (0206 48833) *Contact: John Hitchman*	•						•
CONSETT: Derwentshire Industrial Development Agency, Berry Edge Road, Consett, Co Durham DH8 5EU (0207 509124) *Contact: J. G. Carney*	•	•	•	•	•	•	•
CORBY: Corby Industrial Development Centre, Douglas House, Queens Square, Corby, Northants NN17 1PL (0536 62571) *Contact: R. G. Jackson*	•		•	•			
COVENTRY: Coventry Business Centre, Christchurch House, Greyfriars Lane, Coventry CV1 2GY (0203 552781/22775) *Contact: John Simpson*	•	•	•				
CREWE: SCOPE (South Cheshire Opportunity for Private Enterprise), SCOPE House, Weston Road, Crewe CW1 1DD (0270 582506) *Contact: John Muckersie*	•	•		•	•	•	
DARLINGTON: The Darlington & South West Durham Business Venture Ltd, The Imperial Centre, Grange Road, Darlington, Co Durham DL1 5NQ (0325 48081) *Contact: W. I. Carswell*	•						

	EC	BCL	FLG	KPR	MP	YE	MB
DARTFORD: North West Kent Enterprise Agency, 2a Hythe Street, Dartford, Kent DA1 1BT (0322 91451) *Contact: Michael Fitzpatrick*		•	•				•
DEPTFORD: Deptford Enterprise Agency, 146 Deptford High Street, Deptford, London SE8 3PQ (01 692 9204) *Contact: Joe Greenland*	•		•	•			
DERBY: Derby & Derbyshire Business Venture, Saxon House, Heritage Way, Friary Street, Derby DE1 1NL (0332 360345) *Contact: George Bench*	•	•					
DONCASTER: DonBAC – The Doncaster Enterprise Agency & Business Advice Centre, 19–21 Hallgate, Doncaster DN2 3NA (0302 340320) *Contact: Brian Crangle*	•	•	•				
DUDLEY: Dudley Business Venture, Stanton House, 10 Castle Street, Dudley, West Midlands DY1 1LQ (0384 231283/4/5) *Contact: J. G. Standish*	•	•	•	•	•		•
EALING: Enterprise Ealing Ltd, 69/71 Broadway, West Ealing W13 3PT (01 840 2667) *Contact: Gordon Foss*		•		•	•	•	
EASINGTON: Easington Industrial Enterprise Ltd, 38 Armstrong Road, North East Industrial Estate, Peterlee, Co Durham SR8 5AE (091 5866555) *Contact: D. Battensby*	•	•	•		•		
EDMONTON: Enfield Enterprise Agency, 2–3 Knights Chambers, 32 South Mall, Edmonton Green, London N9 0TL (01 807 5333) *Contact: Alan Wilks*	•		•		•		
ELLESMERE PORT: Entep Trust Ltd, 72a Whitby Road, Ellesmere Port, South Wirral L65 0AA (051 356 3555) *Contact: Peter Metcalfe*	•		•	•		•	

	EC	BCL	FLG	KPR	MP	YE	MB
EXETER: Business Enterprise Exeter, 39 Marsh Green Road, Marsh Barton, Exeter EX2 8PN (0392 56060) *Contact: E. Sheridan*		•			•		
FINCHLEY: Barnet Enterprise Trust Ltd, Hertford Lodge, East End Road, Finchley, London N3 3QE (01 346 2187) *Contact: Peter Lovell*	•	•		•			
FINSBURY PARK: North London Business Development Agency, 35/37 Blackstock Road, Finsbury Park, London N4 2JF (01 359 7405/6/7) *Contact: Manny Cotter*	•	•		•	•	•	
FLEETWOOD: Wyre Business Agency Ltd, WIBEC, 19–21 Copse Road, Fleetwood, Lancs FY7 6RP (03917 79279) *Contact: Michael Burton*	•	•		•	•	•	
FOLKESTONE: Shepway Business Advisory Panel Ltd, 24 Cheriton Gardens, Folkestone, Kent CT20 2AS (0303 59162) *Contact: A. T. Pearce*			•	•			•
FROME: Frome & Mendip Enterprise Agency, South Parade, Frome, Somerset BA11 1EJ (0373 73101) *Contact: Geoff Stringer*	•	•	•	•	•		•
GATESHEAD: Design Works (Gateshead) Ltd, c/o 60 Grainger Street, Newcastle Upon Tyne NE1 5JG (01 261 7856) *Contact: Robert Walmsley*	•				•		
GLASTONBURY: PAD Enterprise Agency, Workface, Market Place, Glastonbury, Somerset BA6 9HL (0458 34220) *Contact: R. Ripper*	•				•	•	
GLOUCESTER: Gloucester Enterprise Agency, 90 Westgate Street, Gloucester GL1 2NZ (0452 501411) *Contact: Jack Tester*	•						•

	EC	BCL	FLG	KPR	MP	YE	MB
GRANTHAM: South Lincolnshire Enterprise Agency Ltd, Station Road, Grantham, Lincs NG31 6HX (0476 68970) *Contact: Mrs Jacqueline Smith*	•	•	•	•	•		
GRAVESEND: Gravesend Enterprise Agency, 22 Wrotham Road, Gravesend, Kent DA11 0PA (0474 327118) *Contact: Jim Pritchard*		•	•	•			•
GRAYS: Thurrock Local Enterprise Agency Ltd, 79a High Street, Grays, Essex RM17 6NX 0375 374362) *Contact: Derek Price*		•			•	•	
GREAT YARMOUTH: Great Yarmouth Business Advisory Service Ltd, Queens Road Business Centre, Queens Road, Great Yarmouth, Norfolk NR30 3HT (0493 850204) *Contact: John Jennings*	•				•		
GRIMSBY: The Grimsby & Cleethorpes Area Enterprise Agency Ltd, Norwich Union House, 27 Osborne Street, Grimsby, South Humberside DN31 1EY (0472 241869) *Contact: G. J. Mellor*							
GUERNSEY: Guernsey Enterprise Agency, States Arcade, Market Street, St Peter Port, Guernsey C1 (0481 710043) *Contact: E. J. Gaudion*			•				
HACKNEY: Hackney Business Venture, 130–150 Hackney Road, London E2 7QL (01 739 7941) *Contact: Paul Chaplin*			•			•	
HALIFAX: Calderdale Small Business Advice Centre (CaSBAC), OP 53, Dean Clough Office Park, Dean Clough, Halifax HX1 1XG (0422 69487) *Contact: Alan H. Craddock*	•	•	•	•			
HAMMERSMITH: Hammersmith & Fulham Business Resources Ltd, 5th Floor, The Town Hall, King Street, Hammersmith, London W6 9JU (01 741 7248) *Contact: David Mitchell*	•	•	•				

	EC	BCL	FLG	KPR	MP	YE	MB
HARLOW: Harlow Enterprise Agency Ltd, 19 The Rows, The High, Harlow, Essex CM20 1DD (0279 38077) *Contact: John Greener*	•		•	•		•	
HARROW: The Harrow Enterprise Agency Ltd, 2 Courtfield Avenue, Harrow, Middx HA1 2LW (01 427 6188) *Contact: David Welch*	•	•					
HARTLEPOOL: Hartlepool Enterprise Agency Ltd, Suite 7, Municipal Buildings, Church Square, Hartlepool, Cleveland TS24 7ER (0429 221216) *Contact: Alan Humble*	•		•				
Hartlepool New Development Support Ltd, Old Municipal Buildings, Upper Church Street, Hartlepool, Cleveland TS24 7ET (0429 266522 ext. 374/179) *Contact: Ron Preece*	•	•		•			
HASTINGS: Hastings Business Venture Ltd, 18 Cornwallis Gardens, Hastings, East Sussex TN34 1LP (0424 433333)	•	•	•	•	•	•	
HATFIELD: Welwyn & Hatfield Enterprise Agency Ltd, 5 Queensway House, Town Centre, Hatfield, Hertfordshire AL10 0NR (07072 67635) *Contact: J. Ken Sumeray*	•	•				•	
HEMEL HEMPSTEAD: The Dacorum Enterprise Agency, Swallowdale Lane, Hemel Hempstead HP2 7EL(0442 232333) *Contact: Tom Hughes*	•		•			•	•
HEREFORD: Herefordshire Enterprise Agency Ltd, Berrows Business Centre, Bath Street, Hereford HR1 2HE (0432 276898) *Contact: Derek O. Herbert*	•						
HONITON: East Devon Small Industries Group, 115 Border Road, Heath Park, Honiton, Devon EX14 8BT (0404 41806) *Contact: Albert Johnson*	•		•	•	•	•	

	EC	BCL	FLG	KPR	MP	YE	MB
HUDDERSFIELD: Kirklees & Wakefield Venture Trust, Commerce House, New North Road, Huddersfield HD1 5JP (0484 531352) *Contact: Clive Pawson*	•					•	
HULL: Hull Business Advice Centre, 24 Anlaby Road, Hull, North Humberside HU1 2PA (0482 27266) *Contact: Peter Haysom*	•	•				•	
HUNTINGDON: Huntingdon Enterprise Agency Ltd, 49 High Street, Huntingdon, Cambs PE18 6AQ (0480 50028) *Contact: Bill Parker*	•					•	
IPSWICH: IPSENTA, 30a Lower Brook Street, Ipswich, Suffolk IP4 1AL (0473 59832) *Contact: David Hennell*	•	•				•	
ISLE OF WIGHT: Isle of Wight Enterprise Agency Ltd, 6 Town Lane, Newport, Isle of Wight PO30 1JU (0983 592120)	•	•			•		
ISLINGTON: Manor Gardens Enterprise Centre, 10–18 Manor Gardens, London N7 6JY (01 272 8944) *Contact: Patrick Quarry* .	•		•		•	•	
JERSEY: Jersey Business Venture, 15 Broad Street, St Helier, Jersey C1 (0534 35168) *Contact: H. W. Hall*		•					
KENDAL: The Cumbria Rural Enterprise Agency, 44–46 Lound Road, Kendal, Cumbria LA9 7DZ (0539 26624) *Contact: John Peat*					•	•	
KENSINGTON & CHELSEA: Business Resource Centre, 9 Thorpe Close, London W10 5X (01 969 9455) *Contact: Barry Tay*	•	•	•	•	•	•	•
KETTERING: Kettering Business Venture Trust Ltd, Douglas House, 27 Station Road, Kettering, Northants NN15 7HH (0536 513840) *Contact: Harry Stevenson*	•	•					

	EC	BCL	FLG	KPR	MP	YE	MB
KING'S LYNN: West Norfolk Enterprise Agency Trust Ltd, 7 King Street, King's Lynn, Norfolk PE30 1ET (0553 760431) *Contact: John Fincham*	•	•					
KIRKBY: Knowsley Enterprise Agency, Admin Building, Admin Road, Knowsley Industrial Park (North), Kirkby L33 7TX (051 548 3245) *Contact: F. G. Crawley*		•					
LANCASTER: Business for Lancaster Ltd, 32b St Leonard's House, St Leonardgate, Lancaster LA1 1NN (0524 66222) *Contact: Gordon C. Peebles*	•	•		•			
LAUNCESTON: Enterprise Tamar, National School, St Thomas Road, Launceston, Cornwall PL15 8BU (0566 5632) *Contact: David Stanbury*	•		•		•	•	
LEEDS: Leeds Business Venture Ltd, Commerce House, 2 St Alban's Place, Wade Lane, Leeds LS2 8HZ (0532 446474/457583) *Contact: Derek Varley*		•	•			•	•
LEICESTER: Leicester Business Venture Ltd, 30 New Walk, Leicester LE1 6TF (0533 554464) *Contact: Alan Lee*	•						
LETCHWORTH GARDEN CITY: Letchworth Garden City Business Centre, Avenue One, Business Park, Letchworth Garden City, Herts SG6 2HB (0462 678272) *Contact: Stephen Brockman*	•	•		•			
LEYLAND: South Ribble Business Venture Ltd, 176 Towngate, Leyland, Lancs PR5 1TE (0772 422242) *Contact: Derek Wakefield*	•		•	•	•	•	
LINCOLN: Lincoln Enterprise Agency, Innovation Centre, West Yard, Ropewalk, Lincoln LN6 7DQ (0522 40775) *Contact: Denis Wilson*	•				•	•	•

	EC	BCL	FLG	KPR	MP	YE	MB
LIVERPOOL: Business in Liverpool Ltd, Merseyside Innovation Centre, 131 Mount Pleasant, Liverpool L3 5TF (051 709 1231/1366) *Contact: S. C. Stevenson*							
Merseyside Education Training Enterprise Ltd (METEL), 6 Salisbury Street, Liverpool L3 8DR (051 207 2281) *Contact: Judith Manifold*	•	•			•		
LONDON: (see also under London Boroughs) **London Enterprise Agency (LEntA)**, 4 Snow Hill, London EC1A 2BS (01 236 3000) *Contact: Brian Wright*	•	•	•	•	•	•	•
LOUGHTON: Forest Enterprise Agency Trust, Feat House, Rear of Swimming Pool, Traps Hill, Loughton, Essex IG10 1SZ (01 508 7435) *Contact: Gerry F. Clarke*	•		•	•	•		
LOWESTOFT: Lowestoft Enterprise Trust Ltd, 19 Grove Road, Lowestoft, Suffolk NR32 1EB (0502 63286)				•	•		
LUTON: Bedfordshire Community Enterprise Agency (BECENTA), Enterprise House, 7 Gordon Street, Luton, Beds LU1 2QP (0582 452288) *Contact: Derek Upcott*	•			•	•	•	
MACCLESFIELD: Macclesfield Business Ventures, Venture House, Cross Street, Macclesfield SK11 7PG (0625 615113) *Contact: Graham Sanger*	•	•	•		•		
MAIDSTONE: The Maidstone Enterprise Agency Ltd, 25a Pudding Lane, Maidstone, Kent ME14 1PA (0622 675547) *Contact: Ian Dumbreck*				•		•	
MANCHESTER: Manchester Business Consortium, PO Box 21, Hyde, Cheshire SK14 1HA (061 368 0685) *Contact: Richard Nash*	•	•		•			

	EC	BCL	FLG	KPR	MP	YE	MB
Manchester Business Venture, c/o Manchester Chamber of Commerce and Industry, 56 Oxford Street, Manchester M60 7HJ (061 236 0153) *Contact: Derek Gower*	•					•	•
Agency for Economic Development Ltd, 8/12 Parisian Way, Moss Side Centre, Moss Lane East, Manchester M15 5NQ (061 226 9434) *Contact: Volney Harris*	•		•	•	•		
MANSFIELD: Mansfield Enterprise Partnership, The Old Town Hall, Market Place, Mansfield, Notts NG18 1HX (0623 21773) *Contact: Peter Slack*	•				•		
MIDDLESBROUGH: Cleveland Enterprise Agency Ltd, 52/60 Corporation Road, Middlesbrough, Cleveland TS1 2RN (0642 222836)	•		•				
Cleveland Youth Business Centres, 6 North Street, Middlesbrough, Cleveland TS2 1JL (0642 240656) *Contact: Mike Reaney*	•	•	•		•	•	
MILTON KEYNES: Milton Keynes Business Venture, Civic Offices (Level 3), 1 Saxon Gate East, Central Milton Keynes MK9 3JH (0908 660044) *Contact: John Carpenter*	•	•	•		•	•	•
MORDEN: Merton Enterprise Agency Ltd, 12th Floor, Crown House, London Road, Morden, Surrey SM4 5DX (01 545 3067) *Contact: Harry Corben*	•						
MORPETH: Northumberland Business Centre, Southgate, Morpeth, Northumberland NE61 2EH (0670 511221) *Contact: Graham Adams*	•		•	•	•		
NEWARK: Newark Enterprise Agency, The Firs, 67 London Road, Newark, Notts NG24 1RZ (0636 640666) *Contact: Brian Tindale*	•				•	•	

	EC	BCL	FLG	KPR	MP	YE	MB
NEWCASTLE: The Tyne & Wear Enterprise Trust Ltd (ENTRUST), Portman House, Portland Road, Newcastle Upon Tyne NE2 1BL (091 261 4838) *Contact: John Eversley*	•		•		•		
Project North East, 60 Grainger Street, Newcastle Upon Tyne NE1 5JG (091 261 7856) *Contact: David Irwin*	•		•			•	
Newcastle Youth Enterprise Centre, 25 Low Friar Street, Newcastle NE1 5UE (091 261 6009) *Contact: Chris Smith*	•		•	•	•	•	
St Thomas Street Workshops, St Thomas Street, Newcastle NE1 4LE (01 232 4895) *Contact: Jeff Boden*					•		
NEWTON ABBOT: Teinbridge Enterprise Agency, The Tindle Centre, St Marychurch Road, Newton Abbot, Devon TQ12 4UQ (0626 67534) *Contact: Leslie Saye*				•	•		
NORTHAMPTON: Northamptonshire Enterprise Agency Ltd, Elgin House, Billing Road, Northampton NN1 5AU (0604 37401) *Contact: David Mann*	•		•	•	•		
NORTHWICH: Vale Royal Small Firms Ltd, Wallerscote House, Winnington Lane, Northwich, Cheshire CW8 4EG (0606 77711) *Contact: Barry Lee*	•	•			•	•	
NORWICH: Norwich Enterprise Agency Trust Ltd, 112 Barrack Street, Norwich NR3 1TX (0603 613023) *Contact: Garry Flatres*	•	•	•			•	
NOTTINGHAM: Nottingham Business Venture, City House, Maid Marian Way, Nottingham NG1 6BH (0602 470914) *Contact: Gordon Mackenzie*	•		•				

	EC	BCL	FLG	KPR	MP	YE	MB
OLDHAM: Oldham Enterprise Agency, Unit 26, The Acorn Centre, Barry Street, Oldham OL1 3NE (061 665 1225) *Contact: Roy Newton*	•	•	•				
ORMSKIRK: The West Lancashire Enterprise Trust Ltd, The Malt House, 48 Southport Road, Ormskirk, Lancs L39 1LX (0695 78626) *Contact: Dr James W. Smith*	•	•		•	•		
OXFORD: Thames Business Advice Centre, 8th Floor, Seacourt Tower, West Way, Oxford, Oxon OX2 0JP (0865 249279) *Contact: B. J. Hills Spedding*	•	•	•		•	•	•
PADDINGTON: Westminster Enterprise Agency Ltd, Beauchamp Lodge, 2 Warwick Crescent, London W2 6NE (01 286 1740) *Contact: Bob MacLean*							
PAULTON: Wansdyke Enterprise Agency, Business Advice Centre, High Street, Paulton, Bristol BS18 5NW (0761 415400) *Contact: Reginald Clark*	•	•	•	•			
PENDLE: Pendle Enterprise Trust Ltd, 19/23 Leeds Road, Nelson, Pendle, Lancs BB9 6SZ (0282 698001) *Contact: Ron Morrish*	•					•	•
PETERBOROUGH: Peterborough Enterprise Programme, Broadway Court, Broadway, Peterborough, Cambs PE1 1RP (0733 310159) *Contact: John Duckworth*	•	•	•			•	•
PLYMOUTH: Enterprise Plymouth Ltd, Somerset Place, Stoke, Plymouth PL3 4BB (0752 569211) *Contact: Fred Parker*	•	•	•		•	•	
POOLE: Dorset Enterprise Agency Ltd, 1 Britannia Road, Lower Parkstone, Poole, Dorset BH14 8AZ (0202 748333) *Contact: Paul Cook*	•		•		•		•

	EC	BCL	FLG	KPR	MP	YE	MB
PORTSMOUTH: Portsmouth Area Enterprise, 27 Guildhall Walk, Portsmouth, Hampshire PO1 2RY (0705 833321) *Contact: Bill Summer*	•	•			•		
PRESTON: Preston Business Venture, 43 Lune Street, Preston, Lancashire PR1 2NN (0772 25723) *Contact: Paul Ardern*	•	•	•		•		
RAWTENSTALL: Rossendale Enterprise Trust Ltd, 29 Kay Street, Rawtenstall, Rossendale, Lancs BB4 7LS (0706 229838) *Contact: Bruce Harris*	•	•	•	•	•		
READING: Berkshire Enterprise Agency, The Old Shire Hall, The Forbury, Reading, Berks RG1 3EJ (0734 585715) *Contact: Roy Hale*	•		•	•	•		
REDDITCH: Redditch Enterprise Agency Ltd, Rubicon Centre, Broad Ground Road, Lakeside, Redditch, Worcs B98 0EN (0527 501122) *Contact: Ron Herd*	•	•	•	•	•		
RICHMOND: Richmond & Northallerton Business Venture Ltd, 13 Market Place, Richmond, North Yorks (0748 6262) *Contact: Alan Slater*	•	•	•	•	•		•
ROCHDALE: Metropolitan Enterprise Trust Rochdale Area Ltd (Business Help), c/o TBA Industrial Products Ltd, PO Box 40, Rooley Moor Road, Rochdale, OL12 7EQ (0706 356250)						•	
ROMFORD: The North East Thames Business Advisory Centre, Marshalls Chambers, 80a South Street, Romford, Essex RM1 1RP (0708 766438) *Contact: Ulrik Middelboe*	•				•		

	EC	BCL	FLG	KPR	MP	YE	MB
ROTHERHAM: Rotherham Enterprise Agency Ltd, 2nd Floor, All Saints Buildings, Corporation Street, Rotherham, South Yorks S60 1NX (0709 382121 ext 3463) *Contact: E. H. Lunness*	•	•			•	•	
RUISLIP: Hillingdon Enterprise Agency Ltd, 400a Long Lane, Hillingdon, Middx UB10 9PG (0895 73433)							
RUNCORN: Business Link Ltd, 62 Church Street, Runcorn, Cheshire WA7 1LD (09285 63037/73549) *Contact: Bernard Burton*	•		•	•	•	•	
ST ALBANS: St Albans Enterprise Agency (STANTA), Unit 6G, St Albans Enterprise Centre, Long Spring, Porters Wood, St Albans, Herts AL3 6EN (0727 37760) *Contact: K. J. Hughesman*					•		
ST AUSTELL: Restormel Local Enterprise Trust Ltd, Lower Penarwyn, St Blazey, Par, Cornwall PL24 2DS (072681 3079) *Contact: A. G. Tourell*	•		•	•	•	•	
ST HELENS: The Community of St Helens Trust Ltd, PO Box 36, St Helens, Merseyside WA10 3TT (0744 696771) *Contact: Dr R. G. Halford*	•	•	•	•	•		
SALE: Trafford Business Venture, Third Floor, Six Acre House, Town Square, Sale, Cheshire M33 1XZ (061 905 2950) *Contact: John Stembridge*	•	•					
SALFORD: Salford Hundred Venture Ltd, Stamford House, 361 Chapel Street, Salford, Manchester M3 5JY (061 835 1166) *Contact: M. T. Finnie*	•				•		
SALISBURY: South Wiltshire Enterprise Agency, 48a New Street, Salisbury, Wilts SP1 2PH (0722 411052) *Contact: Dick Turpin*							

	EC	BCL	FLG	KPR	MP	YE	MB
SCARBOROUGH: Scarborough, Filey & District Business Development Agency Ltd, 4th Floor, Skipton Chambers, 32 St Nicholas Street, Scarborough, North Yorks YO11 2HF (0723 354454) *Contact: Norman H. Swain*	•		•	•	•		
SHEFFIELD: Sheffield Enterprise Agency (SENTA), 61–69 Leavygreave Road, Sheffield S3 7RB (0742 755721) *Contact: Barrie Briggs*	•	•	•		•		
SHILDON & SEDGEFIELD: Shildon & Sedgefield District Development Agency Ltd, BREL Offices, Byerley Road, Shildon, Co Durham DL4 1PU (0388 777917) *Contact: John William Robson*	•	•	•	•			
SKIPTON: The Yorkshire Dales Enterprise Agency Ltd (DEAL), 21 High Street, Gargrave, Nr Skipton, North Yorks BD23 3RW *Contact: Mike Trestrail*							
SOLIHULL: Solihull Business Enterprise Ltd, Vulcan House, Vulcan Road, Lode Lane Industrial Estate, Solihull, West Midlands B91 2JY (021 704 1456) *Contact: Fred Smallman*							
SOUTH SHIELDS: The Tyneside Economic Development Company Ltd (TEDCO), Business Enterprise Centre, Eldon Street, South Shields, Tyne & Wear NE33 5JE (091 455 4300) *Contact: M. G. Taylor*			•		•	•	
SOUTHAMPTON: Southampton Enterprise Agency, Solent Business Centre, Millbrook Road West, Southampton, Hants SO1 0HW (0703 788088) *Contact: John Townsend*			•	•		•	
SOUTH HUMBER: South Humber Business Advice Centre Ltd, 7 Market Place, Brigg, South Humberside DN20 8HA (0652 57637/8) *Contact: Derek Marshall*	•		•	•			

	EC	BCL	FLG	KPR	MP	YE	MB
SOUTHEND-ON-SEA: Southend Enterprise Agency Ltd, Commerce House, 845 London Road, Westcliff-On-Sea, Essex SS0 9SZ *Contact: Gordon Barrett*	•						
SOUTHPORT: Southport Marketing & Enterprise Bureau Ltd, Pavilion Buildings, 99–105 Lord Street, Southport PR8 1RJ (0704 44173/43977) *Contact: Peter Meakin*	•	•		•			
STAFFORD: Stafford Enterprise Ltd, 7/8 Mill Street, Stafford ST16 2AJ (0785 57057) *Contact: John Cooper*							
STEVENAGE: Stevenage Initiative Ltd, Business & Technology Centre, Bessemer Drive, Stevenage, Herts SG1 2DX (0438 315733) *Contact: M. G. Amos*	•	•	•			•	•
STOCKPORT: Stockport Business Venture Ltd, PO Box 66, Crossley Road, Heaton Chapel, Stockport SK4 5BH (061 432 3770) *Contact: Bill Hurren*	•						
STOKE-ON-TRENT: North Staffs & District Business Initiative, Commerce House, Festival Park, Etruria, Stoke-on-Trent, Staffs ST1 5BE (0782 279013) *Contact: Tony Brookes*	•	•	•				
SUDBURY: Sudbury Enterprise Agency, Guthrie House, 67 Cornard Road, Sudbury, Suffolk CO10 6XB (0787 73927) *Contact: David Cackett*	•				•		
SUNDERLAND: Sunderland Youth Enterprise Centre, 1–2 John St, Sunderland SR1 1UA (091 5109191) *Contact: Vincent T. Wright*	•					•	•
SUTTON: Sutton Enterprise Agency Ltd, 11 Lower Road, Sutton, Surrey SM1 4QJ (01 643 9430) *Contact: John Jardine*	•						

	EC	BCL	FLG	KPR	MP	YE	MB
SWINDON: Swindon Enterprise Trust, 54 Victoria Road, Swindon, Wilts SN1 3AY (0793 487793) *Contact: R. H. D. Hardy*	•		•	•	•	•	
TELFORD: Shropshire Enterprise Trust Ltd, National Westminster Bank Chambers, The Green, Church Street, Wellington, Telford, Shropshire TF1 1DN (0952 56624/47046) *Contact: E. A. Houghton*	•						
TIVERTON: Mid Devon Enterprise Agency, The Factory, Leat Street, Tiverton, Devon EX16 5LL (0884 255629) *Contact: Mike Robins*	•	•			•		
TONBRIDGE: Great Weald Enterprise Agency, 34a High Street, Tonbridge, Kent TN9 1EJ (0732 360133) *Contact: Ron Booth*	•	•	•			•	•
TOTNES: South Hams Agency for Rural Enterprise (SHARE), 4a Leechwell Street, Totnes, Devon TQ9 5SX (0803 684200) *Contact: Alan Littlewood*				•	•	•	•
TOWER HAMLETS: Tower Hamlets Centre for Small Business Ltd, 76 Wentworth Street, London E1 7SE (01 377 8821) *Contact: Ian R. Lorkin*				•	•		
TWICKENHAM: Richmond Upon Thames Enterprise Agency Ltd, 55 Heath Road, Twickenham, Middx TW1 4AW (01 891 3742) *Contact: Brian Parkinson*				•	•		
WALSALL: Walsall Small Firms Advice Unit Ltd, Jerome Chambers, Bridge Street, Walsall, West Midlands WS1 1EX (0922 646614/646639) *Contact: David Porter*	•	•	•	•			
WALTHAMSTOW: Waltham Forest Enterprise Agency Ltd, 125a Hoe Street, Walthamstow, London E17 4RX (01 521 3316/7) *Contact: Tony Butler*	•	•	•	•			

	EC	BCL	FLG	KPR	MP	YE	MB
WARRINGTON: Warrington Business Promotion Bureau, Barbauld House, Barbauld Street, Warrington WA1 2QY (0925 33309) *Contact: Brian Rick*	•	•	•	•		•	
WARWICK: Warwickshire Enterprise Agency, Northgate South, Northgate Street, Warwick CV34 4JH (0926 495685) *Contact: C. D. Edwards*	•	•	•	•			
WATFORD: Watford Enterprise Agency, The Business Centre, Colne Way, Watford, Herts WD2 4ND (0923 247373) *Contact: Ken Hards*	•				•	•	
WEMBLEY: Brent Business Venture Ltd, 12 Park Lane, Wembley, Middx HA9 7RP (01 903 7300/7329) *Contact: Anthony Ure*	•		•	•		•	
WEST BROMWICH: Sandwell Enterprise Ltd, Sandwell Business Advice Centre, Victoria Street, West Bromwich, Sandwell, West Midlands B70 8ET (021 569 2231/2562) *Contact: A. W. Woodhouse*	•	•	•	•			
WHITBY: Whitby & District Business Development Agency Ltd, 3 Bagdale, Whitby, North Yorks YO21 1QL (0947 600827) *Contact: Peter Edwin Horn*	•		•		•	•	
WIGAN: Wigan New Enterprise Ltd, 45 Bridgeman Terrace, Wigan, Lancashire WN1 1TT (0942 496591) *Contact: Fred Bamber*	•	•	•			•	
WISBECH: Fens Business Enterprise Trust Ltd (FenBET), 5 Ely Place, Wisbech, Cambs PE13 1EU (0945 587084) *Contact: David A. Rigley*	•		•			•	
WOKING: Surrey Business Enterprise Agency Ltd, 19 High Street, Woking, Surrey GU21 1BW (04862 28434) *Contact: Matt Huber*		•		•		•	

	EC	BCL	FLG	KPR	MP	YE	MB

WOLVERHAMPTON:
Wolverhampton Enterprise Ltd,
Exchange Street, Wolverhampton WV1
1TS (0902 312095)
Contact: Phil Wilson
— EC •, FLG •, KPR •, MP •

WORCESTER: Worcester Enterprise
Agency, First Floor, Marmion House,
Copenhagen Street, Worcester WR1 2HB
(0905 612412)
Contact: Gordon Moone
— EC •, BCL •, KPR •

WORKINGTON: Enterprise West
Cumbria, Thirlmere Building, 50
Lakes Road, Workington, Cumbria CA14
8NF (0900 65656)
Contact: T. Winterbottom
— EC •, BCL •, FLG •, KPR •, MP •, YE •

WORTHING: West Sussex Area
Enterprise Centre Ltd, 69a Chapel
Road, Worthing, West Sussex (0903
31499)
Contact: Len Crowhurst
— EC •, BCL •, FLG •, KPR •, YE •, MB •

YEOVIL: The Enterprise Agency,
(South Somerset & West Dorset), 5 St
Johns House, Church Path, Yeovil,
Somerset BA2 0HF (0935 79813)
Contact: Michael Warne
— EC •, FLG •, MB •

YORK: York Enterprise Ltd, York
Enterprise Centre, 1 Davygate, York
YO1 2QE (0904 646803)
Contact: Richard Foster
— EC •, FLG •, MP •, YE •

The Vale of York Small Business
Association, York Enterprise Centre,
1 Davygate, York YO1 2QE (0904 641401)
Contact: G. Elliott
— EC •, BCL •

WALES

AMMAN VALLEY: Dinefwr
Enterprise Co, Business Centre,
Margaret Street, Ammanford, Dyfed
(0269 3707)

	EC	BCL	FLG	KPR	MP	YE	MB
BARGOED: Economic Development Partnership of the Rhymney Valley, Enterprise Centre, Bowen Industrial Estate, Aberbargoed, Bargoed, Mid Glamorgan CF8 9EP (0443 821222) *Contact: A. Shapland*	•	•	•	•	•	•	
BRIDGEND: Ogwr Partnership Trust Ltd, Enterprise Centre, Bryn Road, Tondu, Bridgend, Mid Glam CF32 9BS (0656 724414) *Contact: Gareth Bray*	•	•	•		•	•	
CARDIFF: Cardiff & Vale Enterprise, Enterprise House, 127 Bute Street, Cardiff CF1 5LE (0222 494411) *Contact: Peter Fortune*	•		•	•	•	•	•
DEESIDE: Deeside Enterprise Trust Ltd, Park House, Deeside Industrial Park, Deeside, Clwyd CH5 2NZ (0244 815262) *Contact: Peter Summers*	•		•	•			
HAVERFORDWEST: Pembrokeshire Business Initiative (PBI), Lombard Chambers, 14 High Street, Haverfordwest, Dyfed SA61 2LD (0437 67655/6) *Contact: Richard Packman*	•		•	•			
HOLYWELL: Delyn Business Partnership Ltd, Greenfield Business Park, Bagilt Road, Holywell, Clwyd CH8 7HN (0352 711747) *Contact: Neville Clive*	•				•		
LLANDRINDOD WELLS: Powys Self Help, Old Town Hall, Temple Street, Llandrindod Wells, Powys LD1 5DL (0597 4576) *Contact: Barrie Cooper*	•		•	•		•	•
LLANELLI: Llanelli Enterprise Co Ltd, 100 Tostre Road, Llanelli, Dyfed, South Wales SA15 2EA (0554 772122) *Contact: David Williams*	•	•	•			•	•

	EC	BCL	FLG	KPR	MP	YE	MB
MERTHYR TYDFIL: Merthyr-Aberdare Development Enterprise Ltd, The Enterprise Centre, Merthyr Industrial Park, Pentrebach, Merthyr Tydfil, Mid Glam CF48 4DR (0443 692233) *Contact: Jeff Pride*	•	•	•	•	•	•	
NEATH: Neath Development Partnership Enterprise Ltd, 7 Water Street, Neath SA11 3EP (0639 54111/ 54112) *Contact: A. R. Morgan*			•				
NEWPORT: Newport Enterprise Agency Ltd, Enterprise Way, Off Bolt Street, Newport, Gwent NP9 2AQ (0633 54041) *Contact: Alan Prosper*	•	•	•	•	•	•	
RUTHIN: Clwydfro Enterprise Agency, Llysfasi, Ruthin, Clwyd LL15 2LB (097888 414) *Contact: Arwyn L. Jones*	•		•	•			
SWANSEA: West Glamorgan Enterprise Trust Ltd, 12a St Mary's Square, Swansea, West Glamorgan SA1 3LP (0792 475345) *Contact: G. W. Atkins*	•	•	•		•		•

NORTHERN IRELAND

	EC	BCL	FLG	KPR	MP	YE	MB
ARMAGH: Armagh Business Centre, 2 Loughgall Road, Armagh BT61 7NH (0861 525050) *Contact: S. Hartley*	•					•	•
BANGOR: North Down Development Organisation, Enterprise House, Balloo Industrial Estate, Bangor, Co Down BT19 2QT (0247 271525) *Contact: D. Dunstall*	•				•		
BELFAST: Action Resource Centre, 3 Botanic Avenue, Belfast BT7 1JG (0232 234504/231730) *Contact: Robin McConkey*	•		•				

	EC	BCL	FLG	KPR	MP	YE	MB
Brookfield Business Centre Ltd, Brookfield Mill, 333 Crumlin Road, Belfast BT14 7EA (0232 745241) *Contact: Fr Myles Kavanagh*	•				•		
Glenand Youth & Community Workshop Ltd, Blackstaff Road, Kennedy Way Industrial Estate, Belfast BT11 9DT (0232 301483) *Contact: P. Crossey*					•		
CARRICKFERGUS: Carrickfergus Enterprise Ltd, 75 Belfast Road, Carrickfergus, Co Antrim BT38 8PH (09603 69528) *Contact: D. R. Waite*	•				•		
COLERAINE: Coleraine Enterprise Agency, 3 Gateside Road, Coleraine, Co Londonderry BT52 2PB (0265 55464) *Contact: Ray Young*	•				•		
DOWNPATRICK: Jobspace (NI) Ltd, 45 Saul Road, Downpatrick, Co Down BT30 6PA (0396 6416) *Contact: Hugh McKirgan*	•				•	•	
DRAPERSTOWN: Workspace Draperstown Ltd, 7 Tobermore Road, Draperstown, Magherafelt BT45 7AG (0648 28113) *Contact: Mr Patsy McShane*	•				•	•	
DUNMURRY: Glenwood Enterprise Ltd, Springbank Industrial Estate, Pembroke Loop Road, Dunmurry BT17 0QL (0232 620150) *Contact: Aidan Fitzpatrick*					•		
ENNISKILLEN: Fermanagh Enterprise Ltd, Project House, Regal Pass, Enniskillen, Co Fermanagh (0365 27348) *Contact: Martin Maguire*	•	•	•		•	•	
LARNE: Larne Enterprise Development Co, Ledcom Industrial Estate, Bank Road, Larne, Co Antrim BT40 3AW (0574 70742) *Contact: Ken Frayne*	•				•	•	

	EC	BCL	FLG	KPR	MP	YE	MB
LONDONDERRY: Ebrington Business Centre Ltd, Ebrington Gardens, Waterside, Londonderry BT47 1EH (0504 43885) *Contact: R. Gillespie*	•				•	•	
North West Ulster Enterprise Agency, 1–3 Clarendon Street, Londonderry BT48 7EP (0504 265817) *Contact: Dr Vera Furness*							
Foyld Factory Space Ltd, Enterprise House, Little James Street, Londonderry BT48 7BG (0504 364015) *Contact: Denis Feeney*	•		•		•	•	
NEWRY: Newry & Mourne Enterprise Agency, Enterprise House, 5 Downshire Place, Newry BT34 1DZ (0693 67011) *Contact: Frank Dolaghan*	•	•	•		•	•	
OMAGH: Omagh Enterprise Co Ltd, Gortrush Industrial Estate, Derry Road, Omagh, Co. Tyrone BT79 7XH (0662 49494) *Contact: Liam McDonald*	•			•	•	•	
PORTADOWN: Craigavon Industrial Development Organisation, Craigavon Enterprise Centre, Carn Industrial Estate, Portadown BT63 5RH (0762 333393) *Contact: Kevin Lowe*	•			•	•	•	•
STRABANE: Strabane Industrial Properties Ltd, Ballycolman Industrial Estate, Strabane, Co. Tyrone BT82 9PH (0504 884518) *Contact: Christina Mullen*				•		•	

SCOTLAND

	EC	BCL	FLG	KPR	MP	YE	MB
ABERDEEN: Aberdeen Enterprise Trust, First Floor, Seaforth Centre, 30 Waterloo Quay, Aberdeen AB2 1BS (0224 582599) *Contact: Anne Minto*	•	•				•	•

	EC	BCL	FLG	KPR	MP	YE	MB
ALLOA: Alloa & Clackmannan Enterprise Trust (ACE), 70 Drysdale Street, Alloa, Clackmannanshire FK10 1JA (0259 217171) *Contact: Tony Deeley*	•	•	•		•	•	
ARBROATH: Arbroath Venture Trust, 115 High Street, Arbroath DD11 1DP (0241 70563)	•	•					
AYR: Ayr Locality Enterprise Resource Trust Ltd (ALERT), 88 Green Street, Ayr KA8 8BG (0292 264181) *Contact: D. Malcolm Troup*	•	•	•				
BATHGATE: Bathgate Area Support for Enterprise Ltd (BASE), 19 North Bridge Street, Bathgate, West Lothian EH48 4PJ (0506 634024) *Contact: Michael Fass*	•	•	•	•	•	•	
COATBRIDGE: Monklands Business Enterprise Trust, Unit 10, Coatbridge Business Centre, Main Street, Coatbridge (0236 23281) *Contact: Terry Currie*	•	•	•	•			•
CROSSGATES: South Fife Enterprise Trust Ltd, 6 Main Street, Crossgates, Fife KY4 8AJ (0383 515053) *Contact: David Blues*	•	•			•		•
CUMBERNAULD: Cumbernauld & Kilsyth Enterprise Trust Ltd, 5 South Muirhead Road, Cumbernauld G67 1AJ (0236 739394) *Contact: Ian Long*	•			•		•	
CUMNOCK: Cumnock & Doon Enterprise Trust, Cumnock & Doon Enterprise Centre, Block 3, Caponacre Industrial Estate, Cumnock, Ayrshire KA18 1LD (0290 21159/25303) *Contact: Alex Neil*	•			•	•	•	
DALKEITH: Midlothian Campaign, 115 High Street, Dalkeith, Midlothian EH22 1AX (031 660 5849) *Contact: Frank Binnie*	•	•	•	•		•	•

	EC	BCL	FLG	KPR	MP	YE	MB
DUMBARTON: Dumbarton District Enterprise Trust, Block 2/2 Vale of Leven Industrial Estate, Dumbarton, Dunbartonshire G82 3PD (0389 50005/ 55424) *Contact: Ralph Risk*	•	•					
DUMFRIES: The Enterprise Trust for Nithsdale: Annandale/Eskdale and the Stewartry, Heathhall, Dumfries DG1 1TZ (0387 56229) *Contact: Cyril Rankin*	•				•	•	
DUNDEE: Dundee Enterprise Trust Ltd, West Hendersons Wynd, Dundee DD1 5BY (0382 26002) *Contact: David Morrison*				•	•	•	•
EAST KILBRIDE: East Kilbride Business Centre, PO Box 1, 10th Floor, Plaza Tower, East Kilbride G74 1LW (03552 38456) *Contact: Burt Miller*	•			•	•	•	
EDINBURGH: Edinburgh Venture Enterprise Trust (EVENT), 2 Canning Street Lane, Edinburgh EH3 8ER (031 229 8928) *Contact: Alf Laing*	•	•	•			•	
Leith Enterprise Trust, 25 Maritime Street, Leith, Edinburgh EH6 5PW (031 553 5566) *Contact: James A. Prettyman*	•	•	•	•			
Edinburgh Old Town Trust, Advocate's Close, High Street, Edinburgh (031 225 8818) *Contact: Brig. James Wilson*				•			
ELGIN: Moray Enterprise Trust, 5 North Guildry Street, Elgin IV30 1JR (0343 49644) *Contact: Dick Ruane*	•					•	
FALKIRK: Falkirk Enterprise Action Trust (FEAT), Suite A, Haypark, Marchmont Avenue, Polmont FK2 0NZ (0324 716173) *Contact: Peter White*	•	•	•	•	•		•

	EC	BCL	FLG	KPR	MP	YE	MB
FRASERBURGH: Fraserburgh Ltd, Old Station Yard, Dalrymple Street, Fraserburgh AB4 5BH (0346 27764) *Contact: Ian Moir*	•		•	•			
GLASGOW: Glasgow Opportunities, 7 West George Street, Glasgow G2 1EQ (041 221 0955) *Contact: Tony Eadsforth*	•	•	•			•	•
The Greater Easterhouse Partnership, 40 Township Centre, Easterhouse, Glasgow G34 9BP (041 771 591) *Contact: William Craw*	•		•		•		
Barras Enterprise Trust, 244 Gallowgate, Glasgow G4 0TS (041 552 7258) *Contact: Martin Caldwell*	•		•	•			
GLENROTHES: Glenrothes Enterprise Trust Ltd, North House, North Street, Glenrothes, Fife KY7 5NA (0592 757903/759584) *Contact: Erik Hendry*	•		•				
GREENOCK: Inverclyde Enterprise Trust Ltd, 64/66 West Blackhall Street, Greenock PA15 1XG (0475 892191/2/3) *Contact: Ewen Macaulay*	•		•	•		•	
HAMILTON: LIFE, 116 Cadzow Street, Hamilton, Lanarkshire ML3 6HH (0698 66622) *Contact: Peter Agnew*	•		•			•	
INVERNESS: Highland Opportunity Ltd, Development Dept, Highland Regional Council, Glenurquhart Road, Inverness IV3 5NX (0463 234121 ext 402) *Contact: Hugh Black*	•	•	•				
KILBURNIE: Garnock Valley Development Executive Ltd, 44 Main Street, Kilburnie, Ayrshire KA25 7BY (0505 685455) *Contact: Bill Dunn*	•	•	•	•	•	•	

	EC	BCL	FLG	KPR	MP	YE	MB
KIRKINTILLOCH: Strathkelvin Enterprise Trust, 10 Rochdale Place, Kirkintilloch G66 1HZ (041 777 7171) *Contact: Donald MacInnes*	•	•	•		•	•	
LEVEN: Levenmouth Enterprise Trust, Unit 17b/20a Hawkslaw Trading Estate, Riverside Road, Leven, Fife KY8 4LT (0333 27905) *Contact: Arthur Murphy*	•		•				•
MOTHERWELL: Motherwell Enterprise Trust, 28 Brandon Parade, Motherwell ML1 1UJ (0698 69333) *Contact: John Murphy*	•	•	•	•	•	•	
NEWTON STEWART: Wigtown Rural Development Co Ltd, Royal Bank Building, 44 Victoria Street, Newton Stewart, Wigtownshire DG8 6BT (0671 3434) *Contact: William Phillips*	•	•	•				•
PAISLEY: Paisley & Renfrew Enterprise Trust, 26 High Street, Paisley PA1 2BZ (041 889 0010) *Contact: David Logan*	•		•	•			
PITLOCHRY: Highland Perthshire Development Co Ltd, 21 Bonnethill Road, Pitlochry, Perthshire PH16 5BS (0796 2697) *Contact: Dr R. G. Taylor*	•			•			
SALTCOATS: Androssan, Saltcoats & Stevenston Enterprise Trust (ASSET), 21 Green Street, Saltcoats, Ayrshire KA21 5HQ (0294 602515) *Contact: Kenneth Fraser*	•		•	•	•	•	
STIRLING: Stirling Enterprise Park, John Player Building, Stirling FK7 7RP (0796 63416) *Contact: Derek Gavin*	•	•	•		•	•	

LOCAL COUNCILS

Local authorities have continued their enthusiastic support for the small business sector. Some useful facts have emerged from two studies, one by Chris Miller of Birmingham University's Centre for Urban and Regional Studies, and the other on London Boroughs, by the London Research Centre. These show that some local authorities are doing much more than others. The only way to check what is happening in your area is to talk to your council's Industrial Development Officer. The following facts might be useful as background information when talking with him. Chris Miller's stratified survey of 86 local authorities in England and Wales showed that only three were not providing some kind of specific assistance to small firms. The main ways in which local authorities seem to be helping are described below.

Policies   Complaints that past policies had frequently harmed or restricted the development of many small businesses have been taken seriously. For example, 75 of the local authorities in this sample were making provision for small enterprise developments. They were, for example, identifying disused buildings and converting them into 'nursery units' for use by small firms; 66 were relaxing controls on industry and for example, allowing light industry into residential areas; 64 were giving priority to industrial and commercial planning applications; and 41 of the authorities were operating a policy of local 'bias' in their own purchasing of goods and services. A smaller number were trying to link this policy with their efforts to encourage small firms by themselves by providing a ready market for some products. Others run local business-to-business exhibitions so that people can see what is available locally.

Advice and Information   Local authorities are also aware of the difficulties experienced by many small businessmen in dealing with the 'Bureaucracy'. Many have tried to improve the co-ordination and administration of their services that relate to business. This is often through the employment of an Industrial Development Officer (72% of the sample had one) or through a small firms advice/information service (67%).

Here are some examples of local authority activities in this area. Northamptonshire County Council has set up INPUT to encourage the development of new firms. It runs small business exhibitions; it is establishing small marketing clubs with the aim of encouraging more inter-trade amongst local companies (these consist of six one-hour sessions when the principal of five small industries will discuss small industry problems); and it has also held 'Search for the Entrepreneur' campaigns.

Wirral Borough Council, in Cheshire, joined force with a local enterprise agency in April 1988 to set up a regional Business Expansion Scheme fund. The initial capital available is £300,000.

Coventry City Council is also involved in launching the Coventry Venture Capital fund, providing £200,000 for promising manufacturing companies.

The London Borough of Bexley operate a Small Business Development Centre providing information on premises and advice and counselling for would-be and existing small businessmen. Similarly, Brent runs a Business Information Centre; Hackney a Business Promotions Centre; and Tower Hamlets, a Small Business Centre.

Tamworth District Council runs small business workshops to provide advice on how to set up and/or develop new enterprises.

Rhymney Valley District Council runs seminar forums to discuss problems experienced by local industrialists.

St Helen's Metropolitan District Council has set up, in conjunction with other local bodies such as banks, firms and unions, the St Helen's Trust to help small businesses. It is an Enterprise Trust which acts as a kind of switchboard, helping new businesses to make contact with local sources of facilities available in the major firms and institutions.

It also provides advice on how to raise funds commercially, and in some cases provides 'seed capital'. It works alongside new businesses through all the formative stages, providing information or advice on such matters as business management, opportunities and markets.

Norwich City Council and Wakefield Metropolitan District Council have also been involved in setting up Enterprise or Venture Trusts to assist small businesses through activities similar to those of the St Helen's Trust. Kensington and Chelsea Council runs a Resource Centre, providing advice on setting up a business and has run local education workshops on 'How to Start a Business'. It has also provided a workshop/retail project, where people can work during the week and open the units up as shops at the weekends.

Somerset County Council's Economic Development Unit published a booklet entitled *Help for the Small Firm*, a guide to sources of assistance for the small firm. Bedford Borough Council offers new businesses a £500 grant for each new job created in the borough.

Loans and Grants   Some local authorities also provide loans and grants to certain types of new and small businesses. This activity tends to be limited to metropolitan, county, district councils and London boroughs, although a few shire county councils do provide some financial assistance (see table overleaf).

Many of the local authorities offer their loans and/or grants specifically for small firms. There are also some new initiatives being developed. For example, Scunthorpe District Council considers the financing of business development plans for small companies and the payment of grants to cover part of a small firm's bank loan interest. North Yorkshire County Council has a Small Business Grant Scheme under which companies employing fewer than 20 skilled workers will be eligible for grants up to £1,000 per annum for three years. In exceptional circumstances this could be raised to £2,000.

In West Yorkshire, Bradford Council provides unsecured loans or redeemable preference shares of up to £15,000 for firms with less than 30 employees. A further extension of this concept is to be for councils to consider setting up their own Business Expansion Schemes (see Finance Section). Lancaster County Council, using ratepayers' money owns Lancashire Enterprise Ltd, which has invested £6.6m in local business ventures.

Loans and Grants by Local Authorities (%)

KEY

MD	Metropolitan districts
SC	Shire counties
SD	Shire districts
LB	London boroughs
%	% of total authorities surveyed

Contributions	MD	SC	SD	LB	%
Land acquisition	58	9	24	18	27
Construction of industrial premises	75	27	18	45	34
Purchase of industrial buildings	75	18	13	36	28
Provision or improvement of services to industrial land	67	18	13	27	26
Provision or improvement of services to industrial buildings	67	18	13	27	26
Plant and machinery	67	27	11	27	27
Relocation from outside authority's area	33	5	5	18	12
Relocation within authority's area	67	5	5	18	16
Provision of rent-free periods for new or relocated firms on council land property	75	23	53	45	30

Finance for Co-operatives   Local authorities also provide finance for co-operatives. Of the authorities surveyed 28% were providing financial assistance to co-operatives (58% of metropolitan districts, 5% of shire counties, 21% of shire districts, and 45% of London boroughs). Cleveland County Council and the London Borough of Greenwich have set up Co-operative Development Agencies to encourage the development of co-operatives (see section on Co-operatives for more information on CDAs).

Analysis Studies   A number of local authorities now undertake analyses of particular relevance to small firms. Of the authorities surveyed 74% had carried out studies of the particular needs of small firms; and 23% of authorities had instigated investigations of gaps in the market for certain products. (This latter activity is mainly undertaken by the county councils and 41% of the shire counties.) As examples, Leicester City investigates new product availability such as through the availability of licences or franchises. Sunderland Metropolitan District has a Business Opportunities Research Unit which provides technical and market research support to small firms. The London Borough of Hackney runs the City Technology Centre, which offers information and advice on developments in new technology.

Enterprise Competitions   Many local authorities have sponsored or co-sponsored competitions for new or existing small businesses with substantial prizes in cash or kind.

You may find it profitable, therefore, to get in touch with your local council's Chief Executives department. Ask to speak to the Industrial Development Officer, and find out what your local authority can do to help you.

More Information   Useful information services and several books on economic activies in local authorities are listed below.

Regional Grants and Assistance Directories   Grants and other assistance available to small businesses from local authorities in England and Wales are detailed in a regional directory from National Westminster Bank. The areas covered are North of England, Midlands/East Anglia, South-East, South-West/Wales, Greater London and the big metropolitan councils. Available from Natwest Marketing Intelligence, Commercial Information Section, 6th Floor, National House, 14 Moorgate, London EC2R 6BS. Price £15.

Economic Development Initiatives and Innovations   Economic development by district councils. Available form Association of District Councils, 9 Buckingham Gate, London SW1E 6LE. Price £3.

A Guide to Local Authority Assistance in London, published in 1987 by the London Research Centre, Economic Activities Group, Room 509, The County Hall, London SE1 7PB (01 633 4293). Prepared for the London Chamber of Commerce, this describes each London Borough's assistance for small firms. Price £2.50.

Local Economic Development Information Service (LEDIS) was launched in April 1982 to provide concise and factual information on local economic employment initiatives being implemented throughout the UK. The service sets out to show how much each initiative costs, how long it took to develop, what the aim of the initiative was and, finally, how successful it was. The Planning Exchange, 186 Bath Street, Glasgow G2 4HL (041 32 8541) can provide further details of the service.

PROPERTY SERVICES

Finding suitable premises is one of the main problems that many people starting up a new business encounter. Apart from availability, these problems include finding somewhere the appropriate size, in the right location, on a flexible lease, with the services already connected.

An added bonus would be shared secretarial, telex, fax and book-keeping facilities – on site. When the first edition of the *Small Business Guide* was produced in 1982, premises fitting this description were virtually non-existent. Now Enterprise Agencies, local councils, science parks, Government agencies, British Coal and British Steel Enterprises, and a growing number of commercial providers supply business parks and centres.

Public Sector
English Estates   This is the trading name of The English Industrial Estates Corporation, a statutory body which develops and markets industrial and commercial property in England. The Welsh and Scottish Development Agencies and the Local Enterprise Development Unit in Northern Ireland carry out a similar role in their respective countries. Their principal services include the provision of:

- Beehive Workshops, who operate small workshop units from 500 sq ft, let with full services on simple tenancy agreements at attractive weekly rentals
- Larger factories for manufacturing, service, warehousing or distribution based companies
- Purpose built units for high technology use, near to universities
- A full professional design and build service for individual or specific property needs

74

■ A business support service for small and medium sized businesses who are tenants or prospective tenants. Advice is given on all aspects of running a business, including start-up, expansion, marketing, finance and grants.

Further information can be obtained from any of the offices below or, if outside England, from one of the agencies above:

Ashbourne: Millbank House, 34 St John's Street, Ashbourne, Derbyshire DE6 1GH (0335 44616)

Chatham: Pembroke, Chatham, Kent ME4 4UF (0634 830010)

Cockermouth: Lakeland Business Park, Cockermouth, Cumbria CA13 0QT (0900 827161)

Consett: Unit 33f, No. 1 Industrial Estate, Medomsley Road, Consett DH8 6SZ (0207 590192)

Doncaster: Hall Cross House, 1 South Parade, Doncaster, South Yorks DN1 2DY (0302 66865)

Gateshead: Methven House, Kingsway, Team Valley, Gateshead, Tyne & Wear NE11 0LN (091 4874711)

Harrogate: 10 North Park Road, Harrogate, North Yorks HG1 5PG (0423 523024)

Hereford: 103/4 East Street, Hereford HR1 2LW (0432 354331/2)

Liverpool: Lancaster House, Mercury Court, Tithebarn Street, Liverpool L2 2QP (051 2363663)

Manchester and North West: 3rd Floor, 75 Moseley Street, Manchester M2 3HR (061 236 9550)

Norwich: Bewick House, 22 Thorpe Road, Norwich, Norfolk NR1 1RY (0603 617006)

Plymouth: 5 Derriford Park, Derriford, Plymouth PL6 5QZ (0752 795598)

Sleaford: 28 Handley Street, Sleaford, Lincolnshire NG34 7TQ (0529 306219)

Thornaby: Forster House, Allensway, Thornaby, Stockton-on-Tees, Cleveland TS17 9HA (0642 765911)

Truro: Castle House, Pydar Street, Truro, Cornwall TR1 2UJ (0872 40505)

Yeovil: 25 Hendford, Yeovil, Somerset BA20 1UN (0935 29601)

Private Sector

A growing number of organisations specialise in providing small office and workshop facilities, usually with shared services such as telex, fax, etc, and sometimes with business advisory services. Some of these are listed below:

ENGLAND

BRISTOL: Avondale Workshops, Woodland Way, Kingswood, Bristol BS15 1QH (0272 603871)

COUNTY DURHAM: British Steel (Industry) Ltd, Berry Edge Road, Consett, Co Durham DH8 5EU (0207 509124) *Contact: Mrs Joyce Robson*

HARTLEPOOL: Hartlepool Workshops, Usworth Road Industrial Estate, Usworth Road, Hartlepool, Cleveland TS25 1PD (0429 265128) *Contact: Mrs Barbara Elsdon*

LIVERPOOL: Brunswick Enterprise Centre, Brunswick Business Park, Liverpool L3 4BD (051 708 0952)

LONDON: Brune Street Workshops, 16 Brune Street, London E1 (01 248 3796) *Contact: LEntA Business Space* Small workshops, studios and offices ranging from 224 sq ft

Spitalfields Workspace Ltd, 9 Heneage Street (off Brick Lane), London E1 5LJ (01 377 9262) *Contact: Mrs F. J. Budd* Studios/light industrial workshops and office accommodation

Long Street Unit Workshops, London E1 (01 488 2546) *Contact: London Industrial plc* Light industrial/business units, ranging from 282 sq ft

Whitechapel Technology Centre, Whitechapel Road, London E1 (01 488 2546) *Contact: London Industrial plc* Units of between 240–4,000 sq ft

Old Nichol, 19 Old Nichol Street, Shoreditch, London E2 7HK (01 729 4243) *Contact: Susan Arrowsmith* Units suitable for light industry, crafts and designers

Bow Enterprise Park, Violet Road, London E3 (01 488 2546) *Contact: London Industrial plc* Light industrial units ranging from 485 sq ft

Bootstrap Enterprises, 18 Ashwin Street, Hackney, London E8 3DL (01 254 0775) *Contact: Helen Evans* Workshops and offices ranging from 77 sq ft for worker co-operatives

Ada Street Workshops, London E8 (01 488 2546) *Contact: London Industrial plc* Light industrial units ranging from 700 sq ft

Hackney Enterprise Workshops, 1/3 Roseberry Place, Dalston, London E8 3DD (01 254 2998) *Contact: Raphael Onikosi* Up to 200 sq ft

Cannon Workshops, 5 Cannon Drive, West India Docks, London E14 9SU (01 987 2696) *Contact: Mr Matthews* Rate free until 1992. Ranging from 600 sq ft

Stratford Workshops, Burford Road, Stratford, London E15 2FP (01 519 3646) *Contact: Mrs June Dyke* Ranging from 200 sq ft

24 Ray Street, Clerkenwell, London EC1 (01 836 7580) *Contact: Gillian Harwood* Self-contained offices/studios ranging from 700 sq ft

Rosebery House, 70 Rosebery Avenue, London EC1 (01 248 3796) *Contact: LEntA Business Space* Ranging from 150 sq ft

Finsbury Business Centre, 40 Bowling Green Lane, London EC1R ONE (01 278 0333) *Contact: Mrs Irene Momberg* Studio and office space for 1–10 people

Pennybank Chambers, 33/35 St John Square, Clerkenwell, London EC1 4DM (01 251 0276) *Contact: Mr B. Penny* Workshops ranging from 100 sq ft

Omnibus Workspace, 39/41 North Road, Islington, London N7 9DP (01 607 7021) *Contact: Nancy Hill* Office and studios from 100 sq ft

1 Prince of Wales Passage, 117 Hampstead Road, London NW1 (01 836 7580) *Contact: Gillian Harwood* Self-contained offices/studios from 700 sq ft

Acton Workshops, School Road, Acton, London NW1 (01 961 6191) Units up to 1,600 sq ft

Morrison Yard, 551a High Road, Tottenham, London N17 (01 348 5101) *Contact: Mr Christie*

Rosebery Industrial Park, Rosebery Avenue, Tottenham, London N17 (01 348 5101) *Contact: Mr Holton*

Tottenham Enterprise Centre, 560/568 High Road, Tottenham, London N17 (01 808 3641) *Contact: LEntA Business Space* Retail units, workshops and offices from 80 sq ft

Butlers Wharf Business Centre, 45 Curlew Street, London SE1 (01 403 4184) *Contact: Bill Cheeseman*

Greenwich Business Centre, 49 Greenwich High Road, London SE10 8JL (01 691 4904) *Contact: Mr D. Kumar*

Trinity Business Centre, 305/309 Rotherhithe Street, London SE16 1EY (01 231 0752) *Contact: John Taylor* Small business units from 500 sq ft

Waterside Workshops, 99 Rotherhithe Street, London SE16 4NF (01 237 0017) *Contact: Kate Rowley or Gill Clement* Spaces for crafts people

176/184 Acre Lane, London SW2 (01 733 7010) *Contact: Mrs Margaret Taylor* Small workshops/offices from 185 sq ft

Bridge Studios, Wandsworth Bridge Road, London SW6 (01 736 3001) *Contact: Clare Walsh* Studios from 150 sq ft

100 New Kings Road, London SW6 (01 736 3001) *Contact: Clare Walsh* Offices from 90 sq ft

Abbey Business Centre, Ingate Place, off Queenstown Road, Battersea, London SW8 (01 622 2400) Offices, workshops, storage units

Shakespeare Business Centre, 245a Coldharbour Lane, London SW9 8RR (01 274 7511) *Contact: Melvin Studdy* Offices, light industrial, studios

Brixton Enterprise Centre, Bon Marche Building, 444 Brixton Road, London SW9 (01 274 4000) *Contact: John Carey*

World's End Studios, 134 Lots Road, London SW10 0RJ (01 351 4333) *Contact: Lize Kirwan* Studios and offices from 200 sq ft

266 Fulham Road, London SW10 (01 736 3001) *Contact: Clare Walsh, Local London Group* Serviced offices from 100 sq ft

42 Upper Richmond Road West, London SW10 (01 736 3001) *Contact: Clare Walsh, Local London Group* Offices

Wandsworth Workshops, 86/96 Garratt Lane, London SW18 (01 731 1303) *Contact: Susan Scott-Powell* Workshops from 140 sq ft

Tideway Yard, Mortlake High Street, London SW14 (01 836 7580) *Contact: Gillian Harwood* Self-contained workshops, studios and offices ranging from 350 sq ft

South Bank Business Centre, 140 Battersea Park Road, London SW11 (01 350 1000) *Contact: Julie Foster, Skillion Ltd* Workshops and offices from 142 sq ft

Camberwell Business Centre, 99 Lomond Grove, London SE5 (01 350 1000) *Contact: Julie Foster, Skillion Ltd* Workshops

London House, 68 Upper Richmond Road, London SW15 2RP (01 736 3001) *Contact: Clare Walsh, Local London Group* Small offices

Charterhouse Works, Wandsworth Town Roundabout, Eltringham Street, London SW18 (01 350 1000) *Contact: Julie Foster, Skillion Ltd* Small workshops

Barley Mow Workspace, 10 Barley Mow Passage, Chiswick, London W4 (01 994 6477) *Contact: The Manager* Serviced offices and workshops

1/11 Glenthorne Road, Hammersmith, London W6 (01 736 3001) *Contact: Clare Walsh, Local London Group* Small offices and suites

College House, Wrights Lane, London W6 (01 736 3001) *Contact: Clare Walsh, Local London Group* Offices from 150 sq ft

271/273 King Street, Hammersmith, London W6 (01 736 3001) *Contact: Clare Walsh, Local London Group* Offices

Middle Row Centre, Middle Row, North Kensington, London W10 5AR (01 960 7066) *Contact: Ron Batsford* Workshops from 750 sq ft

Grand Union Studios, Ladbroke Grove, London W10 (01 488 2456) *Contact: London Industrial plc* Studios, workshops and offices from 480 sq ft

Panther House, 38 Mount Pleasant, London WC1X 0AP (01 278 8011) *Contact: Mr Harris* Workshop/office studios from 150 sq ft

Northington House, 59 Grays Inn Road, London WC1X 8TL (01 242 0012) *Contact: Mr Brodie* Offices of 250 sq ft

Covent Garden Market, 41 The Market, London WC2 (01 836 9137) *Contact: Rennie Turner*

12 Flitcroft Street, London WC2 (01 836 7580) *Contact: Gillian Harwood* Offices, studios and workshops

LEntA Business Space, 4 Snow Hill, London EC1A 2DL (01 248 3796) Formed in 1981 to act as a catalyst in the supply of premises and an adviser to those looking for premises in and around London. It has also bought and developed property itself.

Local London Business Centres Plc, London House, 100 New Kings Road, London SW6 4LX (01 736 3001) This group has 23 business centres in and around London, from the City out to Kingston-Upon-Thames. They also plan other centres in major cities throughout the UK.

As well as providing fully serviced units, inclusive of rates and all operating costs, they also provide 24 hour access; secretarial service; telephone answering; facsimile, telex and photocopying; meeting rooms and Telecom Gold.

London Property Register, Room 517, County Hall, London SE1 7PB (01 633 7494) London Property Register is a computerised databank of available business premises, devised primarily to provide low cost assistance to new and existing small businesses. The service also has many wider applications. As well as saving the time it takes to identify and visit estate agents, LPR's impartial London-wide database can provide a good yardstick for comparisons. LPR offers professional advisers the opportunity to extend the range of their services to clients. The databank lists over 10,000 factory, office, warehouse, shop and development land sites throughout London. At any one time there will be over 5,000 on the active list, available from around 400 different sources. LPR obtains information from over 850 estate agents operating in London, the London Borough Councils and other public bodies. Their search tariff is £15 for a simple search of the database by locality, property type and size; £20 for three discrete searches of the database at monthly intervals by locality, property type and size; from £20 per month for monitoring the database for suitable property by locality, property type and size and notifying agents of particular needs.

London Small Business Property Trust, 2/3 Robert Street, London WC2N 6BH (01 222 8186) Set up in 1982 to invest in small business property in the Greater London area. Using some £10m of local authority pension fund money, it can provide finance to help the development of suitable premises for small firms. The Trust is promoted by an associate company of the Chartered Institute of Public Finance and Accountancy, Granby Hunter and URBED (Urban & Economic Development Ltd).

NOTTINGHAM: Sharespace Ltd, 13/15 Bridlesmith Gate, Nottingham NG1 2GR (0602 583851)

SHIPLEY: Saltaire Workshops, Ashley Lane, Shipley (0274 596746)

WEST MIDLANDS: Waterfall Lane, c/o A & J Mucklow, Halesowen Road, Cradley Heath, Warley B64 7JB

WEST YORKSHIRE: Pennine Heritage Ltd, The Birchcliff Centre, Hebden Bridge, West Yorks HX7 8GD (042 284 3626)

SCOTLAND
DUNDEE: Workstart Ltd, Logie Avenue, Dundee DD2 2ER (0382 67951)

GLASGOW: Clyde Workshops, Fullarton Road, Tollcross, Glasgow G32 8YL (041 641 4972)

Govan Workspace, 6 Harmony Row, Glasgow G51 3BA (041 445 2340)

HAMILTON: Hamilton New Enterprise Workshops, Dept of Strathclyde Regional Council, Portland Place, Hamilton (0698 283082)

PAISLEY: Paisley New Enterprise Workshop, Storey Street, Paisley (041 889 0688)

FORT WILLIAM: Enterprise Workshops, Locgaber, Annat Point, Corpach, Fort William, Inverness-shire (0397 7476)

WALES
SWANSEA: The Swansea Business Centre, Alexandra House, Alexandra Road, Swansea SA1 5ED (0792 476076)

Conventional Methods

Do not forget the more obvious ways of finding premises. These still account for the great majority of satisfied customers.

Dalton's Weekly specialises in a wide range of business areas, including both vacant property and going concerns.

Local newspapers often have a special day each week for business premises.

Business transfer agents are analogous to estate agents and are listed in the Yellow Pages.

Local authorities frequently have lists; contact your Industrial Development Officer for advice on local agencies.

Estate agents specialising in business premises are listed in the Yearbook of the Royal Institute of British Architects, available in the commercial section of larger public libraries.

A Guide to Office and Industrial Rental Trends in England and Wales is published free every six months by Jones Lang Wootton, Research Library, 103 Mount Street, London W1Y 6AS (01 493 6040). This will give you some idea of the level of rents in 50 major towns in England and Wales.

Business Location Handbook bi-annual, latest edition 1987/88 from Matrix Publishing Group, York House, Newton Close, Park Farm, Wellingborough, Northants NN8 3UW (0933 673977).

■■■■■■■■■■

ENTERPRISE ZONES

Twenty-five Enterprise Zones have been defined within some inner cities and other neglected urban black spots. The zones can give new businesses substantial financial benefits as well as freedom from control. In this way business both inside and on the perimeter of the zones will be strengthened. The zones are not aimed exclusively at small or new firms, but nevertheless they provide an attractive commercial inducement to locate in them. The first zone to become operational was in the lower Swansea Valley in June 1981, and the last was North West Kent. The facilities, grants and other assistance available within each zone are comprehensively described in a booklet available from:
The Department of the Environment
2 Marsham Street, London SW1P 3EB
(01 212 3434)

Local contact points
ENGLAND
Corby R. Jackson, Director of Industry Corby Industrial Development Centre, Douglas House, Queens Square, Corby, Northants NN17 1PL (0536 62571)
Dudley K. Duesbury Economic Development Unit, Council House, Dudley, West Midlands DY1 1HF (0384 55433 ext. 4975)
Glanford A. L. Lyman Glanford Borough Council, Council Offices, Station Road, Brigg, South Humberside DN20 8EG (0652 52441)
Hartlepool E. Morley, Industrial Development Officer Civic Centre, Hartlepool, Cleveland TS24 8AY (0429 266522)
London (Isle of Dogs) M. Wilson London Docklands Development Corporation, Enterprise House, 41 Millharbour, London E14 9XX (01 515 3000)
Middlesbrough D. Brydon Enterprise Zone Office, Vancouver House, Gurney Street, Middlesbrough, Cleveland TS1 1QP (0642 222279)
NE Lancashire Please refer to individual zone sheets
NW Kent D. Homewood NW Kent EZ Office, Rochester Upon Medway, City Council, Civic Centre, Strood, Rochester, Kent ME2 4AW (0634 732716/727777)

Rotherham *P. Fairholm* Rotherham Metropolitan Borough Council, Dept of Planning, Norfolk House, Walker Place, Rotherham, S Yorkshire S60 1QT (0709 372099)

Salford *P. Henry, Administrative & Industrial Liaison Officer* City of Salford, Civic Centre, Chorley Road, Swinton, Greater Manchester M27 2AD (061 793 3237/061 794 4711)

Scunthorpe *Mrs J. Knox* Scunthorpe Borough Council, Civic Centre, Ashby Road, Scunthorpe, S Humberside DN16 1AB (0724 862141)

Speke *A. Horner* Planning and Land Committee Section Liverpool City Council, Room 214, Municipal Buildings, Dale Street, Liverpool L69 2DH (051 227 3911 ext. 736)

Telford Telford Development Corporation Priorslee, Telford, Shropshire TF2 9NT (0952 613131)

Trafford *R. M. Dodsworth, Industrial Development Officer* Trafford Metropolitan Borough Council, Town Hall, Talbot Road, Stretford, Greater Manchester M32 0TH (061 872 2101)

Tyneside (Gateshead) *B. Cox* Gateshead Metropolitan Borough Council, Civic Centre, Gateshead, Tyne & Wear NE8 1HH (091 4771011)

Tyneside (Newcastle) *A. Clarke* City of Newcastle Upon Tyne, Central Policy Division, Civi Centre, Newcastle Upon Tyne NE99 2BH (091 2328520)

Wakefield *R. Gregory* Economic Development Department, Estates and valuation Section, City of Wakefield Metropolitan District Council, Bishopsgarth, Wakefield, W Yorks SF1 3RA (0924 367111)

Wellingborough *R. H. Entwhistle, Director of Development* Wellingborough Borough Council, Council Offices, Tithe Barn Road, Wellingborough, Northants NN8 1BN (0933 228885)

Workington *M. Gordon, Enterprise Zone Manager* Allerdale District Council, Holmewood, Cockermouth, Cumbria CA13 0DW (0900 65656)

SCOTLAND
Clydebank *Alistair Rew* Scottish Development Agency, Clydebank Task Force, Erskine House, 1 North Avenue, Clydebank Business Park, Clydebank G81 2DR (041 952 0084)

Invergordon *C. Rennie or A. McCreevy* Highlands and Islands Development Board, 62 High Street, Invergordon IV18 0DH (0349 853666)

Tayside (Arbroath) *W. Ferguson, Director of Planning* Angus District Council, County Buildings, Forfar DD8 3LG (0307 65101)

Tayside (Dundee) *G. McHee* Dundee Project Office, Nethergate Centre, Yeaman Shore, Dundee DD1 3BU (0382 29122)

WALES
Delyn *M. Gibson* Delyn Borough Council, Enterprise House, Aber Park, Flint, Clwyd CH6 5BD (03526 4004)

Lower Swansea Valley *Director of Planning* Swansea City Council, The Guildhall, Swansea SA1 4NL (0792 50821 ext. 2701/2723)

Milford Haven Waterway *I. W. R. David, Chief Executive* Preseli District Council, Cambria House, PO Box 217, Haverfordwest, Dyfed SA61 1TP (0437 4551)

NORTHERN IRELAND
Belfast Belfast Enterprise Zone Office, 9–21 Adelaide Street, Belfast BT2 8NR (0232 248449)

81

Londonderry *J. Spence* Londonderry Enterprise Zone Office, Richmond Chambers, The Diamond, Londonderry BT48 6HN (0504 263992)

Freeports

A half-hearted attempt by the Government in 1984 to emulate the entrepreneurial havens of the Far East. Three of the six UK freeports are based on airports (Belfast, Prestwick, Birmingham) and three on seaports (Liverpool, Cardiff and Southampton).

The freeports allow users to process, store and manufacture goods, entering them without paying customs duties and local taxes. Goods can then be exported without duties being paid. This has obvious cash flow advantages to anyone involved in the re-export field.

In the Far East, however, freeports also have a gamut of fiscal and financial incentives such as tax holidays of between five and ten years, generous depreciation allowances, and exemption from wage and welfare laws. So Hong Kong, Singapore and South Korea can relax for the moment at least.

Urban Development Corporations

These started in the north with the Merseyside Development Corporation in 1981. These were followed by Trafford Park, Teesside and Tyne & Wear. 1988 saw the launch of four more covering Bristol, Leeds, Central Manchester and Sheffield. Each has a budget in excess of tens of millions and is responsible for securing the economic regeneration of their area, and to encourage commercial development.

OTHER BUSINESS ASSOCIATIONS

Alliance of Small Firms and Self Employed People Ltd, 33 The Green, Calne, Wilts SN11 8DJ (0249 817003) The alliance aims to represent and publicise the interests of its members at both national and local level. Membership costs £25 per annum (subscription of newsletter for non-members costs £9), and a legal expenses insurance cover is available for a further £20. Members can use the Alliance's Enquiry Services, which gives advice and information on a wide range of tax, legal and employment matters. If they cannot give you an answer they will put you in touch with a consultant who can. The first consultation is free, and thereafter you agree a price with the consultant direct.

Association of British Chambers of Commerce, Sovereign House, 212a Shaftesbury Avenue, London WC2H 8EW (01 240 5831/6) A co-ordinating body for Chambers of Commerce (see Chambers of Industry and Commerce below).

Association of Collegiate Entrepreneurs, Headbourne Worthy Grange, Winchester, Hampshire SO23 7SX (0962 882661) An organisation of university and college educated young business people – including both entrepreneurs and academics.

Association of Independent Businesses, Trowbray House, 108 Weston Street, London SE1 3QB (01 403 4066) This was established in 1968 to promote the cause of the smaller business. The aim of the Association is to remove discrimination against independent businesses in existing and proposed legislation, and so it maintains close contact with both Whitehall and Westminster. Its small national office staff has a limited capacity to answer members' queries on typical problems that face independent businesses. They can also signpost enquirers to other useful sources of advice.

Centre for Employment Initiatives, 140a Gloucester Mansions, Cambridge Circus, London WC2H 8PA (01 240 8901) Established in 1982 to provide practical assistance to organisations who are trying to deal with unemployment problems. They are independent and non-profit orientated. Their quarterly journal *Initiatives* has articles on new local economic development activities.

Centre for Enterprise Development in Rural Areas (CEBRA), Silsoe College, Silsoe, Bedford MK45 4DT (0525 60428) Founded in 1988 to address issues concerned with job and wealth creation in rural areas. They offer practical advice with market research, business plan preparation, counselling, training and post-start up help.

Chambers of Industry and Commerce, Sovereign House, 212a Shaftesbury Avenue, London WC2H 8EW (01 240 5831/6) Apart from playing an important role in providing information and help for existing businesses, chambers of commerce have been a major force in the launching of many of the most prominent and effective Enterprise Agencies. They have also sponsored many local new business competitions. They are a very important source of information, advice and help for new and small businesses. (They should be listed in your telephone directory.)

Confederation of British Industry (CBI), Centre Point, 103 New Oxford Street, London WC1A 1DU (01 379 7400) The Council carries out research and publishes papers concerning the needs of business in general. Through this work they set out to influence government policy towards small business and government sponsored activity in this field.

The Forum of Private Business Ltd, Ruskin Chambers, Drury Lane, Knutsford, Cheshire WA16 6HA (0565 4467) This is a non-profit making organisation with the objectives of promoting and preserving a system of free competitive enterprise in the UK, and also of giving private people a greater voice in the legislations, that affect their business. The forum researches and distributes a Referendum nine times a year, keeping members informed and asking their views on a number of topical and important business issues. It makes government aware of these views both directly and by various public relations activities. The forum also plays a role by initiating training programmes in schools and colleges to show the importance of free enterprise in our society. Voting membership rises to a maximum of £25–500 per annum.

The Institute of Directors, 116 Pall Mall, London SW1Y 5ED (01 839 1233) The Institute represents the interests both of the directors of large companies and owner directors of smaller ones. In particular, it has a service for putting those looking for funds or other resources in touch with those with funds to invest.

Institute of Management Services, 1 Cecil Court, London Road, Enfield, Middx EN2 6DD (01 363 7452)

The Institute of Small Business, 14 Willow Street, London EC2A 4BH (01 638 4937) Offers an advisory service, monthly newsletter and a business appraisal service, free to members.

Intermediate Technology Development Group, Myson House, Railway Terrace, Rugby, Warks CV21 3HT (0788 60631) An independent group who seek to create enterprise in the third world.

Ismaili Business Information Centre (IBIC), 1 Cromwell Gardens, London SW7 2SL (01 581 2071) Founded in 1976 as a non-profit making organisation to aid the thousands of Ismaili Asians expelled from Uganda by Idi Amin. Since then the 10,000-strong UK Ismaili community, with IBIC's assistance, have formed 650 enterprises including stores, hotels, travel agencies and software houses, initially creating more than 2,000 jobs. IBIC's most important contribution, apart from counselling and advice, has been the introduction of a loan guarantee programme run in conjunction with Lloyds Bank, said to be a forerunner of the government's Loan Guarantee Scheme.

The National Federation of Self Employed and Small Businesses Ltd, 32 St Annes Road, West Lytham, St Annes, Lancashire FY8 1NY (0253 720911)
Press and Parliamentary Office: 140 Lower Marsh, Westminster Bridge, London SE1 7AE (01 928 9272)

The Federation is a campaigning pressure group in business to promote and protect the interests of all who are either self-employed or who own or are directors of small businesses. Formed in 1974, it now has some 50,000 members in 300 branches throughout the UK. The federation has the funds to take major test cases of importance to small business through the expensive legal process leading to the House of Lords (or European Court of Human Rights). They have been particularly effective in taxation and VAT matters.

Amongst other benefits, members are covered by a legal expenses compensation cover scheme. The cover includes:

- VAT tribunal representation and costs up to £10,000 per case to appeal in VAT disputes
- Defence of health and safety prosecutions, covering costs of prosecution under the Health and Safety at Work Act, 1974
- In-depth investigation cover to meet accountants' fees in helping to deal with Inland Revenue investigation
- Industrial Tribunal Compensation Awards to meet unfair dismissal awards. (This is supported by a telephone legal advice service)

Full membership costs £24 per annum; £10 joining fee.

National Forum of Small Business Clubs, PO Box 21, Hyde, Cheshire SK14 1HA (061 268 0085) *Contact: Richard Nash* The Forum maintains liaison with about 120 business clubs across the country, and can put you in contact with your nearest one.

Northern Ireland Small Business Institute, The University of Ulster, Newtownabbey, Co Antrim BT37 0QB (0231 65131) The Institute, amongst other things, pioneers new initiatives in the region. Its latest brainchild, the Boston Project (full name DEBI – Development of Entrepreneurs in Boston for Ireland), provided £180,000 of grants to provide 20 small business entrepreneurs from Northern Ireland and the Irish Republic to get up to nine months working experience in Boston Massachusetts.

Scottish Enterprise Foundation, University of Stirling, Stirling FK9 4LA (0786 3171) *Contact: Bob Hale* Founded in 1982 to encourage enterprise programmes and research, its main initiatives are the Graduate Enterprise Programme, Enterprise Agency Directors Programmes and Action Learning in Small Businesses. It houses a new Small Business Resource Centre charged with bringing together teaching materials, publications and research resources.

The Small Business Bureau, 32 Smith Square, London SW1P 3HH (01 222 0330) Formed in 1976, the bureau aims to serve the needs of the small business community. Membership costs £20 per annum and gives you access to its advisory service and a copy of its monthly newspaper *Small Business*. It also represents the small business point of view to Government, organises trade delegations and provides European opportunities through its involvement with EMSU (the European Medium and Small Business Union).

Small Business Centre, University of Warwick, Coventry CV4 7AL (0203 523523) *Contact: David Storey* Funded by the Economic & Social Research Council, the Centre was launched in June 1988 to carry out a continuing study of the economic aspects of small business, including its role in wealth creation; labour market issues such as the type and quality of jobs created; and the organisational aspects of small business including the problems of management. The Centre will also undertake ad hoc research projects in the small business field.

Small Business Research Trust, Francis house, Francis Street, London SW1P 1DE (01 828 5327) The Trust intends to become an independent research organisation for small businesses in the UK. Formed in 1983 with a wide base of industrial, institutional and professional support. Produces regular research reports and surveys of small business sector.

Trade Associations, to be found through Directory of British Associations, CBD Research Ltd, Beckenham, Kent. Most business fields have a trade association, such as the Brewers Society, the Federation of Fish Friers, or the Booksellers Association. They are a useful source of help and advice to potential new entrants to their trade. This directory lists all such associations.

The Union of Independent Companies, 44–46 Fleet Street, London EC4Y 1BN (01 589 9305) *Contact: Alan Randall* This is a non-political organisation formed in 1977 by a number of small independent industrialists in the south west of England. Its aim is to create an environment which will stimulate the independent sector of the economy and generally further the interests of the small independent company, in both the manufacturing and servicing sectors.

The UIC works through small groups who run independent companies in many parliamentary constituencies to research the problems affecting small independent companies and their potential growth and to develop methods of mutual assistance and combination. The UIC has a small effective headquarters in

Fleet Street, London, where it maintains active contact with Whitehall, Westminster and the press. It disseminates literature, information and a monthly newsletter to members.

Women in Enterprise, 26 Bond Street, Wakefield, West Yorkshire WF1 2QP (0924 361789) A voluntary organisation that helps women to start their own business, or develop existing businesses. They published the first directory for this sector, The National Directory of Women's Businesses and Reference Guide 1988. It is a contact directory offering information, specialist articles and addresses and telephone numbers useful to small businesses. It costs £12. The project has been underwritten by the National Westminster Bank.

Women Into Business, c/o Small Business Bureau Launched in October 1986 as a self help and lobbying network for smaller businesswomen and potential entrepreneurs. Has a bi-monthly newsletter, runs a counselling service and organises teach-ins and seminars.

BUSINESS OPPORTUNITIES

If you know what kind of business you want and you plan either to start from scratch or, if you are already in business, to grow from your existing base, then these ideas and opportunities may not be for you. There are, however, a very large number of people who simply know that they would like to work for themselves – quite what at they are not sure.

There is nothing unusual about this phenomenon, sometimes an event such as redundancy, early retirement or a financial windfall may prompt you into searching for a business opportunity, or perhaps into extending the scope of an existing business idea. Business ideas themselves very often come from the knowledge and experience gained in previous jobs, but they take time to germinate. More usually people only really start to think seriously (and usefully) about an idea when it becomes an opportunity.

NEW PRODUCTS OR BUSINESSES

Although you may not know exactly what you want to do, you will have certain resources and skills. Contacting people with complementary 'features' is one way of getting into business, or expanding an existing business.

There are a number of organisations and publications that put people in touch with business opportunities and new products.

Organisations
Accountants Business Network (ABN), is a confidentail service which helps those who wish to sell their businesses to find buyers through the extensive clients and contact networks of leading firms of chartered accountants. Those wishing to buy a business are provided with a one page no-names general profile of the business, supported by a fuller sales memoranda to be sent at a later stage, once both parties have agreed it is worth proceeding. The ABN participating firms include the following, whose local office details will be in your telephone book: Arthur Andersen, Arthur Young, Binder Hamlyn, Clark Whitehill,

Coopers & Lybrand, Deloitte Haskins & Sells, Ernst & Whinney, Grant Thornton, Pannell Kerr Forster, Peat Marwick McLintock, Price Waterhouse, Robson Rhodes, Spicer & Pegler, Stoy Hayward, Touche Ross.

BAR (Agents Register) Ltd, 24 Mount Parade, Harrogate HG1 1BP (0423 60608). Caters for commercial, distributive and buying agents. Membership costs £35. Their publication, *The Guide to Agency Agreements and Contracts* (£5) is a must. You can advertise in their monthly review for an agent to sell your products. See also the Manufacturers' Agents Association later in this section.

The Business Co-operation Centre, Rue de la Loi, 1049 Brussels (322 230 3948). This centre was set up in 1972 to assist small and medium-sized firms to contact and co-operate with companies with similar interests in the EEC. The centre was established on an experimental basis for a period of three years, but proved sufficiently popular to become a permanent service providing information to companies on economic, legal, tax and financial aspects of cross-frontier co-operation and integration. In addition, the centre acts as a marriage bureau for small and medium sized firms, putting potential partners in touch with one another and assisting in preliminary discussions.

Any firm seeking the centre's help is asked to provide certain information about itself, and to define exactly what type of partner or what type of co-operation it wants. All the information supplied, and any queries received, are treated as strictly confidential, and no names are revealed without the agreement of all parties. The centre will search its files for a suitable partner and, if the application cannot be matched, will, if the firm agrees, circulate a summary of its requirements, with no names mentioned to its 'correspondents' in all EEC countries.

The Business Exchange, 21 John Adam Street, London WC2N 6JG (01 930 8965). Set up by Deloitte Haskins & Sells and Grant Thornton, this is a market for buying and selling companies. Data is fed in by chartered accountants, solicitors and actuaries throughout the country.

Business Link-Up, 33 St George Street, London W1R 9FA (01 499 4714). A contact agency for those wishing to find a new partner for a business enterprise.

Christie & Co, 50 Victoria Street, London SW1 (01 799 2121). Through its 20 regional offices, Christie's claims to be the country's leading agent for buying and selling pubs, hotels, nursing homes and newsagents. The company also provides commercial mortgages, insurance, business valuations and a stocktaking service through a subsidiary company.

Corporate Venturing Centre, NEDO, Millbank Tower, London SW1P 4QX (01 211 5912). The centre launched a register in June 1988 so that prospective corporate venturing partners can find each other more easily. Small companies provide details of their business and describe the sort of partnership they are seeking. This information – not including the company's name – is circulated to larger companies, who then decide whether or not to follow up the proposal. Corporate Venturing is a scheme which encourages large companies to establish flexible links with small companies who are looking for the resources, usually money, to exploit new ideas. The link could be by way of a minority shareholding or a joint venture.

LINC (Local Investment Networking Company) LINC is a nationwide business introduction service, run by seven enterprise agencies which help small businesses find capital and management help and for people who want to invest and sometimes work in those firms. The service has been run on a local basis around the country for as long as six years but has now been launched nationwide. LINC offers investors a much wider choice of business opportunities and provides entrepreneurs with more potential sources of finance.

A bulletin is published monthly with details of investment opportunities and companies for sale from all the participating LINC agencies. In some cases it is also possible to match companies and individuals where it is appropriate.

The Investors' Club is for people who wish to invest and sometimes work in small firms. Membership of the club costs £50 per annum which includes annual subscription to the bulletin, inclusion on the investor database and allows attendance at investors' meetings for a small charge (subject to availability of seats). Investors' meetings enable those seeking finance to present their plans and ideas to investors giving a much clearer indication of the business and how it operates. Details of future investors' meetings and locations can be found at the back of the bulletin. To register simply complete the form at the end of the bulletin and return it to the address indicated together with a cheque for the appropriate amount.

Those seeking finance using LINC need to produce a business plan (sample plans available) indicating clearly the amount of finance required. Firms should be prepared to offer an equity share in return for the investment received though in some cases a mixture of equity and loan finance may be possible. Entrepreneurs who need assistance in completing a business plan should consult their nearest LINC office (see below) or local enterprise agency. A one-off registration fee of £30 is payable.

Aberdeen Enterprise Trust, 1st Floor, Seaforth Centre, 30 Waterloo Quay, Aberdeen AB2 1BS (0224 582599) *Contact: Anne Minto*

Cleveland Enterprise Agency Ltd, 52–60 Corporation Road, Middlesbrough, Cleveland TS1 2RN (0642 222836) *Contact: Alec Laidler*

Dudley Business Venture, 1st Floor, Stanton House, 10 Castle Street, Dudley, West Midlands DY1 1LQ (0384 231283/4/5) *Contact: Derek Brind*

London Enterprise Agency, 4 Snow Hill, London EC1A 2BS (01 236 3000) *Contact: David Wood*

Manchester Business Venture, c/o Manchester Chamber of Commerce, 56 Oxford Street, Manchester M60 7HJ (061 236 0153) *Contact: Derek Gower*

The Medway Enterprise Agency Ltd, Railway Street, Chatham, Kent ME4 4RR (0634 830301) *Contact: Guy Sibley*

Merseyside Education Training Enterprise Ltd, Salisbury Street, Liverpool L3 8DR (051 207 2281) *Contact: Judith Manifold*

Northamptonshire Enterprise Agency, 2nd Floor, Elgin House, Billing Road, Northampton NN1 5AV (0604 37401/2) *Contact: David Mann*

Staffordshire Development Association, 3 Martin Street, Stafford ST16 2LH (0785 223121 ext. 7245) *Contact: Peter Wood*

The Manufacturers' Agents Association (MAA), Lonsdale House, 7/11 High Street, Reigate, Surrey RH2 9AA (0737 240141) can advise you on becoming an agent in almost any trade. Membership costs £63.25 (£34.50 subscription, £28.75 entrance fee). If you are choosing this route to self-employment take on more than one agency. And make sure you have a written agreement, preferably using the standard MAA Agreement Form which costs £3.45.

Singer & Friedlander Ltd, 21 New Street, Bishopsgate, London EC2M 4HR (01 623 3000) operates a company register for those who want to buy a company, sell one or merge with suitable partners. The register is confidential. Its fees, on a graduated scale, are payable only on completion of a satisfactory transaction.

Tourism – The National Tourist Board provide a service advising potential investors and operators of new business opportunities. The English Tourist Board annual reports usually list several hundred possible projects (see Section 2 for addresses).

Publications

Business Opportunities Digest 14 Willow Street, London EC2A 4BH. A monthly subscription magazine, price about £39.50 for 12 issues. Introduces and explains business ideas and how to make them work for you.

The Business Search and Insolvency Supplement published by Venture Capital Report Ltd, Boston Road, Henley-on-Thames RG9 1DY. Subscription £40 pa (banker's order) or £45 pa (cheque).

A fortnightly supplement which contains details of businesses in receivership, liquidation, and administration and a list of auctions. All entries in these categories are placed free of charge. Businesses may advertise in For Sale/Wanted section but are charged.

Entrepreneur published by American Entrepreneurs Association, 2392 Morse Avenue, Irvin, CA 92714, USA. Subscription $37.97 pa (to be paid in US funds and drawn on US banks). This monthly publication gives a very invigorating view of American business opportunities, by the hundred.

Homing In from Chris Oliver, 56 London Road, Milborne Port, Sherborne, Dorset DT9 5DW. A newsletter for people working from home containing business ideas, examples and explanations.

How to Buy a Business This is a guide for the small businessman by Peter Farrell, published in 1988 by Kogan Page Ltd, 120 Pentonville Road, London N1. This book examines the advantages and risks of buying a business. It looks at why and when you should buy, how to judge a business's track record, why it is for sale, how to evaluate its assets and what it is worth. Finally there is a chapter on how to finance a purchase. Contents: 1 Why buy? 2 Why is it for sale? 3 What are you buying? 4 Judging the track record. 5 Evaluating the assets. 6 What is the right price? Can you afford it? 7 Paying for it. Price £5.95 pb, £12.95 hb.

Just for Starters A handbook of small-scale business opportunities, by Alan Bollard, published in 1984 by Intermediate Technology Publications, 9 King Street, London WC2E 8HN, price £12.50. A detailed survey of opportunities in the UK market followed by statistical surveys of nearly 50 industries and profiles of 33 of them.

Opportunities, A Handbook of Business Opportunity Search by Edward de Bono, published in 1980 by Penguin Books, 27 Wrights Lane, London W8 5TZ, price £2.25. This will certainly get you started. The whole book is thought-provoking, and the final part, 'Thinking for Opportunities', has a hundred pages that set out to answer two vital questions: 'How do you set about looking for business opportunities?' and 'Where do you start to look for these opportunities?'. It is mind-bending but it will open your eyes. An opportunity only exists when you can see it.

Venture Capital Report Boston Road, Henley-on-Thames RG9 1DY (0491 579999). This is a publication that gives details of entrepreneurs and their business ventures, inviting people with money to invest, often on a partnership basis. £200 per annum.

Which Business by Stephen Halliday, published by Kogan Page, 1987. Summarises sources of new business ideas in Britain and overseas, and gives pointers as to how to evaluate them. Price £5.95.

Working for Yourself by Godfrey Golzen, published by Kogan Page, 120 Pentonville Road, London N1. This is the very successful *Daily Telegraph* book, with its tenth edition being published July 1988. Apart from useful sections on the general mechanics of starting a business, tax, raising money, etc, there is a Directory of Opportunities. In this section you are given an insight into the pros and cons of some 60 different types of business, together with addresses and contact points to follow up those of interest to you. Price £6.95. (This is a good starting point in the opportunity search.)

Newspapers One of the best ways to keep abreast of current business opportunities is to read a selection of national and local papers. Start off with as wide a range as you can afford (or visit your library) to get the flavour of each. Then once you have made a selection, keep searching. Many articles give details of useful follow-up addresses.

Birmingham Mail and Post
Day: Monday–Friday
Section: Business Page, Business & Industrial, Mail and Post

Bradford Telegraph and Argus
Day: Monday–Friday
Section: Industry Page

Coventry Evening Telegraph
Day: Monday–Friday
Section: Business News, plus 16-page supplement every month called 'Business Life'

Daily Express
Day: Monday
Section: Financial Page

Daily Mail
Day: Wednesday
Section: Moneymail, Moneywise, 2 & 3, Questions Answers, Current Accounts

Dalton's Weekly
Day: Thursday
Extensive coverage of businesses for sale and business opportunities, partnerships, etc.

Exchange & Mart
Day: Thursday
Section: Business opportunities

Financial Times
Day: Tuesday
Section: The Management Pages – 2 pages of business opportunities and companies for sale and wanted

The Guardian
Day: Monday
Section: New Enterprise. Frequent stories of small business success and the new sources of help and advice

Hull Daily Mail
Day: Wednesday
Section: Industrial Notebook

The Independent
Day: Thursdays
Section: Small Business

Lancashire Evening Post
Day: Monday
Section: Business Post

Liverpool Post
Day: Monday–Friday
Section: Business News, Business Supplement 1st Wednesday of every month

Manchester Evening News
Day: Monday–Friday
Section: Business World

Newcastle Journal
Day: Monday–Saturday
Section: Business News, Money (Monday), Business Journal (Tuesday, Thursday–Saturday), Northern Business (Wednesday)

Nottingham Evening Post
Day: Monday–Saturday
Section: Business Post, Month Business Magazine

The Observer
Day: Sunday
Section: Observer Business

Daily Telegraph
Day: Monday
Section: Small Business

Sheffield Telegraph
Day: Monday–Saturday
Section: Business, Business extra (Wednesday)

Sunday Telegraph
Day: Sunday
Section: City Page

Sunday Times
Day: Sunday
Section: Business News, Business to Business, extremely comprehensive
range of business opportunities

The Times
Day: Friday (and Saturday – see above)
Section: Your Own Business, new issues in small business field

Western Mail (Cardiff and South Wales)
Day: Monday–Friday
Section: Business News

Wolverhampton Express
Day: Monday–Friday
Section: Business Page

Yorkshire Post
Day: Monday–Saturday
Section: Business Post

CO-OPERATIVES

Although the most commonly known co-operatives are the high
street shops and supermarkets, there is another, lesser-known
variety, the workers' co-operatives – where workers share control
and decision-making equally, and not in relation to their financial
stake. They split off from the more successful retail movement,
reached a peak of 1,000 or so outlets at the turn of the century,
then declined (almost to the point of extinction).

The Industrial Common Ownership Act, 1976, and the
formation of the Co-operative Development Agency (and
subsequently the local CDAs) in 1978 gave workers' co-operatives
a much needed shot in the arm. Various estimates put the number
of workers' co-operatives operating in the UK in 1988 at around
1,600, employing about 30,000 people. About a fifth of all co-
operatives are in the Greater London area. Certainly if the growth
of supporting organisations and agencies is anything to go by, this
seems a conservative estimate. In order to meet the legal
requirements a co-operative must conform to the following rules:

Conduct of business   The members must benefit primarily
from their participation in the business, i.e., as workers, not
merely as investors.

Control   Each member has equal control through the principle
of 'one person one vote'. Control is not related to the size of
financial stake in the business.

Interest repayments   A co-operative cannot pay an unlimited return on loan or share capital. Even in good years, interest payments will be limited in some specified way.

Surplus   This may be wholly retained in the business or distributed in part to the members in proportion to their involvement, e.g., according to hours worked.

Membership   This must be open to anybody satisfying the qualifications of membership.

The main attraction to co-operatives lies in the belief that shared control and decision-making leads to a greater level of work satisfaction. It is an unlikely path to wealth. There may be many partnerships and limited companies that operate close to the lines of a co-operative. They usually recognise that, in order to grow and survive, the door to larger funds than co-operatives can attract must be kept open.

The Co-operative Development Agency and local CDAs are a good starting point in the search for more information on workers' co-operatives.

The Co-operative Development Agency   The agency was established by Parliament in 1978 with all-party support to promote the concept of co-operatives. It gives advice on the mechanics and philosophy of co-operatives to people starting a new business or wanting to convert an existing business that might otherwise be sold or closed down.

Either from the central office or through its growing network of local Co-operative Development Agencies, the CDA can advise on local opportunities for co-operatives, and will evaluate specific projects from a commercial as well as a co-operative point of view. It can also give advice on sources of finance, legal and taxation problems, education, training and publicity. The CDA has no money of its own to finance co-operatives, and those who are able to pay are charged the cost of the advice and assistance given.

Details can be sent on request of a series of publications which cover various aspects of the co-operative movement.

Local Co-operative Development Agencies. A variety of bodies have been set up in local areas to promote co-operatives. Some have full-time staff funded by a local authority; some are based on existing co-operatives; others are run solely by volunteers. None of them is an agent of the national Co-operative Development Agency, but many have close working relationships with it.

Co-operative Development Agencies

Co-operative Development Agency (CDA), Broadmead House, 21 Panton Street, London SW1Y 4DR (01 839 2987/8)

CDA Belfast Office, c/o Greater West Belfast Community Association, 234 Grosvenor Road, Belfast 12 5AW (0232 328295) *Contact: Michael Fenton, Liam Hunter*

CDA Manchester Office, c/o Co-op Union, Holyoake House, Hanover Street, Manchester M60 0AS (061 832 4300 ext. 288) *Contact: Ian Brierley, Tony Marris, Philip Riley*

Antur Teifi, Teifi Valley Business Centre, Aberarad, Newcastle Emlyn, Dyfed SA38 9DA (0239 710238)

Avon CDA, 108a Stokes Croft, Bristol BS1 3UR (0272 428853)

Barnsley CDA, c/o Pete Deakin, 158 Park Road, Barnsley, South Yorks

Basildon District CDA, Unit 27, Cornwallis House, Howards Chase, Basildon SS14 3BB (0268 2822171)

Bedfordshire CDA, Tavistock House, 34 Bromham Road, Bedford MK40 2QD (0234 213571)

Enterprise House, 7 Gordon Street, Luton LU1 2QP (0582 400949)

Berkshire (West) CDA, c/o Maureen Cotter, 2 School Terrace, Reading RG1 3LS (0734 596639)

Birmingham CDA, Zair Works, Co-operative Enterprise Centre, 111–119 Bishop Street, Birmingham B5 6JL (021 622 6973)

Black Country CDA, Lich Buildings, 44 Queens Square, Wolverhampton WV1 1TX (0902 312136)

Bolton NEDA, Lincoln Mill, Washington Street, Bolton, Lancs BL3 5EU (0204 22213)

Brent CDA, 192 High Road, Willesden, London NW10 2PB (01 451 3777)

Brighton Area CDA, 85 London Road, Brighton BN1 4JF (0273 606722)

Calderdale CDA, c/o 'Food & Futures', 49 Halifax Road, Todmorden, Lancs OL14 5BB (070 681 6990)

Cambridge CDA, The Business Advice Centre, 71a Lensfield Road, Cambridge CB12 1EN (0223 60977)

Camden Co-ops Support Group, c/o 57 Chalton Street, London NW1 (01 387 0779)

Cardiff and Vale CDA, Enterprise House, 127 Bute Street, Cardiff CF1 5LE (0222 494411)

Central London CDA, The KIDS Building, 80 Waynflete Square, London W10 6UH (01 968 7744)

Cheshire (North) CDA, Unit 3, Catherine Street, Bewsey Industrial Estate, Warrington (0925 35158)

The Waterloo Centre, Waterloo Road, Widnes, Cheshire (051 423 5583)

Cleveland Co-operative Agency, 10a Albert Road, Middlesbrough, Cleveland TS1 1QA (0642 210224/5)

Old Municipal Buildings, Upper Church Street, Hartlepool, Cleveland TS2X 7ET (0429 66522)

Cornwall CDA, c/o Jenni Thomson, Co-operative Retail Services Ltd, 105 Station Road, St Blazey, Par, Cornwall PL24 2LZ (072681 2446)

Coventry CDA, Unit 15, The Arches Industrial Estate, Spon End, Coventry CV1 3JQ (0203 714076)

Croydon CDA, 34a Station Road, Croydon, CR0 2RB (01 686 1966)

Delyn CDA, c/o Mr S. Hatch, Bryn Mywion Bach, Llanarmon-yn-Ial, Nr Mold, Clwyd (08243 728) (home)

Derbyshire CDA, Sun Alliance House, Curzon Street, Derby, Derbyshire DE1 1LL (0332 380515)

Furness Chambers, 19 Stephenson Place, Chesterfield, Derbyshire S40 1XL (0246 208953)

23 High Street West, Glossop, Derbyshire SK13 8AL (04574 3547)

Devon CDA, 39 Marsh Green Road, Marsh Barton, Exeter EX2 8PN (0392 72223)

Ealing CDA, Charles House, Bridge Road, Southall, Middlesex UB2 4BU (01 574 4724)

Edinburgh CDA, 137 Buccleuch Street, Edinburgh EH8 9NE (031 662 4514)

Edinburgh Federation of Co-ops, c/o Box C, 1st May Bookshop, 43 Candlemaker Row, Edinburgh EH1 2QB (031 225 2612)

Enfield CDA Steering Group, Co-op Hall, 444 Hertford Road, Enfield EN3 5QH (01 804 0823)

Essex CDA, The Essex Business Centre, Chelmer Court, Church Street, Chelmsford CM1 1NH (0245 283030)

Glamorgan (West) Common Ownership Development Agency, 10 St Helens Road, Swansea SA1 4AN (0792 53498)

Glastonbury Co-op Development Group, c/o Assembly Rooms, Glastonbury, Somerset BA6 9DU (0458 35228)

Gloucester CDA, 20 Berkley Street, Gloucester (0452 425093)

Greenwich Employment Resource Unit, 311 Plumstead High Street, London SE18 1JX (01 310 6695/6)

Hackney CDA, 16 Dalston Lane, London E8 3AZ (01 254 4829)

Hammersmith and Fulham CDA, Palingswick House, 241 King Street, London W6 9LP (01 741 2304)

Haringey Co-op Office, 594 High Road, London N17 9TA (01 885 2967)

Haringey Ethnic Young Adult CDA, 23 Hornsey Park Road, London N8 0JU

Harlow CDA, Latton Bush Centre, Southern Way, Harlow, Essex CM18 7BL (0279 446086)

Harrow Co-ops Group, c/o T. Louki, 11 Tenby Avenue, Kenton, Harrow HA3 8RU (01 907 9438)

Hertfordshire Area CDA, c/o Martin Steers, 40 Kings Hedges, Hitchin, Herts SG5 2PZ (0234 45151)

Humberside CDA, 7c Colin Road, Scunthorpe, South Humberside DN16 1TT (0724 850774)

First Floor, Ferensway Chambers, 79 Ferensway, Hull HU2 8LD (0482 28160)

Islington CDA, 177 Upper Street, London N1 1RG (01 226 2783 or 01 359 3010)

Kala Ujamaa, 220 Southbank House, Black Prince Road, London SE1 7SJ (01 582 9424 or 735 8171)

Kingston and Richmond CDA, 58b London Road, Kingston-Upon-Thames, Surrey KT2 6QA (01 549 9159)

Lambeth CDA, The Co-op Centre, 11 Mowll Street, London SW9 6BG (01 582 0003)

Lancashire CDA, Enterprise House, East Cliff, Preston PR1 3JE (0772 203692)

1st Floor, 36 Church Street, Blackburn BB1 5AL (0254 583041)
Whitecross Mill, Whitecross, Lancaster LA1 4XH (0524 388517)
Skelmersdale Enterprise Centre, Unit 6, Gardiners Place, Gillibrands,
Skelmersdale (0695 32799)
Latin American Co-op Development Project, 11 Mowll Street,
London SW9 6BG (01 582 4482)
Leicester and County CDA, 30 New Walk, Leicester, Leics LE1 6TF
(0533 554464/547837)
Manchester (Greater) CDA (GMCDA), 23 New Mount Street,
Manchester M4 4DE (061 833 9496)
c/o Community Routes, Unit 3, Hattersley Industrial Estate, Stockport
Road, Hattersley, Hyde SK14 3QP (061 367 8014)
c/o ORIC, 7 Commercial Road, Oldham, Lancs OL1 1DP (061 626 4130)
c/o 708 Thornhill, Ashfield Valley, Rochdale, Lancs OL11 1SD (0706
353888)
MANCODA, 12 Mosley Street, Manchester M2 3AQ (061 236 1274)
Middlesbrough Co-operative Initiative, 8 Albert Road,
Middlesbrough, Cleveland TS1 1QA (0642 210226/7)
Milton Keynes CDA, Level 3, Civic Offices, 1 Saxon Gate East, Central
Milton Keynes MK9 3JH (0908 660375)
Newham CDA, Essex House, 375 High Street, London E15 4OZ (01 519
2377)
Norfolk and Norwich CDA, The Glass House, 9/13 Wensum Street,
Norwich NR3 1LA (0603 615200)
North West Co-op Development Council, Holyoake House, Hanover
Street, Manchester M60 0AS (061 833 9379)
Northamptonshire CDA, Elgin House, Billing Road, Northampton,
Northants NN1 5AU (0604 37401/2)
Northern Ireland CDA, Canada House, 22 North Street, Belfast,
Northern Ireland BT1 1LA (0232 232755)
Northern Region CDA, Bolbec House, Westgate Road, Newcastle-
upon-Tyne NE1 1SE (091 261 0140)
Planning Department, Central Library, St George Square, Newcastle-
upon-Tyne, South Shields (091 456 8841)
The Industrial Bureau, County Hall, Durham DH1 (091 386 4411 ext 2374)
Economic Unit, Chief Executive's Department, Gateshead Civic Centre,
Gateshead (091 477 1011 ext 2084)
Nottinghamshire CDA, Dunkirk Road, Dunkirk, Nottingham NG7 2PH
(0602 705700)
Oxfordshire CDA, 14b Park End Street, Oxford OX1 1NW (0865 790623)
Plymouth CDA, 138 North Road East, Plymouth PL4 6AQ (0752 223481)
Port Talbot CDA, 2nd Floor, Royal Buildings, Talbot Road, Port Talbot
SA13 1DN (0639 895173)
Portsmouth CDA, Quinnell Centre, 2 Kent Street, Portsea, Portsmouth
PO1 5EH (0705 822211 ext 321)
Powys Self-Help Trust, The Old Town Hall, Temple Street,
Llandrindod Wells, Powys LD1 5DL (0597 4576)
Redditch CDA, Town Hall, Alcester Street, Town Centre, Redditch B98
8AH (0527 64252 ext 3375)
Salford Community Enterprise Development Agency, 9 Broadway,
Salford M5 2TS (061 872 3838)

Scottish Co-op Development Committee, Templeton Business Centre, Templeton Street, Glasgow G40 1DA (041 554 3797)
Royal Bank Buildings, 191 High Street, Kircaldy, Fife (0592 200866)
Aberdeen Business Centre, Willowbank House, Willowbank Road, Aberdeen AB1 2YG (0224 593159)
Sheffield Co-op Development Group, Palatine Chambers, 22 Pinstone Street, Sheffield S1 2HN (0742 734563)
Southampton Area CDA, 56 High Street, Southampton SO1 0NS (0703 223885)
Southwark CDA, 42 Braganza Street, London SE17 3RJ (01 735 6066)
Staffordshire (North) CDA, c/o Mr D. T. Ward, Town Hall, Stoke-On-Trent ST4 1HH (0782 744241)
Sunderland Common Ownership Resources Centre, 44 Mowbray Road, Hendon, Sunderland SR2 8EL (091 565 0476)
Swindon CDA, c/o Sue Phipps, 3 Harding Street, Swindon SN1 5BZ (0793 511802)
Thetford CDA, Unit 8, Doran's Corner, Magdalen Street, Thetford IP24 2AD (0842 65426)
Tower Hamlets CDA, 84 Whitehorse Road, Tower Hamlets, London E1 0ND (01 791 0450)
Tynedale Co-op Development Group, 2c Tanners Yard, Gilesgate, Hexham, Northumberland NE46 3NJ
Vaynor Alternative, Centre House, Cefn Coed, Merthyr Tydfil, Mid Glamorgan (0685 82348)
Wales Co-op Development & Training Centre, Llandaff Court, Fairwater Road, Cardiff CF5 2XP (0222 554955)
Morfa Hall, Church Street, Rhyl, Clwyd LL18 3AA (0745 55336)
24 Bridge Street, Lampeter, Dyfed SA38 7AB (0570 423107)
Enterprise Centre, Merthyr Tydfil Industrial Park, Pentrebach, Merthyr Tydfil CF48 4DR (0443 692233)
Council Offices, Bron Castell, Stryd Fawr, Bangor LL57 1YU (0248 364729)
Waltham Forest CDA, 547 High Road, Leytonstone, London E11 4PB (01 558 6902)
Wansbeck Community Initiatives Centre, Station Villa, Kenilworth Road, Ashington, Northumberland NE63 9XL (0670 853619)
Waveney CDA, Town Hall, Lowestoft, Suffolk NR32 1HS (0502 62111)
Yarmouth CDA, Business Advisory Service, Queens Road, Great Yarmouth NR30 3HT (0493 857648)

Local Authority Offices with Specific Remit to Promote Co-operatives

Barnsley Metropolitan Council, Co-operatives Co-ordinator, Barnsley Metropolitan Council, Barnsley Enterprise Centre, Pontefract Road, Barnsley, S. Yorks (0226 298091)
Calderdale Metropolitan Council, Strategy Section, Chief Executives Dept, Town Hall, Halifax, W. Yorks (0422 57257 ext 2207)
London Borough of Camden, Economic Development Unit, London Borough of Camden Town Hall, Euston Road, London NW1 2RU (01 278 4444)
Cardiff City Council, Industrial Development Officer, Cardiff City Council, 5 Mountstuart Square, Cardiff CF1 6EE (0222 494411)

London Borough of Hammersmith and Fulham, Economic Development Unit, London Borough of Hammersmith & Fulham, Town Hall, King Street, London W6 9JU (01 748 3020)

London Borough of Haringey, Economic Development Unit, London Borough of Haringey, 98/100 High Road, Wood Green, London N22 (01 881 3000)

London Borough of Hounslow, The Civic Centre, Lampton Road, Hounslow, London TW3 4DM (01 570 7728)

London Borough of Lewisham, Employment Promotion Unit, London Borough of Lewisham, Town Hall Chambers, Lewisham, London SE6 (01 690 4343)

Hull City Council, Dept of Industrial Development, City of Hull, 76/78 Lowgate, Hull, W Yorks (0482 222627)

Kirklees Metropolitan Council, Co-operative Development Officer, Employment Development Unit, Kirklees Metroplitan Council, Estate Buildings, Railway Street, Huddersfield, W Yorks HD1 1JU (0484 22133)

Leeds City Council, Co-operative Development Officer, Dept of Industry & Estates, Leeds City Council, 44 The Headrow, Leeds LS1 8EA (0532 463208/463170)

Merthyr Tydfil Borough Council, Self-Employment Initiative Officer, Merthyr Tydfil Borough Council, Town Hall, Merthyr Tydfil, Mid Glamorgan (0685 3201)

Rhymney Valley District Council, Industrial Development Officer, Rhymney Valley District Council, Park Road, Hengoed, Mid Glamorgan CF8 7YB (0443 812241)

South Yorkshire County Council, Employment Promotion & Development Unit, South Yorkshire County Council, County Hall, Barnsley, S Yorks (0226 86141)

West Midlands County Council, Co-op Team, Economic Development Unit, West Midlands Cunty Council, County Hall, 1 Lancaster Circus, Queensway, Birmingham B4 7DJ (021 300 6667)

Other Organisations

The Co-operative Bank plc, Head Office, 1 Balloon Street, Manchester M60 4EP (061 832 3456). In 1978 this bank launched a special start-up scheme aimed at encouraging viable new co-operatives. This consisted of an offer by the bank to match, pound for pound, the capital raised by members. Interest and other charges are at the prevailing commercial rate. Although this offer in itself is not particularly generous (given a sound business proposition any bank would lend in this ratio), their appreciation of the mechanics of a co-operative may make them a more understanding audience.

The Co-op Bank has been looking after the banking requirements of the co-operative movement for over 100 years. The full range of 'clearing bank' services are also available, including the Government Loan Guarantee Scheme. There are also more bank outlets than you may have thought: 75 regional branches (rising to over 100 over the decade) and 1,000 Handybanks.

Co-operative Development Board, 301–344 Market Towers, New Covent Garden, London SW8 5NQ (01 720 2144). Part of the Food from Britain organisation. Provides grants for farmers and growers who are part of co-operatives. Also helps co-operatives with marketing, financial planning, education and legal matters.

The Co-operative Union Ltd, Publication Sales Section, Holyoake House, Hanover Street, Manchester M60 0AS (061 832 4300). Their booklist is probably the most comprehensive on the subject in the UK, covering both the theory and the practice.

The Co-operative Union Ltd, Education Department, Stanford Hall, Loughborough, Leicestershire LE12 5QR (0509 852333). This is the supreme body in the traditional co-operative movement. The Co-operative College is based here, and it offers a variety of courses for managers. In 1982 it launched a new one-year course for mature students from inside or outside the co-operative movement (grants available).

This is also a contact point for the union's 50 full-time and 70 part-time education secretaries. They cover the country and are a useful starting point for anyone wanting to find out more about co-operatives, courses, books and organisations.

Industrial Common Ownership Finance Ltd, 4 St Giles Street, Northampton NN1 1AA (0604 37563). Formed by ICOM (Industrial Common Ownership Movement) in 1973, ICOF Ltd now operates independently. It provides half the money required by co-operatives in short- to medium-term loans from six months to six years, with a monthly repayment after an initial capital holiday. The minimum sum it will consider is £1,000 and the maximum is £50,000, though usually loans start from £2,500.

ICOF have £1 million available for lending, although some of this is allocated to specific areas – eg, £500,000 for West Midlands, £100,000 for West Glamorgan. They have made a total of around 150 loans, totalling some £1.25 million.

Job Ownership Ltd, 9 Poland Street, London W1V 3DL (01 437 5511). Director of Operations: Robert Oaksholt. Job Ownership was formed in 1978 to encourage the formation of all types of worker-owned business.

Apart from promoting the ideas of worker ownership, JOL is a consultancy. It advises people who are considering what sort of co-operative to set up (for there are several quite different forms of worker ownership, of which the JOL model is only one). JOL's advice may include the preparation of a feasibility study/business plan, to help with the presentation to a source of loan funds, or help in forming a network of contacts. Normally they do not charge for initial consultation, and if they do their charges are modest compared with those of more conventional management consultancies.

New University of Ulster, The Co-operative Education, Research and Training Unit, Magee University College, Londonderry BT48 7JL (0504 265621). Director: Ray Donnelly; Declan Jones.

Registry of Friendly Societies, 15 Great Marlborough Street, London W1V 2AX (01 437 9992). The register can give information about the legal requirements of forming a co-operative.

Assistant Registrar of Friendly Societies, 58 Frederick Street, Edinburgh EH2 1NB (031 226 3224)

Wales Co-operative Development and Training Centre, Llandaff Court, Fairwater Road, Cardiff CF5 2XP (0222 554955). Set up in 1983 to provide technical assistance and managerial expertise to develop and support new worker-owned enterprises.

Publications

How to Set up a Co-operative Business published by CDA, revised July 1987. Price £2. A detailed guide to setting up a co-operative business, containing advice about co-operative organisation, with examples and comparisons of the various model structures which provide limited financial liability and corporate status.

Management Accounting for Co-operatives by P. C. Norkett in Management Accounting (UK), February 1983.

The National Directory of New Co-operatives and Community Businesses published by CDA, 5th edition published July 1988. Price £5.50. The CDA's National Directory of Co-operatives has now been completely revised and updated. Listed, once again, by region and sector; it also includes a selection of useful organisations, an extensive bibliography and co-operative statistics.

Running Your Own Co-operative by John Pearce, published in 1984 by Kogan Page Ltd, 120 Pentonville Road, London N1 9JN (01 278 0433). Price £5.95 pb, £9.95 hb.

Work Aid-Business Management for Co-operatives and Community Exchanges by Tony Naughton, published by Beechwood College, Elmete Lane, Roundhay, Leeds LS8 2LQ (0532 720205). Price £2.95. This book covers the legal, accounting, taxation, financial and marketing aspects of running a co-operative.

FRANCHISING

Franchising accounts for about a third of retail sales in the USA including household names such as Coca-Cola, Avis Rent-a-Car and the ubiquitous McDonalds (over 5,000 franchisees in the US alone). It is also viewed as one of the safest types of business (in the USA) with only around 60 firms failing each year. You have, of course, to remember that these statistics only represent franchisors that have been established long enough to get into the statistics in the first place. Many don't even see out their first year.

Between 1984 and 1988 retail franchise outlets in the UK doubled to a total of 20,000. In 1988 the 400 or so franchise organisations are expected to have sales approaching £2.5 billion. These include such names as Prontaprint, Home Tune and Kentucky Fried Chicken. The franchise method involves three elements: a business (franchisor), which grants to others (franchisees) a right or licence (franchise).

Franchising is a marketing technique used to improve and expend the distribution of a product or service. The franchisor supplies the product or teaches the service to the franchisee, who in his turn sells it to the public. In return for this, the franchisee pays a fee and a continuing royalty, based usually on turnover. The advantage to the franchisee is a relatively safe and quick way of getting into business for himself, but with the support and advice of an experienced organisation close at hand. The franchisor can expand his distribution with the minimum strain on his own capital and have the services of a highly motivated team of owner-managers. Franchising is not a path to great riches, nor is it for the truly independent spirit, as policy and profits will still come from 'on high'.

Before taking out a franchise it is essential that you consult your legal and financial advisers. You must also ask the franchisor some very searching questions to prove his competence. You will need to know if he has operated a pilot unit in the UK – an essential first step before selling franchises to third parties. Otherwise, how can he really know all the problems, and so put you on the right track? You will need to know what training and support is included in the franchise package, the name given to the start-up kit provided by franchisors to see you successfully launched. This package should extend to support staff over the launch period and give you access to back-up advice. You will need to know how substantial the franchise company is. Ask to see their balance sheet (take it to your accountant if you cannot understand it). Ask for the track record of the directors (including their other directorships).

In the USA there are specific disclosure rules that oblige a franchise organisation to give very extensive details of its operations to prospective franchisees; details are available from the Federal Trade Commission, 6th and Pennsylvania Avenue, NW, Washington DC 20580.

In the UK there are no such rules; however, the British Franchise Association (more details below) does lay down some guidelines. They can let you know something of the reputation of the organisation you are negotiating with. It might also be useful to ask one of the banking organisations (also listed below) if the franchisor has been vetted by them and given a clean bill of health.

Associations

The British Franchise Association, 75a Bell Street, Henley-on-Thames, Oxon RG9 2BD (0491 578049). The Association was formed in 1977 to establish a clear definition of ethical franchising standards and to help members of the public, press, potential investors and government bodies to differentiate between sound business opportunities and suspect business offers. It currently has some 90 members. Although being a member of the BFA does not guarantee the likely success of a franchise, it does show acceptance of a code of practice. The association will provide a checklist of questions to ask a franchisor and will answer questions on non-BFA companies if they have the information.

The International Franchise Association, 1025 Connecticut Avenue NW, Suite 1005, Washington DC 20036, USA. Founded in 1960, this is a non profit organisation representing 400 franchising companies in the USA and around the world. It is recognised as the spokesman for responsible franchising. It could be particularly useful in providing information on the growing number of 'new' franchises arriving in the UK with claims of USA parentage.

National Franchise Association Coalition, PO Box 366, Fox Lake, Illinois 60020, USA. This was formed in 1975 by franchisees in order to provide a centre for the expression of the franchisees' viewpoint, as distinct from that of the franchisors. No such organisation exists in the UK, but the American experiences provide some interesting lessons. There are areas of problems and dispute even between ethical and established franchise organisations and their franchisees. If you do run into such problems, this association may be able to give you some ideas and advice.

European Franchise Federation, *President: Mr Duncan Whitfield*, Home Tune Ltd, Home Tune House, Guildford Road, Effingham, Nr Leatherhead, Surrey KT24 5QS. (0372 56656)

Belgian Franchise Association, *President: Mrs Betty Huby*, Boulevard de l'Europe 17, Boite 8, B1420 Braine-L'Alleud, Belgium

Dutch Franchise Association, *President: Mr R. van Dijk*, 1213 Vg Hilversum, The Netherlands

French Franchise Association, *President: Mr B. Amstutz-Mahler*, 9 Bd des Italiens, 75002 Paris, France

German Franchise Association, *President: Dr W. Skaupy*, Josephspital Strasse 14, 8000 Munich 2, W. Germany

Italian Franchise Association, *President: Mr G. Bonani*, C so di Porta Nuova 3, 20121 Milano, Italy

Norwegian Franchise Association, *c/o Mr Torleif Karlesen*, Astweitkogen 41, 5084 Tertnes, Norway

Swedish Franchise Association, *President: Mr Peter Westring*, PO Box 5039, S 181 05 Lidingo, Sweden

Swiss Franchise Association, *President: Mr C. Seroude*, c/o Gesplan, 5 Rue Toepffer, Geneva, Switzerland

Franchisors Association of Australia, *Executive Officer: Mr B. Bell*, Suite 7, Ground Floor, Corporation Centre, 123 Clarence Street, Sydney, New South Wales, Australia 2000

Association of Canadian Franchisors, 44 Laird Drive, Toronto, Ontario, Canada M4G 3T2

Japanese Franchise Association, Elsa Building 602, 3-13-12 Roppongi, Minato-Ku, Tokyo, Japan

South African Franchise Association, c/o Johannesburg Chamber of Commerce, Private Bag 34, Auckland Park 2000, South Africa

---

Banks and Financial Institutions

Barclays Bank plc, Marketing Department, 6th Floor, Juxon House, 94 St Paul's Churchyard, London EC4M 8EH (01 248 9155) *Contact: F. P. Salaun*

Black Arrow Finance Ltd, 748 London Road, Hounslow, Middlesex TW3 1SE (01 572 7474) *Contact: W. P. Griffiths*

Bowring UK Ltd, The Bowring Building, Tower Place, London EC3P 3BE (01 283 3100) *Contact: Robert Leather, Director.* Insurance brokers with offices throughout UK. Specialists in arranging group schemes for franchisees and in personal planning (including provision for pensions, life insurance, etc)

First National Securities Ltd, Television House, Mount Street, Manchester M2 5NB (061 834 1107) *Contact: D. Owen*

Lloyds Bank plc, 71 Lombard Street, London EC3P 3BS (01 626 1500) *Contact: Alan Pope*

Midland Bank plc, Business Sector Marketing, Head Office, Poultry, London EC2P 2BX (01 606 9911 ext 2645) *Contact: Roy Manning, Franchise Manager*

National Westminster Bank plc, Small Business Section, 3rd Floor, 116 Fenchurch Street, London EC3M 5AN (01 726 1000) *Contact: P. Stern, Franchise Marketing Manager*

Royal Bank of Scotland, 42 St Andrew's Square, Edinburgh EH2 2YE (031 556 8555) *Contact: Jim Payne*

Education

The following organisations regularly run courses on franchising, intended to explain the process to potential franchisees.

Franchise Development Services Ltd, Castle House, Castle Meadow, Norwich NR2 1PJ (0603 620301) *Contact: Ben Walton (Seminar Organiser)*
Franchise World, James House, 37 Nottingham Road, London SW17 7EA (01 767 1371)
Institute of Marketing and The British Franchise Association, Moor Hall, Cookham, Maidenhead, Berkshire SL6 9QH (06285 24922)

Publications

This field is still dominated by American Publications. The American books listed here have direct relevance to the UK.

Business Format Franchising by Clive Grant. February 1985, The Economist Intelligence Unit, Report No. 185. The main emphasis of this special report is on the substance and nature of business format franchising in the UK. Drawing on a major survey recently commissioned by the British Franchise Association and on its own investigations, the EIU presents a detailed examination of the sector in terms of size, turnover, employment, sources of finance and advice and its participants which straddle a wide range of service and retailing enterprises.

A final chapter considers the impact of franchising on the UK economy and forecasts very rapid growth over the next five years with an increasing number of well-established firms, circumscribed by financial restraints, opting for expansion by the business format route. The Report includes 28 tables, including country comparisons, and a series of appendices.

The Dow Jones–Irwin Guide to Franchises by Peter G. Norback and Crain Norback, May 1983. This is a thorough investigation of franchising, organised by franchise categories. Once again it covers only the American scene, but it does provide some useful pointers.

The Franchise Newsletter produced by Franchise Development Services, Castle House, Castle Meadow, Norwich NR2 1PJ. A monthly publication; free copy on request.

Franchise Opportunities Directory available from Unit 10, Wreford Yard, Ransome Road, Northampton, Tel. 0604 68691. Updated and published each quarter. Gives the names and addresses of around 200 UK franchisors, a couple of lines description of the business and the minimum investment required.

Franchise Opportunity Handbook produced by US Government Printing Office, Administrative Division (SAA), Washington DC 20402, USA. The handbook provides an interesting insight into the official American views on franchising and also gives an idea of the scope of the franchising phenomenon.

Franchise Reporter produced by Franchise Publications, James House, 37 Nottingham Road, London SW17 7EA. Has eight issues a year. It is intended to keep you up to date with UK franchise news between the quarterly issues of *Franchise World.*

Franchise Rights, a Self-Defence Manual for the Franchisee by Alex Hammond. Hammond and Marton, 1185 Avenue of the Americas, New York, NT 10036, USA. The manual contains perceptive insight into franchisee/franchisor relationships – forewarned is forearmed.

Franchise World produced by Franchise Publications, James House, 37 Nottingham Road, London SW17 7EA. Has all the latest news on new franchise opportunities, new consultancies and sources of finance. Each issue has a franchise directory, which describes the franchise organisations and gives some idea of the cost of entry.

Franchising and the Total Distribution System by D. Izraeli. Longman, 5 Bentinck Street, London W1, Tel. 01 935 0121. 1972. It sets franchising in its context in the economic environment. A good backdrop to see where franchising really fits in.

Franchising in the Economy 1986-7 by US Department of Commerce, Bureau of Industrial Economies, Washington DC, USA, January 1987. Although completely based on the USA, it provides an extremely authoritative view of the role of franchising in an advanced industrial economy. It describes the business environment and the successes and failures in each sector of franchising.

A Guide to Franchising by Martin Mendelsohn, 5th edition 1987, Pergamon Press, Headington Hill Hall, Oxford OX3 0BW, Tel. 0865 64881. A very sound introduction to the advantages and disadvantages of franchising. It covers the basic principles including the 'franchise contract' which formalises the relationship between the franchisor and the franchisee.

The INFO Franchise Newsletter, INFO Press, 736 Center Street, Lewiston, YW 14092, USA. Does for the world (mainly North America) what *Franchise Reporter* sets out to do for the UK. INFO gives advance information on what new franchises are intending to start up in the UK, so it is a way of keeping ahead of the game.

Taking Up a Franchise by Colin Barrow and Godfrey Golzen, published by Kogan Page Ltd, 120 Pentonville Road, London N1. Now into its sixth edition, this book reviews the UK franchise scene, lists and describes around 150 franchisors and provides market size, growth and financial data for each company listed. It also shows how to evaluate a franchise opportunity.

Consultancies

Some management consultancies have specialised in the franchising field. They are usually experienced both in launching new franchise businesses and in finding suitable opportunities for those wanting to take out a franchise. They are not necessarily legal and financial experts, so it is still important to get independent professional advice before acting.

The AFL Deeson Partnership Ltd, Ewell House, Graveney Road, Faversham, Kent ME13 8UP (0795 535468) *Contact: Tony Deeson, Sue Koster*

Anglia Franchise Association, 8 Church Street, Harleston, Norfolk IP20 9BB (0379 853833) *Contact: Dennis Wisker, Norman Hulme*

Caltain Associates Ltd, Rothamsted, Broken Gate Lane, Denham, Middlesex UB9 4LB (0895 834200)

Centre for Franchise Marketing, 26 High Street, Merstham, Surrey RH1 3EA (07374 4211) *Contact: John Gooderham, Michael Way*

Franchise and Marketing Management Ltd, 18 Lichfield Street, Walsall, West Midlands WS1 1TS (0922 615351) *Contact: Mike Matthews*

Franchise Concepts, 3 Castle Street, High Wycombe, Bucks HP13 6RZ (0494 32631) *Contact: Bryan Wilkes*

Franchise Development Services Ltd, Castle House, Castle Meadow, Norwich NR2 1PJ (0603 6677024) *Contact: Roy Seaman*

Franchise Investors Ltd, Davidson House, Green Man Lane, Hatton Cross, Feltham, Middlesex TW14 0PZ (01 890 9896) *Contact: Dick Crook*

Franchise Selection and Marketing Ltd, Highpoint, Hyde Lane, Stafford ST18 9BG (0789 3447) *Contact: Peter Morrell*

Frazer/Scott, 28 Blandford Street, Sunderland, Tyne and Wear (0783 625533) *Contact: John Scott*

GB Fast Foods Ltd, 8 Pembridge Road, London W11 3HL (01 229 6698) *Contact: David Acheson, Sandra Young*

Andrew James, Hilltop House, 24 Cairnmuir Road, Edinburgh EH12 6LP (031 334 8040) *Contact: Andrew James*

MMM, 6 Mill Street, Buxton, Norfolk NR10 5JE (060546 212) *Contact: Michael Virgo*

Pannell Kerr Forster, New Garden House, 78 Hatton Garden, London EC1N 8JA (01 831 7393) *Contact: David Hunt*

RSH Consultants Ltd, 3 Jubilee Buildings, Outram Street, Sutton in Ashfield, Nottinghamshire NG17 1DE (0623 515704) *Contact: Ian Herd, Tony Roberts*

Three important questions you should ask anyone offering their services in this field are:

- Has the consultant been involved in successful franchising at a high level?
- Has he demonstrated his ability to advise? Ask to speak to some of his past clients.
- If the consultant is taking commission on the sale of the franchises his client is launching, there could well be an undesirable conflict of interest.

Lawyers listed by members

Adlers, 22–26 Paul Street, London EC2A 4JH (01 481 9100) *Contact: Martin Mendelsohn*

Baker & McKenzie, Aldwych House, Aldwych, London WC2B 4UP (01 242 6531) *Contact: Gabriel Fisher*

Drummond & Co, WS, 31–32 Moray Place, Edinburgh EH3 6BZ (031 226 5151) *Contact: Michael Bell*

Field Fisher & Martineau, Lincoln House, 296–302 High Holborn, London WC1V 7JL (01 831 9161) *Contact: John Nelson-Jones*

Ladas & Parry, 52–64 High Holborn, London WC1V 6RR (01 242 5566) *Contact: Ian Baillie.* Also trade mark agents

Lorenz & Jones, Courtyard House, 30 Worthing Road, Horsham, West Sussex (Horsham 69166) *Contact: Ken Prichard-Jones*

Macfarlanes, 10 Norwich Street, London EC4A 1BD (01 831 9222) *Contact: V. E. Treves*

Mundays, The Bellbourne, 103 High Street, Esher, Surrey KT10 9QE (0372 67272) *Contact: Ray Walley*

Needham & James, Windsor House, Temple Row, Birmingham B2 5LF (021 236 9701) *Contact: John Pratt*

Owen White & Catlin, Gavel House, 90–102 High Street, Feltham, Middlesex TW13 4ES (01 890 2836) *Contact: Anton Bates*

Peters & Peters, 2 Harewood Place, Hanover Square, London W1R 9HB (01 629 7991) *Contact: Raymond Cannon*

Wm F. Prior & Co, Temple Bar House, 23–28 Fleet Street, London EC4Y 1AA (01 353 3571) *Contact: Christopher O'Grady*

Paul Shrank & Co, Carlton House, 66–69 Great Queen Street, London WC2 5BZ (01 831 6677) *Contact: Paul Shrank*

Franchise Directory

Franchising is an extremely dynamic market, so things change very rapidly. Using this directory, at the side of each entry you will see how long the franchise has been established, whether or not it is a BFA member, how many UK outlets it has, and whether or not is has a pilot operation, how much you will need in order to purchase and start up each franchise.

Use the information as a rough guide only. For example, the investment required in a franchise outlet in Oxford Street, London W1, will be very different from that of a similar operation in a small town. If you think the business area is interesting, get more information on all the franchises in that field and compare them. Do use professional advice before entering into any agreements.

KEY
1 Minimum start-up capital
2 1st UK franchise
3 No. of UK franchised outlets
4 No. of UK companies operated (including 'pilots')
5 BFA member

	1	2	3	4	5
A1 Damproofing, New Side Mill, Charnley Fold Lane, Bamber Bridge, Preston PR5 6AA (0772 35228) *Contact: J. Pickup* Specialists in the treatment of woodworm, woodrot and rising damp	£10,000	1985	10	1	No
The Accounting Centre, Elscot House, Arcadia Avenue, London N3 2JE (01 349 3191) *Contact: Ivor Davies* A monthly accounting service to small/medium sized businesses developing nationally with support from banks and firms of accountants	£15,000	1983	25	1	Yes
Anicare Group Services (Veterinary) Ltd, 23 Buckingham Road, Shoreham-by-Sea, W. Sussex BN4 5UA (0273 463022) *Contact: J. Sheridan* Franchisees need to be fully qualified and members of Royal College of Veterinary Surgeons. Anicare links members to central resource for diagnostic, surgical and in-patient facilities	£15,000	1972	8	1	Yes
Apollo Window Blinds Ltd, Johnstone Avenue, North Cardonald Industrial Estate, Glasgow G52 4YM (041 810 3021) *Contact: Mrs Nan Stevenson* Franchisees assemble and retail window blinds to domestic, commercial and trade customers, from high street locations	£20,000	1975	98	—	Yes
Badgeman Ltd, 544 Chiswick High Road, London W4 5RG (01 994 0826) *Contact: David Mackie* Industry leader in the manufacture of high quality personalised lapel badges	£15,000	1980	11	1	Yes

	1	2	3	4	5
The Bath Doctor, Denbigh House, Denbigh Road, Milton Keynes MK1 1YP (0908 270007) *Contact: Mike Robertson* Home based business renovating bathroom suites	£2,500	1982	50	—	Reg.
Beardsley Theobalds Businesses, Leygore Manor, Northleach, Cheltenham GL54 3NY (0451 60667) *Contact: John Hine* Computer-linked business transfer agents and finance brokers	£30,000	1985	11	5	No
Bodyreform, Reform Cosmetics, Natural Beauty Products Ltd, Unit 5, Kingsway Buildings, Bridgend Industrial Estate, Bridgend, Mid Glam CF31 3SD (0656 57101/ 645400) *Contact: A. R. Lees* Franchised retail outlets for Reform natural cosmetics	£25,000	1985	37	5	No
The Bread Roll Company, Unit 6, 224 London Road, St Albans, Herts (0727 35291) *Contact: Mark Dixon* Specialist supplier of rolls and allied products	£16,000	1984	10	0	No
Brewer and Turnbull, Your Friendly Mr Mover, Waverley Freight Terminal, Miller Road, Preston PR1 5QS (0772 797896) *Contact: Max C. Godfrey* Home and overseas removals and storage	£15,000	1984	24	1	No
British Damp Proofing, The Old School, Fleetwood Road, Esprick, Preston PR4 3HJ (039 136 441) *Contact: B. Wainwright* Rising damp and timber decay specialists	£10,500	1984	45	2	Yes
Bruce & Company, 43 Bridge Street, Leatherhead, Surrey KT28 8BN (0372 375161) *Contact: I. W. Lynch* Agents in business transfer market	£15,000	1981	13	1	No

	1	2	3	4	5
Budget Rent-a-Car International Inc, International House, 85 Great North Road, Hatfield, Herts AL9 5EF (07072 68266) *Contact: Keith Harman* Car and van hire business	£75,000	1966	115	2	Yes
Burger King UK Ltd, 20 Kew Road, Richmond, Surrey TW9 2NA (01 940 6046) *Contact: Mrs Farrah Rose* Fast food hamburger restaurants	$25,000	1987	12	—	Yes
Business Transfer Consultants (Franchise) Ltd, 712 Green Lane, Goodmayes, Essex RM8 1YX (01 597 2302) *Contact: Rhonda Brooke-Taylor* Business transfer agents	£30,000	1983	9	1	No
Carpet Master Ltd, Shop Unit 36, Bradford Road, Off Buckingham Avenue, Trading Estate, Slough, Berks SL1 4PG (0753 691584) *Contact: Hugh Jones* Mobile carpet shop	£3,722	1986	3	—	No
Cartons Boulangeries, Unit 2, Telegraph Hill Estate, Laundry Road, Minster, Ramsgate, Kent CT12 4HJ (0843 821940) *Contact: Bob Peel* High class French bakery	£20,000	1986	5	1	No
Chapter and Verse Bookshops, 41 Park Street, Bristol BS1 5NL (0272 214670) *Contact: T. Foss* General and academic bookshop	£75,000				No
Circle 'C' Stores Ltd, 24 Fitzalan Road, Roffey, Horsham, Sussex RH13 6AA (Horsham 61698) *Contact: J. A. Wormull* Convenience stores situated in neighbourhood locations	£25,000	1984	7	15	Reg.
Clarks Shoes, Box 106, 40 High Street, Street, Somerset BA16 0YA (0458 43131 ext. 2399) *Contact: Paul D. Monaghan* Retail outlets selling Clarks shoes	£80,000	1984	27	70	Yes
Cleo Chimney Linings, Westleton, Saxmundham, Suffolk IP17 3BS (072 873 608) *Contact: J. Wilkin* Lining and restoration of chimneys	£11,000	1982	20	1	Yes

	1	2	3	4	5
Coffeeman, 73 Woolsbridge Industrial Park, Wimborne, Dorset BH21 6SU (0202 823501) *Contact: S. Bayless* Supplier of coffee, tea, etc, to commercial outlets	£9,000–15,000	1979	33	1	No
Colour Counsellors, 187 New King's Road, London SW6 4NZ (01 736 8326) *Contact: Virginia Stourton* Interior decoration and supplies	£4,500	1974	65	1	Yes
Command Performance, High End, Troutstream Way, Loudwater, Herts WD3 4LQ (0923 777 636) *Contact: Iain Macaulay* Modern hairstyling salon, sometimes with beauty dept, nail centre, gym/health centre	£50,000	1984	10	3	Yes
Compleat Cookshop, Buckingham Road, Aylesbury, Bucks HP19 3QQ (0296 431296) *Contact: J. Frankling* Fashion housewares retailing	£20,000		15	7	No
Complete Weed Control Ltd, Industrial Estate, Bourton-on-the-Water, Gloucestershire GL54 2EN (0451 20985) *Contact: Mr R. Turner* Weed control service	£20,000	n/a	13	1	Reg.
Computerland, UK Regional Office, 518 Elder House, Elder Gate, Central Milton Keynes MK9 1LR (0908 664244) *Contact: Clive Booth* Network of microcomputer business centres	£200,000	1982	15	—	Yes
Concorde One Hour Photo Labs, 46 Church Street, Enfield, Middx EN2 6AZ (01 367 4762 (day), 01 360 9645 (evenings) *Contact: John Fairley* One-hour high street photo developing and retailing of photographic accessories	£20,000	1985	1	2	No
Countryside Garden Maintenance Services, 164–200 Stockport Road, Cheadle, Cheshire SK8 2DP (061 428 4444) *Contact: Martin Stott* Garden maintenance services	£14,000	1986	3	1	No

	1	2	3	4	5
Coversure Insurance Services, 4 Longstaff Way, Wartford, Huntingdon, Cambs PE18 7XT (0480 413858) *Contact: P. Theakston* Motor, commercial and life assurance consultants	£10,000	1986	1	3	No
Crimecure 30 Ltd, Darley House, Cow Lane, Garston, Watford, Herts WD2 6PH (0923 663322) *Contact: Ann Stunt* Installation of security systems	£7,500	1986	20	1	No
Dampco, 21 Lythalls Lane, Coventry, West Midlands CV6 6FN (0203 687683) *Contact: Ron Ferrans* Treatment of woodworm and dry rot	£10,500	1987	—	—	No
Dampcure Woodcure/30 Ltd, Darley House, Cow Lane, Garston, Watford, Herts WD2 6PH (0923 663322) *Contact: Ann Stunt* Timber and dampness specialists	£9,000	1982	31	1	Yes
Dial a Char, 77 London Road, East Grinstead, Sussex (0342 28391/314764) *Contact: Marcella van Veen* Domestic services	£12,500	1983	13	3	No
Dyno-Electrics, 143 Maple Road, Surbiton, Surrey KT6 4BJ (01 549 9711) *Contact: T. Fellowes, P. Woodward* Emergency repair and installation service	£1,250	1984	16	1	Yes
Dyno-Rod, 143 Maple Road, Surbiton, Surrey KT6 4BJ (01 549 9711) *Contact: D. Tonchin, C. Smith* Pipework maintenance service	£12,000	1965	86	5	Yes
Everett Masson & Furby Ltd, 18 Walsworth Road, Hitchin, Herts SG5 9SP (0462 32377) *Contact: Ian Littlewood* Business and commercial property agents	£20,000	1971	19	2	Yes
Exchange Travel, Exchange House, Parker Road, Hastings, East Sussex TN34 3UB (0424 423571) One of UK's foremost retail travel multiples concentrating primarily on holiday and leisure sales	£25–£30,000	1984	40	22	Yes

	1	2	3	4	5
Fastframe Instant Picture Framing, 28 Blandford Street, Sunderland, Tyne & Wear SR1 3JH (091 565 2233) *Contact: Margaret Hewison* High street picture framing	£35,000	1984	44	3	Yes
Fatso's Pasta Joint, 3 Palace Gate Parade, Hampton Court, East Molesey, Surrey KT8 9BN (01 783 1664) *Contact: Ron Patmore* Pasta restaurant	£70,000	1987	0	2	No
Fersina International, Cestrum House, Industry Road, Carlton, Barnsley, S. Yorks S70 3NH (0226 728310) *Contact: Ian Woodward* Sale, manufacture and installations of upvc doors, windows and conservatories	£30,000	1981	50	1	No
Fidelity Franchising Ltd, Le Brun House, 3a Chislehurst Road, Orpington, Kent BR6 0DE (0689 38498) *Contact: Geoffrey Birch* Electrical spares and repairs	£12,000	1987	0	1	No
Fires and Things, Heat House, 4 Brighton Road, Horsham, West Sussex RH13 5BA (0403 56227) *Contact: B. D. Simpson* Retails everything from fireplaces and stoves to pokers through retail shops	£25,000	1985	4	3	No
Fixit Mobile Fastening Centre, 98 Braemar Avenue, South Croydon, Surrey CR2 0QB (01 668 4567) *Contact: F. A. Gear* Sale of fixings, fastenings, hand tools and power tools from mobile vehicle	£3,500	1986	2	—	No
Foto Inn, 19a Acton Park Estate, The Vale, London W3 7QE (01 743 2131) *Contact: Sally Levy* Fast photo processing service	£85,000	n/a	1	6	No
The Frame Factory, 67 Vivian Avenue, London NW4 3XE (01 202 2499) *Contact: Stephen Godfrey* Picture framing, posters and art supplies	£30,000		6	2	No
Freezavan Ltd, Fleet Estate Office, Fleet, Nr Spalding, Lincs PE12 8LR (0406 22727) *Contact: Roy Lowe* Leading frozen food home delivery service	£7,000	1986	16	11	No

	1	2	3	4	5
Garden Building Centres Ltd, Coppice Gate, Lye Head, Bewdley, Worcs DY12 2UX (0299 266361) *Contact: Ian Jackson* Sale of garden buildings from garden centres	£25,000	1986	3	3	No
The Gold Vault Ltd, 26 Skelty Park Road, Skelty, Swansea SA2 9AS (0792 207194) *Contact: S. A. Ramsey-Williams* Purchasers of used precious metals, suppliers of dental products	£2,000	1985	n/a	n/a	No
Herbal World Natural Body Care, North Eastern Chambers, Station Square, Harrogate, N. Yorks HG1 1SY (0423 525865) *Contact: T. Cottier* Retailer of natural body care products and ancillary items	£35,000	1987			No
Highway Windscreens, Unity House, Southend Road, Woodford Green, Essex IG8 8HD (01 551 214) *Contact: J. C. Frankling* Mobile windscreen replacement	£6,000	1979	11	7	No
House of Something Different, 12–16 Church Hill, Loughton, Essex (0584 811515) *Contact: R. Padwick* Fireplaces, etc, for DIY home improvement	£30,000		4	4	No
Hyde-Barker Travel, Market Street, Mansfield, Nottinghamshire NG18 1SR (0623 31121) *Contact: M. A. Hyde-Barker* Retail travel agency	£35,000+	1985	1	7	No
Infopoint, 4–5 Hanborough Business Park, Long Hanborough, Oxfordshire OX7 2LH (0993 881991) *Contact: Philip Flook* Information cards for tourists	£5,450	1987	—	4	No
Intacab Ltd, Service House, West Mayne, Basildon, Essex SS15 6RW (0268 415891) *Contact: Mel Lilley* Operate taxis and private hire cars	£80,000				No

	1	2	3	4	5
In-Toto Ltd, Wakefield Road, Gildersome, Leeds LS27 0QW (0532 524131) *Contact: Malcolm Eccleston* Quality fitted kitchens	£25,000+	1980	31	1	Yes
Isodan (UK) Ltd, 55b Colebrook Road, Royal Tunbridge Wells, Kent TN4 9DP (0892 44822) *Contact: S. John Holt* System for filling external cavity walls with insulation material	£7,500	1975	61	—	No
Kall-Kwik Printing, Kall-Kwik House, Pembroke Road, Ruislip, Middx HA4 8NW (0895 632700) *Contact: Mrs Anne Wright* Complete printing, copying and design service	£79,000	1979	111	—	Yes
Knightsguard UK Ltd, 14–16 Tonbridge Road, Maidstone, Kent ME16 8RP (0622 686362) *Contact: G. Phelps* Manpower security	£10,000	1986	9	—	No
Knobs & Knockers Franchising Ltd, 36–40 York Way, London N1 9AB (01 278 8925) *Contact: John R. Staddon* Leading retailers of speciality brassware and home design merchandise	£55,000	1986	—	53	Assoc
Kwik Strip, Units 1–2, The 306 Estate, 242 Broomhill Road, Brislington, Bristol BS4 5RA (0272 772470) *Contact: I. M. Chivers* Process for stripping/restoration market	£8,500	1983	17	1	No
The Late Late Supershop (UK) Ltd, CWS Ltd, PO Box 53, New Century House, Manchester M60 4ES (061 834 1212 ext 5416) *Contact: Mrs Kathryn Sharp* Convenience retailer	£75,000+	1985	2	1	Yes
Maps Marketing Ltd, 160 Molesworth Road, Stoke, Plymouth, Devon (0752 556688/660030) *Contact: J. W. Macleod* Simple advertising and promotion at low cost	£3,000	1986	2	4	No

	1	2	3	4	5
Micrex Microfilm Express Ltd, Microfilm House, Thrupp Lane, Radley, Oxfordshire OX14 3NG (0235 22275) *Contact: Bryan Baillie* Microfilm service centre	£40,000	1987	0	1	No
Midas (Great Britain) Ltd, 107 Mortlake High Street, London SW14 8HH (01 878 7803) *Contact: Ken Phillips* Automotive aftermarket retailer of brakes and exhausts, etc.	£100,000+	1967	9	34	Yes
Midland Waterlife, 154–156 High Street, Bromsgrove, Worcestershire (0527 70676) *Contact: Richard Edge* Retail aquatic centres	£25,000	1986	1	1	No
Mixamate Concrete, Bourne Way, Hayes, Kent BR2 7EY (01 462 8011) *Contact: Peter Slinn* Providers of mixed concrete	£15,000				Yes
Mr Lift, The Lifthouse, Gloucester Road, Almondsbury, Bristol BS12 4HY (0454 618181) *Contact: Rupert Crook* Hires, sells and services forklift trucks	£82,500	1985	3	3	Reg.
Mr Slade Dry Cleaning, Mr Slade Franchises Ltd, Maritime Chambers, 1 Howard Street, North Shields, Tyne and Wear NE30 1AR (0632 596421) *Contact: Eunice Hesslegrave* Dry cleaning business	£15,000	1983	11	15	No
National Vacuum Cleaner Services, Hampton House, 5 Hampton Pier Avenue, Herne Bay, Kent CT6 8EW (0227 374656) *Contact: Dennis Wall* Service and repairs of floor cleaning machines	£4,474	1983	42	0	No
Natural Life Health Foods Ltd, 15 Queen Street, Salisbury, Wiltshire SP1 1EY (0584 811518) *Contact: Ron Padwick* Health food retailers	£70,000	1986	4	1	No

	1	2	3	4	5
New Moves, 15 South Street, Exeter EX1 1DZ (0392 219922) *Contact: Mike Biswell* Estate agency services	£15,000	New			No
Oasis Trading, 7–8 Cave Street, Oxford OX4 1BA (0865 723561) *Contact: Andrew Thomas* Wholesaler and retailer of imported merchandise	£30,000+	1980	12	8	No
The Original Art Shop, 28 Hemmells, Laindon, Essex SS15 6ED (0268 415822) *Contact: Mike Francis* Retail shop offering original pictures	£35,000	1982	4	21	Reg.
Perfect Pizza, 65 Staines Road, Hounslow, Middx TW3 3HW (01 577 1711) *Contact: R. Mendoza* UK leading pizza takeaway and delivery franchise	£56,000	1982	57	3	Yes
Pip Instant Printers, Black Arrow House, 2 Chandos Road, London NW10 6NF (01 965 0700) *Contact: Dermot Waters* Instant print shop	£65,000	1982	65	3	Yes
Pizza Express, 29 Wardour Street, London W1V 3HB (01 437 7215) *Contact: Jonathan Dell* Pizza restaurants	£150,000	1972	28	14	Yes
Poppies (UK) Ltd, 31 Houndgate, Darlington DL1 5RH (0325 488699) *Contact: Beverley Clayton* Specialises in domestic help and commercial cleaning	£10,000	1983	45	0	Yes
Potholes, Prospect Road, Alresford, Hampshire SO24 9QF (0962 73 3025) *Contact: C. T. Bayles* Year-round maintenance, repair, refurbishing and coating service to local authorities, etc	£20,000	1983	5	1	No
PRB Self Drive Hire, Unit 8, Cape Road Industrial Estate, Warwick CV34 4JW (0926 499867) *Contact: Mrs H. R. Burnett* Nationwide vehicle hire depots	£12,000	1984	15	3	No

	1	2	3	4	5
Professional Appearance Services, 1 Queen Square, Bath BA1 2HE (0225 312756) *Contact: Malcolm Shaw* National autovaleting of cars	£11,940	1983	10	—	No
Prontaprint, Coniscliffe House, Coniscliffe Road, Darlington DL3 7EX (0325 483333) *Contact: David Pooley* Instant print shop	£55,000	1971	291	1	Yes
Pronuptia de Paris Bridalwear, 70–78 York Way, Kings Cross, London N1 9AG (01 278 0343) *Contact: Alex Henning* Retail bridalwear specialist	£40,000	1978	57	14	Yes
Ryman Ltd, Ryman House, 59 Markham Street, London SW3 3NR (01 351 5671) *Contact: John Wynne Williams* Retailers of office stationery etc	£90,000		2	52	No
Safeclean, Delmae House, Home Farm, Ardington, Wantage, Oxon OX12 8PN (0235 833022) *Contact: Brian Duckett* Complete furnishing care service	£9,750	172	68	—	Yes
Seekers Estate Agency, 200b Haverstock Hill, London NW3 (01 794 7194) Estate agency	£25,000	1981	45	—	No
Serviceman Service Centres, 2nd Floor, Northgate House, High Pavement, Basildon, Essex SS14 1EA (0268 293355) *Contact: Michael P. Timmins* Car servicing, repairs, tuning, MOT testing	£42,000		9	3	No
Servicemaster, 50 Commercial Square, Freemans Common, Leicester LE2 7SR (0533 548620) *Contact: Philip Tait* Leading cleaning organisation	£9,000	1959	187	—	Yes
Signtalk Ltd, 266 Church Street, Blackpool, Lancs FY1 3PZ (0253 293774) *Contact: K. L. Harber* Suppliers of range of business promotional and incentive products	£5,000	1986	4	1	No

	1	2	3	4	5
Silver Shield Windscreens, Wheler Road, Seven Stars Estate, Coventry CV3 3LA (0203 307755) *Contact: John Oliver* 24-hour windscreen replacement service	£18,000	1978	62	—	Yes
Sketchley Franchises Ltd, PO Box 7, Rugby Road, Hinckley, Leic LE10 2NE (0455 38133) *Contact: Keith J. Twymann* Dry cleaning and shoe repair shops	.£77,000	1985	4	479	Yes
Slim Gym Ltd, Bingswood Industrial Estate, Whaley Bridge, Stockport SK12 7LY (06633 4545) *Contact: N. McKechnie* Health and leisure consultants	£50,000	1983	9	—	No
Snap-On-Tools, Palmer House, 150–154 Cross Street, Sale, Cheshire M33 1FU (061 969 0126) *Contact: Mrs Jackie Coulding* Tools for the motor vehicle garage trade	£6,000	1965	314	n/a	Yes
Spud-U-Like, 34–38 Standard Road, London NW10 6EU (01 965 0181) *Contact: Michael Porritt* Fast food retailing business	£50,000	1981	40	5	Yes
Stained Glass Overlay, PO Box 65, Norwich, Norfolk NR6 6EJ (0603 485454) *Contact: D. Hubbard* Designs on glass using coloured films and lead strips	£35,000	1986	—	1	No
Stockcheck, The Courtyard, Harewood Estate, Harewood, Leeds LS17 9LS (0532 886565) *Contact: J. C. Gilpin* Food and liquor stocktaking and stock control	£7,500	1983	13	—	No
Stop-A-Thief!, Unit 9, Avenue 1, Business Park, Letchworth, Herts SG6 2BB (0462 670555) *Contact: Phil Aston* Supplies and fits vehicle security systems	£9,500	1983	22	3	No

	1	2	3	4	5
Subway Sandwiches and Salads (UK) Ltd, PO Box 153, London N11 3JU (01 361 9546) *Contact: Neil Taylor* Sells sandwiches, salads and fast foods	£40,000	1986	1	—	No
Swinton Insurance, 31–33 Princess Street, Manchester M2 4EW (061 236 8697) *Contact: Peter Lowe* Insurance brokers	£18,000	1984	70	150	Yes
System-Text (UK) Ltd, System-Text House, Beavor Lane, London W6 9BL (01 741 7461) *Contact: Derek Fiddaman* Self-adhesive lettering system	£12,750	1987	—	1	No
Team, Haverscroft Industrial Estate, New Road, Attleborough, Norfolk NR17 1YE (0953 454544) *Contact: David Fossey* Distribution of radio, TV and audio equipment to retailer by mobile showroom	£24,000	1984	13	3	Reg.
Thorntons, Derwent Street, Belper, Derbyshire DE5 1WP (077 382 4181) *Contact: R. E. Smith* Retailers and manufacturers of high quality confectionery	£15,000	1968	80	155	Yes
Tie Rack Ltd, 70–78 York Way, London N1 9AG (01 837 6356) *Contact: Ronald Delnevo* Retails ties, scarves, etc	£35,000	1983	80	20	Yes
TNT Parcel Office, TNT House, Long Street, Atherstone, Warwicks CV9 1BS (08277 5311) *Contact: David Hadley* Reception point for parcels delivered by TNT's express parcel services	£3,000	1981	419	—	Yes
Trust Parts, Unit 7, Groundswell Industrial Estate, Crompton Road, Swindon, Wilts SN2 5AY (0793 723749) *Contact: Bob Wilson* Van sales supplying consumable hardware to motor industry	£20,000	1986	—	86	No

	1	2	3	4	5
Tumble Tots (UK) Ltd, Cannons Sports Club, Cousin Lane, London EC4R 3TE (01 621 0904) *Contact: David Thomas* Active physical play programme for pre-school children	£4,000+	1983	60	2	No
The UK School of Motoring Ltd, 2 East Street, Newport, Isle of Wight PO30 1JN (0983 527788) *Contact: Adrian Brewer* Driving school	£3,500	1986	1	2	No
Uticolour, Sheraton House, 35–37 North Street, York YO1 1JD (0904 37798) *Contact: Eric Bottomley* Vinyl bonding process used to repair damaged vinyl and leather coverings	£6,000	1978	36	2	Yes
Vandervells Business Transfer Centre, Vandervell House, 72 London Road, Southampton SO1 2AJ (0703 229271) *Contact: Geoff Vandervell* Business transfer agents	£15,000	1983	5	—	No
VDU Services, VDU House, Brook Road, Wormley, Surrey GU8 5BR (042 879 3733) *Contact: David Cooper* Computer and VDU cleaning	£8,350	New		1	No
Video Events, 12 Harley House, Upper Harley Street, London NW1 4PR (01 935 4430/0873 77379) *Contact: D. Ahern* Professional video filming services	£7,500	1985	4	2	No
Wallspan Bedrooms Ltd, Industrial Estate, Maulden Road, Flitwick, Beds MK45 5BW (0525 716161) Fitted bedroom furniture	—	1975	45	33	No
Wash 'n' Wax, 19 Ainslie Place, Edinburgh EH3 6AU (031 226 2823) *Contact: Colin McCraith* Mobile vehicle valet service	£6,000	1986	8	1	No
Weightguard Franchise Ltd, Henlow Grange Health Farm, Henlow, Beds SG16 6DP (0462 811111) *Contact: Elizabeth Knight* Slimming clubs	£1,300	1984	35	24	No

	1	2	3	4	5
Welder Health and Fitness, Craven House, Station Road, Godalming, Surrey GU7 1JD (04868 25544) *Contact: Michael J. Stearn* Distributor and retailer of health and fitness equipment, etc	£30,000	1983	4	3	No
Wetherby Training Services, 15 Victoria Street, Wetherby, W. Yorks LS22 4RE (0937 63940) *Contact: D. G. Button* Secretarial and computer training centres	£6,000	1976	98	1	Yes
Wimpy, 10 Windmill Road, London W4 1SD (01 994 6454) *Contact: Mike Chambers* Fast food retailer	£400,000	1958	364	33	Yes
Young's Formal Wear for Men, 70–78 York Way, Kings Cross, London N1 9AG (01 278 0343) *Contact: Alex Henning* Formal wear hire specialist	£40,000	1978	57	14	Yes

EXPLOITING HIGH, AND NOT SO HIGH, TECHNOLOGY

Technology presents considerable opportunities to inventors and users alike. It also presents a number of problems. Inventors have difficulty in communicating their ideas to commercial organisations. These ideas are often a long way from being a recognisable product at the time when most help (financial or otherwise) is needed. A growing number of institutions, organisations and services now aim to provide just this understanding and assistance.

On the other hand, there are many small businesses which could make considerable use of new technology, if only they knew how. Micro-computers are the most obvious development, where dull, repetitive tasks can be done quickly, leaving the entrepreneur free to perform more important tasks.

The following material should give you an appreciation of what is happening to solve these technological communication problems.

SCIENCE PARKS, INNOVATION AND TECHNOLOGY CENTRES

In 1973 an experiment began to encourage the growth of technical innovation in the USA. The basic idea was to bring inventors, entrepreneurs and academics together physically on or near the college campus. By adding some government funds to provide buildings, materials and equipment, it was hoped that the right environment to identify and stimulate new products and services would then be created. Although at the start these 'Innovation Centres' would be heavily subsidised, they were expected to become substantially self-supporting. This, no doubt, was the motivation in ensuring that a good business school was on the campus too (a lesson that UK emulators have not universally followed). The American experiment seems to show that the college-industry centres can and do flourish. By 1978 these centres had played a major part in forming some 30 new and largely technology-based businesses. They employed on average 40 people each, and some had sales returns of well over $1 million per annum. By the end of 1983, some 40 centres were operating around the USA based on such colleges as Carnegie-Mellon and the Massachusetts Institute of Technology.

In the UK (and elsewhere) similar deliberations were taking place. For example, in 1969 a decision was taken to encourage the expansion of science-based industry close to Cambridge. This would take advantage of the considerable concentration there of scientific expertise, equipment and libraries. The resultant Science Park was officially opened in 1975.

A growing number of organisations are now concerned with improving the lot of the inventor-entrepreneur. Some of these seem to offer little more than premises and a sympathetic ear. Others are rather less than high-technology based. However, most of them are extremely young, at least half have expressed a desire to provide practical as well as technological help to small, new innovation-based businesses. This situation represents a considerable improvement when compared to the UK inventors' lot in the 1970s.

There are now over 30 Science Parks in the UK, clustered under the loose umbrella of the UK Science Parks Association, 44 Oaks Road, Sutton Coldfield, West Midlands, B74 2TL, tel. 021 308 8815.

KEY
1 Opening date
2 Rent per sq foot (from)
3 Number of companies
4 Range of unit size
5 Venture capital fund
6 Grants available

	1	2	3	4	5	6
Aberystwyth Science Park, Aberystwith, Powys SY23 4AH (0970 615779) *Contact: Conrad Jenkins* Established as a joint venture between the University College of Wales, Aberystwyth and Mid-Wales Development.	1983	£2.50	5	500–2000	Yes	Yes
Antrim Technology Park, Thomas Street, Ballymena BT43 6BA (0266 3655) *Contact: George Dillan* Wholly owned by Industrial Development Board for Northern Ireland. Has access to a wide range of support services from the Universities.	1985	£4.00	4	2000	No	Yes
Aston Science Park, Love Lane, Aston Triangle B7 4BJ (021 359 0981) *Contact: Harry Nicholls* Established as a joint venture by the City of Birmingham, Lloyds Bank and Aston University, and is managed by Birmingham Technology Ltd. Venture Capital fund specialists in start-up situations for hi-tech companies.	1983	£4.75	41	150–5000	Yes	No
Belasis Hall Technology Park, Billingham, Cleveland TS23 4AZ (0642 522111) *Contact: George Hunter* Owned jointly by ICI and English Estates North. Expertise of ICI available to tenants.	1988		—	150–10000	No	Yes

	1	2	3	4	5	6
Birmingham Research Park, Vincent Drive, Edgbaston, Birmingham B15 2SQ (021 471 4977) *Contact: Dr Derek Burr* Managed by Birmingham Research Park Ltd, which is owned by Birmingham City Council and University of Birmingham. Provides accommodation for companies wishing to use University expertise.	1986	£5	13	350–3000	Yes	No
Bolton Technology Exchange, Queensbrook, Bolton BL1 4AY (0204 361708) *Contact: David Bromley* Developed by English Estates, with the assistance of Bolton Metropolitan Borough Council and the Bolton Institute of Higher Education.	1985	£3.82	17	500–3500	No	No
Brunel Science Park, Uxbridge, Middlesex UB8 3PH (0895 72192/74000) *Contact: Peter Russell* The University, who own the Science Park, is only interested in letting accommodation to tenants who have, or are likely to, collaborate with it.	1983	£11	17	185–30000	Yes	No
Cambridge Science Park, Trumpington Road, Cambridge CB2 2LD (0223 841841) *Contact: John Tweddle* Established by Trinity College to provide accommodation from starter units to developments by companies on 125 yr leases.	1970	—	66	400–	Yes	Yes
Cardiff Business Technology Centre, c/o South Glamorgan City Council, County HQ, Newport Road, Cardiff (0222 499022) *Contact: Duncan Winnard* Formed by South Glamorgan County Council and University College Cardiff, and now aided by a major local private concern.	1988	—	—	130–775	No	No

	1	2	3	4	5	6
Chilworth Research Centre, Chilworth Manor, Southampton SO9 1XB (0703 767420) *Contact: Shirley Smith* Established by the University of Southampton, the Development Trust, and the Southampton Economic Development Corporation. Planning restrictions prevent mass production but light manufacturing is permitted if environmentally compatible. Some research activity is obligatory.	1986	—	18	250	No	No
Durham Mount Joy Research Centre, Durham DH1 3SW (091 3844173) *Contact: John Turner* Developed by English Estates with the University of Durham, Durham City Council and Durham County Council.	1985	—	14	200	No	Yes
Heriot-Watt University Research Park, Riccarton, Edinburgh EH14 4AP (031 449 7070) *Contact: Ian Dalton* Wholly owned by the University. The general criteria for tenant selection is that there is a significant proportion of R&D in the business, and a willingness to collaborate with the University.	1972	£5.50	30	1500	Yes	No
Highfields Science Park, University of Nottingham, University Park, Nottingham NG7 2RD (0602 506101) *Contact: John Webb* Nottingham City Council and the University of Nottingham are partners in this development.	1984	—	24	200	No	No
Listerhills Science Park University of Bradford, 29 Campus Road, Bradford BD7 1HR (0274 733466) *Contact: Lawrence West* English Estates, the University of Bradford and the City Council are partners in this development.	1982	£3.25+	31	200	No	Yes

	1	2	3	4	5	6
Loughborough Technology Centre, University of Technology, Loughborough, Leicestershire LE11 3TU (0509 263171) *Contact: Prof F. Hales* Funded by the Leicester County Council. All links with the centres of education are initially through Loughborough Consultants Ltd.	1984	£4.00	17	200	No	No
Manchester Science Park, Lloyd Street North, Manchester M15 4EN (061 226 1000) *Contact: Tom Broadhurst* Shareholders are Manchester City Council, University of Manchester, Ciba-Geigy plc, Ferranti plc, Fothergill & Harvey plc, Granada TV Ltd.	1983	—	12	230	Yes	Yes
Menai Technology Enterprise Centre (MENTEC), Deiniol Road, Bangor, Gwynedd LL57 2UP (0248 354103) *Contact: Dafydd Jones* Backed by the Welsh Office, MENTEC is a joint venture by University College of North Wales, Gwynedd County Council and Arfon Borough Council.	1987	£3.18	3	660	Yes	Yes
Merseyside Innovation Centre Ltd, 131 Mount Pleasant, Liverpool L3 5TF (051 708 0123) *Contact: Arthur Rimmer* This is a limited company, with connections with the University of Liverpool and Liverpool Polytechnic.	1981	—	12	300	No	Yes
Newlands Centre University of Hull, Cottingham Road, Hull HU6 7RX (0482 465510) *Contact: David Geekie* Financed by English Estates, with help from Hull City Council.	1984	£50pw for 590sq'	12	590	No	Yes

	1	2	3	4	5	6
NEWTECH, Deeside Industrial Park, Deeside, Clwyd CH5 2NU (0244 822881) *Contact: John Allen* Jointly developed by the Clwyd County Council and the North East Wales Institute, with construction by the Welsh Development Agency. NEWTECH assists in arranging patent cover for innovation.	1985	—	10	600	No	No
Portsmouth Advanced Technology Centre, Anglesea Road, Portsmouth, Hants PO1 3DJ (0705 827681) *Contact: Prof Terry Duggan* Company being formed by Hampshire County Council, Portsmouth City Council and other interested parties to develop this centre.						
Reading University–Industry Link, Whiteknights, PO Box 217, Reading RG6 2AH (0734 875123) *Contact: Ted Bell* Organisation set up to facilitate contributions by the University to companies.	1986	—	—	—	—	—
Riddlesdown Science Park, Portland House, Aldermaston, Berks RG7 4HP (07356 78201) *Contact: B. N. Crowley* Site to be built at Whyteleafe, Croydon.	1990	—	—	—	—	—
St Johns Innovation Park Cambridge, St John's College, Cambridge CB2 1TP (0223 338627) *Contact: Dr C. Johnson* Accommodation for technological companies, and provides close links with the University.	1986	—	12	190	No	No
Salford University Business Enterprises Ltd, Salbec House, Salford M6 6GS (061 736 8921) *Contact: Geoff Mortimer* The University and its Business Services company have collaborated with English Estates to build the Business Park.	1988	—	—	—	Yes	Yes

	1	2	3	4	5	6
Sheffield Science Park, Palatine Chambers, Pinstone Street, Sheffield S1 2HN (0742 766755) *Contact: Dr Brigitte Pemberton* The first phase is owned by Sheffield City Council, and a mixture of public and private finance is used for the rest of the site.	1988	—	—	—	No	No
South Bank Technopark, 90 London Road, London SE1 6LN (01 928 2900) *Contact: Jeffe Jeffers* The site is financed by the Prudential Corporation, and managed by representatives of the company, South Bank Polytechnic and other interested parties.	1987	—	46	200	No	No
Surrey Research Park, PO Box 112, Guildford, Surrey GU2 5XL (0483 579693) *Contact: Dr Malcolm Parry* Owned by the University's Foundation Trust.	1986	—	27	600	No	No
University of East Anglia Science Park, Norwich, Norfolk NR4 7TJ (0603 56161) *Contact: David Williamson* Not yet established.						
University College of Swansea Innovation Centre, Singleton Park, Swansea SA2 7PP (0792 295556) *Contact: Sidney Brailsford* Established by the Welsh Development Agency and the University College of Swansea	1986	—	13	300	No	No
University of Warwick Science Park Ltd, Barclays Venture Centre, Sir William Lyons Road, Coventry CV4 7EZ (0203 418535) *Contact: David Rowe* Jointly owned by the University of Warwick, Coventry City Council, Warwickshire County Council and West Midlands Enterprise Board.	1984	—	38	450	Yes	Yes

	1	2	3	4	5	6
West of Scotland Science Park, Glasgow G20 0SP (041 946 7161) *Contact: Linda Stark* Jointly owned by the Scottish Development Agency and the Universities of Glasgow and Strathclyde	1983	—	16	350	Yes	Yes

FINANCIAL AND ADVISORY SERVICES FOR TECHNOLOGY

Apart from science parks, there are a number of other organisations and services useful to the innovator. In this section you can find out how to meet other inventors; how to get someone else to do all the work of developing, patenting and marketing your product, and then pay you a fee; how to find financial institutions that understand technology and can give more than just financial help. (See also Section 6.)

Hi-tech Sources of Finance

A growing number of financial institutions are prepared to take the plunge and invest in high-technology businesses. Some are prepared to go further and put management and production expertise at the entrepreneur's disposal. Naturally these efforts are not philanthropic. They are intended to improve the chances of success and so 'insure' the investors stake.

Advent Eurofund Ltd, Whitley Chambers, 41 Don Street, St Helier, Jersey (0534 75151). *Contact: Ian Cuming*

Alta Berkeley Associates, 25 Berkeley Square, London W1X 5HB (01 629 1550) *Contact: Brian Wood*

Baronsmead Ltd, Clerkenwell House, 67 Clerkenwell Road, London EC1R 5BH (01 242 4900) *Contact: Mr Sharp or Miss Allen*

British Technology Group, 101 Newington Causeway, London SE1 6BU (01 403 6666). (Funded by national government.) In 1981 the British Technology Group was formed out of the late National Enterprise Board and the National Research Development Corporation. The two organisations have a combined portfolio of 400 investments in industrial companies.

In addition, about 200 research and development projects are being funded at British universities.

BTG can provide finance for technical innovation in any field of technology. This finance is available to any company or individual entrepreneur, either as equity or loan capital. BTG is the main channel for exploiting technology from universities, polytechnics, research councils and government research establishments. It has a portfolio of 1,800 UK patents, 600 licences and over 400 revenue earning innovations.

For small companies they have two schemes:

■ The Small Company Innovation Fund (SCIF). This was established in September 1980 to provide finance where the business as a whole is innovative. Despite having advanced only £1 million spread over two dozen projects since its inception, BTG are keen to hear from innovative entrepreneurs needing the services of SCIF.

■ Oakland Finance Ltd, established in March 1981, provides loans of up to £50,000 for technological or more traditionally based companies.

Clydebank Enterprise Fund, Erskine House, 1 North Avenue, Clydebank Business Park, Clydebank (041 952 0084/5/6). This is a joint venture between the Bank of Scotland and the SDA to promote through low interest loans enterprising business projects within Clydebank and the Enterprise Zone. The fund offers unsecured loans up to £25,000 at a 5% rate of interest.

Granville Venture Capital, 8 Lovat Lane, PO Box 202, London EC3R 8BP (01 621 1212)

Greater London Enterprise Technology, 63–67 Newington Causeway, London SE1 6BD (01 403 1742) *Contact: Michael Cooley.* As well as having funds to invest in technology based ventures in London, in April 1987 they set up a £500,000 fund for product development. This is to enable innovatory products from companies and universities to realise their commercial potential. Marketing and financial advice is also provided to support the ventures they back.

Innovation-Linked Investment Scheme (ILIS), offers assistance to independent small and medium-sized firms (up to 500 employees) that are developing innovative products or processing in the high-tech field. Further details from your nearest Department of Trade and Industry.

INTEX Executives (UK) Ltd and EP Woods Investments Ltd, Chancery House, 53/64 Chancery Lane, London WC2A 1QU (01 831 6925/01 242 2263). *Contact: Mr C. Brown*

Oakland Management Holdings Ltd, Ramsbury House, High Street, Hungerford, Berkshire RG17 0LY (0488 83555). *Contact: Gordon Kenneth*

PA Development Ltd, Bowater House East, 68 Knightsbridge, London SW1K 7LJ (01 589 7050). *Contact: Mr Peter Grundy*

3i Ventures, is the high-technology arm of Investors in Industry plc, 91 Waterloo Road, London SE1 8XP (01 928 7822). Generally its approach is effective for situations calling for investments of £200,000 or more. In whatever form its funds are provided it expects them to be at substantial risk. Other than in exceptional circumstances they ask for a significant but minority shareholding in the business.

Advisory Services for Technology

American Inventors Corporation, 82 Broad Street, Dept SL Westfield, Massachusetts 10186, USA. They offer a link between UK inventors and American Industry via a free confidential disclosure registration and an initial consultation in London to discuss your business idea.

Association of Innovation Centre Executives (AICE), PO Box 6, Beverley, North Humberside HU17 7RL (0964 550490). *Contact: Dr W. K. Donaldson* Co-ordinates the efforts of British innovation centres whose founding purpose is to offer a valuable resource to people with ideas for original or improved products.

Supported variously by local authorities, central government, higher education and the private sector, AICE innovation centres offer – often free or at merely nominal cost – services commercial unavailable at affordable prices. These include technical and commercial appraisal; advice on legal protection; design or redesign; prototype manufacture and assessment; sourcing of materials, information or further help; negotiation with potential manufacturers or sponsors; marketing assistance.

Their offices are at:

BIRMINGHAM: Birmingham Innovation and Development Centre Ltd, Essex House, 27 Temple Street, Birmingham B2 5DB (021 643 3430) *Contact; J. U. Shearn*

CORNWALL: Cornwall Innovation Centre, Wesley Street, Camborne, Cornwall TR14 8DS (0209 717111/842201) *Contact: R. H. Stapleton*

EDINBURGH: Technology Products, Scottish Development Agency, Rosebery House, Haymarket, Edinburgh EH12 5EZ (031 337 9595) *Contact: Campbell Thomson*

GLASGOW: Strathclyde Regional Council, Chief Executive's Department, Industrial Development Unit, 20 India Street, Glasgow G2 4PF (041 227 3861) *Contact: John Downie*

HULL: Hull Innovation Centre, Guildhall Road, Queens Gardens, Hull HU1 1HJ (0482 226348) *Contact: Mrs Dawn Smith*

LIVERPOOL: The Merseyside Innovation Centre Ltd, 131 Mount Pleasant, Liverpool L3 5TF (051 708 0123) *Contact: Arthur Rimmer*

LONDON: London Innovation Trust, PO Box 919, Lofting Road, London N1 1XL (01 607 8141) *Contact: Richard Fletcher*

Innovations Adviser; London Enterprise Agency, 4 Snow Hill, London EC1A 2DL (01 236 3000) *Contact: G. Gills*

MID-GLAMORGAN: Welsh Development Agency, Business Development Centre, Treforest Industrial Estate, Pontypridd, Mid-Glamorgan CF37 5UT (0443 841777) *Contact: K. J. Page*

NOTTINGHAM: Centre for Product Development, The Lenton Business Centre, Lenton Boulevard, Nottingham N47 2BY (0602 782200)

SHROPSHIRE: Industrial Development Unit, Telford Industrial Centre, Stafford Park 4, Telford, Shropshire TF3 3BA (0952 610329) *Contact: David Chiva*

SOMERSET: Somerset Innovation Centre, c/o RDC, 1 The Crescent, Taunton, Somerset TA1 4EA (0823 276905) *Contact: D. R. Patten*

TYNE AND WEAR: North East Innovation Centre, Saltmeadows Road, Gateshead, Tyne and Wear NE8 3AH (091 490 1222) *Contact: Dr J. A. Hedley*

WEST YORKS: Calderdale Innovation Centre, Dean Clough Industrial Park, Halifax, West Yorks HX3 5AX (0422 42825) *Contact: P. N. Bissell*

University of Bath, School of Management, Claverton Down, Bath BA2 7AY (0225 826826). *Contact: Graham Ray (accountant) or Nicholas Crawford (marketing and new products)* This is the home of a Levhume trust funded research project into how small firms can make use of technology and product licensing to help them expand.

The Chartered Institute of Patent Agents, Staple Inn Buildings, High Holborn, London WC1V 7PZ (01 405 9450). The institute itself does not run an advisory service, although it will give advice on patents, trade marks and designs where possible. It publishes The Register of Patent Agents (price £2.00), which lists the names and business addresses of all the patent agents qualified to practise before the Patent Office.

The Institute runs a free advisory clinic staffed by patent agents, which is held on Tuesday evenings from 5.00 to 7.00 p.m. (by appointment only in half hour sessions).

The patent agent will be able to give advice on all aspects relating to making application for patents, trade marks and designs, as well as on infringement of these or of protection and on passing off matters. He may also be able to give advice on the exploitation of any invention protected by patent, although this is not specifically within his field of operation. The patent agents will work to a fixed scale of charges relating to the work done, in the same way as a solicitor charges, rather than taking a share in the commercial success of an invention.

Co-operative Research Grants Scheme, Science Research Council, Polaris House, North Star Avenue, Swindon (0793 26222). This scheme promotes co-operation between firms who wish to develop new products that require research beyond their capabilities, and academics in universities and polytechnics. The SRC will support the academic contribution but the firm must pay its share.

The Design Council, 28 Haymarket, London SW1Y 4SU (01 839 8000). A number of Design Advisory Officers are available to advise on design of products and to investigate the technical problems of an existing product. These Records of Engineering

Expertise hold information about sources of specialist technical advice of use to engineering designers.

The Design Council has four regional offices at the following addresses:

- The Design Council: Scottish Design Centre, 72 St Vincent Street, Glasgow G2 5TN (041 221 6121).

- The Design Council: Design Centre Wales, Pearl Assurance House, Greyfriars Road, Cardiff CF1 3JN (0222 395811/2).

- The Design Council: Midlands, Norwich Union House, 31 Waterloo Road, Wolverhampton WV1 4BP (0902 773631).

- The Design Council: Northern Ireland, 9–15 Bedford Street, Belfast (0232 338452).

If you employ between 60 and 1,000 people you could have up to 15 days' free design consultancy and a further 15 days at half price.

For details of this contact John Benson, Department of Industry, PO Box 702, London SW20 8SZ (01 930 8655).

Information Marketing Ltd, 22 Strand Street, Poole, Dorset BH15 1SB (0202 665131). Has a product databank that links inventors with manufacturers and investors. Also office at 4 Derriman Avenue, Sheffield S11 9LA (0742 620751). *Contact: Dr Rogers*

Institute of International Licensing Practitioners Ltd, Suite 78, Kent House, 87 Regent Street, London W1R 7HF (01 439 7091). Licensing practitioners can help you find customers to licence your invention to, if you cannot exploit it yourself. They keep a register of members and their specialist areas of expertise. Copies are available from the secretary.

The Institute of Inventors, 19 Fosse Way, Ealing, London W13 0BZ (01 998 3540/4372/6372). This is a self-supporting institute run by inventors for inventors. It can help with patent application, prototypes and commercialisation of suitable inventions.

The Institute of Patentees and Inventors, Suite 505a, Triumph House, 189 Regent Street, London W1RV 7WF (01 242 7812). The institute was founded in 1919 to further the interests of patentees and inventors. It gives advice and guidance to members on all aspects of inventing, from idea conception to innovation and development. Its journal, *Future*, comes out quarterly and helps to keep members up to date. Its *New Patents Bulletin* acts as a liaison with industry, bringing members' inventions to the notice of specialised manufacturing firms. Exhibitions of new inventions are organised frequently by IPI.

Inventerprise North, Suite 3b, Sunlight House, Quay Street, Manchester M3 3JY (061 832 7358). Launched in 1987, Inventerprise North is a free service of Manchester Business Venture, open to all enterprise agency clients in the North West region. The service was the brainchild of Marks & Clerk Chartered Patent Agents, and Arthur Young chartered accountants. They have a group of advisers covering the protection, financing and marketing aspects of inventions. As well as appraising an invention's chances of commercial exploitation, their advice can extend right through to product launch – or licensing off the rights to another company.

The National Westminster Bank, operate a technical advisory service which can prepare a report on the technical viability of a product or a project, using outside academics and research institutes. The customer and the bank share the costs of this work equally. To find out about the service contact your local branch initially.

New Technology Appraisal Project, Interwork, Cranfield Institute of Technology, Cranfield, Beds MK43 0AL (0234 752767). *Contact: Nick White* Using this scheme, managers of Lloyds, National Westminster and Barclays can refer new technology projects to Interwork for appraisal. Any business, whether an existing or new customer of the bank, which requires finance, could qualify for this free feasibility study. Users get a copy of the report sent to the bank.

PA Technology, Cambridge Laboratory, Melbourn, Royston, Herts SG8 6DP (0763 61222). Their major role is the development of commercially successful products for companies.

The service begins with a clear definition of the commercial and market constraints and extends through initial concept development, technical and commercial feasibility studies, ergonomic design and styling, prototype design and construction, production and manufacturing engineering, market research and market launch, packaging and supporting graphics. Each project is managed by an experienced team of senior consultants who are recognised authorities in their field and have in-depth experience in international project and business development.

Research Engineers Ltd, 11 Orsman Road, Shoreditch, London N1 5RD (01 739 7811). This organisation specialises in making prototypes for inventors.

Technology Exchange Ltd, is a non-profit company limited by guarantee formed to assist the smaller manufacturing enterprise to find new products and processes by licence and also to help them find manufacturers elsewhere for their own development. Under the EEC SPRINT programme the Exchange has a collaboration with Regional Development Authorities in Belgium, Spain, Greece, France, Denmark and Ireland.

They maintain close links with the major databanks in the USA, Europe and Japan and the Development Authorities, Universities and Research Establishments around the world. A catalogue of offers and requests for technology is published quarterly and circulated to licensing agents, journals and managing directors seeking new products in many countries.

The Exchange links with organisations seeking technology for developing countries and obtains early notification of development needs involving the supply of capital plant and licenseable technology.

For further information contact the Technology Exchange Ltd, South Bank Technopark, 90 London Road, London SE1 6LH (01 922 8815).

Transmission Systems Ltd, Airport Road, St Brelade, Jersey (0534 45626) *Contact: Derek Bernard* TSL's business was originally based on its involvement with the *Workmate* workcentre project which is licensed to Black & Decker and manufactured and marketed by them throughout the world with enormous success.

From the various ideas submitted to TSL by outside inventors, they select those which would appear to pass the following criteria:

1 Appear to be technically and economically feasible
2 Appear to hold out the prospect of effective potential protection by Patents and/or Design Registrations
3 Seem to hold out the prospect of sufficient commercial potential to justify the high risks involved
4 Are of a nature and size which is likely to be within TSL's capacity within a reasonable time frame

If an Invention Submission appears to satisfy these criteria then TSL will make the inventor a specific offer setting out the basis on which it would be prepared to become involved in the project. Each project tends to be different but it is not unusual for the agreement to give the inventor 50% of any net royalties arising from the product sales – that is after development, patent and administrative expenses have been deducted.

This may be one of the few ways in which an inventor with little money or commercial expertise can hope to achieve commercial success with his invention without taking on extra risks, such as borrowing substantial sums of money in order to do the job on his own.

At any one time TSL will have between 20 and 30 'live' projects ranging from automotive differentials and sophisticated mechanical transmissions, to family board games.

In the first instance anyone wishing to consider this approach should write to TSL and ask for their Invention Submission Form.

RESEARCH ASSOCIATIONS

There are some 50 research organisations in the UK, which are the centres of knowledge in their respective fields. If the product or idea that you are developing (or want to use) comes within their sphere of interest, they may well be of use. They have extensive information systems, and can usually guide enquirers to appropriate sources of data or other help.

ASLIB (Association for Information Management), Information House, 26–27 Boswell Street, London WC1N 3JZ (01 430 2671) *Contact: Dr Dennis Lewis, Director*

BHRA Fluid Engineering, Cranfield, Beds MK43 0AJ (0234 750422) *Contact: I. Cooper*

Brick Development Association, Woodside, Winkfield, Windsor, Berks SL4 2DX (0344 885651) *Contact: Robert Lloyd-Jones*

British Ceramic Research Association, Queens Road, Penkhull, Stock-On-Trent ST4 7LQ (0782 45431) *Contact: Dr D. James, Director*

British Glass Industry Research Association, Northumberland Road, Sheffield S10 2UA (0742 686201)

The British Internal Combustion Engine Research Institute Ltd, 111–112 Buckingham Avenue, Slough SL1 4PH (0753 27371) *Contact: I. Brown, Director*

British Leather Manufacturers Research Association, King's Park Road, Moulton Park, Northamptonshire NN3 1JD (0604 494131) *Contact: Dr R. L. Sykes, Director*

Building Service Research & Information Association, Old Bracknell Lane West, Bracknell, Berks RG12 4AH (0344 426511) *Contact: Dr D. P. Gregory, Director*

Construction Industry Research and Information Association, 6 Storey's Gate, London SW1P 3AU (01 222 8891) *Contact: Dr P. Bransby*

Cranfield Unit for Precision Engineering, Cranfield Institute of Technology, Cranfield, Beds MK43 0AL (0234 750111) *Contact: Professor P. A. McKeown, Director*

Fire Insurers' Research & Testing Organisation, Melrose Avenue, Boreham Wood, Herts WD6 2BJ (01 207 2345) *Contact: Dr Denney, Manager*

HATRA (Hosiery and Allied Trades Research Association), Thorneywood, 7 Gregory Boulevard, Nottingham NG7 6LD (0602 623311/2) *Contact: Mr Harrison*

Machine Tool Industry Research Association, Hulley Road, Macclesfield, Cheshire SK10 2NE (0625 25421/3 and 2618) *Contact: L. K. Lord*

National Computing Centre, Oxford Road, Manchester M1 7ED (061 228 6333) *Contact: John Aris*
London Office: 11 New Fetter Lane, London EC4A 1PU (01 353 4875) *Contact: Mrs Fleming, Regional Officer*
The Paint Research Association, Waldegrave Road, Teddington, Middx TW11 8LD (01 977 4427/9) *Contact: J. A. Bernie*
Paper & Board, Printing & Packaging Industries Research Association, Roundalls Road, Leatherhead, Surrey KTY22 7RU (0372 376161) *Contact: B. W. Blunden*
Production Engineering Research Association of Great Britain, Melton Mowbray, Leicestershire LE13 0PB (0664 64133) *Contact: R. A. Armstrong*
Rubber and Plastic Research Association, Rapra Technology Ltd, Shawbury, Shrewsbury, Shropshire SY4 4NR (0939 250383) *Contact: Dr M. Copley*
Shoe & Allied Trades Research Association, Satra House, Rockingham Road, Kettering, Northamptonshire NN16 9JH (0536 410000) *Contact: Mr J. Graham Butlin, Director*
Timber Research and Development Association, Stocking Lane, Hughenden Valley, High Wycombe, Bucks HP14 4ND (0240 24301) *Contact: J. G. Sunley, Director*
WIRA (Woollen Industry Research Association), Wira House, West Park Ring Road, Leeds LS16 6QL (0532 781381) *Contact: Dr Munro*

Other institutes include:

British Association for the Advancement of Science, Fortress House, 25 Savile Row, London W1X 1AB (01 734 6010)
The Research and Development Society, 47 Belgrave Square, London SW1X 8QX (01 235 6111)

COMPUTERS

If you have not already bought a computer then there are a number of organisations, periodicals and books that may help you to make the best decisions. You will need to know something of what a computer can and cannot do, and exactly what work you want done. If your business is or is likely to involve repetitions, routinised, time-consuming and usually boring tasks, the chances are that a computer could do them better. Typically, small businesses put their book-keeping, management accounts, payroll, mailing and price lists and, more recently, wordprocessing functions on to a computer. Systems are available to analyse customers: how long they take to pay up; how much on average they order; and when their next order is due.

Finding your solution Once you have decided what you want done, then you have to find the software and hardware to meet your needs. The software is the program or instructions that have to be given to the computer in order to process your data and produce the information you want.

Finding out about software means reading the computer magazines, talking to manufacturers and users, going to exhibitions and getting demonstrations from software houses.

An increasing number of 'standard' software packages are available for specific trades and professions. Packages include those for small shops, such as pharmacies, and for medical practices and estate agents. Your trade association will be watching these developments, and they should be able to help you find out more. Keeping a watch in your trade magazine will also show you what enterprising people are getting up to in this area. It is highly likely that your needs and the available software will not quite match. In this case you will need to customise the software to your own requirements by writing, or having written, additional programs.

Finally, you will have to decide on the hardware – the computer itself. Your choice of software will pre-select the computer best suited to your needs, but you can still choose whether to buy (or lease) your own, or to use a computer bureau on a time-sharing basis.

It is very likely that the complexities and unfamiliarity of the field, combined with overwhelming apparent choice of systems, will leave you confused. Help is at hand, either from the following organisations, or by referring to the publications listed afterwards.

Organisations

Association of Computer Clubs (ACC), 12 Poplar Road, Newtown, Powys SY16 2QQ. ACC maintains a database of the hundreds of computer clubs around the UK. If you want local, unbiased views from those who are familiar with the computer (or software) you are thinking of buying, or who can help you with teething problems with new equipment, then make contact with a Computer Club in your area. Should the ACC not come up with a local contact, look for information from your library, local business directories or computer dealers. Your local Chamber of Commerce or Trade Association may well be able to help too.

The Association of Professional Computer Consultants, 109 Baker Street, London W1M 2BH. (01 267 7144) Founded in 1982, the Association's Code of Professional Conduct ensures that members' clients receive objective, impartial advice and services. Members are not allowed to supply (directly or indirectly) hardware or software, nor are they allowed to write software themselves for sale to their clients. They must not benefit from sales and agency commissions, introductory commissions, or trading links with computer industry suppliers. Contact the Association with details of your problem(s) and the sort of expertise you need and they will send you details of experienced independent and professional consultants, usually in your area.

Computer Companies Most major computer hardware companies run training or information centres. The addresses of a number of manufacturers who will send you information on their products and services are given below:

ACT UK (Apricot), ACT House, 111 Hagley Road, Edgbaston, Birmingham, West Midlands B16 8LB (021 454 8585)

Amstrad plc, PO Box 462, Brentwood, Essex CM14 4CF (0277 262326)

Apple Computer, Eastman Way, Hemel Hempstead, Herts HP2 7HQ (0442 60244)

Black Box, PO Box 80, Reading, Berks RG2 0PS (0734 866800)

British Olivetti, 86–88 Upper Richmond Road, Putney, London SW15 2UR (01 785 6666)

Commodore, Commodore House, The Switchback, Gardner Road, Maidenhead, Berks SL6 7XA (0628 770088)

Compaq Computer, Ambassador House, Paradise Road, Richmond, Surrey TW9 1SQ (01 940 8860)

Data General, Hounslow House, 724–734 London Road, Hounslow, Middx TW3 1PD (01 572 7455)

Digital Equipment, Digital Park, Imperial Way, Reading, Berks RG2 0TE (0734 868711)

Epson UK, Dorland House, 388 High Road, Wembley, Middx HA9 6UH (01 902 8892)

Grid Computer Systems, Unit House, 33 London Road, Reigate, Surrey RH2 9PY (073 72 41211)

Hewlett Packard, Nine Mile Road, Wokingham, Berks RG11 3LL (0344 773100)

IBM (UK), PO Box 32, Alencon Link, Basingstoke, Hants RG21 1EJ (0256 56144)

International Computers Ltd, ICL House, Putney, London SW15 1SW (01 788 7272)

NCR, 206–216 Marylebone Road, London NW1 6LY (01 723 7070)

RAIR, 145–157 St John Street, London EC1V 4QJ (01 250 3535)

Sanyo, Sanyo House, Otterspool Way, Watford, Herts WD2 8JX (0923 46363)

Sharp Electronics (UK), Sharp House, Thorp Road, Newton Heath, Manchester M10 9BE (061 205 2333)

Sinclair Research Ltd, 25 Willis Road, Cambridge CB1 2AY (0223 81211)

Tandon Computer (UK) Ltd, Unit 19, Hunt End, Dunlop Road, Redditch, Worcs B97 5XP (0527 46800)

Tandy Corporation, Radio Shack, Tameway Tower, Bridge Street, Walsall, West Midlands WS1 1LA (0992 648181)

Texas Instruments, Manton Lane, Bedford, Beds MK41 7PA (0234 67366)

Torch Computers, Abberley House, Great Shelford, Cambridge CB2 5LQ (0223 841000)

Victor Technology, Unit 1, The Valley Centre, Gordon Road, High Wycombe, Bucks HP13 6EQ (0494 461600)

Computer Helpline operated by Stoy Hayward Associates, the major accountancy practice. Their phone-in service offers free advice to businesses considering buying a computer. The Helpline number is 01 486 5888, and it operates between 09.30 and 17.30, Monday to Fridays.

Computer Services Association (CSA), Hanover House, 73/74 High Holborn, London WC1V 6LE (01 405 2171). The CSA is the Trade Association whose members offer bespoke and packaged software, data preparation, processing, consultancy, value-added network services, education and training, facilities management, third party maintenance, telecommunications and office automation. Their free Business Advisory Service will put you in touch with companies supplying the computing services you are looking for.

Data Protection Registrar Office of the Data Protection Registrar, Springfield House, Water Lane, Wilmslow, Cheshire SK9 5AX (0625 535711). The Registrar operates a telephone enquiry service for those concerned as to whether or not they should register. Alternatively, information packs on the Act are available from Post Offices, and your Trade Association, Chamber of Commerce or local Microsystems Centre, should be able to advise you.

Federation of Microsystems Centres Independent of computer suppliers and operating under a strict Code of Conduct, precluding computer sales and any commission payments, the Federation of Microsystems Centres was established in 1981 throughout Britain by the Department of Trade and Industry, National Computing Centre and Local Authorities, to provide impartial and expert advice to anyone thinking of first-time and subsequent computer purchase – and training.

They offer a free initial discussion service to help clarify ideas and reduce the potential for inevitable pitfalls. Advice is offered at all stages – feasibility, requirements analysis, system selection, purchase negotiation and contracts, implementation, planning, training and acceptance.

Their training service is designed to help you and your staff to get the best out of your system, whether your company is large or small. They offer highly flexible programs, tailored to your needs, either using your own system or in the well-equipped training rooms at individual Centres.

In addition to structured training, a constantly updated library of self-study computer related courses is available.

The Centres always keep a representative range of the most modern computers and applications for you to try out. Advice is also available on Government Grants which may benefit you. Phone 01 232 2353 or contact your local Centre direct:

Birmingham Microsystems Centre, Birmingham Polytechnic, Wellhead Lane, Perry Barr, Birmingham B42 2TE (021 356 1008)

Bristol Microsystems Centre, Bristol ITeC, St Anne's House, St Anne's Road, Bristol BS4 4AB (0272 779247)

Cheltenham Microsystems Centre – GLOSCAT, Park Campus, Merestones Road, The Park, Cheltenham, Glos GL52 2RR (0242 532055)

Coventry Microsystems Centre, Henley College of Further Education, Henley Road, Bell Green, Coventry CV1 1ED (0203 621333)

Dorset Microsystems Centre, Ground Floor, Holland House, Oxford Road, Bournemouth BH8 8EZ (0202 298622)

Dublin Microsystems Centre, College of Commerce, Rathmines Road, Dublin, Irish Republic (0001 970666)

East Midlands Microsystems Centre, Trent Polytechnic, Burton Street, Nottingham NG1 4BU (0602 418248)

Greater Manchester Microsystems Centre, Salbec House, 100 Broughton Road, Salford M6 6GS (061 736 5843, ext 303)

Hampshire Microsystems Centre, Basingstoke Technical College, Worting Road, Basingstoke RG1 1TN (0256 54141)

Hertfordshire Microsystems Centre, De Havilland College, Elstree Way, Borehamwood, Herts WD6 1JZ (01 953 6024)

Merseyside Microsystems Centre, Merseyside Innovation Centre, 131 Mount Pleasant, Liverpool L3 5TF (051 708 0123)

Milton Keynes Microsystems Centre, Information Technology Exchange, Midsummer House, 428 Midsummer Boulevard, Central Milton Keynes MK9 2HE (0908 668866)

Newcastle Microsystems Centre, Federation Administration Unit, 3rd Floor, Erick House, Princess Square, Newcastle Upon Tyne NE1 8ER (091 232 2353)

North Wales Microsystems Centre, Newtech Square, Deeside Industrial Park, Deeside, Clywd CH5 2NU (0244 822 881)

Norwich ITeC, Hi-Tech House, 10 Blackfriars Street, Norwich NR3 1SF (0603 620341)

South Wales Microsystems Centre, Polytechnic of Wales, Room 38, Maes-yr-Eglwys Annexe, St Illtyd's Road, Upper Church Village, Pontypridd, Mid Glam CF38 1EB (0443 201933)

South Yorkshire Microsystems Centre, Sheffield City Polytechnic, Dyson House, Suffolk Road, Sheffield S1 1WB (0742 20911, ext 2173)

Strathclyde Microsystems Centre, Paisley College of Technology, 72 George Street, Paisley, Renfrewshire PA1 2LF (041 887 1241, ext 379)

Ulster Microsystems Centre, University of Ulster at Jordanstown, Shore Road, Newtownabbey, Co Antrim, N. Ireland BT37 0QB (0232 365131, ext 2675)

Washington Microsystems Centre, Armstrong House, Armstrong Road, District 2, Washington, Tyne & Wear NE37 1LH (091 417 8517)

West Yorkshire Microsystems Centre, Queenswood House, Beckett Park, Leeds LS6 3QS (0532 759741)

Information Technology Centres ITeCs, as they are generally called, were first launched as an experiment in 1982, with the objective of encouraging unemployed youngsters to understand and make use of new technology. There are now 178 ITeCs covering the whole country. They still have a major training role with young people and are an important source of employees to local businesses.

In addition they market their skills to surrounding firms, offering drop-in training facilities in such fields as using business software packages.

ITeCs are supported in various ways by the Department of Trade and Industry, and Training Commission and Local Councils. The address of your nearest ITeC will be in the telephone directory.

The National Computing Centre The National Computing Centre is the UK Centre for Information Technology. Backed by, and in co-operation with, government, the IT industry and IT users, NCC directs technical programmes, administers national schemes and develops products and services to promote the effective use of Information Technology.

The following five services are of particular interest to new computer users:

■ *Enquiry desk* for micro software – advice on the appropriate software packages for your system and organisation

■ *Micro software evaluation* – a new service for the independent evaluation and certification of micro software packages to a common standard

■ *Software products scheme* – through which NCC has administered the allocation of £40m to the development and marketing of 322 innovative software products

■ *Selection testing service* – available on-site and at 15 locations throughout the UK, selection testing offers objective aptitude testing for all types of computer staff

■ *Training* – NCC run regular courses in most aspects of computers throughout the year at venues in London, Manchester, Glasgow, Bristol and Birmingham

Head office: (061 228 6333)
London and South East: (01 353 4875)
Midlands: (021 236 6283)
North and North Wales: (061 228 6333)
Northern Ireland: (0232 665997)
Scotland: (041 204 1101)
South West and South Wales: (0272 277077)

Open College Freepost, PO Box 35, Abingdon, Oxon OX14 3BR (0235 555 444). The Open College is a new national approach to training with the emphasis on open learning allowing you to learn what you want, when, where and how. Information Technology is one of the subject areas in which the Open College will be providing courses.

Open University Associate Student Central Office, Box 76, Milton Keynes MK7 6AN (0908 74066). The Open University has a home study course, 'Selecting a Business Computer System', which takes up about five hours per week over three months.

PICKUP (Professional, Industrial and Commercial Updating), The Adult Training Promotion Unit (01 934 0888). PICKUP (initiated by the Department of Education and Science) is there to help business people and their employees keep up with the latest technology and business skills. The scheme is operated by colleges, universities and polytechnics and can take any form. A particular feature of the PICKUP Programme is that your business needs are identified and met through training specifically tailored to your organisation. To find out your local PICKUP contact phone PICKUP's national inquiry point: The Adult Training Promotion Unit.

Trade Association Your trade association will be able to keep you abreast of computing developments in your trade or industry. The 'Directory of British Associations', published by CBD Research Limited, Beckenham, Kent, lists all Trade Associations. The directory is in most reference libraries.

Publications

Choosing and Using Business Micro Software by Ed Kevin Townsend, published by Gower, 1986. Price £18.50.

Handbook of New Office Technology by John Derrick and Philip Oppenheim, published by Kogan Page, 1986 (2nd edition). Price £9.95 (p/b) £13.95 (h/b).

How to Buy a Business Micro Computer by R. S. Welsby, published by Gower, 1985. Price £18.50.

How to Choose and Use Business Micro Computers and Software by Paul Beck, published by Telegraph Publications/Surrey Books, 1984. Price £5.95.

Introducing VDUs to the Office published by Business Equipment Trade Association, 8 Southampton Place, London WC1A 2EF. Available by mail order only. Price £5.50 (cheque/postal order made payable to 'BEITA').

So You've Bought a Computer a users' guide published in July 1987 by Colin and Paul Barrow to accompany the Yorkshire TV series of that name, price £1. Copies available from Community Education Unit, Yorkshire Television Ltd, The Television Centre, Leeds LS3 1JS.

So You Think Your Business Needs a Computer by Khalid Aziz, published by Kogan Page, 1986. Price £6.95.

Visual Display Units published by Health & Safety Executive, available from HMSO outlets. Price £5.

The Word Processing Handbook by John Derrick and Philip Oppenheim, published by Kogan Page, 1984. Price £6.95 (p/b) £12.95 (h/b).

INDUSTRIAL ORGANISATIONS

Further sources of information on the application of technology are listed below:

British Safety Council, 62–64 Chancellors' Road, London W6 9RS (01 741 1231)

British Standards Institution, 2 Park Street, London W1A 2BS (01 629 9000)

Cambridge Information and Research Services Ltd, Grosvenor House, High Street, Newmarket CB8 9AL (0638 663030)

Ergonomics Information Analysis Centre, Department of Engineering Production, University of Birmingham, PO Box 363, Birmingham B15 2TT (021 414 3344)

Institute of Management Services, 1 Cecil Court, London Road, Enfield, Middx EN2 6DD (01 363 7452) *Contact: Diane Coxon* Leaders in the work study field; their technical information service can give advice to small businesses

Institute of Operational Research, Tavistock Centre, 120 Belsize Lane, Hampstead, London NW3 5BA (01 435 7111)

Institute of Production Control, National Westminster House, Wood Street, Stratford Upon Avon, Warwicks CV37 6JS (0789 205266)

Institute of Production Engineers, 66 Little Ealing Lane, London W5 4XX (01 579 9411)

Institute of Scientific Information, 132 High Street, Uxbridge, Middx UB8 1DP (0895 30085)

Intermediate Technology Development Group, 103/105 Southampton Road, London WC1B 4HH (01 436 9761)

NIFES Consulting Group, Head Office, Nifes House, Sunderland Road, Broad Heath, Altrincham, Cheshire (061 928 5791) and at Birmingham (021 456 1531); Bishop's Stortford, Herts (0279 58412); Leeds (0532 505943); Newcastle-Upon-Tyne (091 213 0189); Nottingham (0602 625841); Aberdeen (0224 642343); and Glasgow (041 332 2453)

Paisley College of Technology, Technology and Business Centre (041 887 1241) *Contact: John Wylie* Major resource in Scotland for small and medium sized businesses for management development and technology, including advanced manufacturing systems.

RIPACS, 229 King's Road, Reading, Berks RG1 4LS (0734 661234)

Technical Indexes Ltd, Willoughby Road, Bracknell, Berks RG12 4DW (03444 26311). Specialists in producing or disseminating technical information. Founded in 1965, they provide essential technical data to design engineers, draughtsmen and buyers in the following fields: electronic engineering, chemical engineering, laboratory equipment, materials handling, engineering components and materials, British Standards, defence standards, American industry standards, Mil Specs, American catalogues and Japanese catalogues.

FINDING OUT ABOUT YOUR MARKET

Marketing and market research is a key element in the success of every new business venture. There are a large and growing number of organisations and publications aimed at satisfying this need.

In contrast to the raising of money, where problems and their solutions can be treated in a relatively general way, everyone's products and markets are specialised, if only geographically so. Unless you are prepared to spend a lot of cash early on, perhaps even before you are sure whether you have a product or service to sell, you will have to find out about your market yourself. Your marketplace is made up of customers, actual and potential; competitors; suppliers; distribution channels; and communication media. In order to succeed, you will have to find out all you can about these elements of your marketplace and use that knowledge to your advantage. There is a vast amount of information freely available, or at a comparatively low cost – much cheaper than the cost of a relatively small mistake, which could be fatal early in the life of a business.

There are also many organisations which, though not expressly set up to help you, have services, facilities or resources that you can tap, and so improve your knowledge and skills.

To make this complex subject digestible it is divided into six topics. 'The Information Available' will give you a flavour of the great mass of data on companies, at home and overseas, and on products and markets. There are almost 4,000 current British directories and this section pulls together the ones of most use to you.

'Finding the Information' tells you how to make use of the country's substantial information and library services. The main business libraries in London, for example, are the most extensive in their fields in Europe.

'Marketing Organisations and their Services' provides details of the prominent professional bodies in the field together with some other organisations of special interest, and, where appropriate, how they might help you.

There are also sections on exporting and importing, giving details of important organisations and services.

The final topic covers general marketing books and periodicals that can give you a broad background knowledge on the subject. These books have been chosen as much for their readability as for their direct usefulness. (See also Section 7 for legal issues in marketing.)

THE INFORMATION AVAILABLE

You will need a regular flow of information on your market to help you make decisions about such matters as what to sell, at what price, your likely competitors, or to find what is going on in markets overseas. You will also need to know something on the size, shape, rate of growth and profitability of your chosen market.

In this section the hundred or so key directories, indexes, reference works and services that hold much of this valuable raw marketing data are identified and described. The ready availability of these publications has been as much a consideration in including them as their usefulness.

Interpreting that information is a harder problem, but some of these reference works contain analyses of the data provided. Otherwise, organisations in the other sections in this book may be able to help, particularly those offering a counselling or advice service, such as Enterprise Agencies, the Marketing Initiative, or the Warwick Statistical Service.

This section is divided into four areas: Company and Product Data, UK; Company and Product Data, Overseas; Market and Industry Data, UK; and Market and Industry Data, Overseas.

Company and Product Data provides information on home and overseas companies, their products or services, profiles and profitability. Market and Industry Data provides information on the markets serviced by those companies, their size, growth and other characteristics. There are a number of reference sources that do not rest easily in one section, and they will have been placed in the most suitable location and cross-referenced in order to help you find your way round.

Company and Product Data The range of readily held data on UK companies is bewildering and on overseas companies only a little less so. At first glance many of the directories and information sources seem to duplicate one another's efforts, or at any rate to overlap. However, once you are faced with a particular problem their differences become apparent. *Kelly's Business Directory* is a most useful tool for finding suppliers or competitors on a national basis.

The Retail Directory will tell you, street by street, the names and business of every shop, and another section will tell you each buyer's name. None of these will tell you much about who owns the business or about their financial performance. This information is given in *Who Owns Whom* and the Extel Card services, respectively. If you want to compare one company with another in the same line of business, *Jordans* or *ICC Business Ratios* are two useful sources. To find out what has been said in the press about a company, you could use *McCarthy's Information Services* or *Research Index*. If you want to confine your search to comment in the *Financial Times*, then their monthly index provides a cross-reference by company, general business area and by personality. If you want to know who has gone bankrupt lately, then *The London Gazette* gives out an official notice.

For overseas companies, much the same information is available, but some of the sources' names are different. There is very little you cannot find out about a company or business if you set your mind to it. The publications listed below are not exhaustive, but they are among the most important and authoritative.

Company and Product Data, UK

The Centre for Interfirm Comparison Ltd, 8 West Stockwell Street, Colchester, Essex CO1 1HN (0206 762274) This is a non-profit-making organisation, established in 1959 by the British Institute of Management and the British Productivity Council to meet the need for a neutral expert body to conduct interfirm comparisons on a confidential basis, and to help managers to improve business performance. Participating firms feed a range of information into the centre, who in turn feed out yardsticks for them to compare systematically the performance of every important aspect of their business with other similar firms. Together with the yardstick ratios come written reports on the findings and ideas for action – but only, of course, to the participating firms, and even then only on a 'comparative' basis so that no one company's data can ever be identified. The uniqueness of this method rests in part on the data itself. It goes far beyond anything supplied in companies' annual returns to Companies House or production monitor figures.

Thousands of companies, large and small, have participated, and comparisons are made in over 100 industries, trade, services and professions both in the UK and abroad.

The centre publishes a number of free booklets that explain their activities, the ratios they use, why they use those particular ratios and, more importantly, how you can use them to improve performance.

Credit Ratings Ltd, 1 City Road, London EC1Y 1AY (01 251 6675/6) This company provides an ad hoc subscription service Credit Report. The cost varies from £18.50 to £27.50 for each report, depending on whether or not you want commentary. These can normally be provided within 48 hours.

Each Credit Report provides a company profile, financial performance figures for the past two years, and eight credit ratios (including an estimate of how long they normally take to pay their bills). These ratios are then compared with the average for that industry, and are followed by a short commentary bringing important factors to the reader's attention.

Companies Registration Office, This keeps records of all limited companies. For England and Wales these records are kept at Companies House, 55–71 City Road, London EC1 (01 253 9393) and for Scotland at the Registrar of Companies for Scotland, 102 George Street, Edinburgh EH2 3JD. For Northern Ireland the same service is available from The Department of Commerce, Chichester House, 43/47 Chichester Court, Belfast BT1 4PJ (0232 234121)

The records kept include financial statements, accounts, directors' names and addresses, shareholders, and changes of name and structure. The information is available on microfiche at £1 per company, and can be photocopied at 10p per sheet. This service is available to visitors only. There are a number of commercial organisations who will obtain this information for you. Two such organisations are:

- ■ **The Company Search Centre**, 1/3 Leonard Street, London EC2A 4AQ (01 251 2566)

- ■ **Extel**, 37/45 Paul Street, London EC2A 4PB (01 253 3400)

The charges for this service are about £3 to £4.50 for a microfiche of each company, or for a photocopy of the report and accounts, around £9.50.

Extel Quoted Service Cards published each year by the Exchange Telegraph Co Ltd. Cards for each of the 3,000 UK companies quoted on the Stock Exchange contain the following information: name and business of the company together with details of subsidiaries and associates; the date on which the company was registered (formed), along with any change of name or status (eg, private to public); directors – their positions (chairman, managing director, etc) and their shareholdings as well as the names of the company secretary, bankers, auditors and solicitors. Ten years' profit and loss accounts and at least three years' balance sheets are given, together with sources and applications of funds statements. The highest and lowest share price over the ten-year period is also given, as well as the chairman's latest statement on the company position. A news card is published three or four times a year, giving details of dividends declared, board changes, acquisitions, liquidations, loans raised and other elements of operating information. A selection of these cards is held in many reference libraries. Individual cards can be bought for £9 from Extel Statistical Services Ltd, 37/45 Paul Street, London EC2A 4PB (01 253 3400, telex 262687) or Manchester office (061 236 5802).

Extel's Handbook of Market Leaders Brings together details on 750 major quoted companies. Though not a substitute for the cards it does provide a quick reference guide to the financial performance of major companies. Published twice a year, in January and July, at £100 per annum.

Extel Unquoted Service Provides a similar service for some 2,000 ordinary companies and those on the USM, OTC and Third Market. These cards cost £11 each, as considerably more work has to be done to get at this information, and the call for it is less.

Financial Times Index, introduced in 1981, provides a monthly and yearly index to the references to some 35,000 companies. Instead of thumbing through back issues, you can locate the abstract of each story by using the corporate index, the general index covering products and industries, or the personality section covering key people. This series costs £400 per annum, and is available from Research Publications, PO Box 45, Reading RG1 8HS (0734 583247).

First Clue, The A–Z of Finding Out, published by Pan Books Ltd, 18 Cavaye Place, London SW10 9PG. Written by Robert Walker, a Fleet Street journalist, it gives hundreds of first ports of call, in your search for organisations. Price £3.50.

ICC Business Ratios Produce 200 business sector reports analysing the performance of some 12,000 leading UK companies over a three-year period. For each sector (for example, window manufacturers, retail chemists, the toy industry or computer equipment) key performance ratios are shown for each company in the sector and an average for the sector as a whole. You can therefore use this information to compare your performance, actual or projected, against an industry standard. There are nineteen key ratios, and they cover profitability, liquidity, asset utilisation, gearing, productivity and exports. Growth rates are monitored, including sales, total assets, capital employed, average wages and exports. It is thus possible to see quickly which company is growing the fastest in your sector and to compare your growth against the best, the worst or the average. Reports are priced at about £165 each, and further details are available from The Business Ratio Manager, ICC Business Ratios, 28/42 Banner Street, London EC1Y 8QE (01 253 3906)

Jordan's Business Information Service, Jordan House, 21 St Thomas Street, Bristol BS1 6JS (0272 230600) Their Company Search Department can get you information on any UK company in 'Companies House', and their Rapid Reply Service can guarantee despatch within a few hours. Alternatively, if you really are in a hurry, they have a telex and telephone service. They also produce a range of annual business surveys covering some fifty industries.

Jordan's new Companies Service could be particularly useful for a small company looking for sales leads. Over 25,000 new companies are incorporated each year, and Jordan's reports on about half. They eliminate the companies with convenience directors and registered offices (each of which offers no contact point), which leaves several thousand 'genuine' new potential customers each month. Naturally, these companies could be anywhere in the UK, so in order to make the service more useful to small business, they have produced a county by county service, with London split into eight. These selected services cost from £250 to £700 per annum. The whole UK service could cost around £8000, and London alone around £3500. At £1 a 'lead', this could prove a cost-effective way to expand sales.

Kelly's Business Directory, published by Kelly's Directories, Windsor Court, East Grinstead House, East Grinstead, West Sussex RH19 1XB (0342 26972), has an alphabetical list of manufacturers, merchants, wholesalers and firms, together with their trade descriptions, addresses, telephone and telex numbers. In addition, entries are listed by trade classification. A section lists British Importers under the goods they import. Exporters are listed by the products they export and the continent and countries in which they sell. The directory covers 90,000 UK firms classified under 10,000 trade, product or service headings. There is also a Brand and Trade Names section, giving an alphabetical listing of brand and trade names, showing the name of the manufacturer or UK distributor and a brief description of the product.

Kelly's Post Office London Directory provides business listings by street, so a company's immediate neighbours can be identified. It is useful for finding concentrations of a particular type of business, or for finding gaps in provisions of a particular type of business.

Key British Enterprises published by Dunn and Bradstreet Ltd, 26/32 Clifton Street, London EC2P 2LY (01 377 4377). Information on 20,000 UK companies that between them are responsible for 90% of industrial expenditure. KBE is very useful for identifying sales prospects or confirming addresses, monitoring competitors and customers or finding new suppliers. As well as giving the names, addresses, telephone and telex numbers of the main office of each company, it gives branch addresses, products indexed by SIC code, sales turnovers (UK and overseas), directors' names and responsibilities, shareholders, capital structure, trade names and number of employees.

KBE is in two volumes, alphabetical and geographical. By using the directory you can quickly establish the size of business you are dealing with and what other products or services they offer. It is very often important to know the size of a firm. If, for example, your products are confined to certain types of business. A book-keeping service is unlikely to interest a large company with several hundred employees; they would have their own accounts department. Conversely, a very small company may not need a public relations consultant.

Kompass is published in association with the CBI in four volumes: Volumes I and II are indexed by product or service to help find suppliers, indicating whether they are manufacturers, wholesalers or distributors. It can be very useful indeed on certain occasions to be able to bypass a wholesaler and get to the manufacturer direct.

Volume III gives basic company information on the 30,000 suppliers identified from Volume I. These include the addresses, telephone and telex numbers, bankers, directors, office hours and the number of employess.

Volume IV gives financial data on these companies over a three year period giving: turnover, profit before tax, fixed assets, current assets, shareholders' funds and the ultimate holding company, if any.

The London Gazette published by HMSO four times a week, provides the official notices on companies, including bankruptcies and receiverships. It may be too late for you to do much by the time it reaches the Gazette.

McCarthy Information Services, McCarthy Information Ltd, Manor House, Ash Walk, Warminster, Wilts BA12 8PY (0985 215151) Provide a comprehensive press comment service monitoring the daily and financial press. From some 50 papers and journals they extract information on quoted companies each day and unquoted companies each week.

The service is provided on subscription, and a modestly priced Back Copy Service seems the most likely one to appeal to small business. The subscription is £42 per annum, and 82p per page copied. Alternatively, an on-line and microfiche service are also offered.

Research Index is an index to news, views and comments from the UK national daily papers plus around 150 periodicals in every field. The material is chosen carefully to include most items that would interest the business user, both on individual companies and on industries. Over a period of a year it includes around 130,000 items, and since the first edition over a million references have been made.

By using it, even the smallest business can have at its fingertips the knowledge for information retrieval equivalent to the most sophisticated libraries. Published by Business Surveys Ltd, PO Box 21, Dorking, Surrey RH4 2YU (0306 7128670)

The Retail Directory published by Newman, 48 Poland Street, London W1V 4PP (01 439 0335) gives details of all UK department stores and private shops. It gives the names of executives, and merchandise buyers as well as addresses and telephone numbers, early closing days, etc. It also covers multiple shops, co-operative societies, supermarkets and many other retail outlets. If you plan to sell to shops, this is a useful starting point, with around 1,305 department stores and large shops and 4,821 multiple shop firms and variety stores listed in 1,346 pages. If you are already selling retail, this directory could help you expand your prospects list quickly. The directory also identifies high turn-over outlets for main product ranges. There is a useful survey, showing retail activities on each major shopping street in the country. It gives the name and nature of the retail businesses in each street.

A separate volume contains shop surveys for the Greater London area, with 27,830 shops listed by name, street number and trade. The head offices of 1,130 multiples are given, as are 233 surveys showing what sort of shops are in any area. This can be used for giving sales people useful contacts within their territory.

Sell's Directory Sell's Publications Ltd, Sell's House, 55 High Street, Epsom, Surrey KT19 8DW (03727 26376) and the Institute of Purchasing Management. It lists 65,000 firms alphabetically, with name, trade, address, telephone number and telex numbers. Using a classified cross-reference system, it covers 25,000 products and services. There is a guide to several thousand trade names cross-referenced back to each company. The two remaining sections include a contractors' section, advertising firms seeking contract work, and a business information section.

If you only know the trade name and want to find out who

makes the product, then this directory will help you. You can then use it to find competitive sources of supply of similar products or services.

Stubbs Name Matching Service, 6/8 Bonhill Street, London EC2A 4BU (01 377 4377) A new (1983) early warning system to alert companies to customers who might be getting into financial difficulties. A check is made on official, public and commercial records each day on: county court judgements; meetings of creditors; companies that have secured a mortgage or charge on assets; appointment of liquidators; winding up orders and appointment of receivers. You supply Stubbs with the names of the companies you want monitored, customers, competitors or even suppliers. It costs £2.50 per name and the information is sent to you within 48 hours.

In 1987, two further systems – Full Alert and Key Alert – were added to cover sole traders and partnerships, offering a slightly slower and consequently cheaper service.

Who Owns Whom (UK) published by Dun and Bradstreet. Volume I lists parent companies, showing the structure of a group as a whole and the relationship with member companies. Volume II lists subsidiaries and associates showing their parent companies.

Company and Product Data, Overseas

Directory of European Retailers, an annual covering 6,000 department stores, chains, co-ops and variety stores.

DTI Export Data Branch Holds 50,000 status reports on overseas businesses. As well as telling you what the company does, each report gives a guide to the company's local standing and suitability for acting on behalf of a UK business. It is very useful if you want an overseas agent or wish to establish their reliability generally, eg, as a customer (see also Finding the Information, Section 5).

European Companies is a comprehensive guide to sources of information on business enterprises throughout Europe. Published by CBD Research Ltd, 154 High Street, Beckenham, Kent BR3 1EA (01 650 7745).

European Report (A4/6) (published in Europe and available in main UK business libraries) comes out twice a week and provides a brief review of business and economic events.

Extel European Companies Service See listing in UK section for more details. Cards on individual companies cost £11 each.

Funk and Scott International and European Indexes provide a worldwide index to company news appearing in several hundred English language papers and journals. They have an index for the USA too. You can use this service to find out what has been happening to a company that has not shown up in its figures, for example, new products cancelled, strikes, acquisitions, divestments, and board changes.

ICC American Company Information Service, 81 City Road, London EC1Y 1BD (01 251 4941) They can provide reports on 12,000 US public companies. The report includes the Annual Report and Accounts and the IOK Corporate Structure report on subsidiaries, directors, prominent shareholders and company properties. These cost approximately £40 and £30 respectively for each company.

ICC European Company Information Services, 81 City Road, London EC1 1BD (01 251 4942) Through company registries and information services throughout Europe, ICC can provide various reports, including financial accounts, status reports and annual returns on companies registered in Belgium, Denmark, France, Germany, Holland, Norway, Sweden, Channel Islands, Italy, Portugal and Spain. A thousand European company accounts are kept on file in the UK ready for immediate despatch. The cost of the information ranges from £30 to £40 per company.

Jordan's Overseas Company Information (see listing in UK section for address) covers the whole world with an international network of agents and information sources. Information on companies varies from country to country, as does the speed with which that information can be retrieved. Still, this is certainly one of the best ways of finding out about a company that is not included in a general directory either because it is too small or too new. Of course, you may need much more detailed information on a particular company than is normally provided in a directory, and this information service may be able to provide it.

KOMPASS Directories similar to UK directories, are available for Belgium and Luxemburg, Denmark, West Germany, France, Holland, Italy, Australia, Brazil, Indonesia, Morocco, Norway, Singapore, Spain, Sweden and Switzerland (Kompass address given in UK listing).

McCarthy's Australian Service
McCarthy's European Information Service
McCarthy's North American Service
See earlier listing in UK section for more details of above three services.

Principal International Business, published by Dunn and Bradstreet, gives the basic facts about 50,000 businesses in 135 countries. As well as the business name, address and telex and its main activities, it tells you if the company is a subsidiary of a larger corporation; whether they import or export; how many employees they have; their latest sales volume; and the name of the chief executive. Its cover of companies in each country is not great; nearly 8,000 in the USA; 6,000 in Germany; 5,500 in France; 4,000 in Japan; and 2,000 businesses in the UK. This represents only a small percentage of the businesses in any one country, but they are the principal ones.

Standard and Poor's Register of Corporations Directors & Executives. The Corporation Record, Volume I, has a wealth of information on the financial structure and performance of 38,000 of the most significant American corporations. There is also a list of the subsidiary companies cross-referenced to parents. Volume II contains the individual listings of 70,000 people serving as officers of these corporations, together with some personal details on their education and fraternal membership. Volume III contains a series of indexes that complement the first two volumes.

Thomas's Register of American Manufacturers, consists of 16 volumes, making it probably the most comprehensive directory on the market. Volumes 1–8 list products alphabetically, giving the manufacturer's name. Volume 9 and 10 give company names, addresses with zip codes and telephone numbers listed alphabetically, together with branch offices, capital ratings and company officials. An American trademark index is given in Volume 10.

Volumes 11–16, called *Thomcat*, contain catalogues of companies, bound alphabetically and cross-referenced in the first ten volumes. In all a formidable work, this is useful either to find an American source of supply or a potential customer for your product. The catalogues provide an insight into the way in which American companies market their wares.

Wall Street's Corporate and Industry Research Reports, prepared by leading analysts and UK brokerage and institutional investment firms. In-depth analysis and data on 5,000 companies and 150 industries, prepared by 40 research departments. Published by Research Publications Ltd, PO Box 45, Reading RG1 8HF (0734 583247).

Wall Street Journal Index provides a monthly and annual review of published material on the USA. It is in two sections. The first gives company news, and the second gives general business news. Both are alphabetical and provide brief abstracts of the activities in question. It is somewhat similar to what the FT has to say about a company, product or personality.

Who Owns Whom (Australasia and Far East) Details are as below.

Who Owns Whom (Continental Europe) is published in two volumes. The first is similar to the UK volume, and the second volume has a section on foreign investment. (See listing in UK section for more details.)

Who Owns Whom (North American edition) is perhaps the definitive directory of US multinational subsidiaries. Canadian companies are also covered.

Market and Industry Data

Businesses have to take part in censuses in much the same way as do individuals. This information, showing purchasers, stocks, capital expenditure and so on, is available for all the main UK industries, in the Annual Report on the Census of Production. The *Business Monitor Series* covers this and other areas in considerable detail each month and quarter. *Mintel Retail Business* is a monthly publication that examines consumer goods markets. By taking an area at a time it can produce quite comprehensive studies on spending patterns and the underlying reasons for them. The market share held by various businesses is given in *The A–Z of UK Marketing Information Sources* which lists the output of the UK manufacturing industry under thousands of headings.

If you want a piggy back on someone else's research, then *Reports Index* is a quick reference guide to several thousand market studies, carried out on UK products and markets, available for purchase at quite modest prices. If you do not find a reference book in this section covering the field you are interested in, then the Guide to *Official Statistics* from HMSO will probably show you where to find it. Overseas markets are particularly well covered with the *Euromonitor* publications, which provide comprehensive comparative information on European and international markets. *Market Data Reports on European Industries* shows growth and size trends of 24 industries in eight countries over the past seven years. The *International Directory of Published Market Research* provides a useful insight into who has done what in the market research field, and a number of useful indexes on other international data sources are also identified.

Market and Industry Data, UK

The A–Z of UK Marketing Information Sources by Christine Shaw, published in 1984 by Euromonitor Publications Ltd, 18 Doughty Street, London WC1N 2PN.

It provides basic market data for several hundred UK markets, from adhesives to zip fasteners, by product area, market size, production, imports, exports, the main brands, their market share and a market forecast. A good glimpse at a wide range of markets. Price £28.

Annual Abstract of Statistics published by the Central Statistical Office, is the basic source of all UK statistics. Figures are given for each of the preceding ten years, so trends can be recognised. Price £18.50.

ASLIB Directory, Volume I. Information sources in science, technology and commerce, edited by Ellen M. Coldlin, 5th edition, 1982. A valuable reference tool if you need to track down information over a wide range of subjects. This edition has over 3,000 entries from a large number of sources, professional, amateur, big and small. A major factor in including sources was their willingness to make the information available.

BBC Data Enquiry Service, Room 7, 1 Portland Place, London W1A 1AA (01 927 5998). This service is an information broker carrying out research on behalf of clients from outside the Corporation. It draws on internal resources and external sources including companies, organisations, libraries and commercial on-line databases. The internal resources include press cuttings and reference libraries, specialist indexes, as well as indexes to the BBC's radio and television output. The information strengths include economic and social events, biographies, business interests, political affairs, world statistics and company information. Ad hoc enquiries cost £50 per hour (minimum half an hour, £25), excluding VAT, with lower rates of £40 or £30 for subscribers, depending on the subscription.

Benn's Media Directory published by Benn Publications Ltd, Sovereign Way, Tonbridge, Kent TN9 1RW (0732 364422) Published in two volumes. Volume I is the standard reference work on the UK media, giving detailed descriptions. Volume II covers the media in other countries.

British Business published weekly by the Department of Industry and Trade (£1.10) provides basic statistics on UK markets. These include retail sales, cinemas, hire purchase, engineering sales and orders, industries production, catering, motor trade, textiles and manmade fibre turnovers.

British Planning Data Book by Taylor and Redwood, published January 1983 by Pergamon Press Ltd, Headington Hill Hall, Oxford OX3 0BW. Price £22. Wide ranging source of information on Market and Industry topics.

British Rate and Data, 76 Oxford Street, London W1N 9FD. Updated monthly. Whatever market you are interested in, it is almost certain to have a specialised paper or journal. These will be an important source of market data. BRAD lists all newspapers and periodicals in the UK and Eire, and gives their frequency and circulation volume, price, their executives, advertising rates and readership classification.

British Rate & Data Advertisers & Agency List is produced four times a year, and lists all advertising agencies, their executives and their customers' brand names. It also covers market research and direct mail companies.

Business Monitors are the medium through which the Government publishes the business statistics it collects from over 20,000 UK firms. They are the primary, and very often the only source of detailed information on the sectors they cover. The *Monitors* can help businessmen to monitor trends and trace the progress of 4,000 individual products, manufactured by firms in 160 industries. *Monitors* can also be used to rate your business performance against that of your industry and measure the efficiency of different parts of your business.

The *Monitors* are published in three main series. The *Production Monitors* are published monthly, quarterly and annually. The quarterly is probably the most useful, with comprehensive yet timely information. The *Service and Distributor Monitors* cover the retail market, the instalment credit business, the motor trade, catering and allied trades and the computer service industry, amongst others. Finally, there are *Miscellaneous Monitors* covering such topics as shipping, insurance, import/export ratios for industry, acquisitions and mergers of industrial and commercial companies, cinemas and tourism.

The Annual Census of Production Monitors cover virtually every sector of industry, and include data on total purchases, total sales, stocks, work in progress, capital expenditure, employment, wages and salaries. They include analyses of costs and output, of establishments by size, of full- and part-time employees by sex, and of employment, net capital expenditure and net output by region.

You can use the information – particularly that from the size analysis table – to establish such ratios as gross output per head, net output per head, net to gross output, and wages and salaries to net output. With these as a base, you can compare the performance of your own business with the average for firms of similar size and for that with your particular industry as a whole. For example, you can discover your share of the market, and compare employment figures, increases in sales and so on.

Most of the libraries listed later in this section will have a selection of the *Business Monitor Series*. Individual monitors can be bought from HMSO Books, PO Box 569, London SE1 9NH. They are all individually priced.

Family Expenditure Survey, published by HMSO, shows in great detail income and expenditure by type of household for the UK and includes some regional analyses – annual price £15.95.

Guide to Official Statistics is the main guide to all government produced statistics, including *ad hoc* reports. It is published by HMSO. Price £22. However, a brief free guide is available each year from the Press and Information Service, Central Statistical Office, Great George Street, London SW1 3AL (01 270 6363)

Key Note Publications Publishers of the same name at 28–42 Banner Street, London EC1Y 8QE (01 253 3006) produce concise briefs on various sectors of the UK economy.

Each *Key Note* contains a detailed examination of the structure of an industry, its distribution network and its major companies; an in-depth analysis of the market, covering products by volume and value, market shares, foreign trade and an appraisal of trends within the market; a review of recent developments in the industry, highlighting new product development, corporate development and legislation; a financial analysis of named major companies, providing data and ratios over a three-year period together with a corporate appraisal and economic overview; forecasts on the future prospects for the industry, including estimates from *Key Notes*, own database and authoritative trade sources. There is a very useful appendix detailing further sources of information – recent press articles, other reports and journals.

Over 100 market sectors are covered, including such areas as adhesives, after-dinner drinks, bicycles, butchers, commercial leasing, health foods, road haulage, public houses, travel agents and women's magazines.

Marketing and Distribution Abstracts published eight times a year by Anbar Publications Ltd, PO Box 23, Wembley HA9 8DJ (01 902 4489). This surveys 200 journals worldwide and provides an index to abstracts of appropriate articles and reports in the field.

Marketing Surveys Index published by Marketing Strategies for Industry (UK) Ltd, 32 Mill Green Road, Mitcham, Surrey CR4 4HY (01 640 6621). A digest of current market research surveys that are available for sale, worldwide, updated each month. It covers almost every sector of the economy.

McCarthy's Industrial Services provides a similar service on products and markets as their service on quoted and unquoted companies. The industry service is classified into 13 industry groups: agricultural and animal and vegetable raw materials; building and civil engineering; finance; general engineering; electrical and electronic engineering; chemicals and chemical engineering; miscellaneous industrial manufacturers; consumer goods manufacture; transport and transport equipment; marketing; distribution and consumer services; communications and communications equipment; mining and minerals and energy. Within the main industry group lie about 350 subsections. Marketing for example ranges from auto vending, franchising to street markets, as well as the more predictable department stores and supermarket groups.

Press cuttings are provided at 82p per copy. A phone call to McCarthy will tell you how many pages are involved, as naturally the size varies with the volume of news in a given area. The Back Numbers Service seems good value for small businesses (see also page 160).

Mintel is a monthly publication providing reports on the performance of new products and a wide range of specific areas of consumer expenditure. It covers several specific consumer goods markets each month, combining published data and original research to make the studies as exhaustive as possible. Comprehensive data on Leisure and Retail markets is also given. They provide research services and have an on-line service. Further details from Mintel Publications Ltd, KAE House, 7 Arundel Street, London WC2R 3DR.

Office of Population Censuses and Surveys produce demographic statistics for each county in England and Wales from the 1981 census (next census in 1991). These provide data not only on total populations in each area, but also on occupations, economic groups, etc. Similar reports for Scottish and Northern Ireland regions are also available. There is a reference library at OPCS, St Catherines House, 10 Kingsway, London WC2B 6JP (01 242 0262). More information and answers to general enquiries on these reports are also available from this number on ext 2009/2013.

Overseas Trade Statistics published by the Department of Industry and Trade, provide a monthly statement of UK imports and exports by volume and value for each product group and individual country.

The Bill Entry Services operated by HM Customs and Excise, Portcullis House, 27 Victoria Avenue, Southend-on-Sea SS2 6AL (0702 348944) will provide more detailed information for data up to 1986. From that date the service has been privatised and *Data Star*, Plaza Suite, 114 Jermyn Street, London SW1Y 6HJ (01 930 5503) provides the service.

Reports Index More recently Business Surveys Ltd introduced its bi-monthly Reports Index. This is an index to reports in every field published and available for sale. Its sources include Government publications, HMSO as well as non-HMSO, market research organisations, trade and professional associations, public bodies, stockbrokers, educational establishments, EEC, industrial and financial companies. Again the cost is modest. (Address: see Research Index in the UK Company and Product Data section.)

Retail Business published monthly by the Economist Intelligence Unit, covers the economic aspects of the UK retail trade, with emphasis on consumer goods market research, distribution patterns and sales trends.

Retail Intelligence is a quarterly publication also from Mintel, covering the consumer goods marketed in considerable depth.

Social trends, published by HMSO, brings together key social and demographic data on many aspects of the UK economy – useful charts and graphs – annual price £21.

Stockbrokers Research and Information Services compiled by Hilton and Watson, from the Library, Oxford Centre for Management Studies, Kennington, Oxford OX1 5NY. Has the details of research specialisations of 54 leading UK stockbroking firms, who all produce regular analysis of UK market sectors.

UK Market Size published by IMAC Research, Lancaster House, More Lane, Esher, Surrey (0372 63121). This report lists the output of UK manufacturing industry under 3,500 separate headings. It costs £125 and is produced each year.

Market and Industry Data, Overseas

British Business magazine's European Community Information Unit offers a free service to businesses in Britain by answering general enquiries about EEC matters and referring business enquiries to experts in official circles (details in UK section).

Economist Intelligence Unit 40 Duke Street, London W1A 1DW (01 493 6711) produces each quarter some 83 separate reviews covering 160 countries, evaluating growth prospects, assessing opportunities and examining local and international problems. It provides a business-oriented analysis of the economic state of the countries examined.

European Marketing Data and Statistics published by Euromonitor Publications Ltd, is an annual handbook containing comparative information about European Markets. *International Marketing Data and Statistics* is a companion volume that covers North and South America, Asia, Africa and Australasia.

Finding Export Markets published in 1986 by Trade Research Publications, 6 Beech Hill Court, Berkhamsted, Herts HP4 2PR (04427 3951). An excellent guide to methods and information sources worldwide.

Market Search published each year by British Overseas Trade Board in association with Arlington Management Publications Ltd, 87 Jermyn Street, London SW1Y 6JD (01 930 3638). Price £52.50.

The directory is in three parts. Part I is the Master Index, assigning a code number to each product. Part II contains 18,000 study listings in numerical order according to the British Standards Industrial Classification Scheme. This has the advantage of keeping related subjects close together. The studies themselves cover industrial and consumer markets and are briefly described together with the data when they were completed, how much each study costs and who is selling it. Part III gives the names, addresses and phone numbers of the 375 research firms who carried out the studies. The price includes a half yearly update and access to an information hotline.

Statistics – Europe (£47.50) *Africa* (£25.00) *America* (£43.50) *Asia and Australasia* (£48) are four guides to sources of statistics for social, economic and market research. They are published by CBD Research Ltd, Chancery House, 15 Wickham Road, Beckenham, Kent BR3 2JS (01 650 7745).

Subjects Index to Sources of Comparative International Statistics (SISCIS) For any activity or commodity it shows in what form the statistics are presented, in what unit and for what countries. From this it is possible to identify which of 350 major statistical serials contain the required figures. Also published by CBD Research Ltd (see above for address). Price £60.

FINDING THE INFORMATION

Now that you have an idea of the considerable mass of data that is available about companies, their products and markets, the next problem that remains is to track it down. Fortunately many of the directories and publications are kept in reference sections of major libraries up and down the country.

If you know exactly what information you want, then your problem is confined to finding a library or information service that has that information.

Specialist Libraries

Apart from your local library there are hundreds of specialist libraries concentrated in government departments, major industrial companies, trade organisations, research centres and academic institutes.

Two useful publications that will help find out about these are listed below.

ASLIB Economic and Business Information Group Membership Directory, published by the group and available from the London Business School Library, Sussex Place, Regent's Park, London NW1 4SA (01 262 5050). It provides a list of over 300 specialist business libraries throughout the country, and gives a very useful guide to their area of specialist interest.

Guide to Government Departments and Other Libraries is available from the Science Reference Library, 25 Southampton Buildings, Chancery Lane, London WC2A 1AW (01 405 7821). As the title indicates, this book concentrates on libraries in government departments and agencies, and particularly avoids duplicating the ground covered by the ASLIB Directory. The entries are arranged by subject covered, supplemented by an alphabetical index of the libraries, their locations, phone numbers and opening hours.

Not all the libraries covered in these directories are open to the public for casual visits. However, many will let you use their reference facilities, by appointment.

British Institute of Management Library and Management Information Centre Management House, Cottingham Road, Corby, Northants NN17 1TT (0536 204222). Open Monday to Friday, 09.30–17.00. The library houses one of the largest specialist collections of management literature in Europe. This includes much valuable information not generally available. The services are for BIM members who can use the library in person or make enquiries by letter or telephone.

The library also produces extremely valuable reading lists covering a wide range of topics. These provide a selective guide to books, directories and periodicals in any of 170 specific areas. They also publish *A Basic Library of Management* which lists 300 or so of the more useful books in the management field.

Business Statistics Office Library, Cardiff Road, Newport, Gwent NPT 1XG (0633 56111 ext 2973, telex 497121/2) open Monday to Friday, 09.00–17.00. This library keeps all the data produced in published form by the Business Statistics Office, together with a substantial quantity of non-official material. The coverage extends beyond UK statistics to include foreign information and an extensive range of company data and trade directories. The library is freely open to the public, who can enquire personally or by telephone, telex or letter.

Science Reference and Information Service Department of the British Library, 25 Southampton Buildings, Chancery Lane, London WC2A 1AW (01 323 7494/7496; patent enquiries 01 323 7919, telex 266959). This is the national library for modern science and technology, for patents, trade marks and designs. It has the most comprehensive reference section of this type of literature in Western Europe. If you do not have an adequate library close at hand a visit here could save you visits to several libraries. It should also be able to provide you answers if most other places cannot do so.

There are three locations, one at Southampton Buildings (address above) which hold company information, industry, country and market surveys. The other two are listed below.

The Library's resources are formidable. It has 25,000 different journals, with issues back to 1960 on open shelves and the rest quickly available. It has 85,000 books and pamphlets and 20,250,000 patents. It has a worldwide collection of journals on trade marks, together with books on law and design. Most of the major UK and European reports are held, as is trade literature and around 1,000 abstracting periodicals.

The services are equally extensive. It is open from Monday to Friday, 09.30–21.00, and on Saturday from 10.00–13.00. You can visit without prior arrangement or a reader's ticket. Telephone requests for information, including the checking of references, are accepted. Once at the library, staff are available to help you find items and to answer general queries. Scientific staff are also on hand for specialised enquiries. There is even a linguist service to help you inspect material written in a foreign language, though for this service you must make an appointment.

The Business Information Service of the British Library
Science Reference and Information Service, 25 Southampton
Buildings, London WC2A 1AW. Set up in 1981 in response to
demand for a national business information service. It specialises
in the provision of market, company, and product information.
Personal callers to the library receive help with their enquiries
from specialist staff, between 09.30–17.00 Monday to Friday and a
free telephone service for brief enquiries is available on 01 323
7464. A charged business information service and an on-line
searching service for more detailed research are also offered.
Further details are available on 01 323 7979.

Official Publication Library The British Library, Great Russell
Street, London WC1B 3DG (01 636 1544 ext 234/5). Open Monday,
Friday and Saturday from 09.30–16.45, and Tuesday to Thursday
09.30–20.45 (please phone first). Virtually all official British
publications are held here, together with an extensive intake from
all other countries of the world from international organisations.
All the UK and major overseas series complementing the
Statistics and Market Intelligence Library are here too. An
extensive worldwide collection of legislative publications and a
complete set of all current UK electoral registers are kept here.

The Newspaper Library The British Library, Colindale Avenue,
London NW9 5HE (01 200 5515). A comprehensive set of British
(national and local) newspapers and most major foreign and
commonwealth newspapers are kept here. It is best to telephone
and check they have what you want, or you can send for a
catalogue and price list.

Statistics and Marketing Intelligence Library of the
Overseas Trade Board, 1 Victoria Street, London SW1 (01 214
5444/5, telex 8811074DTHQG). Reading room open 09.30–17.30,
Monday to Friday.

This library is primarily concerned with statistics and
directories from overseas countries and import/export data on
the UK. As such, it is the most important source of international
statistics and business information. It also has a very
comprehensive collection of other UK statistics and directories.

In addition to these special libraries, major chambers of
commerce, such as those in London, Birmingham, Manchester
and Glasgow, have their own substantial business collections.

Local Reference Libraries

For most purposes you will find that one of the major local
libraries with a good business information section will do. Among
the libraries with a strong commitment to business information
and experienced staff are the following:

ABERDEEN: Central Library, Rosemount Viaduct, Aberdeen AB9 1GU (0224 634622) Open 09.00–21.00 Monday–Friday, 09.00–17.00 Saturday

BATHGATE: Business Information Bureau, West Lothian Libraries Dept, Business Development Centre, Waverley Street, Bathgate EH48 4HZ (0506 630843) Provide a free information service for business in their area.

BEDFORD: Central Library, Harpur Street, Bedford MK40 1PG (0234 50931) Open Monday 11.00–19.00; Tuesday–Friday 09.30–19.00; Saturday 09.30–16.30

BIRMINGHAM: Central Libraries, Chamberlain Square, Birmingham B3 3HQ (021 235 4511) Open: Monday and Friday 09.00–20.00; Tuesday–Thursday 09.00–20.00; Saturday 09.00–17.00

BRADFORD: Central Library, Prince's Way, Bradford, W. Yorks BD1 1NN (0274 753600) Open: Monday–Friday 09.00–20.00; Saturday 09.00–17.00

BRISTOL: Central Library, College Green, Bristol BS1 5TL (0272 276121) Open: Monday–Friday 09.30–20.00; Saturday 09.30–17.00

CAMBRIDGE: Central Library, 7 Lion Yard, Cambridge CB2 3QD (0223 65252) Open: Monday–Saturday 09.00–19.00

CHATHAM: Chatham Library, Riverside, Chatham MA4 5SN (0634 43589) Open: Monday, Tuesday, Friday 09.00–19.00; Wednesday, Thursday, Saturday 09.00–17.00

CORNWALL: County Information Library, Union Place, Truro, Cornwall (0872 72702) Open: Monday–Wednesday 09.30–17.00; Friday 09.30–19.00; Saturday 09.30–12.30

COVENTRY: Reference Library, Bayley Lane, Coventry CV1 5RG (0203 25555) Open: Monday–Friday 09.00–21.00; Saturday 09.00–16.30

DURHAM: Branch Library, Reference Department, South Street, Durham DH1 4QS (0385 64003) Open: Monday–Friday 10.00–19.00; Saturday 09.30–17.00

EDINBURGH: Central Library, Reference Section, George IV Bridge, Edinburgh (031 225 5584) Open: Monday–Friday 09.00–21.00; Saturday 09.00–13.00

EXETER: Central Library, Castle Street, Exeter EX4 3PQ (0392 77977) Open: Monday–Friday 09.30–20.00; Wednesday 09.30–16.00; Saturday 09.30–16.00

GATESHEAD: Business Information Office, 1 Walker Terrace, Gateshead, Tyne & Wear NE8 1EB (091 477 6679) A free service provided by the Council's Library Department

GLASGOW: Commercial Library, Royal Exchange Square, Glasgow (041 221 1872) Open: Monday–Saturday 09.30–17.00

INVERNESS: Inverness Branch Library, Reference Section, Farraline Park, Inverness (0463 236463) Open: Monday and Friday 09.00–19.30; Tuesday and Thursday 09.00–18.30; Wednesday and Saturday 09.00–17.00

IPSWICH: Central Library, Northgate Street, Ipswich IP1 3DE (0473 214370) Open: Monday–Thursday 10.00–17.00; Friday 10.00–19.30; Saturday 09.30–17.00

LEEDS: Central Library, Calverley Street, Leeds LS1 3AB (0532 462067) Open: Thursday–Friday 09.00–17.00; Monday–Wednesday 09.00–21.00; Saturday 09.00–16.00

LEICESTER: Library Information Centre, Bishop Street, Leicester LE1 6AA (0533 556699) Open: Monday–Friday 09.00–20.00

LIVERPOOL: Commercial Library, William Brown Street, Liverpool, Merseyside L3 8EW (051 207 2147/0036) Open: Monday–Friday 09.00–21.00; Thursday and Saturday 09.00–17.00

LONDON: City Business Library, Gillett House, 55 Basinghall Street, London EC2B 5BX (01 638 8215) Open: Monday–Friday 09.30–17.00

Deptford Reference Library, 140 Lewisham Way, Deptford, London SE14 6PF (01 692 1162) Open: Tuesday–Friday 09.30–20.00

Holborn Library, 32/38 Theobalds Road, London WC1X 8PA (01 405 2706) Open: Monday–Thursday 09.30–20.00; Friday 09.30–18.00: Saturday 09.30–17.00

Westminster Reference Library, St Martin's Street, London WC2H 7HP (01 930 3274) Open: Monday–Friday 10.00–19.00; Saturday 10.00–17.00

LUTON: Reference Library, Bridge Street, Luton (0582 30161) Open: Monday–Friday 09.00–20.00; Saturday 09.00–17.00

MANCHESTER: Central Library, St Peter's Square, Manchester M2 5PD (061 236 9422) Open: Monday–Friday 09.00–21.00

NEWCASTLE UPON TYNE: Central Library, Princess Square, Newcastle-Upon-Tyne, Northumberland NE99 1HC (0632 610691) Open: Monday–Friday 09.00–21.00; Thursday and Saturday 09.00–17.00

NOTTINGHAM: Central Library, Angel Row, Nottingham NG1 6HP (0602 43591) Open: Monday–Friday 09.30–20.00; Saturday 09.00–13.00

OXFORD: Central Library, Westgate, Oxford OX1 1DJ (0865 815509) Open: Monday–Friday 09.15–19.00; Thursday and Saturday 09.15–17.00

PORTSMOUTH: Central Library, Guildhall Square, Portsmouth PO1 2DX (0705 819311-7) Open: Monday–Friday 10.00–19.00; Saturday 10.00–16.00

SHEFFIELD: Sheffield Business Library, The Central Library, Surrey Street, Sheffield S1 1XZ (0742 734711)

SOUTHAMPTON: Central Library, Civic Centre, Southampton SO9 4XP (0703 238555) Open: Monday–Friday 09.00–19.00; Saturday 10.00–16.00

SWANSEA: Central Reference Library, Alexandra Road, Swansea SA1 5DX (07923 55521) Open: Monday–Wednesday and Friday 09.00–19.00; Thursday and Saturday 09.00–17.00

Before making a special journey it would be as well to telephone and make sure the library has the reference work you want.

Do not neglect your local library. A recent visit to Kensington and Woolwich libraries was a very pleasant surprise. Gloucestershire is also among a growing band of progressive County Libraries aiming to serve local business needs in the information field. Their librarian has produced a very useful guide to their free commercial service for the county's business communities.

Information Services

In addition to the many excellent business libraries up and down the country, there are an increasing number of organisations that

175

will do the searching for you. The benefits to you are twofold: professionals search out the data, and can alert you to sources that you may not have thought of; they save you time, not just the time you would spend searching. If you are not near a good business reference library you may have a considerable and expensive journey to make. Mostly, these organisations have substantial libraries of their own, but Warwick, for example, will search elsewhere if they cannot find it in their stocks. They claim the largest statistics collection in the UK, after the Statistics and Market Intelligence Library in London, and they have access to several on-line bases.

The Financial Times Business Information Service, Bracken House, 10 Cannon Street, London EC4 (01 248 8000). The service offers impartial, authoritative facts – facts about companies, industries, statistics and people. They keep press cuttings on some 25,000 prominent people in industry, politics and business. They also have a Business Information Consultancy, which can offer an on-demand information service to meet individual information requirements.

The service is available to subscribers only. These can be taken out on a six month or annual basis. Prices vary with the level of service required, but start at £400.

Industrial Aids Ltd, Enquiry service at 15 Buckingham Palace Road, London SW1W 0QP (01 828 5036, telex 918666 CRECON G). This service is geared to supply commercial and technical information, such as Who makes what/where/how much? Who is company A's agent in country X? Where are custom manu-facturing sources? Details are given of company financial data, affiliations, product literature, consumption patterns, end users, prices, discounts and trading terms, as well as new legislation and standards, trade and industrial economic statistics, conference papers, proceedings and lists of delegates.

The cost is £45 per hour, excluding VAT. You can use the service by telephone, telex or by letter, and the response is fast.

Market Location Ltd, Warwick Street, Royal Leamington Spa, Warwicks CV32 5LW (0926 34235). *Contact: M. J. Griffiths.* Market Location is a research organisation studying manufacturing industry in the UK. It gathers its information through field research. Its team of researchers travel the country, marking each manufacturing unit on maps and conducting a face-to-face interview with a representative of the company in order to obtain accurate, first-hand information.

The data gathered is published on a series of large-scale maps with accompanying indexes, giving the company name, address and telephone number; the name of the location manager and his position; the activity of the company and its SIC main-order heading; the size of the workforce and its group structure.

Clients of Market Location are usually companies with a sales force selling to manufacturing industry. They use the service to improve their sales performance by finding new prospects, by increasing salesmen's call rates, reducing travelling expenses, and eliminating potentially abortive cold-calling.

Market Location produces statistics tables for each county, showing the number of factories, broken down by SIC code and number of employees (including percentages).

Copies of the statistics tables for all the counties researched cost £50.

The Marketing Shop, 18 Kingly Court, Kingly Street, London W1R 5LE (01 434 2671, telex 2625437) This organisation provides a wide range of marketing services, but its Information Service is perhaps the most useful facility for small businesses. It can provide data on practically any topic, either using its own library or outside sources, and will also monitor the media for information on companies, products or markets. Charges are £75 an hour for ad hoc work. The more usual arrangement is for customers to take a block of hours to be used over the year. Block fees start at around £500 which works out at £35 per hour. In general they give quotes for any research they do.

Warwick Business Information Services, University of Warwick Library, Coventry CV4 7AL (0203 523251, telex 31406) *Contact: Jennifer Carr or David Mart* The service offers a range of commercial and economic information based on published sources including international statistics, both official and non-official, market research, periodicals, reports, directories, company reports and on-line services. The service can be particularly helpful to a small business with information on market size and share, locating particular types of company and finding out about them, tracing recent articles on a particular product or process, on consumer expenditure data, imports and exports, economic conditions, price trends, advertising expenditure and production and sales figures.

The service will also undertake analysis of the data in question, and provide a written report on their desk research. In general, enquiries are dealt with on the telephone, telex or by post; however, personal visits are welcomed. If you telephone beforehand, documents can be assembled for you to look at.

Annual subscribers to the service pay £330 for 10 hours search time and publication. Occasional users of the service can get information or research assistance on an ad hoc basis at a cost of £50 per hour pro rata, with a minimum charge of £10. All in all, it is very good value.

Their monthly journal, *Market & Statistics News*, provides a regular source of information on statistical and marketing topics, and costs £25 per annum.

The service holds regular one-day seminars on Information Sources for Business Planning and Market Research.

On-line Databases There are now nearly 3,000 databases via 500 services, worldwide. These are listed and described in the definitive on-line directory available from Cuadra Associates, 2001 Wishire Boulevard, Suite 305, Santa Monica, California WA. Closer to home, ASLIB, 26–27 Boswell Street, London WC1N 3JZ (01 430 2671) can help on most aspects of on-line searching.

Useful business databases include:

- [ ] **Datasolve**, 99 Staines Road West, Sunbury-On-Thames, Middx TW16 7AH (0327 85566). Sells the 'World Reporter' which contains reports from the *Financial Times, Economist,* BBC World Service, etc. They also offer 'World Exporter', a foreign market intelligence service

- [ ] **Dialog**, Learned Information, PO Box 8, Abingdon, Oxfordshire OX13 6EB (0865 730969). A major publisher of technical, business and financial information, worldwide. Their EUSIDIC Database Guide lists most databases

- [ ] **Echo**, 177 Route d'Esch, 1471 Luxembourg (352 488041). Technical and commercial information on the EEC

- [ ] **Fintext**, a financial information service on British Telecom's Prestel service. Offers guidance on sources and uses of finance, tax planning and management advice, pension schemes, guides to computer hardware and software, and the London Enterprise Agency's LINK marriage bureau – a business introduction service bringing investors and fund seekers together

- [ ] **Mead Data**, 1 St Katherine's Way, London E1 9UN (01 488 9187). Publishes, amongst others, an international legal information service, LEXIS

- [ ] **Pergamon Infoline**, Achilles House, Western Avenue, London W3 0UA (01 992 3456). Publishes Key British Enterprises, Who Owns Whom and various management and marketing abstracts

Abstracting Services If you do not know exactly what you are looking for but know the subject area, then you need to find out what is in print on that subject. Simply to scan the shelves, apart from being time-consuming, will not produce direct results. Only a fraction of the books, periodicals, directories and other reference works are likely to be in any one library. For these reasons you need to use one of the main abstracting systems. An abstract is a brief summary of the publication itself, usually just enough to let you know if it is worth reading. Only a few are mentioned here, but one or more such services are available at many major county libraries. Alternatively, you could search the one that best suits your needs by reading:

Inventory of Abstracting and Indexing Services Produced in the UK by Ed Burgess, published by the British Library Research and Development Department. This is the definitive guide to abstracting and indexing services. Otherwise, useful abstracting services are listed below.

Anbar Bibliography gives details of the main business management books published each year. Anbar Publications, 65 Wembley Hill Road, Wembley, Middx HA9 8DJ (01 902 4489).

Anbar Abstracting Journals cover accounting and data processing; marketing and distribution; personnel and training; top management; work study and O&M.
   These abstracts are a selective guide through the literature, provided by subject experts, and include brief summaries of the articles listed from the 200 or so journals searched.

British National Bibliography published weekly by the British Library Bibliographic Services Division, provides a subject list of all books published in Britain.

Business Periodicals Index published annually by G. H. W. Wilson (New York), provides a guide to articles published in some 300 international business journals, and are indexed by the service.

London Business School Small Business Bibliography arranged under appropriate subject headings, lists and indexes about 2600 books and articles on small business management. First published in 1980, it is updated at nine-monthly intervals.

SCIMP (Selective Co-operative Index of Management Periodicals) is distributed by Manchester Business School Library, but covers mainly European periodicals.

It may be useful to know something of other types of written information that is not generally published. Two such abstracts are:

Current Research in Britain, from the British Library Documents Supply Centre. There is a section on business and management with a comprehensive guide to current research in every university and polytechnic, many colleges and other institutions, indexed by topic and college.

Selected List of UK Theses and Dissertations in Management Studies compiled by N. R. Hunter, University of Bradford Library.

A useful book on researching for business information is:

The Manager's Guide to Getting Answers The Library Association, 7 Ridgmount Street, London WC1E 7AE (01 636 7543). Available from DMS Ltd, Sheldon Way, Larkfield, Maidstone, Kent ME20 6SE (0622 882000). Price £5.75.

MARKETING ORGANISATIONS AND THEIR SERVICES

The organisations that look after the interests of professional marketeers can also give considerable help to newcomers and small businesses. At least two of these organisations, the Institute of Marketing and the British Overseas Trade Board, have unrivalled libraries and information banks in their respective fields. The Institute of Marketing, with its unique low-cost advisory service, is one particularly useful organisation. Many others, including the Market Research Society and the Institute of Management Consultants, provide specialist members' directories. These can put you in touch with someone with recent experience in the areas of your concern. Although you will have to pay for their services, you will improve the chances of solving your problem first time round.

Education is also a strong point of many organisations. The Institute of Sales and Marketing and the British Direct Marketing Association hold frequent short courses on most aspects of sales and marketing, as does the Institute of Marketing itself.

Some new and localised organisations are also listed here, if their services seem unique and important. The Small Firms Service, the SDA, WEDA and LEDU can also help with marketing expertise (see Section 2).

The Advertising Association, Abford House, 15 Wilton Road, London SW1V 1NJ (01 828 2771). The association was formed in 1926, and is primarily a federation of organisations with a major interest in advertising. As such it sets out to promote greater awareness of the effectiveness and purpose of all types of 'paid-for-space' in the media. Two services of possible interest are its publications of advertising expenditure statistics and forecasts in all media, and its education programme, run through CAM, listed below.

British Consultants Bureau, Westminster Palace Gardens, 1-7 Artillery Row, London SW1P 1RJ (01 222 3651). This is an independent, non-profit making association of British consulting firms of all disciplines. BCB's main purpose is to promote the interest of British consultants overseas. However, the bureau publishes a comprehensive directory, giving detailed information about all their members, their experience and their expertise. This is available to commercial firms.

The British Direct Marketing Association, Grosvenor Gardens House, 35 Grosvenor Gardens, London SW1W 0BS (630 7322). The association brings together the three main groups of people who influence the way in which products and services are marketed direct to customers. These groups are: direct mail houses, who prepare and market lists of prospective customers; financial, insurance, commercial and manufacturing firms; publishers and professional organisations that market direct (i.e., not via retailers), and advertising agencies and consultancies that specialise in direct marketing methods.

The BDMA is growing rapidly both in size and stature. It has played an important role in helping the customer to choose whether or not he wants to receive more advertising mail through the post. Its education programmes of short courses and workshops, covering the use of direct mail, is extensive. In October 1982 the first Diploma in Direct Marketing programme was launched at Kingston Polytechnic.

The BDMA also produces a number of useful books that introduce the subject to the novice, or sharpen up older hands.

British Institute of Management, Management House, Cottingham Road, Corby, Northants NN17 1TT (0536 204222). Their services to members include information and advisory functions, and a research and education programme. They also have a Centre for Physical Distribution Management, which covers transport, warehousing, inventory control, materials handling and packaging matters.

This is more an institute for professional managers than just for marketeers, but its wider vision is particularly useful for small businesses.

British List Brokers Association, Springfield House, Princess Street, Bedminster, Bristol BS3 4EF (0272 666900). *Contact: Graham Cooper.*

Communication Advertising and Marketing Education (CAM) Foundation, Abford House, 3rd Floor, 15 Wilton Road, London SW1V 1NJ (01 828 7506). This is the authoritative body on what and where to study in the marketing field.

The Design Initiative by the DTI offers subsidised expert advice on design from product concept to corporate image (see under Enterprise Initiative, Section 2).

Direct Selling Association, 44 Russell Square, London WC1B 4JP (01 580 8433).

Institute of Management Consultants, 33 Hatton Garden, London EC1N 8DL (01 242 1803/2140). The institute has 3,300 individual members, and publishes the journal *Consult*. As a free service to industry it operates a client enquiry service, putting enquirers in contact with members with appropriate skills.

Institute of Marketing, Moor Hall, Cookham, Maidenhead, Berks SL6 9QH (06285 24922). The institute has nearly 23,000 members and is the largest and most comprehensive body in the field. It has a substantial library and a wide range of publications. There are few subjects in the field to which the institute cannot provide a useful pointer.

The Marketing Initiative from the DTI provides subsidised professional help with all aspects of marketing including market research, strategy review, pricing and distribution. See under Enterprise Initiative – section 2.

Industrial Market Research Association, 11 Bird Street, Lichfield, Staffs WS13 6PW (0543 263448). The association represents over 1,000 members of the profession of Industrial Market Research in the UK. Although it does produce a directory of members, this is not generally available.

Institute of Public Relations, Gate House, St John Square, London EC1M 4DH (01 253 5151). The institute is mainly concerned with keeping professional standards high and promoting general awareness of the role of public relations.

Institute of Sales Promotion, Panstar House, 13–15 Swakeleys Road, Ickenham, Middx UB10 8DF (08956 74281/2). This is the recognised professional body of their branch of marketing. Their *Consultants Register* is available to non-member prospective clients, as is their information service, which holds a comprehensive reading list on the subject.

Mail Order Traders Association of Great Britain, 25 Castle Street, Liverpool L2 4TD (051 236 7581).

The Market Research Society, 175 Oxford Street, London W1R 1TA (01 439 2585). This is the professional body for those concerned with market, social and economic research. It has 3,500 members and is the largest body of its kind in the world.

Apart from a programme of education, research and publications of primary interest to members, the society produces a directory of organisations providing market research services. The directory provides background information on the 210 research agencies, their executives, experience and the size in sales turnover. Some of the organisations are quite small, with turnovers below £50,000 per annum, whereas others have a turnover of several million pounds. They also publish the *International Research Directory.*

The Marketing Society, Derwent House, Stanton House, 206 Worple Road, London SW20 8PN (01 879 3464). The society was formed 20 years ago. One of its main objectives is to raise the reputation and understanding of marketing among general management, government, the Civil Service, trade unions and educationalists.

Ministry of Defence, Small Firms Advice Division, Room 318, Lacon House, Theobald's Road, London WC1X 8RY (01 430 5849). Established in December 1986 to help and advise small companies who want to enter the defence market and to point them to the right contacts within the MoD.

The Newspaper Society (Marketing Dept), Bloomsbury House, Bloomsbury Square, 74–7 Great Russell Street, London WC1 BDA (01 636 7014). *Contact: Marilyn Beadle or Mary Segal.* Single point of entry to book advertising in any of 1,000 local newspapers. They offer a computerised database service that can provide all relevant facts and figures about these local papers and the areas in which they operate.

Public Relations Consultants Association, Premier House, 10 Greycoat Place, London SW1P 1SB (01 222 8866 ext 2354/5). The association produces a wide range of guidance papers and other publications, which extend from the useful – *Selecting a PR Consultancy and Consultancy/Client Agreement* – to the esoteric *How to Set Up for a Royal Visit.*

It publishes together with the *Financial Times* the most authoritative book in the field, *Public Relations Yearbook.* This gives profiles of 150 PR consultancies and their clients. There are also several useful articles on other aspects of public relations.

Small Firms Marketing Centre, London Road, Warmley, Bristol BS15 5JH (0272 677807). The centre has a small full-time staff and a team of part-time specialist consultants on tap. It was established in 1983 to provide practical help to small and young enterprises at a modest cost.

Their range of service includes: Market Research and Assessment; Preparing a Market Plan; Product Design; Advertising and Promotion; Market Contacts – and general Marketing Advice. *Contact: Rona Wagstaffe and Angela Davis.*

SPECIALIST SERVICES FOR EXPORTING

The British Overseas Board, with its wide range of expertise and services, is of considerable use to first-time exporters. Apart from a wealth of information and statistics, its Market Entry Guarantee Scheme can provide an important part of the funding which a small firm needs to enter a new market.

The Institute of Export is the professional body in the field, and two other services are particularly interesting. Scanmark, run from Buckinghamshire College of Higher Education, undertakes research into overseas markets at a fraction of the cost of the commercial research organisations. The Export and Overseas Trade Advisory Panel Ltd performs a rather different role. Using their panel of expert advisers, they not only help you to evaluate an overseas market opportunity but will guide you through the red tape, too.

SITPRO (the Simplification of International Trade Procedures Board) will also be able to help with export documentation systems that will save exporters time and money, and the BBC Service to Exporters is always keen to hear interesting exporting stories.

Organisations

Berlitz, 321 Oxford Street, London W1A 3BZ (01 629 7360). Perhaps the best known name in the language business.

The Brain Exchange, Aiesec Great Britain Ltd, Ukin House, Phipp Street, London EC2A 4NR (01 739 9847). Can provide an overseas business studies student to work on your project for between 8 weeks and 18 months. Administrative fee of £150 and student must be paid £120 per week (London) or £90 (outside London).

BBC Data Enquiry Service, Room 7, 1 Portland Place, London W1A 1AA (01 927 5998). This service draws on the worldwide resources of the BBC to provide up-to-the-minute accurate information, fast. It can provide information on the social, economic and political aspects of every country in the world. It can also supply career details of leading foreign politicians and other public figures overseas.

BBC Service to Exporters, Export Liaison Unit, BBC External Services, Bush House, London WC2B 4PH (01 257 2039). Which of your products could make a good story? Which programme would be the right one for you? Any overseas enquirers will be put in touch with you.

British Overseas Trade Board, 1–19 Victoria Street, London SW1H 0ET (01 215 7877). The board provides a considerable amount of information, advice and help to the exporter. In particular it gathers, stores and disseminates information on overseas markets; gives advice and help to indivdual firms; organises collective trade promotions; and stimulates export publicity.

The board really does know all there is to know about the process of exporting, and it can help with some of the costs. For example, it can provide up to £20,000 towards the costs of carrying out market research studies overseas. They can also help with finding a representative abroad, getting overseas status reports, tariffs and regulations and subsidised trade missions and fairs.

The board's Export Intelligence Service, Lime Grove, Eastcote, Middx (01 866 8771) costs around £60 per annum to receive their notices. These will keep you up to date on events in any market area you choose. The service publishes a very comprehensive booklet outlining its services, and can provide more information on any area of particular interest.

Regional offices

North Eastern Regional Office, Stanegate House, 2 Groat Market, Newcastle-Upon-Tyne NE1 1YN (091 232 4722, telex 53178)
Yorkshire and Humberside Regional Office, Priestley House, 1 Park Row, Leeds LS1 5LF (0532 443171, telex 557925)
West Midlands Regional Office, Ladywood House, Stephenson Street, Birmingham B2 4DT (021 632 5222, telex 337919)
North West Regional Office, Sunley Tower, Piccadilly Plaza, Manchester M1 4BA (061 236 2171, telex 667104)
East Midlands Regional Office, Severns House, 20 Middle Pavement, Nottingham NG1 7DW (0602 56181, telex 37143)
South West Regional Office, The Pithay, Bristol BS1 2PB (0272 262666, telex 44214)
Scottish Regional Office, Alhambra House, 45 Waterloo Street, Glasgow G2 6AT (041 248 2855, telex 777883)
Welsh Regional Office, New Crown Buildings, Cathays Park, Cardiff CF1 3NQ (0222 825097)

British Knitting and Clothing Export Council, 7 Swallow Place, London W1R 7AA (01 493 6622). Advises members on export sales and marketing matters in the knitting and clothing fields.

The Defence Export Services Organisation, Room 707, Stuart House, 23/25 Soho Square, London W1V 5FJ (01 632 4826). Helps British firms market their defence products overseas.

Durham University Business School, Export Unit, Mill Hill Lane, Durham BH1 3LB (091 374 2000). *Contact: Bill Ferguson.* The Unit was set up in 1980, particularly to help small firms to enter export markets. They are developing a national network of export centres, so there may be one nearer to you than Durham. Also see the Education Section for other institutions running courses in exporting (page 281).

EC Business Centres, Electronically linked to the EC database in Luxembourg. Users will be able to get information on research and development opportunities, legal requirements, standards and tender opportunities throughout the EEC. Other services include the ability to match British companies with possible joint venture partners in the EEC. The Centre can be contacted at London (01 730 8115), Birmingham (021 454 6171), Glasgow (041 248 7806) and Newcastle (091 232 6002).

The European Project, Department of Languages, Napier Polytechnic, Sighthill Court, Edinburgh EH11 4BN (031 444 2266). *Contact: J. R. Megson.* Language/marketing students are available to carry out 2 week marketing tasks in one European market. No fees are charged, but firms using students are expected to make a £200 contribution to expenses.

Export Buying Offices Association, c/o Portman Ltd, 360 Oxford Street, London W1A 4BX (01 493 8141). Assists in the exporting of consumer products to the department stores of the world – who are its members.

Export Credit Guarantee Department (ECGD), ECGD is the government department responsible to the Secretary of State for Trade & Industry for providing export credit insurance for British manufacturers and merchants. It also insures new overseas investment against political risks (Head office and regional offices listed in Organisations & Publications for Finance section).

Export Houses See under their heading in Section 6. These provide the most comprehensive range to exporters and potential exporters.

Exporters Workshops are held by the Small Firms Group of the London Chamber of Commerce, 69 Cannon Street, London EC4N 5AR (01 248 4444). Provides information, education and contacts to help small firms to start exporting. Your local chamber may do the same.

The Institute of Export, 64 Clifton Street, London EC2A 4HB (01 247 9812). The institute aims to contribute to profitable exporting by providing a forum for the exchange of experience and information between exporters. It also promotes education and training throughout the whole field of exporting. Its regular journal, *Export*, is a good way of getting into the export picture. Price £20 for 10 issues.

Institute of Freight Forwarders Ltd, Redfern House, Browells Lane, Feltham, Middx TW13 7EP (01 844 2266).

Institute of Linguists, 24a Highbury Grove, London N5 2EA (01 359 7445). Will advise on industrial and technical translations – ask for the Translator's Guild.

International Chamber of Commerce, Centre Point, 103 New Oxford Street, London WC1A 1QB (01 240 5558). Publishes a range of booklets in overseas payments and documentation.

The London Chamber of Commerce, runs residential beginners' courses in French, Arabic, German, Spanish and Portuguese, Italian, Japanese and Mandarin Chinese, which guarantee to teach you to speak and write 450 words of the new language in six days. It does not sound a lot, perhaps, but when used in multiple combinations 450 words provide an extremely useful basic preliminary vocabulary of expressions and phrases. Also available are intermediate and advanced courses in French and intermediate courses in German and Spanish.

The courses have been designed by Professor Robert Boland specifically for the mature student, and make a complete departure from the school language lab routine.

For more information contact LCCI, 69 Cannon Street, London EC4A 5AB (01 248 4444 ext 337).

The Post Office provides an introductory offer for first-time users of their Overseas Direct Mail Service. Contact the Customer Care unit at Main Post Offices.

Scanmark, Buckinghamshire College of Higher Education, High Wycombe, Bucks HP11 2JZ (0494 444640). Established in 1974, Scanmark is a team of postgraduate students in the final year of an export marketing course. Their first disciplines include accountancy, agriculture, business studies, chemistry, economics and psychology. They also have a combined fluency in French, Spanish, German, Russian, Italian and Portuguese.

Recognised by the British Overseas Trade Board and the London Chamber of Commerce, Scanmark has carried out over 100 research projects in 20 countries.

Its clients have included small businesses launching their first product, and larger companies moving into new markets. This really is a low-cost way of getting the fundamental facts on overseas markets.

Simplification of International Trade Procedures Board, SITPRO, Almack House, 26/28 King Street, London SW1Y 6QW (01 930 0532, telex 919130 SITPRO G). This is an independent body set up by the Department of Trade. Its objective is to simplify trade documents and procedures and so make international trade easier for British companies.

The board would like to know of any persistent problems in international trade documents and procedures, to help it decide on future priorities for action. SITPRO News is available on request. SITPRO also produces a range of publications, one of which, *Top Form* (price £7.00), is a useful guide through a complex process.

The board has an advisory consultancy service which will visit sites and help with specific problems.

Technical Help for Exporters from the British Standards Institution, Linford Wood, Milton Keynes MK14 6LE (0908 220022). Marketing any product overseas means that you will have to comply with the laws of the land (safety and environmental); national standards; certification practices; and customer needs. This service can supply detailed information on foreign regulations; identify, supply and assist in the interpretation of foreign standards and other technical requirements; provide translations; and help with obtaining foreign approval.

A technical enquiry service is operated specifically to deal with the day-to-day problems of exporters, many of which are answerable over the telephone. The charge depends on the amount of research and the time involved.

Simple enquiries are dealt with free of charge. A range of fees is charged for more detailed and difficult enquiries.

Technical Translations International Ltd, Imperial House, 15/19 Kingsway, London WC2B 6UU (01 240 5361).

Publications

Barclays Bank International, Barclays House, 1 Wimborne Road, Poole, Dorset BH15 2BB (0202 671212) Barclays Bank International produces a series of booklets entitled 'Support for World Trade': *An Introduction to Exporting and Importing; Documentary Letters of Credit; Foreign Exchange for Export/ Import; An Introduction to Importing.* The publications deal in detail with such subjects as how to find markets abroad; where to obtain reliable, up-to-date information about those markets; the

British Overseas Trade Board and export factoring; the Export Credits Guarantee Department; buyer/supplier credits; documentary letters of credit; and bills of exchange. Specimen documents and diagrammatic guides complement the text.

These booklets were produced not only for companies thinking of exporting for the first time but also for those already established in the overseas markets. They explain, in a clear, concise manner, the steps along the export road. Copies of the booklets are available to companies through any branch of Barclays or by writing to the Marketing Department (address above).

The Business Traveller's Handbook: How to get along with people in 100 countries, compiled by Foseco Minsep Ltd. Gives complete advice on etiquette and codes of behaviour in over 100 countries. An ideal handbook for the business traveller who wants to create the best possible impression. Available from Graham & Trotman Ltd, Sterling House, 66 Wilton Road, London SW1V 1DE (01 821 1123). Paperback price £9.50; hardback £13.50.

Croner's Reference Book for Exporters, from Croner House, 173 Kingston Road, New Malden, Surrey KT3 3SS (01 942 8966). This is a loose leaf and regularly updated service that keeps exporters up to date on all exporting procedures. It is available on a ten day free approval offer. Price £60.50.

Directory of Export Buyers in the United Kingdom, 1987, by Tookey and published by Trade Research Publications, 6 Beech Hill Court, Berkhamsted, Herts HP4 2PR (04427 3951). The conventional wisdom of successful exporting recommends that you should travel abroad to contact buyers. However, firms abroad are increasingly establishing buying offices in this country in order, amongst other reasons, to look for new sources of supply. It is estimated that orders for about 20% of British exports are negotiated and signed in the UK, and mainly by people listed in this directory. The entries are indexed by countries bought from, products bought and foreign firms bought for. Price £45.

Doing Business, A series of comprehensive guides to the economic and commercial climate in most of the developed economies, published in 1987. Free from Ernst & Whinney, Becket House, 1 Lambeth Palace Road, London SE1 7EU (01 928 2000).

The Europa Year Book 1987, A world survey (28th edition), Europa Publications Ltd, 18 Bedford Square, London WC1B 3JN. In two large volumes this annual provides factual information about every country in the world, and 1650 of the principal international organisations. Price (UK) the set £130.

Export for the Small Business, by Henry Deschampneufs 1984, published by Kogan Page Ltd, 120 Pentonville Road, London N1 (01 278 0433). Price £6.95.

Export Handbook, published each year. This is an invaluable guide from the British Overseas Trade Board for all seeking to explore and boost their export potential. It provides an introduction to governmental and non-governmental services, which give advice and assistance and gives much useful information on UK import and export regulations, overseas tariffs, credit insurance and finance, freight forwarding and international transport. Available from HMSO Bookshops and Agents (see Yellow Pages). Price £6.

Exporting Step by Step To Success, by Brian Ogley, published by Harper & Row on behalf of the Small Business Research Trust, 1988. Deals in plain English with each stage in the export process from assessing the market to financing the sale.

Handbook of International Business, edited by Ingo Walter, published in 1982 by John Wiley, Baffins Lane, Chichester, Sussex PO19 1UD (0243 784531). It contains 44 sections covering virtually every area of international business. Price £75.

Selecting Agents and Distributors, by J. Thorn in Industrial Marketing Digest (UK) Volume 8 No. 1 (1983) warns of the pitfalls and problems and suggests how to overcome them.

The Small Firms Service of the Department of Employment, produces a free booklet, *How to Start Exporting.* It is a very useful 26 pages, and includes a market checklist to help choose which market to tackle first. There is also a reading list and a section giving other useful organisations.

The service's counselling and information service can also provide practical advice on exporting for beginners.

Both the booklet and the counselling service can be reached on Freefone Enterprise.

SPECIALIST SERVICES FOR IMPORTING

British Importers Confederation, 69 Cannon Street, London EC4N 5AB (01 248 4444). The confederation was founded in 1972, and represents some 3,500 importers. It is the only organisation protecting the interests of importers whatever the goods concerned.

Membership fees are modest and members include a significant number of one-man importers or smaller firms, as well as such companies as Shell and Unilever.

Because of its close relationship with the UK Government and the EEC Commissions, the confederation is usually aware of likely changes in import procedures long before they occur. This knowledge and other information form an important part of the service that the confederation can provide for small businesses.

Croner's Reference Book for Importers, accurately spells out the regulations and procedures to import goods of any nature into the UK. It covers import controls, exchange controls, VAT, marketing of goods, customs and excise, and transit and transhipment insurance. The book is in loose-leaf form and the service includes a regular supply of amendments. From Croner Publications Ltd, Croner House, 173 Kingston Road, New Malden, Surrey KT3 3SS (01 942 8966). Price £38.90.

Directory of British Importers, published by the British Importers Confederation and Trade Research Publications of 6 Beech Hill Court, Berkhamsted, Herts HP4 2PR (04427 3951). The directory gives a considerable amount of information about importing firms, and whether you simply want to find out more about your competitors or to find an alternative source of supply, this directory will give you the answers. Price £39.

Importing for the Small Business, by Mag Morris (1984). Published by Kogan Page Ltd, 120 Pentonville Road, London N1. Price £5.95.

Importing Handbook, published by the British Importers Confederation and Trade Research Publications (address above), 2nd edition 1984. Price £15.

See also *The Exporting Handbook* in previous section.

BOOKS AND PERIODICALS ON MARKETING

Advertising, What It Is and How to Do it, by Roderick White, published by McGraw-Hill Book Co (UK) Ltd, Shoppenhangers Road, Maidenhead, Berks SL6 2QL (0628 23431) in association with the Advertising Association. Starting from 'Should you advertise and if so how much?' the book covers media, agencies, ad designs and choice, economics and the law. It tells you what questions to ask, and whether and where the answers can be provided. Price £10.95.

Advertising and Public Relations, by Alison Corke (ex Saatchi & Saatchi) 1986, published by Pan Books. Price £2.95.

All About Selling, by Alan Williams, published in 1983 by McGraw-Hill. A first-class review of all aspects of the selling process. Price £9.95.

Basic Marketing, 3rd edition, 1988, by Tom Cannon, published by Cassell. A first-class backdrop to modern marketing matters. Price £8.95.

Campaign, Haymarket Publications Ltd, 22 Lancaster Gate, London W2 (01 402 4200). A weekly mainly concentrating on advertising and agency matters. Price 60p.

The Creative Handbook, published by British Media Publications, Windsor Court, East Grinstead, W. Sussex RH19 1XA (0342 26971). Listing of all creative services, e.g., illustrators, model makers, photographers, cartoonists, etc. Annual. Price approx £35.

The Effective Use of Advertising Media, by Martyn P. Davis, published by Hutchinson in 1988, price £9.95. A comprehensive and useful guide to the various advertising media and to how to choose the most appropriate one for your business.

Exhibition Bulletin, from the London Bureau, 266/272 Kirkdale, Sydenham, London SE26 4RZ (01 778 2288). Provides a monthly list of all exhibitions in the UK.

Focus, The European Journal of Advertising and Marketing launched January 1982. More details from Advertising Age's Focus, Crain Communications Inc, 20/22 Bedford Row, London WC1 4EB (01 831 9621). Price £17.50 per annum.

How to Promote Your Own Business, A guide to low budget publicity by Jim Dudley, published in 1988 by Kogan Page Ltd, 120 Pentonville Road, London N1. Price £7.95.

How to Win More Business by Phone, by Bernard Katz, published in 1985 by Business Books (address below). Everything about telephone selling, a vital technique no small businessman can be without. Price £6.95.

Introducing Marketing, by Christopher, McDonald and Wills, Pan Books Ltd, 18 Cavaye Place, London SW10 9PG (01 373 6070). 1980. Refreshing, practical and set firmly in the UK environment. Price £3.95.

Managing for Results, Peter F. Drucker, Pan, 1967. Not strictly marketing, but a classic with many important pointers for the person running his own business. Price £2.95.

Managing the Sales Team, January 1982, by Neil Sweeney, published by Kogan Page, 120 Pentonville Road, London N1. It presents 12 management tasks and 100 management skills of use to small organisations with a sales force. Price £11.95.

Map Marketing Ltd, 92–194 Carnwath Road, London SW6 3HW (01 736 0297). Offer a range of Bartholomews Maps, showing area, district and sector post codes. The range of 63 maps covers the whole of the UK priced at £12.95 each. The maps are laminated so you can write on and rub off information. Useful for sales and territory planning.

Marketing, A weekly subscription only publication from Haymarket Publications (address above). Price 60p weekly and £40 per annum.

Marketing for Business Growth, by Theodore Levitt, published by McGraw-Hill Book Co (UK) Ltd, Shoppenhangers Road, Berks SL6 2QL (0628 23431). An extremely readable book on the strategic level. Price £28.95.

Marketing for the Small Business, by Derek Waterworth, published by Macmillan, 1987. Examines all elements of marketing including market research, pricing, promotion and finance.

Marketing, Management, Analysis, Planning and Control, by Philip Kotler, published by Prentice Hall, 66 Wood Lane End, Hemel Hempstead, Herts HP2 4RG (0442 585312) 5th edition, 1984. The most lucid and comprehensive book on the subject. Generally accepted as the standard text, and though illustrated liberally with American examples, the theory is both readable and understandable. Price £18.95.

The Marketing Research Process, by Margaret Crimp, published by Prentice-Hall, 2nd edition, 1986. Useful coverage of the whole area of market research in such a way that the layman will have no trouble in understanding it. Price £12.95.

Self-Starter Series: Marketing, by Cameron, Rushton and Carson, published in 1988 by Penguin, 27 Wrights Lane, London W8 7TZ. One of a series designed to help you develop skills and proficiency in a variety of subject areas. Price £3.95.

Marketing Week, 60 Kingly Street, London W1R 5LH. In most newsagents. It provides a general review of main current marketing topics. Price 50p.

Selling to the Ministry of Defence, a free booklet published in December 1986 to help small firms to compete for MoD business. Available from Room G179, Ministry of Defence, St Christopher House, Southwark Street, London SE1 0TD (01 921 2606).

Selling to the Public Sector, a free guide from the Department of Trade and Industry, details the main public sector buyers, explains what products and services each organisation buys and how it does business. Available from DTI Policy Division 3, Room 544, 1–19 Victoria Street, London SW1H 6ET.

Successful Retailing Through Advertising, by Eric Lowe, published by McGraw-Hill in 1983. It is a step-by-step approach to improving retailers' sales and profits, and advertising. Price £9.95 (see also pages 265–6 for books on the legal aspects of marketing).

RAISING THE MONEY

PREPARING YOUR CASE

There does not seem to be a shortage of money to finance the launching of new businesses and the growth of existing ones. What are scarce are good, small company propositions. At least, that is the argument put forward by the financial institutions themselves. There is certainly an element of truth in this view, but the quality of the propositions owes much to the poor groundwork and planning of some budding entrepreneurs.

The starting point for any search for funds is to determine how much is needed, and then to demonstrate the security that the likely investor will then enjoy.

The accepted way in which proposals for funds are put forward is through a Business Plan. The Business Plan brings together the marketing and operational aspects of the business or proposed business, and expresses these actions in terms that a financial institution will understand. Not surprisingly, these institutions will expect the plan to contain financial statements both actual and projected.

Banks as Advisers

As well as being a possible source of money, the banks, through their national network of branch managers, can help with the preparation and evaluation of business plans.

They see hundreds of new business proposals each year and are a mine of local knowledge.

If you want advice on your business plan, and they are usually only too pleased to help, you need some facts to hand first.

The National Westminster Bank has prepared a business plan presentation checklist, which is reproduced below.

CHECKLIST

About you

- ☐ Very brief synopsis for your own banker, detailed for approach to others: age, education, experience

- ☐ Personal means, e.g. property, liabilities guarantees. Other business connections

- ☐ For a type of business new to you, or start-up situation, outline experience, ability and factors leading up to your decision

Your Business

- ☐ Brief details of: when established, purpose then and now, how the business has evolved, main factors contributing to progress

- ☐ Reputation, current structure and organisation. Internal accounting system

- ☐ Past 3 years' audited accounts if available, and latest position

- ☐ Up to date Profit and Loss figures, including details of withdrawals

- ☐ Borrowing history and existing commitments, e.g. HP, leasing loans, bankers

- ☐ Description of major assets, and any changes

Your key personnel

- ☐ Age, qualifications, experience, competence, of directorate/ senior management. Directors' bankers

- ☐ Emergency situation, someone to run the business in your absence

- ☐ List of principal shareholders/relationships

Your purpose

- ☐ Explain fully your business plan, the use to which the money will be put, e.g. expansion, diversification, start-up

- ☐ Describe the practical aspects involved and the how and when of implementation

☐ Diagrams, sketches, photographs, etc are usually helpful, e.g. property purchase and conversion to your use

☐ Consider: planning permission, legal restrictions, government policy

☐ Contingency plans for setbacks: reliability of supplies/raw materials/alternative sources, other factors outside your control, e.g. weather

☐ Relevance to existing operations (if any), opportunity for shared overheads, disruption of current business

☐ Personnel, are more staff required, availability of specialist skills/training. Management ability for expanded/different operation?

Your market

☐ Estimated demand, short and long term. External verification of market forecasts, e.g. from trade associations, market research publications

☐ Competition, who from, likely developments

☐ Describe your competitive advantages, e.g., quality, uniqueness, pricing (justify), location–local/national

☐ Marketing included in costings?

☐ If new, or technology based or highly specialised business – detail and perspective necessary

Note A banker does not need to know how it works (though he may be interested), just that what it does is reliable and has good sales prospects

Your profit

☐ Demonstrate how profits will be made, include detailed breakdown of costs, timing, projected sales, orders already held

☐ Profit projections should attempt to cover the period of a loan, however sketchy

☐ For capital investment – profit appraisal. Capital allowances, e.g. new small workshop scheme

☐ Everything included in costings? e.g. tax, stamp duty, legal fees, bank interest

The amount

- [ ] State precisely the amounts and type of finance required and when it will be needed. Is type of finance correct? e.g. overdraft to finance working capital, term loan for capital expenditure

- [ ] Is the amount requested sufficient? e.g. increased working capital requirements/margin for unforeseen circumstances

- [ ] Detail the amount and form of your contribution to the total cost

- [ ] Justify all figures – Cash flow forecast for next 12 months: show maximum range. All outgoings considered, e.g. net VAT, holiday pay, bank interest and repayments, personal drawings

Repayment

- [ ] Relate projected profitability and cash flow to expected repayments. Justify fully the term requested. Is it long enough?

- [ ] How quickly will the business generate cash? Is a repayment 'holiday' necessary and what turnover needs to be achieved to break-even?

- [ ] Consider the worst situation, feasibility of contingency plans, irretrievable losses

- [ ] Interest rate – What is the effect of variation in base rate on plans?

Security

- [ ] What assets are/will be available as security?

- [ ] Are any assets already used for security elsewhere?

- [ ] Independent/realistic valuation of assets offered. Leasehold considerations, any unusual features/saleability. Support for guarantees

- [ ] Agreement of other interested parties/realistic awareness of loss of asset

- [ ] Insurance, e.g. life, property, business

If you can provide a satisfactory and comprehensive answer to most of these points, you will certainly find yourself at the head of most queues for funds.

Your first point of contact should be the local branch of any bank you choose. If you have any difficulties then speak to the bank's small firms adviser. These are listed later in this section.

Accountants and Your Business Plan

You might think of accountants as people who can only help once your business has got off the ground, or if you run into tax problems.

Nothing could be further from the truth. Most accountancy firms can help you with your initial business plan. Ernst & Whinney, for example, produce a free booklet entitled 'How to present a financial case to a bank'. Some have departments that only look after new and small businesses. Usually the first consultation is free and at least one major accountancy firm offers new businesses a discounted rate of fees, up to the time they can appoint their own accountant. The type of services an accountant can offer in the businesses planning field include:

☐ Help in preparing cash flows, forecasts and budgets
☐ A critical appraisal of your business plan
☐ Advice on the most suitable legal forms for your business
☐ Raising capital
☐ Obtaining Government grants and assistance
☐ Feasibility studies
☐ Staff recruitment and employment advice
☐ Training in book-keeping and the use of computers

The following firms are amongst those that have departments, groups or partners responsible for providing services to new and small businesses. Whilst only the head offices of these are given below, they all have branches throughout the UK that can give a similar service locally.

Arthur Andersen & Co., 1 Surrey Street, London WC2R 2TS (01 836 1200) *Contact: J. Ormerod*
Arthur Young, Rolls House, 7 Rolls Buildings, Fetter Lane, London EC4A 1NH (01 831 7130) *Contact: Nick Pasricho*
Binder Hamlyn, 8 St Bride Street, London EC4A 4DA (01 353 3020) *Contact: Rodney Graves*
Coopers and Lybrand, Plumtree Court, London EC4A 4HT (01 583 5000) *Contact: Tony Trembeth*
Dearden Farrow, 1 Serjeant's Inn, London EC47 1JD (01 353 2000) *Contact: Tom Simmons*
Deloitte Haskins & Sells, Hillgate House, 128 Queen Victoria Street, London EC4P 4JX (01 248 3913) *Contact: Richard Murphy*
Ernst & Whinney, Becket House, 1 Lambeth Palace Road, London SE1 7EU (01 928 2000) *Contact: Peter Gillett*
Grant Thornton, Grant Thornton House, Melton Street, Euston Square, London NW1 2EP (01 383 5100) *Contact: Miss S. Palmer*

Hodgson Impey, Spectrum House, 20–26 Cursitor Street, London EC4A 1HY (01 405 2088) *Contact: I. G. Pratt*

Neville Russell, Regent House, Heaton Lane, Stockport, Cheshire SK4 1BS (061 477 4750) *Contact: J. C. G. Pickering*

Peat Marwick McLintock, 1 Puddle Dock, Blackfriars, London EC4V 3PD (01 236 8000) *Contact: J. R. Hustler*

Price Waterhouse, Independent Business Group, Southwark Towers, 32 London Bridge Street, London SE1 9SY (01 407 8989) *Contact: Brian Hunter*

Spicer and Pegler, Friary Court, 65 Crutched Friars, London EC3N 2NP (01 480 7766) *Contact: David Robinson*

Touche Ross & Co, Chartered Accountants, Hill House, 1 Little New Street, London EC4A 3TR (01 353 8011) *Contact: Rony Herron*

Other help to prepare your financial plans

The Small Firms Service, The Rural Development Commission and the Enterprise Agencies listed in Section 2, and the DTI through its Business Planning Initiative, can also help you put together a proposal to raise money, as can some of the bodies listed under Venture and Development Capital.

Many of the courses run at the colleges listed in Section 8 will take you step-by-step through the process of preparing your case for finance. In all about 1,000 organisations that could help you in your plans to raise money, are listed in the guide.

Books that can help you with business plans are included at the end of this section.

WHAT ARE THE DIFFERENT TYPES OF MONEY?

Small businesses need to borrow money for a variety of reasons: in order to start up, expand, relocate, to start exporting or importing, to innovate or carry out research and development, or to meet the unexpected, such as the collapse of a major customer or supplier. The level of borrowing that you can secure will be related in some way to your abilities, the nature of your business and how much you have put into the business. Few lenders like to see themselves much more exposed to financial risk than the owner(s), who after all expect to make the most gain.

In the eye of most lenders, finance for the small business fits into two distinct areas: short-term, which does not necessarily mean that you only want the money for a short-term, but rather the life of the asset you are buying is itself relatively short; and long-term, which is the converse of that. The table below may help you get a clearer picture.

Now of course, starting up or expanding a small business will call for a mix of short-term and long-term finance. You may be able to get all this from one source: more likely, though, once you start to trade you will find that different sources are better organised to provide different types of money.

All methods of financing have important implications for your tax and financial position, and appropriate professional advice should always be taken before embarking on any financing exercise.

Term	Business need (e.g.)	Financing method
Short (up to 3 years)	For raw materials or finished goods; to finance debtors; equipment with a short life or other working capital needs; for dealing with seasonal peaks and troughs; to start exporting; or to expand overseas sales	Overdrafts, short-term loans, factoring, invoice discounting, bill finance, trade credit, export & import, finance
Medium to Long (3+ years)	Acquiring or improving premises; buying plant and machinery with a long life; buying an existing business, including a franchise; for technological innovations or developing a 'new' product or idea	Mortgage, sale and leaseback, loan finance, long-term leasing, hire purchase, equity & venture, finance, public sector finance

Overdrafts   Bank overdrafts are the most common type of short-term finance. They are simple to arrange; you just talk to your local bank manager. They are flexible with no minimum level. Sums of money can be drawn or repaid within the total amount agreed. They are relatively cheap, with interest paid only on the outstanding daily balance.

Of course, interest rates can fluctuate. So what seemed a small sum of money one year can prove crippling if interest rates jump suddenly. Normally you do not repay the 'capital'. You simply renew or alter the overdraft facility from time to time. However, overdrafts are theoretically repayable on demand, so you should not use short-term overdraft money to finance long-term needs, such as buying a lease or some plant and equipment. Overdrafts are more usually used to finance working capital needs, stocks, customers who have not paid up, bulk purchases of materials and the like.

Term Loans (short, medium and long)   These are rather more formal than a simple overdraft. They cover periods of 0–3, 3–10 and 10–20 years respectively. They are usually secured against an existing fixed asset or one to be acquired or are guaranteed personally by the directors (proprietors). As such, this may involve you in a certain amount of expense with legal fees and arrangement or consultants' fees. So it may be a little more expensive than an overdraft, but unless you default on the interest charges you can be reasonably confident of having the use of the money throughout the whole term of the borrowing.

The interest rates on the loan can either be fixed for the term or variable with the prevailing interest rate. A fixed rate is to some extent a gamble, which may work in your favour, depending on how interest rates move over the term of the loan. So, if general interest rates rise you win, and if they fall you lose. However, a variable rate means that you do not take that risk. There is another benefit to a fixed rate of interest. It should make planning ahead a little easier with a fixed financial commitment, unlike a variable overdraft rate, in which a sudden rise can have disastrous consequences.

Government Loan Guarantees for Small Businesses   These were first introduced in March 1981 and are still available. To be eligible for this loan, your proposition must have been looked at by an approved bank and considered viable, but should not be a proposition that the bank itself would normally approve. You can be a sole trader, partnership, co-operative or limited company wanting funds to start up or to expand. The bank simply passes your application on to the Department of Industry, using an approved format. (If your loan request is for less than £15,000 the bank can give approval directly.)

This is an elementary business plan, which asks for some details of the directors, the business, their cash needs and profit performance or projection of the business. There are no formal rules on size, number of employees or assets, but large businesses and their subsidiaries are definitely excluded from the scheme. The other main exclusions are businesses in the following fields: agriculture, horticulture, banking, commission agents, education, forestry (except tree harvesting and sawmilling), house and estate agents, insurance, medical and veterinary, nightclubs and licensed clubs, pubs and property, travel agencies, libraries, sport, gambling, authors and artists, postal services and public administration.

The loans can be for up to £75,000 and repayable over 2 to 7 years. It may be possible to delay paying the capital element for up to two years from the start of the loan. However, monthly or quarterly repayments of interest will have to be made from the outset. The loan itself, however, is likely to be expensive. Once approved by the Department of Trade, the bank lends you the money at bank rate and the Government guarantees the bank 70% (this rises to 85% in inner city areas) of its money if you cannot pay up.

In return for this the government charge you a 2% 'insurance' premium on the 70% of the loan it has taken on risk. Borrowers would be expected to pledge all available business assets as a security for the loan, but they would not necessarily be excluded from the scheme if there are no available assets.

Directors will not be asked to give personal guarantees on security. However, all their personal assets, including their home, must be fully committed already, on conventional loans, before a loan guarantee could be considered.

There are now some 23 banks operating the scheme, and by mid 1988 some 20,000 loans worth £650 million had been granted. The average loan has remained at about £33,000 for the past two years. Although the failure rate on loans was high in the early days of the scheme, new monitoring and appraisal systems introduced in 1984 have resulted in a very creditable 70% success rate.

The rule certainly seems to be to ask for as much as you need, plus a good margin of safety. Going back for a second bite too soon is definitely frowned upon. You do not have to take all the money at once. At the discretion of your bank manager, you can take the money in up to four lots. However, each lot must be 25% or more.

Encouraging, too, is the evidence that these loans were fairly evenly split between 'start-ups' and growing your businesses.

One final point on term loans. Banks tend to lump overdraft facilities and loans together into a 'total' facility, so one is often only given at the expense of the other.

Mortgage Loans   These operate in much the same way as an ordinary mortgage. The money borrowed is used to buy the freehold on the business premises. That then acts as the main security for the loan, with regular repayments made up of interest charges and principal paid to the lender.

The main suppliers are the insurance companies and pension funds, who generally prefer to deal in sums above £50,000. Some of the smaller companies will lend as little as £5000, particularly if the borrower is a policyholder. As well as the regular payments, a charge of about 2% will be made to cover the survey, valuation and legal work in drawing up agreements. (See National Association of Pension Funds.)

Sale and Leaseback   This involves selling the freehold of a property owned by a business to a financial institution, which agrees to grant you a lease on the premises.

The lender will want to be sure that you can afford the lease, so a profit track record will probably be needed, and all expenses involved in the negotiations are met by the borrower. The borrower then has the use of the value of the asset in immediate cash to plough into the business.

The tax aspects of sale and leaseback are complex and work more in the favour of some types of business than others, so professional advice is essential before entering into any arrangement.

As with other forms of finance, it is a competitive market and a few 'quotes' are worth getting.

Trade Credit   Once you have established creditworthiness, it may be possible to take advantage of the trade credit extended by suppliers. This usually takes the form of allowing you anything from seven days to three months from receiving the goods, before having to pay for them.

You will have to weigh carefully the benefit of taking this credit against the cost of losing any cash discounts offered. For example, if you are offered a 2.5% discount for a cash settlement, then this is a saving of £25 for every £1,000 of purchases. If the alternative is to take six weeks' credit, then the saving is the cost of borrowing that sum from, say, your bank on overdraft. So if your bank interest is 16% per annum, that is equivalent to 0.31% per week. Six weeks would save you 1.85%. On £1,000 of purchase you would only save £18.50 of bank interest. This means that the cash discount is more attractive. However, you may not have the cash or overdraft facility, so your choice is restricted.

Bill Financing   This is rather like a post-dated cheque which can be sold to a third party for cash, but at a discount. Once you have despatched the goods concerned to your customer you can draw a trade bill to be accepted by him on a certain date. This, in effect, is a commitment by him to settle his account on that date, and he is not expected to pay until then. You can sell this bill to a bank or a discount house and receive immediate cash. Of course, you have to pay for this service. Payment takes the form of a discount on the face value of the bill, usually directly related to the creditworthiness of your customer. It has several advantages as a source of short-term finance.

Firstly, it is usually competitive with bank overdrafts. Secondly, you can accurately calculate the cost of financing a transaction, because the discount rate is fixed and not subject to interest rate fluctuations. This is particularly important if the time between despatch of the goods and payment by the customer is likely to be several months. Thirdly, by using bill finance, you can free up overdraft facilities for other purposes. For example, you can get on with making up more products for other customers – something you may not have been able to do if you were waiting for the last customer to pay.

Factoring   This is an arrangement which allows you to receive up to 80% of the cash due from your customers more quickly than they would normally pay. The factoring company buys your trade debts and provides a debtor accounting and administration service. In other words, it takes over the day-to-day work of invoicing and sending out reminders and statements. This can be a particularly helpful service to a small expanding business. It can allow the management to concentrate on growing the business, with the factoring company providing expert guidance on credit control, 100% protection against bad debts, and improved cash flow.

You will, of course, have to pay for factoring services. Having the cash before your customers pay will cost you a little more than normal overdraft rates. The factoring service will cost between 0.5% and 3.5% of turnover, depending on volume of work, the number of debtors, average invoice amount and other related factors. You can get up to 80% of the value of your invoice in advance with the remainder paid when your customer settles up, less the various charges just mentioned.

If you sell direct to the public, sell complex and expensive capital equipment or expect progress payments on a long-term project, then factoring is not for you.

If you are expanding more rapidly than other sources of finance will allow, then this may be a useful service. All other things being equal, it should be possible to find a factor if your turnover exceeds £25,000 per annum, though the larger firm will look for around £100,000 as the economic cut-off point.

Invoice Discounting   This is a variation of factoring open to businesses with a net worth of £30,000. Unlike factoring, where all your debtors are sold to the factor, in this service only selected invoices are offered. This can be particularly useful if you have a few relatively large orders to reputable, 'blue chip' type customers in your general order book.

Up to 75% of the value of the invoices can be advanced, but you remain responsible for collecting the money from your customers. This you forward to the discounting company, who in turn sends you the balance less a charge on the assigned invoices. This charge will be made up of two elements. You will pay interest on the cash advanced for the period between the date of the advance and your refunding the discount company. You will also have to pay a factoring charge of between 0.5 and 0.75%.

The twist is that, if your customer does not pay up, you have to repay the discount house their advance. Unlike normal factoring, however, your customer will never know that you discounted his invoice.

Export Finance   This is a specialist subject in itself. The range of possibilities open to the exporter is described in considerable detail in the Bank of England booklet referred to at the end of this section. The central feature of most forms of export financing is ECGD (Export Credits Guarantee Department) credit insurance. This is a government-backed credit insurance policy that gives cover against the failure of your foreign customers either to take up the goods you have despatched or to pay them. The cover includes loss caused by war and trade sanctions. Although the government themselves do not provide export finance, ECGD credit insurance will put you in a highly favourable position with, for example, your bank. They in turn would be able to provide finance with a greater degree of security than they could normally expect. (ECGD addresses are at the end of the section.)

Some banks, notably the Midland, operate a Smaller Exporters Scheme providing ECGD-backed post-shipment finance for small exporters who may find it uneconomic to take out an ECGD policy on their own. In certain cases, an Export house may be willing to manage your overseas business for you, acting as your agent in finding customers, or even as a merchant actually buying the goods from you for re-sale in certain overseas markets.

Import Finance   This includes such elements as a produce or merchandise advance. In this case the imported goods themselves are offered as security for a loan. There are some obvious limitations on the type of goods that could be accepted. Fruit and vegetables, and other perishable goods or commodities in volatile markets are excluded. However, under the right circumstances up to 80% of the value of sold goods and 50% of unsold goods can be realised in cash quite quickly.

Leasing   This is a way of getting the use of vehicles, plant and equipment without paying the full cost at once. Operating leases are taken out where you will use the equipment for less than its full economic life – for example, a car, photocopier or vending machine. The lessor takes the risk of the equipment becoming obsolete and assumes responsibility for repairs, maintenance and insurance. As you, the lessee, are paying for this service, it is more expensive than a Finance lease, where you lease the equipment for most of its economic life and maintain and insure it yourself.

Leases can normally be extended, often for fairly nominal sums, in the later years.

The obvious attractions of leasing are that no deposit is needed leaving your working capital for more profitable use elsewhere. Also, the cost of leasing is known from the start, making forward planning more simple.

Hire Purchase   This differs from leasing in that you have the option at the start to become the owner of the equipment after a series of payments have been made. The interest is usually fixed and often more expensive than a bank loan. However, manufacturers (notably car makers) often subsidise this interest, so it pays to shop around both for sources of HP finance and manufacturers of equipment.

Private Equity Finance   This is only relevant if your business is or is shortly to become a limited company, and it refers to the sale of ordinary shares to investors. Unlike other forms of 'borrowing', where interest has to be paid whether or not the business makes a profit, shares usually only attract a dividend when the business is profitable.

This makes it extremely important to get as large an equity base as possible at the outset. Although it does mean giving up some control, you may gain some valuable business expertise, and your reputation can be enhanced if the investors are respected themselves.

Apart from equity finance you provide yourself, you can attract outside investment from outside sources.

Individuals Unlike publicly quoted companies, which have a stock exchange facility, you will have to find investors yourself. Recent tax changes – in particular, those incorporated in the Government's 'Business Expansion Scheme' (described below) – have made it attractive for high taxpayers to invest in new business. Several organisations have been established to acquire such funds and find suitable investments.

Institutions Such as 3i's, subsidiaries of the clearing banks and venture capital organisations, provide equity capital, usually for companies with exceptionally high growth potential. In general, equity financing from people other than those known well by you is the most difficult to raise.

The Business Expansion Scheme   Introduced in April 1983, replaces the Business Start Up Scheme. It is designed to make it attractive for UK income taxpayers to invest in new or growing businesses. It is now intended to run indefinitely.

The investors at whom the scheme is aimed are UK taxpayers who are not connected with the business they are going to invest in. They cannot be paid directors or employees of the business, nor can they own more than 30% of the business. They could, however, be unpaid directors or take fees for professional services. The investor gets tax relief on up to £40,000 invested in any one year. The minimum investment is £500 and the funds must be left in for at least five years. The effect of this scheme is that a top-rate taxpayer could be putting as little as £6,000 of his own money into a business in return for a £10,000 share, the balance being effectively paid by the Inland Revenue. Your solicitor, accountant or bank manager may be able to put you in touch with interested individuals.

Alternatively, a number of financial institutions are offering 'portfolio' facilities to investors. This means that investors put their funds into an approved organisation which seeks out potential investment opportunities on their behalf. This spreads their risk, and gives them the benefit of 'professional' management.

Many of the institutions keep a 'register' of business proposals that they have not invested in. People with funds can use the register to seek out private investment opportunities. So it is well worth sending your business plan.

Public Equity Finance   1983 saw the establishment of the Unlisted Securities Market (USM), followed by the Third Market in 1987, as major sources of finance for small and growing companies. These markets work in a similar way to the Stock Exchange, in offering shares to a wide public market. There is no minimum size for a company looking for such a Quote, although a three year track record is expected. Under certain conditions the Stock Exchange will let a completely new venture come in. A company entering the market in this way can expect to pay expenses of between 5% and 10% of the amount raised.

To find out more contact either the Stock Exchange, or a stockbroker.

Venture Capital   This is start-up capital usually associated with businesses involved in technological and technical innovation. The sums involved are usually up to £100,000 over periods of five years or more. With this capital usually comes management expertise, often in the form of a board member from the financial institution. So you are going to have to be able to work with him, and probably give a personal guarantee for the sums involved.

Perhaps the greatest benefit coming from the provider of venture capital is their expertise at keeping your financial structure in line with your changing needs.

Development Capital   These are funds to help established firms grow and diversify. Like venture capital, the period involved is five years or so, and the investing institution expects to be able to sell its stake either to the directors or possibly through an eventual Stock Exchange quotation. Generally you will need to have a pre-tax profit of £30,000 per annum and be looking for more than £50,000 additional finance. The investor will want to put a director on your board – as much to help you and the company as to keep an eye on its investment.

Management Buy-Outs   This is not a type of money. It is however an increasingly popular activity that involves the existing managers of a business buying out the business from its owners. As both the business and the managers will have a 'track record', it may be easier to find equity finance for such ventures; an increasing number of financing organisations have moved into this field.

Public Sector Sources   These include central and local government, certain agencies and EEC funds. There are many different types of funds available, with differing types of eligibility. In the main, they are concentrated on providing regional and local assistance, encouragement for specific industries, ranging from agriculture to encouraging tourism in Wales; and assistance for specific purposes such as research and development, employment or exporting. The booklet Financial Incentives and Assistance for Industry referred to at the end of this section covers this subject comprehensively.

Individual schemes of particular relevance and importance to small businesses are explained under the appropriate sponsoring bodies heading, in the section headed 'Where you can get the money'.

WHERE YOU CAN GET THE MONEY

There are now several hundred institutions that provide start-up and development capital for new and small businesses. They are clustered into a score or so groups, usually called 'houses'. Some of them, as their names imply, provide only one type of finance. However, in the main, they cover a spread of the different types. The functions of each 'house' are briefly described, before their main members are listed.

For most of us, borrowing money usually means either a visit or a letter to our local bank manager. Although he is by no means the only source of finance for a new or small business, the local bank manager is a good starting point.

Clearing Banks This is the general name given to the high street bankers. We immediately think of the big four banks – Barclays, Lloyds, Midland and the National Westminster – when we think of 'clearers'. However, there are another dozen or so that fit within the general meaning of 'clearing and domestic deposit bank'.

The banks offer a wide range of services in their own right. Through wholly or partially owned subsidiaries they cover virtually every aspect of the financial market. These services include overdrafts, term loans, trade bill finance, factoring, leasing, export and import finance, the Government Loan Guarantee Scheme, and equity financing.

In addition to providing a source of funds, the clearing banks have considerable expertise in the areas of tax, insurance and financial advice generally. Very little of this expertise will rest in your local branch office. The bank's regional and main head offices are where these centralised services are provided.

As you probably already have a bank account, this may be your starting point in looking for money for business. Do not forget, however, that the banks are in competition with one another and with other lenders. So shop around if you do not get what you want first time. Incidentally their charges to commercial customers vary too, so ask for figures before signing up.

The banks are becoming quite adventurous in their competition for new and small business accounts, and now all the clearers offer some special inducement to attract new small business accounts. For example, the Co-operative Bank offers free banking, even to companies with an overdraft, provided it is kept within agreed limits.

Some of the banks have a small firms specialist, one of whose tasks is to help new, small business clients get the best out of their banking services. To get an opinion from one of these specialists would be a good way of finding the possibilities of getting finance and how best to go about it.

Clearing and Other Domestic Deposit Banks

Allied Irish Banks Ltd, 64/66 Coleman Street, London EC2R 5AL (01 588 0691) *Contact: Declan Flynn*

Bank of Ireland, 36 Queen Street, London EC4R 1BN (01 329 4500) *Contact: Area Manager*

Bank of Scotland, PO Box 725, Orchard Brae House, 30 Queensferry Road, Edinburgh EH4 2NU (031 339 3758) *Contact: David MacLaren*

Barclays Bank plc, Corporate Division, Corporate Marketing, 54 Lombard Street, London EC3P 3AH (01 626 1567) *Contact: Peter Clark*

Clydesdale Bank plc, (a member of the Midland Banking Group) 30 St Vincent Place, Glasgow G1 2HL (041 248 7070) *Contact: A. K. Denholm*

Co-operative Bank plc, 1 Balloon Street, Manchester M60 4EP (061 832 6262) *Contact: J. Cowburn*

Coutts & Co, (a member of the National Westminster Bank Group) 440 Strand, London WC2R 1QS (01 379 6262) *Contact: A. Beale and J. Lucas*

Girobank plc, 10 Milk Street, London EC2V 8JH (01 600 6020) *Contact: David Barber*

Lloyds Bank plc, Head Office, PO Box 215, 71 Lombard Street, London EC3P 3BS (01 626 1500) *Contact: R. I. Bardell*

Midland Bank plc, Small Business Unit, Mariner House, Pepys Street, London EC3N 4DA (01 260 7954) *Contact: Stuart White*

National Westminster Bank plc, Domestic Banking Division, Commercial Banking Services, 8th Floor, Finsbury Court, 101–107 Finsbury Pavement, London EC2A 1EH (01 726 1000) *Contact: Andy Lord and Malcolm Keeping*

Northern Bank Ltd, (a member of the Midland Bank Group) Corporate Finance Department, PO Box 183, Donegall Square West, Belfast BT1 6JS (0232 245277) *Contact: A. O'Hanlon*

The Royal Bank of Scotland, PO Box 183, 42 St Andrews Square, Edinburgh EH2 2YE (031 556 8555) *Contact: J. Byers*

Ulster Bank Ltd, (a member of National Westminster Bank Group) 35–39 Waring Street, Belfast BT1 2ER (0232 235232) *Contact: T. McCurly*

Yorkshire Bank plc, 20 Merrion Way, Leeds LS2 8NZ (0532 441244) *Contact: D. Mortimer*

British Merchant Banking and Securities Houses

Association Formerly the Accepting Houses, provide some or all of these services: domestic and international banking; credit finance, export credits, leasing, debt factoring, medium term finance, buyouts and some development capital for the small firm. They are unlikely to be interested in propositions for amounts less than £50,000, but they are worth a try. The Accepting Houses Committee is at Granite house, 101 Cannon Street, London EC4N 5BA (01 283 7332)

Baring Brothers & Co Ltd, 8 Bishopsgate, London EC2N 4AE (01 283 8833)

Brown, Shipley & Co Ltd, Founders Court, Lothbury, London EC2R 7HE (01 606 9833)

Charterhouse Bank Ltd, 1 Paternoster Row, St Pauls, London EC4M 7DH (01 248 4000)

Robert Fleming & Co Ltd, 25 Copthall Avenue, EC2R 7DR (01 638 5858)

Guinness Mahon & Co Ltd, 32 St Mary at Hill, London EC3P 3AJ (01 623 9333)

Hambros Bank Ltd, 41 Tower Hill, London EC3N 4HA (01 480 5000)

Hill Samuel & Co Ltd, PO Box 20, 100 Wood Street, London EC2P 2AJ (01 628 8011)

Kleinwort Benson Ltd, PO Box 560, 20 Fenchurch Street, London EC3P 3DB (01 623 8000)

Lazard Brothers & Co Ltd, PO Box 516, 21 Moorfields, London EC2P 2HT (01 588 2721)

Samuel Montagu & Co Ltd, 10 Lower Thames Street, London EC3R 6AE (01 260 9000)

Morgan Grenfell & Co Ltd, PO Box 56, 23 Great Winchester Street, London EC2P 2AX (01 588 4545)

Rea Brothers Ltd, Alderman's House, Alderman's Walk, London EC2M 3XR (01 623 1155)

N. M. Rothschild & Sons Ltd, PO Box 185, New Court, St Swithin's Lane, London EC4P 4DU (01 280 5000)

J. Henry Schroder Wagg & Co Ltd, 120 Cheapside, London EC2V 6DS (01 382 6000)

Singer & Friedlander Ltd, 21 New Street, Bishopsgate, London EC2M 4HR (01 623 3000)

S. G. Warburg & Co Ltd, 33 King William Street, London EC4R 9AS (01 280 2222)

Discount Houses These are the specialist institutions that provide bill financing. There are eight members of the London Discount Market Association, whose Honorary Secretary is Mr S. J. Dare, 39 Cornhill, London EC3V 3NU (01 623 1020). Bill financing is a bit of a long shot as a source of finance for a small business. Although bills may be as little as a few thousand pounds, the average is nearer £25,000. Nevertheless, given a good proposition, discount houses will be happy to listen. Quin Cope & Co Ltd may be the most responsive at the small end of the bill market.

Alexanders Discount plc, 65 Cornhill, London EC3V 3PP (01 626 5467)

Cater Allen Ltd, 1 King William Street, London EC4N 7AU (01 623 2070)

Clive Discount Company Ltd, 1 Royal Exchange Avenue, London EC3V 3LU (01 283 1101)

Gerrard & National Ltd, 33 Lombard Street, London EC3V 9BQ (01 623 9981)

King & Shaxon Ltd, 52 Cornhill, London EC3V 3PD (01 623 5433)

Quin Cope & Co Ltd, 150 Leadenhall Street, London EC3V 4SD (01 626 2121)

Seccombe Marshall & Campion plc, 7 Birchin Lane, London EC3V 9DE (01 283 5031)

Union Discount Co Ltd, 39 Cornhill, London EC3V 3NU (01 623 1020)

Export Houses There are some 800 export houses operating in the UK, offering almost every service possible to exporters and foreign importers. Some 230 of them belong to the British Export Houses Association, and they are actively interested in working with small firms.

Three types of company will find an export house particularly useful: those that are considering exporting for the first time; secondly, those that want to expand outside their existing overseas markets; and thirdly, those that have to extend credit to their customers to a greater extent than they are willing or able to do (this may be to meet competition or currency problems).

Export houses are specialists in financing and servicing exports and are divided into four main types.

Export agents and managers sell a manufacturer's goods in selected countries where they have expert knowledge. They work very closely with their clients, and can in effect become the manufacturer's own export department. This can save a small company money and provide a greater level of expertise than could realistically be afforded. Payment for these services is usually by commission, but sometimes a retainer or even a profit-sharing scheme can be used.

Confirming houses, buying or independent houses and stores buyers work as follows. Confirming houses represent foreign buyers in the UK and can confirm, as a principal, an order placed by that buyer with a British supplier. Buying or independent houses buy, pay for and ship goods for their overseas principals. A stores buyer is a particular type of buying house dealing only with departmental stores. Being linked to such houses costs you nothing but can open up many new overseas markets for your products.

Merchants, as the word implies, both buy and sell as a principal. They specialise in certain products and markets. One of the largest sells in 120 different countries. Others operate in a much narrower sphere. Dealing with a merchant is little different from selling in the UK and, even better, there is no credit risk.

Finance houses can provide you with non-resource finance and allow your foreign buyer time to pay. This gives the exporter absolute security and makes the deal attractive to an overseas buyer. Normally only the foreign buyer pays a commission for the service.

The British Export Houses Association, 16 Dartmouth Street, Westminster, London SW1H 9BL (01 222 5419) is the best starting point for contacting an export house. The association secretary is Mr H. W. Bailey. They provide a Directory of British Export Houses, which tells you all about each house and its particular expertise. Last edition was brought out in 1986/87 and a new edition will be released in 1990. Alternatively you can include full details of your requirements in the association's monthly Export Enquiry circular. This will cost £25.00 plus VAT for the first insertion, and £10.00 plus VAT for each repeat. The circular goes to all members and is considered to be a very effective way of communicating quickly in a rapidly changing environment.

Some export houses:

Adam & Harvey Ltd, 15/16 Bonhill Street, London EC2P 2EA (01 628 7711)
Balfour Williamson & Co Ltd, Roman House, Wood Street, London EC2Y 5BP (01 638 6191)

British Markitex Ltd, PO Box 52, Deneway House, Potters Bar, Herts EN5 1AH (0707 57281)

Coutinho Caro & Co Ltd, Walker House, 87 Queen Victoria Street, London EC4V 4AL (01 236 1505)

Dalgety Export Services Division, St Dunstan House, 201 Borough High Street, London SE1 1HX (01 407 4400)

Inchcape Exports Ltd, Sir John Lyon House, 5 High Timber Street, Upper Thames Street, London EC4V 3JC (01 248 1995)

W. H. Jones & Co (London) Ltd, Tower House, 17 Oakleigh Park North, London N20 9AP (01 445 5006)

Keep Brothers Ltd, PO Box 48, The Rotunda, New Street, Birmingham B2 4NQ (021 631 2211)

Lewis & Peat (Merchanting) Ltd, 32 St Mary at Hill, Eastcheap, London EC3P 3AJ (01 623 6222)

Matheson & Co Ltd, 142 Minories, London EC3N 1QL (01 528 4000)

Scholefield Goodman & Sons Ltd, 135 Edmund Street, Birmingham B3 2HS (021 236 7471)

UAC International Ltd, Brandon House, 180 Borough High Street, London SE1 1LR (01 378 0656)

United City Merchants Ltd, UCM House, 3/5 Swallow Place, London W1A 1BB (01 629 8424)

Some finance houses:

Brownjohn & Howard, 5 The Drive, Hove, East Sussex BN3 3JE (0273 778408)

Charterhouse Bank Ltd, 1 Paternoster Row, St Paul's, London EC4M 7DH (01 248 4000)

Grindlay Brandts Export Finance plc, Minerva House, Montague Close, London SE1 9DH (01 378 2121)

Manufacturers Hanover Export Finance Ltd, City Tower, 40 Basinghall Street, London EC2V 5DE (01 600 5666)

Trade Finance International Ltd, 50 Gresham Street, London EC2V 7A (01 606 3000)

Factoring Companies These financial institutions provide a full sales accounting service, often including credit management and insurance against bad debts. Factoring Companies have reported significant increases in business in recent years. The Association of British Factors is at Hind Court, 147 Fleet Street, London EC4A 2BU (01 353 1213).

ABF members charge between 0.75 and 2.5% of gross turnover for the sales ledger package and around bank overdraft rate for finance charges. They will advance about 80% of invoice price almost immediately the invoice is raised. They generally only consider customers with £100,000 per annum turnover, but may consider good cases from £50,000.

Members of the Association of British Factors:

Alex Lawrie Factors Ltd, (Shareholder: Lloyds Bank plc) Beaumont House, Beaumont Road, Banbury, Oxford OX16 7RN (0295 67788)

Arbuthnot Factors Ltd, (Shareholders: Arbuthnot Latham Bank Ltd and Yorkshire Bank) Arbuthnot House, Breeds Place, Hastings, East Sussex TN34 3DG (0424 430824)

Century Factors Ltd, (Shareholders: Close Brothers Group and management) Southbrook House, 25 Bartholomew Street, Newbury, Berks RG14 5LL (0635 31703)

Credit Factoring International Ltd, (Shareholders: National Westminster Bank plc) Smith House, PO Box 50, Elmwood Avenue, Feltham, Middx TW13 7QD (01 890 1390)

Griffin Factors Ltd, (Shareholders: Midland Bank plc) 21 Farncombe Road, Worthing, West Sussex BN11 2BW (0903 205181)

H&H Factors Ltd, (Shareholders: Heller Ltd and Hambros Bank) Randolph House, 46/48 Wellesley Road, Croydon, Surrey CR9 3PS (01 681 2641)

International Factors Ltd, (Shareholders: Lloyds Bank) PO Box 240, Sovereign House, Queen's Road, Brighton, Sussex BN1 3WZ (0273 21211)

Security Pacific Business Finance (Europe) Ltd, (Shareholders: Security Pacific EuroFinance Inc) 126 Dyke Road, Brighton, Sussex BN1 1TE (0273 21177)

UDT Commercial Finance Ltd, (Shareholders: TSB Group) Boston House, The Little Green, Richmond, Surrey TW9 1QE (01 940 4646)

Invoice Factors

The Association of Invoice Factors, 109/113 Royal Avenue, Belfast BT1 1FF (0232 224522), *Mr A. M. Selig.* This may be a better bet for a small business. Their members' average client has a turnover of £100,000 per annum, and they would be prepared to look at propositions from £1,000 per month gross sales value. They advance 70 to 80% of the value of the invoice, and charge between 0.5 and 3.5% for maintaining the sales ledger. Between advancing you the money and getting it in from your client, their financing rate charges are similar to overdraft rates.

Members of the Association of Invoice Factors:

Anpal Finance Ltd, PO Box 37, Kimberley House, Vaughan Way, Leicester LE1 9AZ (0533 516006)

Bibby Financial Services Ltd, Norwich House, Water Street, Liverpool L2 8UW (051 236 0492)

Borg-Warner Financial Services Ltd, 18 Market Place, Hitchin, Herts SG5 1DS (0462 31541)

Clifton Mercantile Co Ltd, 115 Gloucester Place, London W1H 3PJ (01 486 0541)

Gaelic Invoice Factors Ltd, Finlay House, 10-14 West Nile Street, Glasgow G1 2PP (041 248 4901)

Hayes Securities Ltd, 17 Mount Ephraim, Tunbridge Wells, Kent TN4 8AE (0892 40815)

Hogg-Poynton Factors Ltd, 129 Wellington Road South, Stockport, Cheshire SK1 3TS (061 477 1470)

Kintyre Securities Ltd, The Computer Centre, Benmhor, Campeltown, Argyll PA28 6DN (0586 54488)

London Wall Factors Ltd, Barkhill House, Shire lane, Chorleywood, Herts WD3 5NR (09278 5199/4133)

Ulster Factors Ltd, 113 Royal Avenue, Belfast BT1 1FF (0232 324522)

Leasing Companies These may be a little more adventurous in dealing with new and small businesses than other sources of finance. The Equipment Leasing Association is the main organisation in this field. It is located at 18 Upper Grosvenor Street, London W1X 6PB (01 491 2783).

Most leasing companies are subsidiaries of much larger financial institutions, including the clearing banks. Some of them operate in specialist markets. Many would not look at anything under £1 million. A phone call to the association will put you in touch with a selection of appropriate companies. Three companies that have a spread of business between a few hundred pounds and £50,000 are Anglo Leasing, First Co-operative Finance and Schroder Leasing.

Allied Irish Finance Company Ltd, (A member of Allied Irish Banks Group) Wembley Hill House, 10–12 Neeld Parade, Wembley Hill Road, Wembley, Middx HA9 6QU (01 903 1383) *Contact: N. Osgood*

Anglo Leasing plc, (A subsidiary of J. Rothschild Holdings plc) Anglo House, 2 Clerkenwell Green, London EC1R 0DH (01 253 4300) *Contact: L. Silman*

ANZ Finance Ltd, (A member of the ANZ Group) Minerva House, PO Box 7, Montague Close, London SE1 9DH (01 378 2121) *Contact: C. Gordon*

Arbuthnot Leasing International Ltd, (A subsidiary of Arbuthnot Latham Bank Ltd) 131 Finsbury Pavement, Moorgate, London EC2A 1AY (01 628 9876) *Contact: R. Butler*

Atlantic Computer Systems Ltd, Winchmore House, Fetter Lane, London EC4A 1BR (01 583 9481) *Contact: N. K. Scott*

BAII Leasing Ltd, (A member of the BAII Group) 1 London Bridge, London SE1 9QU (01 378 7070) *Contact: S. Udale*

Banque Paribas, 68 Lombard Street, London EC3V 9EH (01 929 4545) *Contact: Alison J. Stokes*

Barclays Mercantile Industrial Finance Ltd, (A member of the Barclays Bank Group) Elizabethan House, Great Queen Street, London WC2B 5DP (01 242 1234) *Contact: B. C. Hassell*

Baring Brothers & Co Ltd, 8 Bishopsgate, London EC2N 4AE (01 283 8833) *Contact: A. B. Swann*

BNP Finance Ltd, (A subsidiary of Banque Nationale de Paris) 8–13 King William Street, London EC4P 4HS (01 626 5678) *Contact: M. S. Harland*

Boston Leasing Ltd, (A subsidiary of the First National Bank of Boston) Bank of Boston House, 5 Cheapside, London EC2P 2DE (01 236 2388) *Contact: P. Burrows-Smith*

British Credit Trust Ltd, (A Bank of Ireland Company) British Credit House, 34 High Street, Slough SL1 1ED (0753 74211) *Contact: T. G. O'Neill*

BUHAL Leasing Ltd, (A subsidiary of Banco Hispano Americano Ltd which is a member of the Banco Hispano Americano Group) 15 Austin Friars, London EC2N 2DJ (01 628 4499) *Contact: R. Soper*

Capital Leasing Ltd, (A member of the Bank of Scotland group) 4 Melville Street, Edinburgh EH3 7NZ (031 453 1919) *Contact: A. D. Nichol*

Carolina Leasing Ltd, (A subsidiary of Carolina Bank Ltd) 26 Austin Friars, London EC2N 2EH (01 588 9133) *Contact: A. C. Moir*

Chartered Trust plc, (A subsidiary of Standard Chartered plc) 24/26 Newport Road, Cardiff CF2 1SR (0222 473000) *Contact: A. C. Webb*

Citicorp, Cottons Centre, Hays Lane, London SE1 2QT (01 234 5678) *Contact: M. Fewings*

City Leasing Ltd, (A member of the Morgan Grenfell Group) 23 Great Winchester Street, London EC2P 2AX (01 588 4545) *Contact: R. M. Maslinski*

Combined Lease Finance plc, The Quadrant, 4 Clifton Street, London EC2A 4BT (01 247 5463) *Contact: A. R. Barnes*

Concord Leasing Ltd, Concord House, 61 High Street, Brentford, Middx TW8 0AA (01 568 3321) *Contact: K. J. Salsbury*

Continental Illinois National Bank & Trust Co of Chicago, 162 Queen Victoria Street, London EC4V 4BS (01 236 7444) *Contact: D. Kileforth*

Corporate Funding Ltd, (A subsidiary of Hoogovens UK Ltd and a member of the Hoogovens Groep BV) Carrier House, Warwick Row, London SW1E 5ER (01 828 5656) *Contact: T. Shaw*

CPS Leasing Ltd, (A subsidiary of CPS Computer Group plc) Marble House, Cocksparrow Street, Warwick CV34 4ED (0926 496291)

Dataserv Ltd, (A subsidiary of Dataserv Inc) Queen Anne's Court, Windsor, Berks SL4 1DG (0753 868133) *Contact: P. N. Sampson*

DNC Leasing Services Ltd, (A subsidiary of Den norske Creditbank plc) 20 St Dunstan's Hill, London EC3R 8HY (01 621 1111) *Contact: S. G. Smith*

Eastlease Ltd, (A member of the Norwich Union Insurance Group) 8 Surrey Street, Norwich, Norfolk NR1 3ST (0603 622200) *Contact: P. Phillips*

ELCO Leasing Ltd, (A consortium leasing company managed by Hambros Bank Ltd for the shareholders Allied Breweries UK Ltd, Allders Ltd, Hambros Leasing Ltd) 41 Bishopsgate, London EC2P 3AA (01 588 2851) *Contact: A. G. Mallin*

First Co-operative Finance Ltd, (A member of the Co-operative Bank Group) 1 Balloon Street, Manchester M60 4EP (061 832 3300) *Contact: M. Cluett*

Forward Trust Group Ltd, (A subsidiary of Midland Bank plc) Crown House, 145 City Road, London EC1V 1J (01 251 9090) *Contact: A. Outten*

Girobank plc, 10 Milk Street, London EC2V 8JH (01 600 6020) *Contact: R. W. Rumins*

GKN Sankey Finance Ltd, (A member of the GKN group of companies) PO Box 6, Dudley Street, Bilston, West Midlands WV14 0JF (0902 405261) *Contact: D. C. Smart*

Guinness Mahon Leasing Ltd, PO Box 442, 32 St Mary at Hill, London EC3P 3AJ (01 623 9333) *Contact: Mrs S. Goodsell*

Hambros Leasing Ltd, 41 Tower Hill, London EC3N 4HA (01 480 5000) *Contact: A. G. Malin*

Hewlett Packard Finance Ltd, Miller House, The Ring, Bracknell, Berks RG12 1XN (0344 424898) *Contact: J. A. Pearson*

Hill Samuel Leasing Co Ltd, (A member of the Hill Samuel Group) 100 Wood Street, London EC2P 2AJ (01 628 8011) *Contact: J. Hirsch*

IBL plc, Wentworth House, 1 Station Parade, Virginia Water, Surrey GU25 4BD (0990 23344) *Contact: G. R. Rozwadowski*

IBM UK Financial Services Ltd, PO Box 41, North Harbour, Portsmouth, Hampshire PO6 3AU (0705 321212) *Contact: P. R. Nichols*

Investors in Industry plc, (3i Asset Finance) 91 Waterloo Road, London SE1 8XP (01 928 7822) *Contact: Miss J. E. Cunningham*

Kleinwort Benson Ltd, 20 Fenchurch Street, London EC3P 3DB (01 623 8000) *Contact: D. R. Soper*

Landhurst Leasing Ltd, 6/7 Queen Street, London EC4N 1SP (01 236 8702/6) *Contact: E. J. Ball*

Lazard Equipment Leasing Ltd, (A subsidiary of Lazard Brothers & Co Ltd) 21 Moorfields, London EC2P 2HT (01 588 2721) *Contact: I. Wiseman*

Lease Plan UK Ltd, (A subsidiary of Lease Plan Holding NV) Thames Side, Windsor, Berks SL4 1TY (0753 868268) *Contact: N. J. Donkin*

Lloyds Leasing Ltd, (A member of the Lloyds Bank Group) 57 Southwark Street, London SE1 1SH (01 403 1600) *Contact: W. R. Fullelove*

Lombard North Central plc, (A subsidiary of National Westminster Bank plc) Lombard House, 3 Princess Way, Redhill, Surrey RH1 1NP (0737 774111) *Contact: J. G. Woodhouse*

Manex Leasing Ltd, (A member of the Manchester Exchange group of companies) Pembroke House, 40 City Road, London EC1Y 2AX (01 251 9261) *Contact: A. C. L. Brown*

Milestone Leasing Ltd, (A member of the EXCO International Group plc) Warnford Court, Throgmorton Street, London EC2N 2AU (01 638 4191) *Contact: J. Brunyate*

Samuel Montagu Leasing Services Ltd, (A subsidiary of Samuel Montagu & Co Ltd) 10 Lower Thames Street, London EC3R 6AE (01 260 9000) *Contact: T. J. W. Botham*

North West Securities Ltd, (A member of the Bank of Scotland group) North West House, City Road, Chester CH1 3AN (0244 690000) *Contact: J. S. Brown*

Orient Leasing (UK) Ltd, (A subsidiary of Orient Leasing Co Ltd in Japan) Centric House, 391 Strand, London WC2R 0LT (01 831 1455) *Contact: T. Sato*

Orion Leasing Ltd, (A member of the Royal Bank of Canada group) 1 London Wall, London EC2Y 5JX (01 600 6222) *Contact: W. C. Thompson*

P B Leasing Ltd, (A subsidiary of Pitney Bowes Incorporated) Aviation House, 129 Kingsway, London WC2B 6NH (01 404 5555) *Contact: F. V. Shapland*

Rea Brothers Leasing Ltd, Alderman's House, Alderman's Walk, London EC2M 3XR (01 623 1155) *Contact: R. Y. Birley*

Royal Bank Leasing Ltd, (A member of the Royal Bank of Scotland group) 67 Lombard Street, London EC3P 3DL (01 623 4356) *Contact: C. R. Freeborough*

St Michael Finance Ltd, (A subsidiary of Marks & Spencer plc) Michael House, Baker Street, London W1A 1DN (01 935 4422) *Contact: R. C. Gale*

Saturn Leasing Ltd, PO Box 180, Ferroners House, Shaftesbury Place, London EC2Y 8AJ (01 236 1261) *Contact: P. L. Clein*

Saudi International Bank, 99 Bishopsgate, London EC2M 3TB (01 638 2323) *Contact: H. R. Chaplin*

Scandinavian Leasing Ltd, (A subsidiary of Scandinavian Bank Ltd) 2/6 Cannon Street, London EC4M 6XX (01 236 6090) *Contact: S. Northage*

Schroder Leasing Ltd, (A member of the Schroders group of companies) Townsend House, 160 Northolt Road, Harrow, Middx HA2 0PG (01 422 7101) *Contact: B. D. Bullimore*

Shawlands Securities Ltd, (A member of the Frizzell Group Ltd) 8 Christchurch Road, Bournemouth BH1 3NQ (0202 295544) *Contact: R. A. Matthews*

SocGen Lease Ltd, (A member of the Société Générale Banking Group) 13–17 Long Lane, London EC1A 9PN (01 726 6040) *Contact: P. W. West*

Sovereign Leasing plc, Central Buildings, 211 Deansgate, Manchester M3 3NW (061 834 1582) *Contact: M. B. Richards*

Stakis Finance Ltd, (A subsidiary of Stakis plc) 244 Buchanan Street, Glasgow G1 2NB (041 333 0848) *Contact: J. W. Moore*

Standard Chartered Merchant Bank Ltd, (A subsidiary of Standard Chartered plc) 33–36 Gracechurch Street, London EC3V 0AX (01 623 8711) *Contact: J. W. Gratwick*

TSB England & Wales Asset Finance Ltd, (A member of the TSB group) 60 Lombard Street, London EC3V 9EA (01 600 6000) *Contact: A. W. Jukes*

Union Discount Leasing Ltd, (A subsidiary of the Union Discount Company of London plc) 39 Cornhill, London EC3V 3NU (01 623 1020) *Contact: R. M. Munro*

United Dominions Trust Ltd, (A member of the TSB group) Holbrook House, 116 Cockfosters Road, Cockfosters, Herts EN4 0DY (01 449 5533) *Contact: G. W. Robinson*

United Leasing plc, International House, 7 High Street, Ealing, London W5 5DB (01 840 7874) *Contact: S. Geneen*

U S Leasing Ltd, (A member of the United States Leasing International Group) Gateway House, 322 Regents Park Road, London N3 2LP (01 349 4834) *Contact: G. A. Jenkins*

Wang Equipment Services Ltd, (A subsidiary of Wang Laboratories Inc) 1000 Great West Road, Brentford, Middx TW8 9HL (01 568 9200) *Contact: I. Harrison*

S. G. Warburg & Co (Leasing) Ltd, (A subsidiary of S. G. Warburg & Co Ltd) 33 King William Street, London EC4R 9AS (01 280 2222) *Contact: D. M. M. Beever*

Yorkshire Bank Lease Management Ltd, (A subsidiary of Yorkshire Bank plc) 2 Infirmary Street, Leeds LS1 2UL (0532 442511) *Contact: K. A. Webster*

Finance Houses These provide instalment credit for short-term credit facilities such as hire purchase. Their association is at 18 Upper Grosvenor Street, London W1X 9PB (01 491 2783)

Finance Houses Association Members, Hire Purchase:

Abbey National Personal Finance Ltd, (A subsidiary of Abbey National Building Society) Buckingham Road, Bletchley, Milton Keynes MK3 5LD (0908 36611)

Allied Irish Finance Co Ltd, (A subsidiary of Allied Irish Banks Ltd) Wembley Hill House, 10–12 Neeld Parade, Wembley Hill Road, Wembley, Middx HA9 6QU (01 903 1383)

Associates Capital Corporation Ltd, (A subsidiary of Associates Corporation of North America) Associates House, PO Box 200, Windsor, Berks SL4 1SW (0753 857100)

Avco Trust Ltd, (A subsidiary of Textron Corporation) Avco House, Castle Street, Reading, Berks RG1 7DW (0734 586123)

Beneficial Trust Ltd, (A subsidiary of Beneficial Corporation) Prudential House, Wellesley Road, Croydon, Surrey CR0 9XY (01 680 5096)

British Credit Trust Ltd, (A subsidiary of the Bank of Ireland) British Credit House, High Street, Slough SL1 1ED (0753 73211)

Carlyle Finance Ltd, (A subsidiary of Carlyle Trust Ltd) 31 Windsor Place, Cardiff CF1 3UR (0222 371726)

Cattle's Holdings Finance Ltd, (A subsidiary of Cattle's Holdings plc) PO Box 17, Haltemprice Court, 38 Springfield Way, Anlaby, Hull HU10 6RR (0482 564422)

Chartered Trust plc, (A subsidiary of Standard Charted Bank plc) 24–26 Newport Road, Cardiff CF2 1SR (0222 473000)

Citibank Financial Trust Ltd, (A subsidiary of Citicorp) St Martin's House, 1 Hammersmith Grove, Hammersmith, London W6 0NY (01 741 8000)

Club 24 Ltd, (A subsidiary of Next plc) Hepworth House, Claypit Lane, Leeds LS2 8AA (0532 448820)

Copleys Ltd, (A subsidiary of Rea Brothers Group plc) 14 King Street, London EC2V 8EA (01 606 1101)

Credit & Data Marketing Services Ltd, J M Centre, Old Hall Street, Liverpool L70 1AB (051 235 2475)

First Co-operative Finance Ltd, (A subsidiary of Co-operative Wholesale Society Ltd) 1 Balloon Street, Manchester M60 4EP (061 832 3300)

First National Securities Ltd, (A subsidiary of First National Finance Corporation plc) First National House, College Road, Harrow, Middx HA1 1FB (01 861 1313)

Ford Motor Credit Co Ltd, Regent House, 1 Hubert Road, Brentwood, Essex CM14 4QL (0277 224400)

Forthright Finance Ltd, (A subsidiary of Commercial Bank of Wales plc) 114–116 St Mary Street, Cardiff CF1 1XJ (0222 396131)

Forward Trust Group Ltd, (A subsidiary of Midland Bank plc) 145 City Road, London EC1V 1J (01 251 9090)

HFC Trust & Savings Ltd, (A subsidiary of Household International Inc) Cory House, The Ring, Bracknell, Berks RG12 1BL (0344 424727)

Hill Samuel Leasing Co Ltd, (A member of the Hill Samuel Group) 100 Wood Street, London EC2P 2AJ (01 628 8011)

Hitachi Credit (UK) Ltd, (A subsidiary of Hitachi Ltd) Hitachi Credit House, Stables Courtyard, Church Road, Hayes, Middx UB3 2UH (01 561 8486)

House of Fraser plc, 1 Howick Place, London SW1P 1BH (01 834 1515)

Industrial Funding Trust Ltd, (A member of Anglo Irish Bank Corporation plc) 70/74 City Road, London EC1Y 2BJ (01 253 7272)

Investors in Industry plc, 91 Waterloo Road, London SE1 8XP (01 928 7822)

JCB Credit Ltd, The Mill, Rocester, Staffordshire ST14 5JW (0889 590800)

Lloyds Bowmaker Ltd, (A subsidiary of Lloyds Bank plc) 9–13 Grosvenor Street, London W1X 9FB (01 491 3236)

Lombard North Central plc, (A subsidiary of National Westminster Bank plc) Lombard House, 3 Princess Way, Redhill, Surrey RH1 1NP (0737 774111)

London Scottish Bank plc, Arndale House, Arndale Centre, Manchester M4 3AQ (061 834 2861)

Lynn Regis Finance Ltd, (A subsidiary of Mabey Holdings Ltd) 10 Tuesday Market Place, King's Lynn, Norfolk PE30 1JL (0553 691331)

Medens Ltd, (A subsidiary of Brown Shipley & Co Ltd) Medens House, Station Way, Crawley, West Sussex RH10 1HH (0293 518877)

Mercantile Credit Co Ltd, (A subsidiary of Barclays Bank plc) Elizabethan House, Great Queen Street, London WC2B 5DP (01 242 1234)

Moorgate Mercantile Holdings plc, Moorgate House, 312 High Road, Tottenham, London N15 4BX (01 801 3361)

Nationwide Anglia Trust Ltd, (A subsidiary of Nationwide Anglia Building Society) The Old Meeting House, Lower Dagnell Street, St Albans, Herts AL3 4PC (0727 32241)

North British Finance Group Ltd, (A subsidiary of Yorkshire Bank plc) PO Box 82, Paragon House, Ferensway, Hull HU1 3BL (0482 23815)

North West Securities Ltd, (A subsidiary of the Bank of Scotland) North West House, City Road, Chester CH1 3AN (0244 690000)

RoyScot Trust Ltd, (A subsidiary of the Royal Bank of Scotland Group plc) RoyScot House, The Promenade, Cheltenham, Gloucester GL50 1PL (0242 36141)

St Michael Financial Services Ltd, (A subsidiary of Marks and Spencer plc) Michael House, 57 Baker Street, London W1A 1DN (01 935 4422)

Sears Financial Services Ltd, (A subsidiary of Sears plc) PO Box 809, 23 Harbet Road, London W2 1JL (01 629 1234)

Security Pacific Holdings Ltd, (A subsidiary of Security Pacific Corporation) 308–314 Kings Road, Reading, Berks RG1 4PA (0734 61022)

Shawlands Securities Ltd, (A subsidiary of Frizzell Group Ltd) 8 Christchurch Road, Lansdowne, Bournemouth, Dorset BH1 3NQ

Trinity House Finance plc, (A Thorn EMI company) Trinity House, Trinity Lane, Waltham Cross, Herts EN8 7DS (0992 31988)

UCB Financial Services Ltd, (A subsidiary of Compagnie Bancaire) UCB House, Railway Approach, Wallington, Croydon, Surrey SM6 0DY (01 773 3111)

United Dominions Trust Ltd, (A subsidiary of TSB Group plc) Endeavour House, 1 Lyonsdown Road, New Barnet, Herts EN5 1HU (01 440 8282)

Vernons Finance Corporation, (A subsidiary of Vernons Organisation Ltd) Vernons Building, Mile End, Liverpool L5 5AF (051 207 3181)

The Wagon Finance Corporation plc, (A subsidiary of MAI plc) Argyle House, Joel Street, Northwood Hills, Middx HA6 1NW (09724 26199)

Welbeck Finance plc, Welbeck House, Bond Street, Bristol BS1 3LB (0272 277442)

Wrenwood Group Finance Ltd, Lancaster House, Blackburn Street, Radcliffe, Manchester M26 9TS (061 723 1628)

Yorkshire Bank Finance Ltd, (A subsidiary of Yorkshire Bank plc) 2 Infirmary Street, Leeds LS1 2UL (0532 442511)

Investment Trust Companies Invest mainly in public equity shares. Some will provide equity finance for private companies, perhaps for amounts down to £25,000.

The Association of Investment Trust Companies is at 6th Floor, Park House, 16 Finsbury Circus, London EC2M 7JJ (01 588 5347) Members of the Association who may consider smaller companies are:

The Ailsa Investment Trust plc, 15 St James's Place, London SW1A 1NW (01 493 8111)

Alliance Investment plc, Meadow House, 64 Reform Street, Dundee DD1 1TJ (0382 201700)

The Alva Investment Trust plc, Royal London House, 22–25 Finsbury Square, London EC2A 1DS (01 638 0317)

The Baillie Gifford Japan Trust plc, 3 Glenfinlas Street, Edinburgh EH3 6Y (031 225 2581)

The Edinburgh Investment Trust plc, Dunedin House, 25 Ravelston Terrace, Edinburgh EH4 3EX (031 315 2500)

Electra Investment Trust plc, 65 Kingsway, London WC2B 6QT (01 831 6464)

The First Scottish American Trust plc, Belsize House, West Ferry, Dundee DD5 1NF (0382 78244)

The Fleming Enterprise Investment Trust plc, 25 Copthall Avenue, London EC2R 7DR (01 638 5858)

The Fleming Mercantile investment Trust plc, 25 Copthall Avenue, London EC2R 7DR (01 638 5858)

Gartmore European Investment Trust plc, Gartmore House, 16–18 Monument Street, London EC3R 8AJ (01 623 1212)

Globe Investment Trust plc, Electra House, Temple Place, London WC2R 3HP (01 836 7766)

Govett Strategic Investment Trust plc, Shackleton House, 4 Battle Bridge Lane, London SE1 2HR

Grahams Rintoul Investment Trust plc, 5–10 Bury Street, London EC3A 5AT (01 623 8224)

Greenfair Investment Co plc, 3 Finsbury Avenue, London EC2M 2PA (01 638 5757)

Hambros Investment Trust plc, 41 Tower Hill, London EC3N 4HA (01 480 5000)

'Investing in Success' Equities plc, James House, 1 Babmaes Street, London SW1Y 6HD (01 925 0555)

Investors Capital Trust plc, 1 Charlotte Square, Edinburgh EH2 4DZ (031 225 1357)

Kleinwort Charter Investment Trust plc, 20 Fenchurch Street, London EC3P 3DB (01 623 8000)

Lancashire & London Investment Trust plc, Neptune House, Triton Court, 14 Finsbury Square, London EC2A 1BR (01 256 8873)

Moorgate Investment Trust plc, 9 Upper Belgrave Street, London SW1X 8BD (01 235 4802)

Murray International Investment Trust plc, 7 West Nile Street, Glasgow G1 2PX (041 226 3131)

Rights & Issues Investment Trust plc, Dauntsey House, Frederick's Place, Old Jewry, London EC2R 8HN (01 606 2167)

The River Plate & General Investment Trust plc, 11th Floor, Knightsbridge House, 197 Knightsbridge, London SW7 1RB (01 225 1044)

St Andrew Trust plc, 29 Charlotte Square, Edinburgh EH2 4HA (031 225 3811)

The Scottish American Investment Co plc, 45 Charlotte Square, Edinburgh EH2 4HW (031 226 3271)

The Second Alliance Trust plc, Meadow House, 64 Reform Street, Dundee DD1 1JT (0382 210700)

The Smaller Companies International Trust plc, 4 Melville Crescent, Edinburgh EH3 7JB (031 226 4931)

TR Trustees Corporation plc, Mermaid House, 2 Puddle Dock, London EC4V 3AT (01 236 6565)

Updown Investment Co plc, 12 Tokenhouse Yard, London EC2R 7AN (01 588 2828)

Business Expansion Funds   There are now over 30 schemes launched. Some will invest in start-ups, even down to £30,000. Some keep registers putting individual investors in touch with specific companies.

So if you are looking for equity capital it will pay to put your proposal forward, even if the fund itself will not invest.

Capital for Companies Ltd, Coverdale House, 14 East Parade, Leeds LS1 2BH (0532 438043) *Contact: B. A. Anysz*

Capital Ventures Ltd, The Priory, 37 London Road, Cheltenham, Glos GL52 6HA (0242 584380) *Contact: D. Fredjohn/P. Underhill*

Castleforth Fund Managers Ltd, 150 Strand, London WC2R 1JP (01 240 6887) *Contact: J. D. B. Workman*

Centreway Business Expansion Fund: Midland and Northern, 1 Waterloo Street, Birmingham B2 5PG (021 643 3941) *Contact: A. J. Cross*

Charterhouse Business Expansion Fund Management Ltd, 6 New Bridge Street, London EC4V 6JH (01 248 4000) *Contact: Richard Duncan*

Community of St Helen's Trust, PO Box 36, St Helen's, Merseyside (0744 696770) *Contact: David Boult*

Electra Risk Capital plc, 65 Kingsway, London WC2B 6QT (01 831 6464) *Contact: Peter Rowledge*

FPG Ltd, 1 Fredericks Place, London EC2R 8HR (01 600 3677) *Contact: M. Kinney*

Granville Business Expansion Finance: Granville & Co Ltd, 8 Lovat Lane, London EC3R 8BP (01 621 1212) *Contact: Wendy Pollecoff*

Hodgson Martin Ventures Ltd, 4a St Andrew Square, Edinburgh EH2 2BD (031 557 3560) *Contact: A. Hodgson/R. Martin*

Industrial Technology Securities Ltd, Church Lane House, Church Lane, Chalfont St Peter, Bucks SL9 9RE (0753 885524) *Contact: I. M. Cohen*

Johnson Fry plc, Princes House, 36 Jermyn Street, London SW1Y 6DT (01 439 0924) *Contact: Charles Fry*

Lazard Development Capital Fund: Lazard Development Capital Ltd, 44 Baker Street, London W1M 1DH (01 935 2731) *Contact: N. Faulkner/D. Hudson*

Mercia Venture Capital Scheme: Mercia Venture Capital Ltd, 126 Colmore Row, Birmingham B3 3AP (021 223 3404) *Contact: R. P. Barnsley*

Minster Trust 1983/4 Business Expansion Fund: Minster Trust Ltd, Minster House, Arthur Street, London EC4R 9BH (01 623 1050) *Contact: H. J. H. C. Hildreth*

Quester Capital Management Ltd, 2 Queen Anne's Gate Buildings, Dartmouth Street, London SW1H 9BP (01 222 5472) *Contact: A. Homes/J. Spooner*

Sabrelance Ltd, 48 Westminster Gardens, Marsham Street, London SW1P 4JG (01 821 0817) *Contact: D. L. Shaw*

Ulster Venture Capital Ltd, Sinclair House, 89 Royal Avenue, Belfast BT1 1BP (0232 248490/246678) *Contact: G. Lomas*

Public Sector Finance There are over 100 different schemes operating, offering a wide range of assistance to new and small businesses. The important services and publications that will keep you up-to-date in this rapidly changing field are listed at the end of this section.

One scheme worthy of special mention is the Enterprise Allowance Scheme, under which unemployed people are encouraged to start their own business. They are paid £40 per week for a maximum of 52 weeks.

The scheme is open to people who:

■ Are receiving unemployment or supplementary benefit
■ Have been unemployed for at least 13 weeks
■ Are over 18 and under retirement age
■ Have at least £1,000 to invest in the business
■ Agree to work full-time in the business (at least 36 hours per week)

The business you plan to set up should be:

■ New – if you have already started your business you are ineligible
■ Independent – you should not be a subsidiary of or supported by another business

- Small – applications will not be accepted from people who intend to employ more than 20 workers during the first three months of the operation
- Suitable for public funding – businesses involving sex, religion, politics or gambling, for example, are excluded

If you think you may be eligible contact your nearest job centre.

Business Competitions   Competitions are one of the few absolutely free sources of money open to you. Over £1 million a year is given away in this manner, to people in Britain with soundly based business ideas. These competitions are usually sponsored by banks, local councils and big companies offering prizes ranging from a few hundred pounds up to £30,000. The prize will also probably include a package of help and advice and, dependent on the nature of the sponsoring organisation, a useful piece of business equipment such as a microcomputer or a rent free work unit.

These competitions are usually announced in the press. Regular sponsors of such events include:

Sponsor	Competition	Prize Fund
Bank of Ireland	Start Your Own Business	£30,000
Churchill College, Cambridge	Small Business Essay Prize (3,000 awards)	£400
Daily Telegraph and National Westminster Bank	Business Venture Award	£20,000
Design Council	Design Award for Small Firms	£10,000
Lloyds Bowmaker & Accountancy Age	National Award for Small Business	£25,000

Venture and Development Capital   The UK now has the largest and most diverse venture capital market, outside the USA, with over £2bn currently invested. Many companies in this directory are subsidiaries of the clearing banks, insurance companies, pension funds, overseas banks; and even the Bank of England and the Government. Some of them can provide a range of services beyond equity and loan finance, although in general that is their speciality. A brief description of Investors in Industry (3i's), the largest of these institutions will give a flavour of the whole sector.

Investors in Industry (3i's), part of Finance for Industry, was formed in 1945 and now claims to be the major source of long-term finance for new and small businesses.

3i's shareholders are the Bank of England (15%) and the English and Scottish clearing banks (85%). It operates as a private sector organisation concerned exclusively with private-sector business. However, it also administers funds with low interest rates from the European Investment Bank (EIB), the European Coal and Steel Community (ECSC), and participates in the Government's loan guarantee scheme.

The corporation currently has over £1bn invested in some 4,000 companies, £200 million of which is advanced to over 1,000 businesses each year.

Funds for individual investments range from £5,000 up to £2 million. About 70% of these were for £100,000. Indeed, about half of all loans are for less than £50,000.

Finance is provided through long-term loans, or in the form of ordinary or preference shares, or in any combination of these. 3i's takes an equity stake in about a third of cases, the balance being term loans.

3i's close relationship with the clearing banks makes the negotiation of security cover easier. This is particularly true when, for example, the clearer already has a charge on the business's assets.

3i's main areas of activity are financing new businesses, providing funds for expansion, and arranging management buy-outs. 3i's have completed over 400 buy-outs, and claim to be the pioneers of the technique. More recently they have moved into the leasing and hire-purchase fields. This spread of facilities often allows 3i's to propose the best financial package for the company's current needs, and the regional office structure can make it convenient to do business with them. However, there are another 100 or so players in the market, who may be equally attracted to your proposal.

Institutions giving long-term finance

KEY
1 Will invest less than £50,000
2 Start-up funds
3 Minimum stake
4 Non-exec dir.
5 Industry pref
6 No. of ventures per annum

	1	2	3	4	5	6
Abingworth plc, 26 St James Street, London SW1A 1HA (01 839 6745) *Contact: Anthony Montagu*	No	No	1%	Pos	High Tech	12
Advent Ltd, 25 Buckingham Gate, London SW1E 6LD (01 630 9811) *Contact: David Cooksey*	No	Yes	1%	Pos	High Tech	15
Alan Patricof Assoc Ltd, 24 Upper Brook Street, London W1Y 1PD (01 493 3633) *Contact: Ronald Cohen*	No	Yes	1%	Yes	High Tech	10
Allied Irish Investment Bank plc, c/o Pinners Hall, 8/9 Austin Friars, London EC2N 2AE (01 920 9155) *Contact: Brian Stephens*	No	No	10%	Yes	Yes	4
Alta Berkeley Associates, 25 Berkeley Square, London W1X 5HB (01 629 1550) *Contact: Mark Diskin*	No	Yes	10%	Pos	High Tech	10
Barclays Development Capital Ltd, Pickfords Wharf, Clink Street, London SE1 9DG (01 407 2389) *Contact: Lucinda Horler*	No	No	—	No	No	20
Baring Brothers Hambrecht & Quist Ltd, Suite 34, 140 Park Lane, London W1Y 3AA (01 408 0555) *Contact: Richard Onians*	No	Yes	1%	Yes	No	12
Baring Capital Investors Ltd, 140 Park Lane, London W1Y 3AA (01 408 1282) *Contact: Otto van de Wyck*	No	No	1%	Yes	No	5
Baronsmead Associates Ltd, 59 London Wall, London EC2M 5TP (01 638 6826) *Contact: Richard Hargreaves*	No	Yes	10%	Yes	No	10
Birmingham Technology Ltd, Love Lane, Birmingham B7 4BJ (021 359 0981) *Contact: Derek Harris*	Yes	Yes	1%	No	High Tech	5

	1	2	3	4	5	6
British Linen Bank Ltd, 12 Melville Street, Edinburgh EH3 7NS (031 243 8470) *Contact: Brian Finlayson*	No	Pos	0–49%	Yes	No	16
British Technology Group, 101 Newington Causeway, London SE1 6BU (01 403 6666) *Contact: David James*	No	Yes	Yes	—	Yes	—
Brown Goldie & Co Ltd, 16 St Helen's Place, London EC3A 6BY (01 638 2575) *Contact: Cameron Brown*	Yes	No	2%	Yes	No	6
Candover Investments plc, Cedric House, 8/9 East Harding Street, London EC4A 3AS (01 583 5090) *Contact: Roger Brooke*	No	No	5%	Yes	No	16
Capital Partners International Ltd, Kingsmead House, 250 Kings Road, London SW3 5UE (01 351 4899/5511) *Contact: Christoph von Luttitz*	Yes	Yes	10%	No	No	2
Capital Ventures Ltd, 37 London Road, Cheltenham, Glos GL52 6HA (0242 584380) *Contact: Simon Smith*	No	Yes	Flex	Yes	No	60
Causeway Capital Ltd, 21 Cavendish Place, London W1M 9DL (01 631 3073) *Contact: Lionel Anthony*	No	Yes	1%	Yes	No	15
Centreway Development Capital Ltd, 1 Waterloo Street, Birmingham B2 5PG (021 643 3941) *Contact: John Naylor*	No	Yes	No	Yes	No	8
Chartfield & Co Ltd, 24–26 Baltic Street, London EC1Y 0TB (01 608 1451) *Contact: Nicholas Branch*	Yes	Yes	25%	Yes	Yes	15
Charterhouse Development Capital Ltd, 7 Ludgate Broadway, London EC4V 6DX (01 248 4000) *Contact: Robert Smith*	No	Yes	1%	Yes	High Tech	8
Charterhouse Venture Fund, 10 Hertford Street, London W1Y 7DX (01 409 3232) *Contact: Dr. John Walker*	No	Yes	25%	Yes	Health Care	5
CIN Venture Managers Ltd, PO Box 10, Hobart House, Grosvenor Place, London SW1X 7AD (01 245 6911) *Contact: R. Hall*	Yes	Yes	Min	Yes	No	35

	1	2	3	4	5	6
Citicorp Venture Capital Ltd, PO Box 200, Cottons Centre, Hays Lane, London SE1 2QT (01 234 5678) *Contact: Michael Smith*	No	Yes	1%	Yes	No	10
Close Investment Management Ltd, 36 Great St Helens, London EC3A 6AP (01 283 2241) *Contact: Jonathan Thornton*	No	No	2%	Yes	No	12
County NatWest Ventures Ltd, Drapers Gardens, 12 Throgmorton Avenue, London EC2P 2ES (01 638 6000) *Contact: R. M. Drummond*	No	Yes	Min	No	No	59
Dartington & Co Venture Capital Investments, Bush House, 72 Prince Street, Bristol BS1 4QD (0272 213206) *Contact: Sue Watson*	No	No	15%	No	No	8
Development Capital Corporation Ltd 103 Mount Street, London W1Y 5HG (01 491 0767) *Contact: Janus Heath*	Yes	Yes	1%	Yes	No	8
Development Capital Group Ltd, 44 Baker Street, London W1M 1DH (01 935 2731) *Contact: Neil Falkner*	No	Yes	Min	Yes	No	40
Equity Capital for Industry, Brettenham House, Lancaster Place, London WC2E 7EN (01 606 1000) *Contact: Tony Lorenz*	Yes	Yes	1%	No	No	20
Robert Fleming Venture Capital Unit, 25 Copthall Avenue, London EC2R 7DR (01 638 5858) *Contact: Jill Singleton*	No	No	n/a	No	No	12
Foreign & Colonial Ventures Ltd, 1 Laurence Pountney Hill, London EC4R 0BR (01 623 4680) *Contact: James Nelson*	No	Yes	1%	Yes	No	15
Gartmore Investment Management, 16/18 Monument Street, London EC3 (01 623 1212) *Contact: Michael Walton*	No	Yes	5%	Yes	No	10
Granville & Co, 8 Lovat Lane, London EC3R 8BP (01 621 1212) *Contact: David Steeds*	No	Yes	10%	Yes	No	6

	1	2	3	4	5	6
Grosvenor Venture Managers Ltd, Commerce House, 2/6 Bath Road, Slough, Berks SL1 3RZ (0753 32623) *Contact: David Beattie*	No	No	10%	Yes	No	13
Guinness Mahon Development Capital Ltd, 32 St Mary at Hill, London EC3P 3AJ (01 623 9333) *Contact: Stephen Hill*	Yes	Yes	11%	Yes	No	32
Hambros Advanced Technology Trust plc, c/o Top Technology Ltd, 20/21 Tooks Court, Cursitor Street, London EC4A 4LB (01 242 9900) *Contact: H. E. Fitzgibbons*	No	No	20%	No	High Tech	10
Hodgson Martin Ventures Ltd, 36 George Street, Edinburgh EH2 2LE (031 226 7644) *Contact: Sheila Mackie*	No	No	10%	Yes	Low Tech	8
Innotech Ltd, 28 Buckingham Gate, London SW1E 6LD (01 834 2492) Contact: R. O. Hay	Yes	Yes	10%	Yes	High Tech	3
Investors in Industry plc, 91 Waterloo Road, London SE1 8XP (01 928 7822) *Contact: Ian Menzies*	Yes	Yes	0%	Pos	No	1000

Regional offices:

Aberdeen: 38 Carden Place, Aberdeen AB1 1UP (0224 638666) *Contact: Keith Mair*

Birmingham: 112 Colmore Row, Birmingham B3 3SA (021 236 9531) *Contact: Peter Williams*

Brighton: 47 Middle Street, Brighton BN1 1AL (0273 23164) *Contact: Hugh Richards*

Bristol: Pearl Assurance House, Queens Square, Bristol BS1 4LE (0272 277412) *Contact: John Kingston*

Cambridge: Science Park, Milton Road, Cambridge CB4 4FZ (0223 420031) *Contact: Jim Martin*

Cardiff: Harlech House, 20 Cathedral Road, Cardiff CF1 3SF (0222 394541) *Contact: Chris Rolands*

	1	2	3	4	5	6
Edinburgh: 8 Charlotte Square, Edinburgh EH2 4DR (031 226 7092) *Contact: Mike Pacitti*						
Glasgow: 9th Floor, Pegasus House, 375 West George Street, Glasgow G2 4AR (041 248 4456) *Contact: Sandy Walker*						
Guildford: The Billings, Walnut Tree Close, Guildford, Surrey GU1 4UL (0483 301773) *Contact: Roger Pett*						
Hull: Suite 7, Unit 12, The Avenues, Bishop Lane, Hull HU1 1NJ (0482 27066) *Contact: David Wilkinson*						
Leeds: 34 Park Cross Street, Leeds LS1 2QH (0532 430511) *Contact: David Wilkinson*						
Leicester: St Johns House, East Street, Leicester LE1 9NN (0533 555110) *Contact: David Wilson*						
Liverpool: Silkhouse Court, Tithebarn Street, Liverpool L2 2LZ (051 236 2944) *Contact: Robert Toomey*						
Manchester: Virginia House, 5 Cheapside, Manchester M2 4WG (061 833 9511) *Contact: Charles Richardson*						
Milton Keynes: 388 Silbury Court, Silbury Boulevard, Milton Keynes MK9 2LQ (0908 66818) *Contact: Clive Brook*						
Newcastle: Scottish Life House, Archbold Terrace, Jesmond, Newcastle upon Tyne NE2 1DB (091 281 5221) *Contact: Colin Chadburn*						
Nottingham: 38 The Ropewalk, Nottingham NG1 5DW (0602 412766) *Contact: Alan Lewis*						
Reading: St Giles House, 25 King's Road, Reading, Berks RG1 3AR (0734 584344) *Contact: Marc Gillespie*						
Sheffield: 11 Westbourne Road, Sheffield S10 2QQ (0742 680571) *Contact: Paul Gilmartin*						

	1	2	3	4	5	6
Southampton: Capital House, 11 Houndwell Place, Southampton SO1 1HU (0703 32044) *Contact: Stephen Denford*						
Watford: Arliss Court, 24 Clarendon Road, Watford WD1 1JY (0923 33232) *Contact: Mike Piper*						
Kleinwort Benson Development Capital Ltd, 20 Fenchurch Street, London EC3P 3DB (01 623 8000) *Contact: Barry Dean*	No	No	Any	Yes	No	14
Lloyds Development Capital Ltd, 40/66 Queen Victoria Street, London EC4P 4EL (01 248 4275) *Contact: Ron Hollidge*	No	No	10%	Yes	No	16
Managed Technology Investors, 70 St Albans Road, Watford, Herts ED1 1RP (0923 50244) *Contact: Dr Paul Castle*	No	Yes	30%	Pos	High Tech	3
March Investment Fund, 33 King Street, Manchester M2 6AA (061 834 9720) *Contact: Richard Marshall*	No	Pos	1%	Yes	No	4
Mercia Venture Capital Ltd, 126 Colmore Row, Birmingham B3 3AP (021 233 3404) *Contact: R. P. Barnsley*	No	Yes	25%	Yes	No	5
Mercury Asset Management, 33 King William Street, London EC4R 9AS (01 280 2800) *Contact: D. R. Llewellyn*	No	Yes	Yes	Yes	No	21
Midland Montagu Ventures Ltd, 10 Lower Thames Street, London EC3R 6AE (01 260 9911) *Contact: David Hutchings*	No	No	5%	No	No	16
Murray Johnstone Ltd, 7 West Nile Street, Glasgow G1 2PX (041 226 3131) *Contact: David McLellan*	No	Yes	No/ min	No	No	19
Newmarket Venture Capital Ltd, 14/20 Chiswell Street, London EC1Y 4TY (01 638 2521) *Contact: Caroline Vaughan*	No	Yes	1%	Yes	High Tech	3
Northern Investors Co Ltd, Centro House, 3 Cloth Market, Newcastle-Upon-Tyne NE1 1EE (0632 327068) *Contact: Michael Denny*	Yes	Yes	5%	Yes	No	6

	1	2	3	4	5	6
Norwich Union Venture Capital Ltd, PO Box 53, Surrey Street, Norwich NR1 3TE (0603 683803) *Contact: G. T. Evans*	No	Yes	Yes	No	No	8
Oakland Management Holdings Ltd, Ramsbury House, High Street, Hungerford, Berks RG17 0LY (0488 83555) *Contact: Gordon Kenneth*	No	Yes	1%	Yes	No	20
Oxford Seedcorn Capital Ltd, 213 Woodstock Road, Oxford OX2 7AD (0865 53535) *Contact: John Laurie*	Yes	Yes	10%	No	High Tech	3
PA Development Ltd, Bowater House East, 68 Knightsbridge, London SW1X 7LJ (01 589 7050) *Contact: Max Silver*	No	No	25%	Yes	No	5
Phillips & Drew Development Capital, Triton Court, 14 Finsbury Square, London EC2A 1PD (01 628 6366) *Contact: Ian Hawkins*	No	Yes	5%	Yes	No	10
Prelude Technology Investments Ltd, The Innovation Centre, Science Park, Milton Road, Cambridge CB4 4GF (0223 423132) *Contact: Dr R. Hook*	Yes	Yes	10%	Yes	Scie	6
Prudential Venture Managers Ltd, Audrey House, Ely Place, London EC1N 6SN (01 831 7747) *Contact: Paul Brooks*	No	Yes	5%	Pos	No	15
Quayle Munro Ltd, 42 Charlotte Square, Edinburgh EH2 4HQ (031 226 4421) *Contact: R. Legget*	No	No	—	No	Not High Tech	7
Rainford Venture Capital Ltd, Rainford Hall, Crank Road, Crank, St Helens, Merseyside WA11 7RP (0744 37227) *Contact: D. Johnston*	No	Yes	10%	Yes	No	2
N. M. Rothschild Asset Management Ltd, PO Box 528, Five Arrows House, St Swithin's Lane, London EC4N 8NR (01 280 5000) *Contact: J. L. Curnock Cook*	No	Yes	10%	No	Bio Tech	7
Rothschild Ventures, New Court, St Swithin's Lane, London EC4P 3DU (01 280 5000) *Contact: Jeremy Dawson*	No	Yes	—	—	No	7

	1	2	3	4	5	6
St James Venture Capital Fund Ltd, Cleveland House, 19 St James Square, London SW1Y 4JE (01 839 2264) *Contact: Simon Hochhauser*	No	Yes	5%	Pos	Tech	5
Schroder Ventures, 20 Southampton Street, London WC2 7QG (01 379 5010) *Contact: Jon Moulton*	No	Yes	1%	Pos	No	15
Scottish Development Agency, 120 Bothwell Street, Glasgow G2 7JP (041 248 2700) *Contact: Donald Pleasance*	Yes	Yes	Flex	Yes	Energy Related	150
Seed Capital Ltd, 20 Baldwin Street, Bristol BS1 1SE (0272 272250) *Contact: Lucius Cary*	Yes	Yes	25%	Yes	Innov	4
Sharp Technology Fund, Edmund House, 12 Newhall Street, Birmingham B3 3ER (021 200 2244) *Contact: L. C. N. Bury*	No	Yes	1%	Yes	Tech	6
SUMIT plc, Edmund House, 12 Newhall Street, Birmingham B3 3ER (021 200 2244) *Contact: John Kerr*	No	Yes	varied	Yes	No	5
SYNTECH Information Technology Fund, Barnes Thomson Management Ltd, 19 Bedford Row, London WC1R 4EB (01 405 1326) *Contact: K. Barnes*	No	Yes	10%	Yes	Info Tech	5
Thompson Clive & Pts, 24 Old Bond Street, London W1X 3DA (01 491 4809) *Contact: Colin Clive*	Yes	Yes	1%	Yes	Tech	20
Transatlantic Capital Ltd, 55 Gracechurch Street, London EC3V 0BN (01 280 3190) *Contact: Gordon Dean*	Yes	Yes	2%	Yes	Bio Tech	6
Venture Founders Ltd, 50/51 Conduit Street, London W1R 9FB (01 434 9781) *Contact: Charles Cox*	No	Yes	5%	Yes	No	8
Venture Link Portfolio Management Ltd, 6/7 Queen Street, London EC4N 1SP (01 236 6891) *Contact: John V. Hatch*	No	Yes	1%	Pos	No	10
Welsh Development Agency, Pearl House, Greyfriars Road, Cardiff CF1 3XX (0222 222666) *Contact: Stephen White*	Yes	Yes	n/a	No	No	

CONTROLLING THE MONEY

Even with a good business plan and a reasonably willing provider of funds, your financial problems are not over. Indeed, in one sense they are just about to begin. Before you take on outside investors or lenders you only have your own money to lose. With other people's funds you will have to give an account of 'stewardship' as well as keep records to meet the needs of the Inland Revenue and the Customs and Excise.

In fact, you will probably have to show how you propose to control the finances of the business before anyone will part with any funds. They will want to know how you will keep track of the business.

There are four elements to successful financial control. Firstly, you should plan ahead. Have a budget that sets out clearly what you expect to happen over the next 12 months month by month. This should be expressed in terms of money out and money in.

Secondly, you need management information that shows you what has actually happened at each stage in your plan.

Thirdly, you need to compare your budget or plan with the actual position.

Fourthly, you need to be able to use this comparison to take action – to control the business.

The single greatest reason that new and small businesses go out of business is lack of good financial control.

Choosing a Book-Keeping and Accounting System

In order to get financial control you need to install a book-keeping system BEFORE YOU START TRADING. This should tell you how much you have in the bank; how much you owe; and how much you are owed (a bare minimum). All the systems reviewed can do this.

The following is a brief survey of some of the more 'popular' book-keeping systems. They are divided into five categories: 'shoe boxes': do it yourself books; halfway houses; accountants only and computer based systems.

'Shoe box' systems This is for the simplest businesses, which need relatively little financial control beyond cash, bank accounts, accounts payable and accounts receivable.

At its simplest you need four shoe boxes, a bank paying-in book and a cheque book (the last two can tell you how much you have in the bank). You keep two boxes for unpaid invoices (one for sales, one for purchases, services and so on). You transfer the invoices into the other two boxes (one for sales, one for purchases, etc) when each invoice is paid. By adding all the invoices in one box (sales, unpaid invoices) you can find out how much you are owed, and by adding another (purchases unpaid) you find out how much you owe.

You keep every record relating to the business, too.

This is a perfectly adequate system unless you need some form of cash control or some profit information and you need it fast. It is, however, not too good on credit control.

Essentially, this system is only for the smallest firms.

The DIY system These are normally hardback, bound books with several sections to them, each part ruled and already laid out for the entries. Each one has a set of instructions and examples for each section.

All the systems mentioned here have some advantages and disadvantages in common:

Advantages Each one tries to assist the small business person by allowing some measures of financial control, especially over cash and bank balances. They almost always include VAT sections and Profit and Loss sections. They aim, in the large part, to make an accountant unnecessary, or at least to minimise your expense in that area.

Disadvantages None of these systems will work unless it is kept up regularly – which means weekly at a minimum, and preferably daily. As a drawback this cannot be over-emphasised. Unless you currently regularly keep a diary, these books are probably not for you. If not kept properly, they can cost you more in accountancy fees rather than less. Other disadvantages are that they often assume some prior knowledge from the user, even though they give instructions. Their instructions sometimes leave much to be desired relying largely on worked examples that are difficult to follow. They compartmentalise people and business, and they tend to ignore such expenses as 'use of home as office' (for example, home telephone bills) many of which may be tax allowable. Finally, many people also find that they would rather not use these books as the basis for dealing with their Inspectors of Taxes, and would rather have their accountants do this. In these circumstances you are going to need an accountant anyway, and your inspector is much more likely to pay attention to him in any case.

The following tables show the basic information for some of the most common systems, and the conclusions as to their relative usefulness.

Finco Small Business Book-Keeping System This system is slightly more expensive, but it has two years' supply of forms (compared to others which provide only one), and gives a large amount of financial control for a relatively small sum. This is first choice.

The Kalamazoo Set Up is the second choice. It would have been first choice, but for its price. You probably also need training to be able to use it, even with their book as support. It has been chosen because it can give the best financial control, if used properly. In addition, it can save time through being a single-write system (entering up to three records simultaneously).

DIY Accounting Books, Comparison Table

Name and availability	Cost band	Financial control provided	Records provided
Ataglance, Ataglance Publications, 16 Sawley Avenue, Lytham St Annes, Lancs FY8 3QL (0253 727107)	A	Bank	Payments, receipts, VAT
Collins Self Employed Account Book, W. H. Smith & other stationers	A	Bank, debtors, creditors	Payments, receipts, VAT, subcontract
Collins Complete Traders Account Book, W. H. Smith & other stationers	A	Bank	Payments, receipts, VAT
Evrite Traders Account Book, Commercial stationers, or Evrite Publishing Co Ltd, Hill Street Chambers, St Helier, Jersey, Channel Islands	A	Bank, debtors	Payments, receipts, VAT
Finco Small Business Book-Keeping System, Broadwood View, Chester le Street, Co Durham DH3 3NG (091 3880421)	B	Bank, cash, debtors, creditors, wages	Receipts, payments, sales, purchases, payroll, VAT
Kalamazoo Set Up Pack, Kalamazoo Business Systems, Mill Lane, Northfield, Birmingham B31 2RW (021 475 2191)	C	Bank, cash, debtors creditors	Receipts
Simplex 'D' Cash Book, Commercial stationers, or George Viner (Dist) Ltd, Simplex House, Mytholmbridge Mills, Mytholmbridge, Holmfirth, Huddersfield HD7 2TA	A	Bank, cash	Receipts payments, profit & loss

Cost band legend: A = up to £25
B = £25–75
C = £76–150

General Comments

Ataglance Few instructions, mostly related to VAT. But if you are thinking of opening a fish and chip shop they have prepared a special book-keeping ledger, costing £1.98.

Collins Self Employed Account Book This seems to be aimed at sub-contractors and is reasonably comprehensive, but the instructions may call for prior knowledge.

Collins Complete Traders Account Book For retail outlets only. The instructions are somewhat limited.

Evrite Traders Account Book Brief instructions. Relies on worked examples. Assumes prior knowledge. Debtor control in total only (not by individual customers).

Finco Small Business Book-Keeping System Simple instructions, two years' supply of record sheets, loose-leaf. This is more easily adaptable to any business (there is less compartmentalisation), and gives detailed control over individual amounts outstanding, both receivable and payable. Because it is loose-leaf, your accountant can take the relevant records without depriving you of your control. It can also be used in conjunction with your accountant's microcomputer.

Kalamazoo Set Up This is the most comprehensive system (as well as the most expensive). It provides everything that all other systems give you, two years' supply of records (loose-leaf) and a debtors/creditors ledger. Your £92 also buys you a basic book-keeping book which gives information on how to keep it up (and why you need to). The book is by John Kellock, *A Practical Guide to Good Book-Keeping and Business Systems*, and is available separately.

Simplex 'D' Cash Book This is the best known of this type of book. Its instructions are short, and it uses worked examples. There are separate books for VAT and wages, as well as a separate book, *Simplified Book-Keeping for Small Business* at £3.

Halfway House Systems The halfway-house systems lie between a simple DIY system and an 'accountant only' system. Pre-printed stationery tends to be used, but in loose-leaf form. They are more flexible than the DIY, and tend to be cheaper than using an accountant only. However, they do require some knowledge on the part of the person who keeps the books. Again, this need not be daunting, as your accountant can probably train you (or your office girl or boy) to keep them up. The major problem is that you need your accountant before you can use your records for more advanced financial control.

There are two common halfway-house systems on the market: Twinlock and Kalamazoo.

Twinlock available at commercial stationers or the publishers at Twinlock Ltd, 36 Croydon Road, Beckenham, Kent BR3 4BH (01 650 4818).

Kalamazoo only from the publishers at Kalamazoo Ltd, Northfield, Birmingham B31 2RW (021 475 2191).

At the basic level the two systems seem remarkably similar, both in cost and financial control. The minimum systems will cost £200–400 and Kalamazoo offer training with their product. Both are single-write systems (where one writing can enter up to three records). You should talk to your accountant before installing one.

Accountant Only Systems The accountant only systems are those for the more complex (possibly larger) small businesses, and will be designed by your accountant. They often need trained book-keepers to run them. However, the training period can be relatively short (anything from one day upwards). The book-keeper handles the routine matters, and your accountant the non-routine.

Computer Systems There are many small computer systems that will carry out the book-keeping and accountancy functions needed by a small business. But, like all systems, they are only as good as the quality of information put in. The other major problems with computer systems are these: selecting the equipment in a market with many models with claimed advantages; making sure that you have the necessary extra equipment; making sure that you have the software (programs) capable of handling your information and record needs; and, finally, ensuring that you can use the machine efficiently.

Kalamazoo has gone some way towards solving these problems with its complete accounting system for the small business. Launched in 1988 its 'one up system' includes a computer, the software, a printer, disks, a full range of stationery, the usual warranties and 12 months of advisory back-up on software usage. The price, including a day's training at their Birmingham office, is £1,800. For other options contact your nearest Microsystem centre.

ORGANISATIONS AND PUBLICATIONS FOR FINANCE

Organisations

The Association of Authorised Public Accountants, 10 Cornfield Road, Eastbourne, East Sussex BN21 4QE (0323 410412).

The Association of Bankrupts, 4 Johnson Close, Abraham Heights, Lancaster LA1 5EU (0524 64305). *Contact: John McQueen.* They try to give support to those who cannot cope with bankruptcy.

The Association of Certified Accountants, 29 Lincoln's Inn Fields, London WC2A 3EE (01 242 6855).

Banking Information Service, 10 Lombard Street, London EC3V 9AR (01 626 8486). Provides information on banking to the public.

British Insurance Association, Business Finance Information, Aldermary House, 10/15 Queen Street, London EC4N 1TT (01 248 4477). Some insurance companies will provide long term loans, mortgage loans, sale and leaseback arrangements and equity finance for new businesses. Contact the Secretary for more information.

British Venture Capital Association, 1 Surrey Street, London WC2R 2PS (01 836 5702). Acts as a clearing house for people wishing to make contact with a member venture capital company.

Business Grant Services, Spendlove Centre, Enstones Road, Charlbury, Oxon OX7 3PQ (0608 811212). Formerly a corporate insurance broker, they launched their computer based grant advisory service in 1987. Their programme 'Grant Man' will identify any grants a business may be eligible for, after they have completed a short questionnaire explaining their present and projected business plans. They cover all UK and EEC grants.

The Business Planning Initiative from the DTI provides subsidised expert advice on the development of business plans. See under Enterprise Initiative, Section 2.

Chartered Institute of Management Accountants, 63 Portland Place, London W1N 4AB (01 637 2133)

Credit and Guarantee Insurance Co Ltd, Colonial House, Mincing Lane, London EC3R 7PN (01 626 5846). Provides domestic trade credit and can cover commercial risk for exporters.

Dunn & Bradstreet, 26 Clifton Street, London EC2P 2LW (01 377 4377). Provides a payment analysis report to help forecast how quickly certain companies pay their bills.

Ernst & Whinney, Becket House, 1 Lambeth Palace Road, London SE1 7EU (01 928 2000). They use a computerised database of Government Assistance, maintained and constantly updated by the Centre for the Study of Public Policy at the University of Strathclyde. Their information covers the UK, other European countries and the EC. An initial assessment will cost £200.

Export Credits Guarantee Department (ECGD)
Headquarters: PO Box 272, Export House, 50 Ludgate Hill, London EC4M 7A (01 382 7000)

Belfast: 12th Floor, Windsor House, 9–15 Bedford Street, Belfast BT2 7EG (0232 231743)

Birmingham: Colmore Centre, 115 Colmore Row, Birmingham B3 3SB (021 233 1771)

Bristol: 1 Redcliffe Street, Bristol BS1 6NP (0272 299971)

Cambridge: Three Crowns House, 72/80 Hills Road, Cambridge CB2 1NJ (0223 68801)

City of London: Export House, 50 Ludgate Hill, London EC4M 7AY (01 726 4050)

Croydon: Sunley House, Bedford Park, Croydon, Surrey CR9 4HL (01 680 5030)

Glasgow: Berkley House, 285 Bath Street, Glasgow G2 4JL (041 332 8707)

Leeds: West Riding House, 67 Albion Street, Leeds LS1 5AA (0532 450631)

Manchester: 6th Floor, Townbury House, Blackfriars Street, Salford M3 5AL (061 834 8181)

The Financial Information Systems Initiative from the DTI, provides subsidised expert advice on introducing or improving accounting and control systems. See under Enterprise Initiative, Section 2.

Government Assistance Information Service (GAINS), Bank of Scotland, Uberior House, 61 Grassmarket, Edinburgh EH1 2JF (031 229 2555). You put forward your project and the Bank runs it through their GAINS computer program. This produces a printout listing the government assistance you may be eligible for. The service is free.

Institute of Chartered Accountants in England and Wales, PO Box 433, Chartered Accountants Hall, Moorgate Place, London EC2P 2BJ (01 628 7060). The society provides a free booklet, *You Need a Chartered Accountant*.

The Institute of Chartered Accountants in Scotland, 27 Queen Street, Edinburgh EH2 1LA (031 225 5673).

Institute of Credit Management, Easton House, Easton on the Hill, Stamford, Lincolnshire PE9 3NH (0780 56777). The professional body for people interested in credit management. Produce a quarterly journal, *Credit Management*.

Local Councils can very often provide small sums of start-up finance, or money for market research. Contact your local council's Industrial Development Officer.

London Enterprise Agency Their 'LINK' marriage bureau (see Enterprise Agencies) puts people with funds (amongst other resources) in contact with people with business ideas.

The London Society of Chartered Accountants, 38 Finsbury Square, London EC2A 1PX (01 628 2567). The society will put you in touch with an accountant if you ring its client information service.

Management Buy-Out Association, 388/396 Oxford Street, London W1N 9HE (01 491 4929). Founded in 1982 by George Bloomfield, to offer impartial advice to managers contemplating 'buy-outs'.

National Association of Pension Funds, 12/18 Grosvenor Gardens, London SW1W 0DH (01 730 0585). Some pension funds are prepared to invest in promising small businesses. The Secretary of this Association could put you in touch with such a fund.

Prestel Citiservice, Page 5991, provides a weekly update of important changes in the pattern of government finance for new projects. (Service provided by Peat Marwick McLintock.)

Small Business Management Resources Ltd, 13 Great Stuart Street, Edinburgh EH3 7TP (031 225 3567). Financial and management advisers.

The Society of Company & Commercial Accountants, 40 Tyndalls Park Road, Bristol BS8 1PL (0272 738261). 550 membership in the UK, this body specialises in providing accounting services for small businesses. Amalgamated in 1974 from Institute of Co. Accountants, Society of Commercial Accountants, Incorporated Cost & Industrial Accountants and the British Association of Accountants and Auditors.

The Stock Exchange, The Quotations Department, Throgmorton Street Entrance, PO Box 119, London EC2P 2BT (01 588 2355). Can give advice on USM listing and other equity finance.

Regional offices:

Belfast: 10 High Street, Belfast BT1 2BP (0232 21094)

Birmingham: Margaret Street, Birmingham B3 3JL (021 236 9181)

Dublin: 28 Anglesea Street, Dublin 2 (0001 778808)

Glasgow: 69 St George's Place, Glasgow G2 1BU (041 221 7060)

Liverpool: Silkhouse Court, Tithebarn Street, Liverpool L2 2LT (051 236 0869)

Manchester: 4 Norfolk Street, Manchester M2 1DS (061 833 0931)

Trade Indemnity plc, Trade Indemnity House, 12/34 Great Eastern Street, London EC2A 3AX (01 739 4311). Branches at Birmingham, Bradford, Bristol, Glasgow, Leicester, Manchester, Newcastle and Reading. Provides domestic trade credit and can cover commercial risk for exporters.

Publications

An Insight into Management Accounting by John Sizer, published by Penguin 1980. A good all round book for people with some financial knowledge. Price £4.95.

The Business Planning Workbook by Colin and Paul Barrow, published by Kogan Page in 1988, price £7.95. A step by step guide to how to prepare, write up and present a business plan. Using real examples and 20 self-study assignments this model has been tried and tested at some of the UK's leading business schools.

Cost Accounting by A. J. Tubb, first edition 1977, published by Teach Yourself Books, Hodder & Stoughton, Mill Road, Dunton Green, Sevenoaks, Kent TN13 2YA (0732 450111). A very useful book for anyone starting up a manufacturing business who wants to see how to set prices at a level that will not lose money. Price £2.95.

Directory of Grant Making Trusts March 1987, published by Charities Aid Foundation, 48 Pembury Road, Tonbridge, Kent TN9 2JD (0732 356323). Lists 2,300 grant making bodies, their objectives, policies and criteria. The purpose of the directory is mainly to help charities in their search for funds. In certain cases these trusts will make grants to individuals, very often in the educational fields.

Factoring Information Kit a pack of five booklets explaining most aspects of factoring. Free from H&H Factors Ltd, Randolph House, 46/48 Wellesley Road, Croydon, Surrey CR9 3PS (01 681 2641).

Finance for New Projects in the UK, a Guide to Government Grants published by Peat Marwick McLintock, 1 Puddle Dock, Blackfriars, London EC4V 3PD (01 236 8000). Annual.

Finding Money in Brussels, A Businessman's Guide to Sources of European Community Finance, CBI Publication Sales, Centre Point, 103 Oxford Street, London WC1A 1DU.

Financial Management for the Small Business by Colin Barrow, 2nd edition published in 1988 by Kogan Page, 120 Pentonville Road, London N1. This is the Daily Telegraph Guide. It is a comprehensive guide to preparing profit and loss accounts, cash flow statements, financial control ratios, costing, pricing and break-even. Also included are chapters on sources of finance and computerised accounting systems. Price £7.95.

Going Public Introduction to the various stock markets, describing procedures for listing, costs, relative advantages (and disadvantages) and a timetable of events. Free from Ernst & Whinney, Becket House, 1 Lambeth Palace Road, London SE1 7EU.

Grant News published several time a year by Ernst & Whinney. Provides information on recent developments in UK and EC financial assistance available for UK companies.

A Guide to European Community Grants and Loans published by Eurofin, available from Baily Distribution Ltd, Wear Bay Road, Folkestone, Kent CT19 6PH (0303 850501). Manual £45. Regular updating service £95.

Guide to Running a Small Business (The Guardian) published by Kogan Page Ltd, 120 Pentonville Road, London N1. Annual, price £7.95.

Guide to Venture Capital in the UK by Lucius Cary, published in December 1987 by Venture Capital Report Ltd, Boston Road, Henley-on-Thames RG9 1D (0491 579999). A review of venture capital sources – in some detail. Price £25.

How to Collect Money That is Owed To You by Mel Lewis, published by McGraw-Hill Book Co (UK) Ltd, Shoppenhangers Road, Maidenhead, Berks SL6 2QL (0628 23431). April 1982. This is a lively short book on the techniques which any business person can use to achieve prompt payment of money owed to him or her. It has a guide to credit insurance and factoring, examples of contracts, invoices and collection letters, lists of useful addresses and organisations and a guide to telephone collection techniques. It will be of great interest to the smaller trader. Price £9.50.

Industrial Aids in the UK, March 1987, a Businessman's Guide by Gasa Walker and Kevin Allen, available from Centre for Study of Public Policy, McLance Building, University of Strathclyde, Glasgow G1 1XQ (041 552 4400). Describes the different industrial aids in a 'user orientated' manner.

Leasing by T. M. Clark, published in December 1984 by McGraw-Hill. This is a comprehensive guide to all aspects of leasing as a means of financing capital equipment. It traces the development of leasing to its present importance in finance for industry. It also deals with the principles of finance leasing, taxation, government policy, aspects of law and insurance, and with risks and problems involved, offering suggestions for evaluating and accounting for leasing transactions. Price £15.

Management Accounting by Brian Murphy, second edition 1978, published by Teach Yourself Books, Hodder & Stoughton, Mill Road, Dunton Green, Sevenoaks, Kent TN13 2YA (0732 450111). A good book for beginners, it covers all the essential stages of the business plan, together with the elements of financial control systems. Price £2.50.

Management Buy-Outs free from Peat Marwick McLintock, 1 Puddle Dock, Blackfriars, London EC4V 3PD (01 236 8000).

Money for Business published in July 1985 by the Bank of England, Industrial Finance Division, London EC2R 8AH (01 606 4444). A first class and comprehensive guide. Price £3.

A Practical Guide to Good Book-Keeping and Business Systems by John Kellock, published in 1982 by Business Books Ltd, 17/21 Conway Street, London W1P 6JD. Written to accompany the Kalamazoo book-keeping system for small businesses, but a valuable read on its own.

Official Sources of Finance and Aid for Industry in the UK published annually by the National Westminster Bank plc, available from Market Intelligence Unit, 41 Lothbury, London EC2P 2BP (01 726 1000). Price £5.50.

Raising Finance: The Guardian Guide by Clive Woodcock, published by Kogan Page, 120 Pentonville Road, London N1, 3rd edition 1988. A very good and comprehensive book. Price £7.95.

Small Business Software Series McGraw-Hill, Shoppenhangers Road, Maidenhead, Berks SL6 2QL. Six programs and accompanying books to explain different aspects of financial management. Prices from around £30.

Sources of Venture and Development Capital in the UK Describes the main features of the venture capital market in the UK and lists 150 providers, describing the type of investments they undertake. Free from Stoy Hayward, 54 Baker Street, London W1M 1DJ.

Understanding Company Financial Statements January 1982, by R. H. Parker, published by Penguin, 530 Kings Road, London SW10 (01 351 2393). It is an excellent, simple guide to the balance sheet and other important financial statements. Price £4.95.

Venture Capital Report Boston Road, Henley-on-Thames RG9 1DY (0491 579999). The report puts people with funds in touch with people with business proposals.

Working for Yourself Daily Telegraph. Annual, by Godfrey Golzen, Chapter 3, published by Kogan Page Ltd, 120 Pentonville Road, London N1 9JN. Now in its 9th edition.

Working Capital a free guide from the Institute of Chartered Accountants, Moorgate Place, London EC2P 2BJ. Covers forecasting techniques for estimating working capital and practical hints for managing cash flow.

BUSINESS AND THE LAW

Everyone is affected in some way or another by the law, and ignorance does not form the basis of a satisfactory defence. Businesses are also subject to specific laws, and a particular responsibility rests on those who own or manage them. Although an indication of some of the main legal implications is given here, there is no substitute for specific professional advice.

A lawyer will probably know the way in which your particular business will be affected by the laws mentioned here and other laws. In the area of taxation an accountant can earn his fee several times over. Other organisations and professionals who can advise you are listed at the end of each sub-section. Most of the organisations in the first section of this book will be able to give you some guidance in this field.

This section identifies and outlines some 90 of the services or publications that can help you get a better understanding of business and the law. These include a number of relatively inexpensive advisory services. One, for example, will provide, for as little as £25 per annum, on-the-spot advice, back-up research and information, as well as insurance cover to provide professional accounting or legal advice to defend yourself if you are prosecuted under one of the many relevant business laws.

Lawline launched in May 1988 with the endorsement of the Law Society, provides a recorded information service, written by solicitors in jargon-free language on 112 legal problems. Business subjects covered include directors' rights and duties, planning permission and employment contracts. Each topic has its own telephone number, which provides access to about 5 minutes explanation and pointers to further help and advice, 24 hours a day. Off peak, the costs are around 22p per minute; otherwise charges are 35p. A directory of Lawline services and numbers is being delivered free to 1 million homes and it is also available from building societies and solicitors' offices. Alternatively you can telephone 0898 600 600 and ask for your own copy of the directory.

Lawyers for Enterprise, which came into force in June 1988, is a scheme whereby lawyers will give a free initial interview, homing in on specific queries ticked by the client on a special leaflet obtainable from libraries, town halls, enterprise agencies and other small business organisations. Thereafter the client pays in the normal way. The leaflet also lists the 1,000+ solicitors who are part of the scheme. This scheme complements the efforts of the enterprise agency network, whose 300+ chain have 50 lawyers as board members (10 as chairmen). Nine firms of solicitors are also sponsors of enterprise agencies, including Nabarro Nathanson, Ashurst Morris Crisp, Clifford Chance, Freshfields, Herbert Smith, Turner Kenneth Brown and Oppenheimers. Some of these firms are now offering to make available a specific number of consultancy hours, free of charge, to enterprise agency clients.

Four useful books that cover most of the field are listed below. Start with *Law for the Small Business*, that should meet most needs.

Commercial Law by R. M. Goode, August 1985, published by Penguin. Price £18.95.

Law for the Small Business, The Daily Telegraph Guide by Patricia Clayton. Moving into its sixth edition in 1988, it covers the whole field well. Price £7.95.

The Legal 500 (Legalease) PO Box 404, London NW6 1JP. Published March 1988. Price £24.95, compiled by John Pritchard. The Guide gives profiles of the firms and outlines what work they do; gives a region-by-region guide to the leading firms in each part of the country and tips the market leader.

Managing Legal Costs CBI Publication Sales, Centre Point, 103 New Oxford Street, London WC1A 1DU. Price £5. A guide to choosing and using a solicitor and to getting value for money.

███████████████

CHOOSING THE FORM OF THE BUSINESS

At the outset of your business venture you will have to decide what legal form your business will take. There are four main forms that a business can take, with a number of variations on two of these. The form that you choose will depend on a number of factors: commercial needs, financial risk and your tax position. All play an important part. The tax position is looked at in more detail later, but a summary of the main pros and cons is set out on pages 251–2.

Sole Trader If you have the facilities, cash and customers, you can start trading under your own name immediately. Unless you intend to register for VAT, there are no rules about the records you have to keep. There is no requirement for an external audit, or for financial information on your business to be filed at Companies House. You would be prudent to keep good books and to get professional advice, as you will have to declare your income to the Inland Revenue.

Without good records you will lose in any dispute over tax. You are personally liable for the debts of your business, and in the event of your business failing your personal possessions can be sold to meet the debts.

A sole trader does not have access to equity capital, which has the attraction of being risk-free to the business. He must rely on loans from banks or individuals and any other non-equity source of finance.

Partnership There are very few restrictions to setting up in business with another person (or persons) in partnership. Many partnerships are entered into with legal formalities and sometimes without the parties themselves being aware that they have entered a partnership.

All that is needed is for two or more people to agree to carry on a business together intending to share the profits. The law will then recognise the existence of a partnership.

Most of the points raised when considering sole tradership apply to partnerships. All the partners are personally liable for the debts of the partnership, even if those debts were incurred by one partner's mismanagement or dishonesty without the other partner's knowledge. Even death may not release a partner from his obligations, and in some circumstances his estate can remain liable. Unless you take 'public' leave of your partnership by notifying your business contacts, and advertising retirement in *The London Gazette* you will remain liable indefinitely. So it is vital before entering a partnership to be absolutely sure of your partner and to take legal advice in drawing up a partnership contract.

The contract should cover the following points:

Profit sharing, responsibilities and duration This should specify how profit and losses are to be shared, and who is to carry out which tasks. It should also set limits on partners' monthly drawings, and on how long the partnership itself is to last (either a specific period of years or indefinitely, with a cancellation period of, say, three months).

Voting rights and policy decisions Unless otherwise stated, all the partners have equal voting rights. It is advisable to get a definition of what is a policy or voting decision, and how such decisions are to be made. You must also decide how to expel or admit a new partner.

Time off Every partner is entitled to his share of the profits even when ill or on holiday. You will need some guidelines on the length and frequency of holidays, and on what to do if someone is absent for a long period for any other reason.

Withdrawing capital You have to decide how each partner's share of the capital of the business will be valued in the event of either partner leaving or the partnership being dissolved.

Accountancy procedure You do not have either to file accounts or to have accounts audited. However, it may be prudent to agree a satisfactory standard of accounting and have a firm of accountants to carry out that work. Sleeping partners may well insist on it.

Sleeping partners A partner who has put up capital but does not intend to take an active part in running the business can protect himself against risk by having his partnership registered as a limited partnership.

Limited Company The main distinction between a limited company and either of the two forms of business already discussed is that it has a legal identity of its own separate from the people who own it. This means that, in the event of liquidation, creditors' claims are restricted to the assets of the company. The shareholders are not liable as individuals for the business debts beyond the paid-up value of their shares. This applies even if the shareholders are working directors, unless the company has been trading fraudulently or wrongfully.

The Insolvency Act, 1986, amongst other things brings into effect the notion that limited liability is a privilege rather than a right. Under these new rules incompetent as well as fraudulent directors may incur a measure of personal liability for debts incurred in the face of looming insolvency.

Directors found unfit to manage can also be disqualified from holding office elsewhere.

Other advantages for limited companies include the freedom to raise capital by selling shares and certain tax advantages.

The disadvantages include the legal requirements for the company's accounts to be audited by a chartered or certified accountant, and for certain records of the business trading activities to be filed annually at Companies House.

In practice, the ability to limit liability is severely restricted by the requirements of potential lenders. They often insist on personal guarantees from directors when small, new or troubled companies look for loans or credits. The personal guarantee usually takes the form of a charge on the family house. Since the Boland Case, in 1980, unless a wife specifically agreed to a charge on the house, by signing a Deed of Postponement, then no lender can take possession in the case of default.

A limited company can be formed by two shareholders, one of whom must be a director. A company secretary must also be appointed, who can be a shareholder, director, or an outside person such as an accountant.

The company can be bought 'off the shelf' from a registration agent, then adapted to suit your own purposes. This will involve changing the name, shareholders and articles of association.

Alternatively, you can form your own company, using your solicitor or accountant.

Co-operative There is an alternative form of business for people whose primary concern is to create a democratic work environment, sharing profits and control. If you want to control or substantially influence your own destiny, and make as large a capital gain out of your life's work as possible, then a co-operative is not for you.

The membership of the co-operative is the legal body that controls the business, and members must work in the business. Each member has one vote, and the co-operative must be registered under the Industrial and Provident Societies Act, 1965, with the Chief Registrar of Friendly Societies (see also Co-operatives, Section 3).

Forms of business: pros and cons
Sole Trader

Advantages	Start trading immediately
	Minimum formalities
	No set-up costs
	No audit fees
	No public disclosure of trading information
	Pay Schedule 'D' tax
	Profits or losses in one trade can be set off against profits or losses in any other area
	Past PAYE can be clawed back to help with trading losses
Disadvantages	Unlimited personal liability for trading debts
	No access to equity capital
	Low status public image
	When you die, so does the business

Partnership

Advantages   No audit required, though your partner may insist on one

No public disclosure of trading information

Pay Schedule 'D' tax

Disadvantages Unlimited personal liability for your own and your partners' trading debts (except sleeping partners)

Partnership contracts can be complex and costly to prepare

Limited access to equity capital

Death of a partner usually causes partnership to be dissolved

Limited Company

Advantages   Shareholders' liabilities restricted to nominal value of shares

It is possible to raise equity capital

High status public image

The business has a life of its own and continues with or without the founder

Disadvantages Directors are on PAYE

Audit required

Trading information must be disclosed

Suppliers, landlords and banks will probably insist on personal guarantees from directors (except for government loan guarantee scheme)

You cannot start trading until you have a certificate of incorporation

Useful Organisations and Publications

Accountancy bodies are listed, together with their services (see Section 6).

Organisations

The Chief Registrar of Friendly Societies, 15/17 Great Marlborough Street, London W1V 2AZ (01 437 9992)

The Companies Registration Office, Crown Way, Maindy, Cardiff CF43 (0222 388588) and for Scotland: 102 George Street, Edinburgh EH2 (031 225 5774). Both provide information and guidance on registering a limited company.

The Law Society, 113 Chancery Lane, London WC2 (01 242 1222). Their Legal Aid Department publishes booklets which give the name, address and telephone number of solicitors in each area, indicating their area(s) of specialisation, e.g., consumer law, landlord/tenant problems, employment or business problems generally, including tax and insolvency. They are available at libraries or Citizens' Advice Bureaux, and are solely concerned with solicitors willing to undertake legal aid work.

Alternatively, the society will simply give you the names of some firms of solicitors in your area.

Publications

How to Form a Private Company by Alec Just, 30th edition, published by Jordans, Jordan House, 47 Brunswick Place, London N1 (01 253 3030). Price £5.

The Companies Act, 1985 free from Peat Marwick McLintock, 1 Puddle Dock, Blackfriars, London EC4V 3PD (01 236 8000). A succinct publication giving comprehensive coverage of the Act.

Financial and Accounting Responsibilities of Directors free from the Consultative Committee of Accountancy Bodies, PO Box 433, Chartered Accountants Hall, Moorgate Place, London EC2P 2BT. Covers the civil and criminal law as it relates to directors' responsibilities to their companies, shareholders and to third parties.

THE BUSINESS NAME

The main consideration in choosing a business name is its commercial usefulness. You want one that will let people know as much about your business, its products and services as possible. Since 26 February 1982, when the provisions of the Companies Act, 1981 came into effect, there have been some new rules that could influence your choice of name.

Firstly, anyone wanting to use a 'controlled' name will have to get permission. There are some 80 or 90 controlled names that include words such as 'International', 'Bank' and 'Royal'. This is simply to prevent a business implying that it is something that it is not.

Secondly, all businesses that intend to trade under names other than those of their owner(s) must state who does own the business and how the owner can be contacted. So, if you are a sole trader or partnership and you only use surnames with or without forenames or initials, you are not affected. Companies are also not affected if they simply use their full corporate name.

If any name other than the 'true' name is to be used, then you must disclose the name of the owner(s) and an address in the UK to which business documents can be sent. This information has to be shown on all business letters, on orders for goods and services, invoices and receipts, and statements and demands for business debts. Also, a copy has to be displayed prominently on all business premises. The purpose of the Act is simply to make it easier to 'see' who you are doing business with.

Useful Organisations and Publications

Department of Trade, Room 003, Company House, 55 City Road, London EC1Y 1BB (01 253 9393), produce a useful free publication, *Notes for guidance on Business Names and Business Ownership*.

Jordan's Business Information Service, Jordan House, 21 St Thomas's Street, Bristol BS1 6JS (0272 230600). Under the 1982 Company Rules, the onus is on you to object within twelve months to someone else using your business name. For around £60 per annum, Jordans will alert you if anyone tries to register a company using your trading name, via their 'name watching' service.

PROTECTING YOUR IDEAS

Patent law can give you temporary protection for technological inventions. The registration of a design can protect the appearance or shape of a commercial product; copyright protects literary, artistic or musical creations and, more recently, computer programs; trade marks protect symbols, logos and pictures.

The period of the protection which these laws can give varies from five years, for the initial registration of the design, to fifty years after your death, for the copyright on an 'artistic' work. The level and scope of protection varies considerably, and is in the process of change. A flurry of activity in the late seventies set UK patent law on a course to harmonise it with EEC law. So, for example, it is now possible with a single patent application made in the UK to secure a whole series of protections throughout Europe. The Patent Co-operation Treaty will eventually extend that protection to the USA, USSR and Japan.

In practice, however, defending 'intellectual' property is an expensive and complex process for a new or small business.

Patent Protection This covers inventions which are 'truly' novel and are capable of industrial application. Scientific or mathematical theories and mental processes are included in the long lists of unpatentable items. Ideas that may encourage offensive, immoral or antisocial behaviour are also excluded.

Obviously it is important to establish first whether or not your idea is really new. With 20 million or so registered patents it is possible that the idea belongs to someone else, even if it is not being used. A search of patents granted and applied for will give you some idea of the activity in your area of interest. This can be done by studying abstracts of published specifications. These are classified under 400 main headings, with 6,000 'catch' words to guide you. You can get details of the classification key free of charge from the Patent Office. You can then either subscribe to a weekly service that selects and supplies patent specifications under the classification that interests you, or you can carry out a search yourself at the Science Reference Library. Otherwise, you could get a Patent Agent both to investigate your claim and look after your interests.

Registering Designs The shape, design or decorative features of a commercial product may be protectable by registering the design. The laws exclude any shape or appearance which is dictated solely by the production function. Thus, in order to be registerable, a design must be new or original, never published before or, if already known, never applied to the type of product you have in mind.

Unlike patent searches, which you can do yourself, as a design application you have to entrust this work to the officials at the Design Registry.

Copyright The copyright laws protect you from the unlicensed copying of 'original' creative works. Some skill and judgement are required to qualify a work for protection, but the 'originality' itself may be of quite a low order.

The categories protected by copyright include literary works (including not just the obvious, but such items as rules for games, catalogues, advertising copy, etc); dramatic and musical works; artistic works, including maps, graphs, photographs; films, TV and radio programmes, records, tapes and so on.

While the work remains unpublished no legal steps need to be taken to protect it. Once it is published, all you need to do is to add a copyright line to each copy of the work. This must take the form © Barbara Upchurch 1989. If you want to record the date on which a work was completed this can be registered for a fee with The Registrar, Stationers Hall. It is a fairly unusual thing to do, only important if you expect an action for infringement.

It is generally illegal to reproduce copyright work, but less than a substantial part may be used without infringement. The use of the word 'substantial' is more likely to mean important rather than large, though it is up to the courts to interpret.

Trade Marks A trade mark is a symbol by which the goods of a particular manufacturer, merchant or trader can be identified by customers. This can take the form of a word, a signature, a monogram, a picture or logo – or any combination of these. If you have been using an unregistered trade mark so extensively that it is clearly associated in your customers' mind with your brand or product, then you may have acquired a 'reputation' in that mark, which gives you rights under common law.

Otherwise the process of registration is similar to that of patents. First a search must be carried out either in person or having a Trade Mark Agent to act for you. Then, using forms from the Trade Marks Registry, you can apply for registration. Once your application has been accepted by the registry it is advertised in a weekly journal, *The Trade Marks Journal*. If this raises no objections the mark is officially registered. Once your mark is registered you have the right to bring an 'infringment' action if anyone else uses your trade mark. The courts also recognise that a trade mark acts as a protection to your customers. When they ask for a branded product by its trade mark, they can be confident of getting your product and not a 'pirate' product.

Organisations

The British Technology Group, 101 Newington Causeway, London SE1 6BU (01 403 6666) Publicity Department. They can help you with the exploitation and development of your invention. They have financial, technological and commercial resources and expertise.

The Chartered Institute of Patent Agents, Staple Inn Buildings, High Holborn, London WC1V 7PZ (01 405 9450). They can put you in contact with a patent agent in your area, and advise on the subject generally.

The Design Council, 28 Haymarket, London SW1 4DG (01 839 8000).

The Design Registry, Room 1124a, 11th Floor, State House, High Holborn, London WC1R 4TP (01 831 2525). For textiles: The Design Registry, Baskerville House, Browncross Street, New Bailey Street, Salford M3 5PU.Free pamphlet from either office of the Design Registry, *Protection of Industrial Designs* 17 pages. (There are design agents, but no register as such, although either a patent agent or a trade mark agent will be able to act for you.) ·

Institute of Information Scientists, 44/45 Museum Street, London WC1A 1LY (01 831 8003). Formed in 1978, it represents the interest of searchers, and has a register of searchers who will carry out literature searches in the patent field.

The Institute of Inventors, 19 Fosse Way, Ealing, London W13 0BZ (01 998 3540).

The Institute of Patentees and Inventors, Suite 505a, Triumph House, 189 Regent Street, London W1R 7WF (01 242 7812). The Institute looks after the interests of patent holders and inventors. They can provide useful advice and guidance on almost every aspect of 'intellectual' property.

The Institute of Trade Mark Agents, Suite 3/5, 38 Mount Pleasant, London WC1X 0AP (01 833 0875). The Institute can put you in contact with a trade mark agent in your area, and advise you on the subject generally.

Legal Protection Group, Marshalls Court, Sutton, Surrey SM1 4DU (01 661 1491). Can provide insurance at Lloyds, to cover some of the cost of fighting a patent infringer. The worst infringers of small inventors' ideas are international companies who bank on the little man being too poor to embark on a costly legal action, so this £250,000 (approx) a year insurance policy could be worthwhile.

The Patent Office, State House, 66–71 High Holborn, London WC1R 4TP (01 831 2525). Open to the public 10.00–16.00, Monday to Friday. They produce free pamphlets, *Basic Facts* is a simple introduction for inventors and gives a brief rundown on what patents are, how they are obtained and the kind of protection they give. *Introducing Patents* – a guide for inventors is aimed at inventors who need more detailed information. It should help them to decide whether to patent, and if so, whether to apply for a national patent or to try one of the international routes. Some idea of the costs and the various pitfalls that can occur are given. *How to prepare a UK Patent Application* is only for those who have decided to apply for a patent without professional help, at least in the initial stages, but is not intended as a substitute for the services of a patent agent. This booklet is only available on personal request from the Patent Office.

The Register of Trademarks, Patent Office, State House, 66–71 High Holborn, London WC1R 4TP (01 829 6145). 10.00 to 16.00, Monday to Friday. Accepts and advises on the registration of trade marks. Free pamphlet *Applying for a Trademark*, April 1980, 24 pages.

Science Reference Library, 25 Southampton Buildings, London WC2A 1AW (01 323 7919). The Library houses all patent details, and is open from 09.30 to 21.00, Monday to Friday, and on Saturday from 10.00 to 13.00. More details of this library are given in the section on specialist libraries (see page 172).

Provincial Patent Libraries
Belfast: Central Library, Royal Avenue, Belfast BT1 1EA (0232 43233)
Birmingham: Patent Department, Paradise Circus, Birmingham B3 3HQ (021 235 4537/8)
Glasgow: Mitchell Library, Science & Technology Dept, North Street, Glasgow G3 7DN (041 221 7030)

Leeds: Central Library, Calverley Street, Leeds LS1 3AB (0532 462006)

Liverpool: Patent Library, Science & Technology Library, William Brown Street, Liverpool L3 8EW (9051 207 2147)

Manchester: Patent Library, Central Library, St Peter's Square, Manchester M2 5PD (061 236 9422)

Newcastle-Upon-Tyne: c/o Business & Technology Library, Central Library, Newcastle PO Box MC, NE99 1MC (0632 610691)

Sheffield: Commerce and Technology Library, Surrey Street, Sheffield S1 1XZ (0742 734742)

Apart from UK, European, PCT and US specifications, the holdings of these libraries are varied. It is wise to check whether their holdings cover your requirements before going to the library.

Publications

The Inventors Information Guide by T. S. Eisenschitz and J. Phillips, Fernsway Publications, 5 Crane Grove, London N7. A very useful 90 pages covering the whole field – lots of useful addresses too. Price £3.95.

Patents, Trade marks, Copyright and Industrial Designs by T. A. Blanco White and Robin Jacob, in the Concise College Texts Series, published in 1986 by Sweet and Maxwell, 11 New Fetter Lane, London EC4 (01 583 9855). Price £10.50.

See also section on Financial and Advisory Services for Technology, and 'Training to use Patents' in the Other Small Business Courses section.

PREMISES

Buying or leasing a business premises entails a number of important and often complex laws affecting your decisions. To some extent these laws go beyond the scope of the physical premises, into areas such as opening hours and health and safety. (See also Property Services, Section 2.)

Planning Permission An important first step is to make sure that the premises you have in mind can be used for what you want to do. There are nearly a score of different 'use classes', and each property should have a certificate showing which has been approved. The classes include retail, offices, light industrial, general industrial, warehousing and various special classes.

Certain changes of class do not need planning permission – for example, from general industrial to light industrial. Also, changes of use within a class – say, from one type of shop to another – may not need planning permission.

In August 1985 a booklet was issued by the Department of the Environment called *The Small Firm and the Planners*. The circular stated, amongst other things, that if a business premises was put to a 'non-conforming' use, that was not in itself sufficient reason for taking enforcement action or refusing planning permission. Permission should only be refused where the business would cause a nuisance or a safety or health hazard. This in effect means that running a business from home does not necessarily require planning permission.

Once you have taken on a premises, then the responsibilities for 'conforming' fall on your shoulders, so take advice.

Building Regulations Even if you have planning permission, you will still have to conform to building regulations. These apply to the materials, structure and building methods used, in either making or altering the premises. So if you plan any alterations you may need a special approval.

The Lease Before taking on a lease, look carefully at the factors below.

Restrictions If you are taking on a leasehold property, then you must find out if there are any restrictions in the lease on the use of the property. Often shop leases have restrictions protecting neighbouring businesses. The lease will often stipulate that the landlords cannot 'unreasonably' withhold consent to a change in use. He may, however, insist on the premises being returned to its original shape before you leave.

Repairs Most leases require the tenant to take on either internal repairing liability or full repairing leases. Resist the latter if at all possible, particularly if the property is old. If you have to accept a full repairing lease, then it is *essential* to get a Schedule of Condition. This is an accurate record of the condition of the premises when you take it over. It is carried out by your own and the landlord's surveyor. It is one expense you may be tempted to forego – don't.

Rent Reviews However long (or short) your lease is, it is likely that a rent review clause allowing rent reviews every three to seven years will be included. Look very carefully at the formulas used to calculate future rents.

Security of Tenure The Landlord and Tenant Act, 1954, protects occupiers of business premises. When your lease ends you can stay on at the same rent until the steps laid down in the Act are taken. These steps are fairly precise, and you would be well advised to read the Act and take legal advice.

You will get plenty of warning, as the landlord must give you six months' notice in writing, even if you pay rent weekly. The landlord cannot just ask you to leave. There are a number of statutory grounds for re-possession. The two main types of grounds are, firstly, that you are an unsatisfactory tenant, an allegation you can put to the test in court; or secondly, that the landlord wants the premises for other purposes. In that case you must be offered alternative suitable premises. These are obviously matters for negotiation, and you should take advice as soon as possible.

Unified Business Rate From 1990 with a transition period of up to ten years for small businesses, a new and possibly more expensive form of business rates are coming into force. You should certainly be aware of the likely implications for your premises of the Local Government Finance Bill, as the law changing these rates is known.

Health and Safety at Work Whatever legal form your business takes (if you are a sole trader for instance, or a limited company) you will be responsible for the working conditions of all your premises. Your responsibility extends to people who work on those premises, to visitors and to the public. If you have more than five employees, you will have to prepare a statement of policy on health, and let everyone who is working for you know what that policy is. You may also be required to keep records of such events as the testing of fire alarms and accidents.

The main laws concerned are the health and Safety at Work Act (1974), the Offices, Shops and Railway Premises Act (1963) and the Factories Act (1961). Employers' liability is based on the common law, and your responsibilities can be extensive. A catalogue listing more than 2,000 relevant publications covering health and safety legislation is available from HMSO.

The Acts cover, among other matters, fire precautions and certificates; general cleanliness and hygiene; means of access and escape; machine and equipment safety; workspace; temperature; noise; welfare; catering arrangements; security of employees' property; toilet and washing facilities; protective clothing; the appointment of safety representatives and committees; and minimum insurance cover.

Special Trades Restaurants and all places serving food, hotels, pubs, off-licences, employment agencies, nursing agencies, pet shops and kennels, mini cabs, taxis, betting shops, auction sale rooms, cinemas and hairdressers are among the special trades that have separate additional regulations or licensing requirements.

Your local authority Planning Department will be able to advise you on the regulations that apply specifically to your trade. It would be as well to confirm the position whatever you planned to do. They can also tell you if any local by-laws are in force which could affect you.

Opening Hours Sunday trading and opening hours may be the subject of local restrictions. Once again, your local authority Planning Department will be able to advise you whether or not special local rules apply.

Advertising Signs There are some restrictions on the size and form that the name or advertising hoarding on your premises can take. A look around the neighbourhood will give you an idea of what is acceptable. If in doubt, or if you are going to spend a lot of money, take advice.

Organisations

British Institute of Interior Design, 1c Devonshire Avenue, Beeston, Nottingham NG9 1BS (0602 221255).

The Building Centre, 26 Store Street, London WC1E 7BT (01 637 1022). This has the most extensive library and information service on the whole building field, including building regulations and sources of professional advice. Their free information service (01 637 8361) will provide answers to almost any building problem.
Regional centres are at the addresses below:
The Building Centre, 35 King Street, Bristol BS1 4DZ (0272 22953)
Northern Counties Building Information Centre, c/o NFBTE, Green Lane, Durham DH1 3JY (0385 62611)
The Building Centre, Macdata Centre, 47 High Street, Paisley PA1 4AL (041 840 1199)
The Building Centre, 113/115 Portland Street, Manchester M1 6FB (061 236 9802)
The Building Materials Information Service, 22 Broadway, Peterborough PE1 1RU (0733 314239)
The Building Research Establishment, Bucknalls Lane, Garston, Watford WD2 7JR or Scottish Laboratory, Dept of Environment, Kelvin Road, East Kilbride, Glasgow

Design Selection Service, The Design Council, 28 The Haymarket, London SW1Y 4SU (01 839 8000). They offer a service to people looking for a designer to deal with the inside of a premises.

The Environmental Health Department will be able to advise you on particular problems related to using premises for serving or producing food or drink.

The Federation of Master Builders, 33 John Street, London WC1N 2BB (01 242 7583)

Health and Safety Executive, 1 Long Lane, London SE1 4PG (01 407 8911). Apart from supplying pamphlets and reference on the various regulations, they can put you in contact with the nearest of their 21 area office information services. In each of these offices there are groups of inspectors specialising in the specific local industries and their problems.

Incorporated Association of Architects and Surveyors, Jubilee House, Billing Brook Road, Weston Favel, Northants NN3 4NW (0604 404121).

Local Authorities Each has a Planning Department, which can give information and opinions on planning applications and other matters relating to your premises; a Building Control Department, covering building regulations; an Environmental Health Department, covering health and safety at work; and an Industrial Liaison Department, giving general advice to encourage industrial development.

Rating Surveyors Association, Regal House, Mengham Road, Hayling Island, Hants PO11 9BL.

Rating and Valuation Association, 115 Ebury Street, London SW1W 9QT (01 730 7258/7359).

Royal Institute of British Architects, 66 Portland Place, London W1N 4AD (01 580 5533). They have a clients advisory service in London and nine provincial centres. They can deal with all types of enquiry by phone, letter, or even a personal call. The Advisory Service direct line is 01 323 0687.

Royal Institute of Chartered Surveyors, 12 Great George Street, London SW1P 3AD (01 222 7000).

Royal Town Planning Institute, 26 Portland Place, London W1N 4BE (01 636 9107). A contentious or complex planning application may need the services of a planning consultant – perhaps from this institute. They produce a list of consultant firms throughout the UK. Otherwise, 'local knowledge' is the best source of a good surveyor or an architect who will be able to manage most planning and building regulation matters for you.

Rural Development Commission who have advisers who can help with both building regulations and planning permission.

Publications

Land Law in the Nutshell series, published in 1987 by Sweet and Maxwell, 11 New Fetter Lane, London EC4 (01 583 9855). Regularly updated. Price around £3.95.

Selwyn's Law of Health and Safety at Work Butterworths Bookshop, 9–12 Bell Yard, Temple Bar, London WC2 (01 405 6900). Price £7.95.

Planning Directory and Development Guide contains information on planning in central government in the UK, planning consultants, and organisations concerned with or related to the planning process. The information on local government, which forms the bulk of the book, includes names and addresses of chief officers in charge of planning, the names and functions of key planning staff and a summary of the development opportunities existing in each authority area, plus a list of publications relating to planning in the area. Available from Ambit Publications Ltd, 6a College Green, Glos GL1 2LY.

Planning Permission, A Free Guide for Industry from the Department of the Environment, 2 Marsham Street, London SW1P 3EB. Explains the planning control systems to help businesses submit a successful application.

TRADING LAWS

Once you start trading, whatever the legal form of your business, you will have certain obligations to your customers. These are contained in a number of legal acts and some of these are outlined below.

Sale of Goods Act, 1979 This Act states that the seller has three obligations. Firstly, the goods sold must be of merchantable quality – that is, reasonably fit for their normal purpose. Secondly, those goods must also be fit for any particular purpose made known to the seller. This makes you responsible for your advice, if, for example, your customer asks you whether or not a product will perform a particular job. Thirdly, the goods sold must be as described. This would include the colour or size of the goods concerned.

The Food and Drugs Act, 1955 This Act makes it a criminal offence to sell unfit food; to describe food falsely; or to mislead people about its nature, substance or quality. This regulation covers food wherever it is sold, manufactured, packed, processed or stored for sale.

Prices Act, 1974 The Prices Act enables the Government to require prices to be displayed and to control how they are displayed. This requires restaurants, pubs, cafés and petrol stations to display their prices.

Consumer Credit Act, 1974 This Act took eleven years to implement throughout the whole range of credit provided to consumers, but as of 19 May 1985, the final sections came into force. It covers every aspect of trader relationships with customers who buy on credit.

Trade Descriptions Acts, 1968 and 1972 The Acts make it a criminal offence for a trader to describe his goods falsely. These acts cover such areas as declared car mileage on second-hand cars and statement of the country of manufacture on jeans.

Unsolicited Goods and Services Act, 1971 The Act makes it an offence to send goods without a customer's order, in the hope that they will then buy them.

Weights and Measures Acts, 1963 and 1979 The Acts make it an offence not to mark the quantity (weight, volume or, in a few cases, the number) on the contents of most packaged grocery items and many other items.

Unfair Contract Terms Act, 1977 The Act prevents firms from escaping their responsibilities by using 'exclusion clauses' or disclaimers, such as statements saying 'articles left at owner's risk'. The onus is on the trader to prove that his exclusions are fair and reasonable in the circumstances. The notice itself is not enough.

Consumer Protection Act, 1987 This Act safeguards consumers from products that do not reach a reasonable level of safety. Before this Act those injured had to prove a manufacturer negligent before they could successfully sue for damages. Whilst a customer could already sue a supplier without proof of negligence, under the Sale of Goods law, this Act provides the same rights to anyone injured by a defective product whether or not the product was sold to them.

This Act provides an incentive, where one was not yet present, for businesses to ensure that their products provide the safety users or those affected, can reasonably expect.

For manufacturers, the UK national standard for quality assurance systems laid down in BS 5750 is now compulsory reading.

Organisations

Advertising Standards Authority, 2/16 Torrington Place, London WC1E 7HN (01 580 5555). Will put you right on your legal responsibilities if you advertise your goods for sale.

Environmental Health Departments of the local authority will be able to provide advice on all matters to do with food, drink and hygiene.

Office of Fair Trading, Fields House, Breams Building, London EC4A 1PR (01 242 2858). The office provides useful booklets on most aspects of trading law from the consumer's point of view.

The Small Claims Procedure is a useful low cost way to collect money owed to you. Small debts of up to around £500 can be sued for with the minimum of formalities. All County Courts keep a stock of an invaluable book, *Small Claims in the County Court*, written in layman's language. A companion volume, *Enforcing Judgements in the County Court*, is also available.

Trading Standards Department of the local authority can also give you advice on acceptable trading behaviour.

Publications

Consumer Law for the Small Business by Patricia Clayton, published in 1983 by Kogan Page Ltd, 120 Pentonville Road, London N1 (01 278 0433). Covers: Trade Descriptions Acts, Supply of Goods and Services, Health and Safety, Cash and Credit, Quality and Quantity, Unfair Trading and Codes of Practice. Price £7.95.

The Consumer Protection Act, 1988 a short guide, available free from the Department of Trade and Industry.

Fair Deal published by the Office of Fair Trading in July 1988 and available from HM Bookshops, price £2.00. Provides a concise, authoritative and up-to-date summary of the main laws affecting traders.

Guide to the Consumer Protection Act, 1987 free from the Consumer Safety Unit, Department of Trade and Industry, 10/18 Victoria Street, London SW1H 0NN.

Hotel and Catering Law by Davis Field, in the Concise College Texts series, published in 1982 by Sweet & Maxwell, 11 New Fetter Lane, London EC4 (01 583 9855). Price £5.65.

How to Collect the Money That Is Owed To You by Mel Lewis, published by McGraw-Hill Book Co (UK) Ltd, Shoppenhangers Road, Maidenhead, Berks SL6 2QL (0628 23431). 1982. Written for managers in small-to-medium sized businesses, it contains a wealth of ideas for getting payment. It also has a guide to credit insurance and factoring, examples of contracts invoiced and collection letters, lists of useful organisations and addresses and a guide to telephone collection techniques. Price £14.95.

Legal Aspects of Marketing by John Livermore, 4th edition 1984, published by William Heinemann Ltd, 10 Upper Grosvenor Street, London W1X 9PA. Price £9.95.

Product Liability Briefing executive guide published by Whitakers, covers all aspects and is regularly updated.

Sale of Goods and Consumer Credit by A. P. Dobson, in the Concise College Texts series, published by Sweet and Maxwell, 11 New Fetter Lane, London EC4 (01 583 9855). Price £9.95.

EMPLOYING PEOPLE

Apart from the problems of finding the right people to work in your business, and making sure that the conditions under which they will have to work are satisfactory, you may have other responsibilities. Examples are given below.

Terms of Employment Within 13 weeks of starting to work for you, you have to give people a written set of terms of employment. These terms will cover pay, holidays, sick pay and overtime commitments and pay.

Notice of Lay-offs Once an employee has worked for you for over four weeks, they are entitled to at least one week's notice of dismissal. They are also entitled to guaranteed pay up to five days in any three months if you decide to either lay them off or to put them on short time.

Discrimination You cannot discriminate against anyone on colour or racial grounds. The same protection applies to married people. If you employ five people, including part-timers, then you cannot discriminate against them or against any applicant for a job, on the grounds of their sex. There are further laws and protections covering, amongst other considerations, pregnancy, disabled people, minimum wages, union recognition, discipline and wrongful dismissal.

You may find it useful to join an organisation such as the Institute of Personnel Management or the Industrial Society, who can give you timely and cost-effective advice in this field. Such organisations keep absolutely up to date with all the many changes in this field of legislation, a task beyond the resources of most small firms with other, more pressing problems.

Useful Organisations

Advisory, Conciliation and Arbitration Service (ACAS), 27 Wilton Street, London SW1X 2AZ. Although you mainly hear of ACAS in big public disputes between unions and their management, a large part of their work is concerned with preventing disputes and dispensing information. Nearly a quarter of their 12,500+ (pa) advisory visits are to firms with fewer than 50 employees.

They offer advice on recruitment and selection, payment systems and incentive schemes, manpower planning, communications and consultations, collective bargaining and so on.

They also produce free advisory booklets on job evaluation, introduction to payment systems, personnel records, labour turnover, absence, recruitment and selection and introduction of new employees. Their regional offices are at:

Northern Region: Westgate House, Westgate Road, Newcastle-Upon-Tyne NE1 1TJ (091 261 2191) Cumbria, Tyne & Wear, Cleveland, Northumberland and Durham

Yorkshire and Humberside Region: Commerce House, St Albans Place, Leeds LS2 8HH (0532 431371) North Yorkshire, South Yorkshire, Humberside and West Yorkshire

London Region: Clifton House, 83/117 Euston Road, London NW1 2RB (01 388 5100)

South East Region: Clifton House, 83/117 Euston road, London NW1 2RB (01 388 5100) Cambridgeshire, Norfolk, Suffolk, Oxfordshire, Buckinghamshire, Bedfordshire, Hertfordshire, Essex, Berkshire, Surrey, Kent, Hampshire (except Ringwood), Isle of Wight, East Sussex, West Sussex

South West Region: Regent House, 27a Regent Street, Clifton, Bristol BS8 4HR (0272 744066) Gloucestershire, Avon, Wiltshire, Cornwall, Devon, Somerset, Dorset, Ringwood

Midlands Region: Alpha Tower, Suffolk Street, Queensway, Birmingham B1 1TZ (021 631 3434) Northamptonshire (except Corby), Shropshire, Staffordshire (except Burton-on-Trent), West Midlands, Hereford and Worcester, Warwickshire

North West Region: Boulton House, 17/21 Chorlton Street, Manchester M1 3HY (061 228 3222) Lancashire, Cheshire, High Peak District of Derbyshire, Greater Manchester

Midlands Region: Nottingham Office, 66/72 Houndsgate, Nottingham NG1 6BA (0602 415450) Derbyshire (except High Peak District), Nottinghamshire, Leicestershire, Corby, Lincolnshire, Burton-on-Trent

Merseyside Office: Cressington House, 249 St Mary's Road, Garston, Liverpool L19 0NF (051 427 8881)

Scotland: Franborough House, 123/157 Bothwell Street, Glasgow G2 7JR (041 204 2677)

Wales: Phase 1, Ty-Glas Road, Llanishen, Cardiff CF4 5PH (0222 762636)

Industrial Participation Association, 85 Tooley Street, London SE1 2QZ (01 407 9083 or 01 403 6018). The association is concerned with bringing all parties in industry together in a common effort to promote employee participation in a practical and realistic way.

The Industrial Society Peter Runge House, 3 Carlton House Terrace, London SW1Y 5DG (01 839 4300). The society campaigns for the involvement of people at work and argues that increased involvement means greater efficiency and productivity.

Annual membership costs £125 for companies with up to 250 employees, and this gives access to an extensive range of services and publications.

Their Information and Personnel Advisory Services department will answer enquiries from members on any subject in the field of personnel management and industrial relations. Most enquiries are dealt with the same day, though complicated questions that have to be referred to their legal advisers or the medical advisory panel may take about ten days. Of particular interest to small business is the Personnel Advisory Service, which can, in effect, provide you with all the services of a professional personnel manager, from recruitment to redundancy. The fees for this service are about £1,800 per annum.

Institute of Personnel Management, IPM House, 35 Camp Road, Wimbledon SW19 4UW (01 946 9100). The Institute has 33,000 individual members, and has extended its service to businesses through its Company Service Plan. The cost of membership for a company employing up to 75 people would be £120 per annum, an entrance fee of £25 plus VAT. This would give access to the Institute's library, publications, conferences and seminars, and, more importantly, it would allow use of the Information and Advisory Service. This service is staffed by a small team of multi-disciplines specialists, including a legal adviser who is a barrister at law. They can answer or find answers to most problems in this field.

Enquiries can be made by letter, telephone or a personal visit between 09.00 and 17.00 daily, Monday to Friday.

Interestingly enough, of the 800 or so enquiries they handle each month, pay and conditions of employment account for half, followed by employment law, employee relations and then training.

Job Centres As well as providing you with employees, your local Job Centre can also advise you on most aspects of employment law, or at any rate introduce you to other local organisations who can help.

Legal Protection Group, Marshalls Court, Sutton, Surrey SM1 4DU (01 661 1491). Provide an employer's legal protection package. They also undertake commercial legal proceedings insurance, provide legal fees for the protection of patents, copyright, registered designs and trade marks, and in respect of 'passing off' actions.

See also National Federation of Self Employed and Small Business; and Alliance of Small Firms and Self Employed People.

Publications

Croner's Reference Book for Employers, Croner House, 173 Kingston Road, New Malden, Surrey KT3 3SS (01 942 8966). Details all the legal requirements an employer must observe, including unfair dismissal, health and safety at work, rights at work, and training measures. Price £53.50.

The Department of Health & Social Security produces a number of leaflets in the employment field, including one on statutory sick pay.

Employing People, Guidance for Those Setting Up in Business for the First Time is a free booklet from the Department of Industry, Small Firms Service. Your local office can be reached on Freephone Enterprise.

Labour Law by C. D. Drake, published in the Concise College Texts series by Sweet and Maxwell, 11 New Fetter Lane, London EC4 (01 583 9855). It is a sort of A-level crammer which covers all the ground and case law illustrations. Price £8.50.

The Law on Unfair Dismissal, Guidance for Small Firms by Joan Henderson, Free from Job Centres and Department of Employment Small Firms Centres.

INSURANCE

Insurance forms a guarantee against loss. You must weigh up to what extent your business assets are exposed to risk and what effect such events could have on the business if they occurred. Insurance is an overhead, producing no benefit until a calamity occurs. It is therefore a commercial decision as to how much to carry, and it is a temptation to minimise cover. You must carry some cover, either by employment law, or as an obligation imposed by a mortgager.

You will have to establish your needs by discussing your business plans with an insurance broker. Make sure you know exactly what insurance you are buying; and, as insurance is a competitive business, get at least three quotations before making up your mind.

Employer's Liability You must carry at least £2 million cover to meet your legal liabilities for death or bodily injury incurred by any employee during the course of business. In practice, this cover is usually unlimited, with the premiums directly related to your wage bill.

Personal Accident Employer's liability only covers those accidents in which the employer is held to be legally responsible. You may feel a moral responsibility to extend that cover to anyone carrying out an especially hazardous task. You may also have to cover your own financial security, particularly if the business depends on your being fit.

Public Liability This protects employers against legal liability for death or injury to a third party on their property. These events can occur through defects in your premises, negligent acts by your employees or from liabilities arising from the product that you market.

Professional Liability Solicitors, accountants and management and computer consultants are obvious examples. Anyone involved in giving professional advice should consider their possible liability arising from wrongful advice and negligence to their client.

Business Premises, Plant and Equipment Obviously need cover. There are, however, a number of ways of covering them. 'Reinstatement' provides for full replacement cost, whilst 'indemnity' meets only the current market value of your asset, which means taking depreciation off first. There are other things to consider too. Removal of debris, architect's fee, employees' effects and (potentially the most expensive of all) local authorities sometimes insist that replacement buildings must meet much higher standards than the ones they replace.

Stock From raw materials through to finished goods stock is as exposed as your buildings and plant in the event of fire or another hazard. Since 1982 theft from commercial property has exceeded £50 million per annum.

Consequential Loss Meeting the replacement costs of buildings, plant, equipment and stock will not compensate you for the loss of business and profit arising out of a fire or other disaster. Your overheads, employees' wages, etc, may have to continue during the period of interruption. You may incur expenses such as getting sub-contracted work done.

Insurance for consequential loss is intended to restore your business's finance to the position it was in if the interruption had not occurred.

Goods in Transit Until your goods reach your customer and he accepts them, they are still at your risk. You may need to protect yourself from loss or damage in transit.

Commercial Vehicle Policy Although you may have adequate private use cover for your present vehicle, this is unlikely to be satisfactory once you start to use the vehicle for business purposes. That and any other vehicles used in the business should be covered by a commercial use policy.

Fidelity Guarantee and Other Thefts Once in business you can expect threats from within and without. A Fidelity Guarantee can be taken to protect you from fraud or dishonesty on the part of key employees. Normal theft cover can be taken to protect your business premises and its contents.

Useful Organisations These organisations will be able to put you in contact with either a broker or an insurance company that can help you to assess your needs and level of cover.

British Insurance & Investment Brokers Association, BIIBA House, 14 Bevis Marks, London EC3A 7NT (01 623 9043). BIIBA brokers will take a detailed look at a business, see what risks it is running, and put together a package of policies from different insurers to meet exactly the needs of a client.

Credit Insurance Association Ltd, 13 Grosvenor Place, London SW1 (01 235 3550).

Insurance Brokers Registration Council, 15 St Helens Place, London EC3A 6DS (01 588 4387).

Legal Protection Group, Marshalls Court, Sutton, Surrey SM1 4DU (01 661 1491). Specialises in 'Legal Fees' insurance covering such fields as Unfair Dismissal, Sale and Purchase Indemnity and other consumer and employee related legal areas.

National Association of Trade Protection Societies, 4/6 New Street, Leicester LE1 5NB (0533 531951).

Publications

A Businessman's Guide to Liability Insurance available free from the Sun Alliance plc, Bartholomew Lane, London EC2N 2AR.

NATIONAL INSURANCE, PAYE, TAX, VAT AND PENSIONS

This is one field where good professional advice at the outset will more than pay for itself. Although considerable publicity is given to the 'Black Economy', there are also many people paying more tax than they need. However, you will get the best of your professional adviser if you understand the basics yourself.

Tax The tax that you have to pay will depend on the legal form of the business you decide on. As a sole trader or partner you will pay tax under Schedule 'D', Case I or II. If you choose a limited company, then the company will pay corporation tax and the directors will be on Schedule 'E', under the PAYE scheme.

The difference in net tax paid by a sole trader or a company can be very significant, and there are many other factors to take into account. For example, a sole trader can offset any trading losses against other income. Company losses are locked into the company. In the event of losses, a sole trader can even claw back past taxes paid – for example from PAYE in his last job. A company cannot do this.

There is also a difference in when the tax is due. As the director of a company, you pay as you earn. A sole trader or partner can pay tax up to nearly two years after earning the income, depending on his accounting year. For new businesses there are still more factors to consider and some variations on the normal rules.

This is not an area in which to take uninformed guesses.

National Insurance Contributions Once again, the legal form of your business will determine what you pay. A sole trader or partner is self-employed and pays contributions in class 2, which is a weekly sum, and in class 4, based on annual profits. A company director pays as an employee, and his company pays as an employer. So it is quite possible for a small company to pay up to four times the National Insurance contributions that it would have paid, had it been operated as a sole trader or partnership.

As a rule of thumb, if you do not expect to make more than £10,000 per annum profit, you would be better off not trading as a company. But the level of contributions are not the only consideration. For example, the 'employee' director has better benefits out of the National Insurance than the 'self employed' sole trader.

Pay-As-You-Earn (PAYE) Either as an 'employee' director, or in any other form of enterprise employing people, you will be responsible for maintaining the PAYE system. This will involve you in deducting the appropriate tax from your employees' pay and sending it to the Collector of Taxes. If you do not, then you, and not the employee, will be liable for the uncollected tax.

VAT (Value Added Tax) Whatever the legal form of your business, if your turnover exceeds £7,500 in any calendar quarter, or if it exceeds £22,100 in the last four calendar quarters, then you must register for VAT. This has to be done by notifying your local VAT office, within 21 days of the end of the quarter in question. VAT is normally charged at 15%, but some areas are zero-rated and some are exempt. There are also some special rules on exports and imports. VAT is normally accounted for quarterly, but from 1 July 1988 an optional annual accounting scheme came into force.

Before you reach this level of turnover it would be prudent to become better informed (VAT thresholds are usually revised in the Budget).

Pensions Once you are working for yourself, you will have to make your own pension provision (and perhaps provision for those working for you). Fortunately for people in profitable self-employment, there are now a large number of highly tax-efficient pension schemes. By selecting the right scheme you can get tax relief at your highest income tax rate, and so get the Inland Revenue to contribute up to three-quarters of your pension. In addition, it is possible eventually to receive capital gains tax on the profits made on your contributions over the years; and partly as a pension which will be treated as earned income and not be subject to the investment income surcharge.

It is a complex but potentially very rewarding investment, with a considerable difference in performance by the different pension plans. For example, over the period 1970/1980 the best-performing pension 'annuity' turned £500 per annum into an accumulated cash sum of £9,480 and the worst only £5,309.

You can pay up to 17.5% (this has been increased to 20% for those born between 1916 and 1933, and there are also small increases for those born between 1912 and 1915) of your net earnings into an approved pension scheme, so once again good professional advice is a must.

It is also possible, under certain circumstances to use the funds in a self-administered pension fund to finance investments in your own business.

The Pension Mortgage A package that will pay off the mortgage, win full tax relief, and provide at least a small pension into the bargain. It may not even cost any more. Building Societies who offer pension mortgages include: Alliance, Anglia, Cheltenham and Gloucester, Halifax, Leicester and Woolwich.

Employee Buy Outs Employees who borrow money to buy out their company can, under some circumstances, get tax relief on loan interest.

Profit Sharing Companies that can give tax free shares to employees each year up to the value of £5,000, or 10% of their earnings, whichever is the lower.

Organisations

Association of Consulting Actuaries, c/o R. Watson & Sons, 47/49 London Road, Reigate, Surrey RH2 9PG (07372 41144)

Company Pensions Information Centre, 7 Old Park Lane, London W1Y 3LJ (01 493 4757) Publish a free booklet *What Pension Terms Mean*, explaining the 200 or so commonly used words and phrases.

National Association of Pension Funds, 12/18 Grosvenor Gardens, London SW1W 6DH (01 730 0585)

Professional Advisers See Section 6 for accountants and earlier in this section for insurance.

Society of Pension Consultants, Ludgate House, Ludgate Circus, London EC4A 2AB (01 353 1688)

The Tax Payers Society, Room 22, 1st Floor, Wheatsheaf House, 4 Carmelite Street, London EC4Y 0JA (01 583 6020) Business and professional membership costs £35 p.a. and the Society provides these services for members:

1 Free advice on any point of law or practice concerning Income Tax, Corporation Tax, Capital Gains Tax and Capital Transfer Tax. The complexities of these taxes make this service of inestimable value.

2 (a) A newsletter which is sent from time to time to keep members informed on tax affairs.
(b) Booklets published by the Society on current tax subjects.

3 The views of the Society's members are, when appropriate, brought up in Parliament. In particular, an annual letter from the Society is addressed to the Chancellor of the Exchequer prior to the Budget, putting forward suggested tax changes in line with needs of members.   .

Trade and Professional Organisations including those independent business associations given in Section 2, can often point you towards help in this field.

Publications

Business Start-Up Package from the Alliance of Small Firms, 42 Vine Road, East Molesey, Surrey KT8 9LF (01 979 2293). Book II in this five-part series is on tax and National Insurance, 12 pages. Gives you a few useful clues. The others cover law generally and book-keeping and banking. They also run an information and consultancy reference service for members. See also National

Federation of Self Employed and Small Business, which also runs an information service in this field (see Section 2). Price £1.25 each or £6.25 for 5.

Employer's Guide to PAYE leaflet P7.

Employer's Guide to National Insurance Contributions leaflet NP15.

Employer's National Insurance Contributions a free technical bulletin from Hodgson Impey, 4 Kings Arms Yard, London EC2R 7AX.

Grundy's Tax Havens edited by Milton Grundy, The Bodley Head Ltd, 9 Bow Street, London W1X 3RA (01 379 6637) Gives details on a score of tax havens from the Bahamas to Switzerland.

Guide to Running a Small Business, The Guardian Book edited by Clive Woodcock, published by Kogan Page Ltd, 120 Pentonville Road, London N1 (01 278 0433). Chapter 7 has nearly 50 pages of very useful advice in the taxation field. Price £7.95.

Allied Dunbar Tax Guide (formerly Hambro's) published by Longman, 5 Bentinck Street, London W1 (01 935 0121). Produced each year, this has extensive special sections on income from business and professions, partnerships, companies, VAT and a useful section on tax-saving hints. This should be available in most bookshops. Price about £9.

Managing Tax in Your Business by Robert Walters, published by Business Books, Hutchinson House, 17/21 Conway Street, London W1P 6JD (01 387 2811). Well illustrated and plenty of worked examples. Price £14.95. Provides answers to these questions:
- How are businesses and partnerships taxed?
- What reliefs are available?
- When is tax payable?
- What is a capital gain?
- How are dividends treated?
- What is Development Land Tax?
- Do I have to pay if I get planning permission?
- What is a Capital Transfer?
- What is Value Added?
- How do I transfer Assets and Shares?
- What are the pitfalls of converting to a Company?
- Do I have to make a loss, to get tax relief from losses?

National Insurance Guide for the Self Employed leaflet NI, from the Department of Health and Social Security.

Peat Marwick McLintock, 1 Puddle Dock, Blackfriars, London EC4V 3PD (01 236 8000). Free tax booklet from the Librarian.

Pensions for the Self-Employed by N. Toulson, published by Gower Publishing Co Ltd, Gower House, Croft Road, Aldershot, Hants GU11 3HR (0252 331551). A very readable, comprehensive guide to the subject. Paperback price £6.20.

Self Employed Pensions An annual by the Financial Times Business Publishing Ltd. This is the only source of detailed comparative information on pensions for the self-employed. The book analyses nearly 100 schemes, explains different types of pension plans available, and summarises the tax position. It also shows how each pension scheme has performed and makes projections on likely future results. Price £21.50.

Starting in Business is a free pamphlet issued by the Board of the Inland Revenue, and is available from your local tax inspectorate. It provides a simple and basic introduction to most aspects of tax, PAYE, National Insurance and VAT.

Tax Facts updated each year after the Budget, this free publication describes income tax, National Insurance, corporation tax, capital gains tax, development landtax, inheritance tax and VAT. It gives details on tax rates and allowances as well as the Business Expansion Scheme. Available from Kidson's, Columbia House, 69 Aldwych, London WC2B 4DY.

Tax and the Privately Owned Business covers the taxation of sole traders, partnerships and companies and the effects of converting a business into a company. It also outlines the implications of introducing capital into a business and providing for retirement. Free from Ernst & Whinney, Becket House, 1 Lambeth Palace Road, London SE1 7EU.

Thinking of Taking Someone On? Pamphlet on employers' tax responsibility, Inland Revenue (IR 53).

Tolley's Corporation Tax annual from Tolley Publishing Co, 102/104 High Street, Croydon, Surrey CR0 1ND (01 686 0115). A very authoritative guide, concerned only with business taxation. Price £8.75.

Value Added Tax, Scope and Coverage and *The General Guide* are two free publications from HM Customs & Excise local VAT offices. They also have pamphlets on such topics as 'Filling in your VAT return', keeping records and accounts, and visits by VAT officers.

'Which' Tax Saving Guide produced each year, concentrates on personal tax.

DATA PROTECTION

Under this Act it is unlawful for anyone to keep on computer details which could identify living individuals unless they have registered as 'data users'. The registration fee is £22. From 11 November 1988 the 'subject access' provisions of the Act apply, which means people must be provided with access to their files within 40 days of asking.

The Data Protection Registrar, Springfield House, Water Lane, Wilmslow, Cheshire SK9 5AX produces a number of free publications outlining the Act and its consequences.

TRAINING FOR BUSINESS

There are now many opportunities for education and training, at every level, in the business and management field. No formal academic qualifications are required for most of the courses and costs are generally modest. In certain cases, participants may be eligible for grants or subsidised training.

The bulk of the activities are concentrated in universities and colleges throughout the whole of the UK. However, there are a growing number of opportunities for the less mobile to take up some form of home study in the business field in general, and small business opportunities in particular. There is now some reliable evidence to show that people attending small courses can significantly improve their chances of success.

COURSES AT COLLEGES AND OTHER INSTITUTIONS

Our survey has divided the courses on offer into the following main categories.

Short Courses That is, up to 2 weeks, for people considering starting up a business. These are usually of one or two days' duration, and cost around £30, unless the provider is supported by the Training Commission. Such courses are often free. They concentrate on giving an introduction on how to start your own business. The courses as well as providing lectures, give an opportunity for those who have recently started up in business to talk about their experiences. The demand for these courses is very high. Various estimates suggest that upwards of 50,000 people attended such courses during 1986/87. This certainly forms the most cost effective method of finding out very quickly a lot about what is going on in the 'new and small business world'. These courses are frequently run at weekends and sometimes on evenings during the week.

Longer Courses Following on from the introductory, one or two day courses, a number of colleges run programmes lasting up to sixteen weeks. In the main, the longer courses are sponsored by the Training Commission. Their courses, called by such titles as 'Firmstart', New Enterprise Programmes or Small Business

Courses, are run at business schools in universities, polytechnics and colleges throughout the country.

Such courses very often consist of 3 to 4 weeks of classroom content, covering all the main aspects of running a small business. This is complemented by up to 10 further weeks, with business school staff working with the 'entrepreneurs' on the mechanics of starting up their own business. This can involve detailed work on preparing a business plan, raising finance, finding premises, applying for grants or aid, or marketing and market research. During this period the student entrepreneur can be given an allowance of around £40 per week, together with some subsistence allowance, and a grant for market research.

There are other longer courses, on a part-time or linked weekend basis. The former may be one or two evenings each week over 10 weeks or more covering a specific topic such as book-keeping or marketing.

The linked weekends tend to cover the whole field of starting up a business, with individual project work carried out between weekends. In this way participants can bring their problems back to the business school staff and get their advice and help.

Topic Courses These are usually run over a few days or weeks, for those already in business. They cover topics such as: Financial Management, Marketing, Book-keeping, Exporting, Computers, Employing People and Strategy/Business Growth. Also after the budget some colleges hold tax update courses.

Provision on Existing Courses Many courses in colleges are modular or in discrete sections, with, say, a few weeks of one topic given in a fairly concentrated form. The subject may be marketing, finance, computer systems or business law. Although these courses are not aimed specifically at people running small businesses, the subject matter is certainly appropriate. Some colleges encourage people to join in parts of an existing full-time course, so in effect you join a class for a few weeks and learn the topic of particular interest to you.

Business Growth Programmes These programmes are aimed at established new businesses, usually with a turnover in excess of £250,000 per annum, with a view to helping them develop strategies for expansion. They are of particular interest to companies seeking to raise new capital. They are run in the UK at the Cranfield School of Management, and the London and Manchester Business Schools.

Scholarships and Bursaries A limited number of awards for full-time postgraduate courses leading to higher degrees (e.g., Master of Business Administration) and diplomas are made available by the Economic and Social Research Council, Postgraduate Training Division, 160 Great Portland Street, London W1M 6BA (01 637 1499)

Alternatively you could contact your nearest college and see what they have to offer. The situation is constantly changing, and many innovations in education for small business are being introduced.

Future Trends New colleges and courses are coming on stream all the time. As well as using this directory, try your local college or education department and see what they have on offer. Another organisation that keeps abreast of development is:

The UK Small Business Management Education Association, c/o London Business School, Sussex Place, Regents Park, London NW1 4SA (01 262 5050) *Contact: Catherine Gurling*

Training Commission (formerly the Manpower Services Commission) Their training departments at the following locations will be able to advise you on dates and courses in their areas:

Head Office: Moorfoot, Sheffield, S1 4PQ (0742 753275)
Office for Scotland: 9 St Andrew Square, Edinburgh EH2 2QX (031 225 8500)
London: 236 Grays Inn Road, London WC1X 8HL (01 278 0363)
Midlands: Alpha Tower, Suffolk Street, Queensway, Birmingham B1 1UR (021 631 3555)
Northern: Broadacre House, Market Street, Newcastle-upon-Tyne NE1 6HH (091 232 6181)
North West: Washington House, The Capital Centre, New Bailey Street, Manchester M3 5ER (061 833 0251)
South East: Telford House, Hamilton Close, Basingstoke RG21 2UZ (0256 29266)
South West: 4th Floor, The Pithay, Bristol BS1 2NQ (0272 273710)
Wales: 4th Floor, Companies House, Crown Way, Maindy, Cardiff CF4 3UT (0222 802479)
Yorkshire and Humberside: Jubilee House, 33–41 Park Place, Leeds LS1 2RL (0532 446299)

WHERE TO FIND A COURSE

The results of our 1988 survey of the small business education provisions are set out below. As well as showing the nature of the course run and the person to contact, you can see if the programme is run full-time (F) or part-time (P). In the case of topic courses the legend corresponds to the initials of the subject covered. So Financial Management is (FM), Marketing is (M),

Book-keeping is (B), Exporting is (E), Computers is (C), Employing People is (P), Strategy/Business Growth is (S).

We have also identified where advice and consultancy are available, and research activities are underway.

Business Club is the name often given to the regular meetings of small business people for discussions or seminars. These are often hosted by colleges and we have shown those that do. Finally, we have listed whether or not the college has a full-time commitment to the small business field. Very often the task of teaching in this field is divided up amongst people with other important and time consuming commitments.

KEY TO COLUMNS
1 Short courses start-up
2 Long courses start-up
3 Topic courses
4 Prov on existing courses
5 Advice, info & counsel
6 Consultancy services
7 Research activity
8 Business club
9 Special unit

KEY TO INITIALS
F Full-time
P Part-time
FM Financial management
M Marketing
B Book-keeping
E Exporting
C Computers
P Employing people/management
S Strategy/business growth

ENGLAND

	1	2	3	4	5	6	7	8	9
Accrington & Rossendale College of Further Education, Sandy Lane, Accrington, Lancs (0254 393521) *Contact: Mrs K. Belton*	P				•	•		•	
Acton Technical College, Dept of Business & General Studies, Millhill Road, Acton, London W3 8UX (01 993 2344) *Contact: B. Marshall*	P						•		
Airedale & Wharfedale College of Further Education, Small Business Unit, Calverley Street, Horsforth, Leeds LS18 4RQ (0532 581723) *Contact: David Hardy*	P	FP	FM M B C P		•	•		•	•
Basingstoke Technical College, Worting Road, Basingstoke, Hants RG12 1TN (0256 54141) *Contact: B. Gurden*	FP	P	FM M B E C P S	•	•	•		•	
University of Bath, Claverton Down, Bath BA2 7AY (0225 826826) *Contact: N. Crawford*			•			•	•		
Birmingham University, IEBS, Asley Building, PO Box 363, Birmingham B15 2TT (021 414 6692) *Contact: N. Kavanagh*	P			F	•		•	•	•
Blackburn College of Technology & Design, Dept of Management & Professional Studies, Neilden Street, Blackburn BB2 1LH (0254 55144) *Contact: R. Walne*		FP	FM B C P	•	•	•	•	•	•
Blackpool College of Further & Higher Education, Faculty of Business Food & Management, Ashfield Road, Blackpool FY2 0HB (0253 52352) *Contact: P. Lavelle*	FP	FP	FM M B E C P S		•	•			

		1	2	3	4	5	6	7	8	9

Bolton & District Business Club, c/o Bolton Business Centre, Lower Bridgeman Street, Bolton, Lancs (0204 53460)
Contact: Anne Barratt

Bournemouth & Poole College of Further Education, North Road, Parkstone, Poole, Dorset BH14 0LS (0202 747600)
Contact: B. Sutton

Boxtowe College of Further Education, Business Studies Dept, High Road, Chilwell, Beeston, Nottingham (0602 228161)
Contact: G. Gardner

Bradford University, Management Centre, Emm Lane, Bradford (0274 542299)
Contact: Peter Buckley

Bradford & Ilkley Community College, Mgt & Admin Studies Dept, Great Horton Road, Bradford (0274 753298)
Contact: V. Baston

Brighton College of Technology, Pelham Street, Brighton BN1 4FA (0273 685971)
Contact: T. Garnell

Brighton Polytechnic, Mithras House, Lewes Road, Moulescoomb, Brighton (0273 693655)
Contact: Barry Lee Scherer

Bristol University, Wills Building, Bristol BS8 1SS (0272 230557)
Contact: Linda Skinner

Bristol Polytechnic, Coldharbour Lane, Frenchay, Bristol BS16 1QY (0272 656261)
Contact: John Collins

British Institute of Management, Management House, Cottingham Road, Corby, Northants NN17 1TT (0536 204222) (Members only)

Brunel University, Brunel Management Programme, Uxbridge, Middx UB8 3PH (0895 56461)
Contact: K. Alsop

Continuing Education, Uxbridge, Middx UB8 3PH (0895 37188)
Contact: Prof J. Miller

Institution	1	2	3	4	5	6	7	8	9
Bolton & District Business Club								•	
Bournemouth & Poole College of FE		P							
Boxtowe College of FE			•						
Bradford University			All		•	•	•		•
Bradford & Ilkley Community College	P	P	All	F P	•	•	•	•	•
Brighton College of Technology	F P	F P	FM MB CP	?	•	•	•	•	•
Brighton Polytechnic	F P	F P	All			•	•		
Bristol University	F P	F P				•			•
Bristol Polytechnic	F P	F P			•	•	•		
British Institute of Management					•				
Brunel University			FM MC P		•	•			
Continuing Education	F P	F P	FM MB EC PS	•	•	•	•		

	1	2	3	4	5	6	7	8	9
Bucks College of Higher Education, Newland Park, Chalfont St Giles HP17 4AD (02407 4441) *Contact: S. Halliday*		FP	F	•		•	•		
Burnley College of Arts & Technology, Shorey Bank, off Ormerod Road, Burnley (0282 36111) *Contact: E. Beswick*	F	P	FM MB CP L		•	•		•	•
Burton Upon Trent Technical College, Lichfield Street, Burton Upon Trent DE14 3RL (0283 45401) *Contact: Peter Ostle*	P	P	FM MB CP S	F P	•	•	•	•	•
Bury Metropolitan College of Further Education, Business Studies, Management Unit, Bank House, Blackburn Street, Radcliffe M26 9WQ (061 723 2480) *Contact: David Draper*	FP	FP	FM MB CP S		•	•			•
Business & Commerce & Industry Fellowship, 600 House, 16 Middleborough, Colchester, Essex CO1 1QT (0206 561700) *Contact: Stuart Beckwith*	FP		FM MB CP S		•	•	•	•	•
Business Development Unit, Business Advice Centre, 30 New Walk, Leicester LE1 6TF (0533 554464) *Contact: U. Dholakia*	FP	FP	All		•	•	•	•	•
Business Enterprise Training, 10 Woodland Way, Goffs Oak, Waltham Cross, Herts (0707 872905) *Contact: B. Englebright*	P		FM MB CP S		•	•		•	•
Cambridge University, Dept of Geography, Downing Place, Cambridge CB2 3EN (0233 333399) *Contact: Peter Blair, David Keeble*							•		
Carlisle Technical College, Business & Secretarial Department, Victoria Place, Carlisle CA1 1HS (0228 24464)	P	F	FM MB CP S	•	•	•			
Cassio College, Retail Distribution & Services, Langley Road, Watford, Herts WD1 3RH (01 924 0311) *Contact: K. Farrow*	FP	FP	FM MB EC PS		•	•	•	•	
Central London Polytechnic, 35 Marylebone Road, London NW1 5LS (01 486 5811) *Contact: John Stanworth, Robin Tuck*	FP	FP			•	•	•		•
Chelmer Institute of Higher Education, Victoria Road, South Chelmsford, Essex CM1 1NH (0245 350388) *Contact: R. McLarty*	FP	FP	FM MB EC PS		•	•	•	•	•

	1	2	3	4	5	6	7	8	9
Chichester College of Technology, Westgate Fields, Chichester, West Sussex PO19 1SB (0243 786321) *Contact: D. Evans*	P		FM MB CP S		•				
City of Birmingham Polytechnic, Mgt & Business Development Centre, Room G112, Perry Bar, Birmingham B42 2SU (021 331 5202) *Contact: Upkar Pardesi*		P	All	F P	•	•	•	•	•
City University, Centre for Continuing Education, Northampton Square, London EC1V 0HB (01 253 4399 ext 3269) *Contact: Sylvia Tyler*		F P	All			•			
Clarendon College, Pelham Avenue, Mansfield Road, Nottingham (0602 607201 ext 252) *Contact: A. Frances*	P		C						
Coalville Technical College, Bridge Road, Coalville, Leic LE6 2QR (0530 36136) *Contact: J. R. Eastham*	FP	FP	All	F P	•	•	•	•	•
College for the Distributive Trades, 30 Leicester Square, London WC2H 7LE (01 930 6536) *Contact: Allison Roberts*	FP	FP	All	P	•	•	•		
Coombe Cliff Adult Education Centre, Coombe Road, Croydon CR0 5SP (01 868 9191) *Contact: Beryl Osborne*	P		FM MB						
Cornwall College of Further/Higher Ed, Pool, Redruth, Cornwall (0209 712911 ext 2185) *Contact: Tony Sully*	P	P	All	P	•	•		•	
Coventry Polytechnic, Priory Street, Coventry CV1 5FP (0203 24166) *Contact: Jim Saker*	FP	FP			•	•	•		
Cranfield School of Management, Cranfield, Beds MK43 0AL (0234 751122) *Contact: Colin Barrow, Paul Burns, Robert Brown*	FP	FP	All	•	•	•	•	•	•
Crewe & Alsager College of Higher Education, Crewe Road, Crewe CW1 1DW (0270 50266) *Contact: P. Kitchen*		P	M	F P	•	•	•	•	•
Darlington College of Technology, Management & Business Studies, Cleveland Avenue, Darlington, Co Durham DL3 7BB (0325 467651) *Contact: J. Rosser*	F		FM MB CP S	•	•	•		•	

	1	2	3	4	5	6	7	8	9
Dartington Institute, Shinners Bridge, Dartington, Devon TX9 6DX *Contact: Frank Watson*	P	P							
Doncaster Metropolitan Institute of Higher Education, Dept of Management Studies, Barnsley Road, Scawsby, Doncaster DN5 7UD (0302 783421) *Contact: Chris Pike*	F P	F P	FM MB CP S	•	•	•		•	
Dorset Institute, Holland House, Oxford Road, Bournemouth BH8 8EZ (0202 298626/28) *Contact: Prof D. Watkins*	FP	P	All	F P	•	•	•	•	•
Dudley College of Technology, The Broadway, Dudley, West Midlands DY1 4AS (0384 455433) *Contact: A. P. Wilkes*		FP	FM MB C	F	•	•		•	•
University of Durham, Graduate into Enterprise, 14 Old Elvet, Durham BH1 3HP (091 3742253) *Contact: David Absalom*		FP			•	•	•	•	•
Ealing College of Higher Education, St Mary's Road, Ealing, London W5 5RF (01 579 4111) *Contact: Pat Lord*	P		All	P	•	•	•	•	•
East Devon College, Bolham Road, Tiverton, Devon EX16 6SH (0884 254247) *Contact: E. A. Janes, Patricia Webber*	P	P							
East Herts College, The Springs, Turnford, Broxbourne, Herts (0992 466451) *Contact: Tony Jones*	F P	P	?						
East Lancashire Professional Services, Nelson & Colne College, Scotland Road, Nelson, Lancs BB9 7YT (0282 866780) *Contact: P. Thornton*	F		MB						
East Midlands Regional Management Centre, 56 Clarendon Street, Nottingham (0602 410910) *Contact: Gerry Gardner*	F P		All		•	•		•	•
East Surrey College, Gatton Point, Claremont Road, Redhill, Surrey RH1 2JX (0737 772611) *Contact: Kevin O'Leary*	P		All	F P	•	•	•	•	
Essex Institute of Higher Education, Chelmer Court, Church Street, Chelmsford, Essex (0245 233030) *Contact: Roy McLarty*	F P	F P	All	F P	•	•	•	•	•

	1	2	3	4	5	6	7	8	9
Exeter University, Extra Mural Studies, St Luke's, Heavitree Road, Exeter EX1 2LU (0392 74425) *Contact: Prof Daveney*			FM	C					
Fielden House Productivity Centre Ltd, Fielden House, Mersey Road, West Didsbury, Manchester M20 8QA (061 445 2426) *Contact: R. Hutton*	P		FM MB CP S		•	•	•	•	•
Gloucester College of Arts & Tech, Small Business Unit, Oxstalls Lane, Gloucester GL2 9NW (0452 426819) *Contact: C. Bennett*	P	FP	All		•	•		•	•
Great Yarmouth College of Further Education, Southtown, Great Yarmouth NR31 0ED (0493 55261) *Contact: Philip Gunn*	FP	•	FM MB CP		•	•			•
Hall Green Technical College, Business Studies & General Education, Cole Bank Road, Hall Green, Birmingham B28 8ES (021 778 2311) *Contact: E. Owen*	P	P	FM MB EC S	•	•	•			
Halton College of Further Education, Kingsway, Widnes, Cheshire WA8 7QQ (051 423 1139) *Contact: John Palmer*	F	F							
Handsworth Technical College, Soho Road, Handsworth, Birmingham B21 9DP (021 551 6031) *Contact: Masood Rizui*	FP	FP						•	•
Hartlepool College of Further Education, Stockton Street, Hartlepool, Cleveland TS26 0DP (0429 75453) *Contact: Colin Doram*		F	FM MB CP S		•	•		•	
Hatfield Polytechnic, Hertford Campus, Balls Park, Hertford SG13 8QF (0992 558451) *Contact: John Sykes*					•	•	•	•	
Henley Management College, Greenlands, Henley on Thames, Oxon RG9 3AU (0491 571454) *Contact: Prof K. MacMillan*			All		•	•	•		
Highbury College of Technology, Dept of Management Studies, Cosham, Portsmouth PO6 2SA (0705 383131) *Contact: D. Wright*	•		FM	C	•	•	•	•	

	1	2	3	4	5	6	7	8	9
Highlands College, PO Box 142, St Saviour, Jersey, Channel Islands (0534 71065) *Contact: Mrs G. Renouf*	P	P		•	•			•	
Hotel & Catering Training Board, International House, High Street, Ealing, London W5 5DB (01 579 2400) *Contact: Mrs Kym Kennedy*	F	P	FM MP		•	•	•		•
Huddersfield Polytechnic, Queensgate, Huddersfield HD1 3DH (0484 22288 ext 2121) *Contact: John Thompson*	FP	P	All	F	•	•	•	•	•
Humberside College, Higher Education, Cottingham Road, Hull HU6 7RT (0432 41451) *Contact: Mr M. Hird*	F	F	ME C	•	•	•	•		•
Imperial College of Science & Technology, Dept of Management Science, Exhibition Road, London SW7 2BX (01 589 5111) *Contact: Anne Benjamin*					•	•	•		
Isle of Wight College of Arts & Technology, Newport, Isle of Wight (0983 526631) *Contact: John Peck*	P	P	FM MB CP	P	•	•	•		•
Kidderminster College of Further Education, Hoo Road, Kidderminster, Worcs DY10 1LX (0562 820811) *Contact: R. E. Bishop*		P	FM MB CP S		•	•	•	•	•
Kingston Polytechnic, Penrhyn Road, Kingston Upon Thames, Surrey KT2 5SE (01 549 1366) *Contact: James Curran*							•		
Knowsley Small Firms Business Club, c/o Knowsley Central Tertiary College, Rupert Road, Huyton, Merseyside L36 9TD (051 480 6161) *Contact: The Secretary*								•	
Lancaster University, Gillow House, Lancaster LA1 4YX (0524 65201) *Contact: Robert Daniels*							•		
Leeds Polytechnic, 5 Queen Square, Leeds LS2 8AY (0532 439726) *Contact: Martyn Robertson*	F	P	All	F	•	•	•		•
Leek College of Further Education, Stockwell Street, Leek, Staffs ST13 6DB (0538 382506) *Contact: D. A. Jagger*	P	P	S		•	•	•	•	

	1	2	3	4	5	6	7	8	9
Leicester Polytechnic, 30 New Walk, Leicester LE1 6TF (0533 554464) *Contact: Director – Small Firms Centre*	P	P	All		•	•		•	•
Leigh College, Railway Road, Leigh, Lancs NN7 4AH (0942 608811) *Contact: N. Pemberton*		P			•	•		•	
Lewes Technical College, Business Education Dept, Mountfield Road, Lewes, East Sussex (079 16 6121) *Contact: J. Breeze*		P	FM M C B P S	•					
Lincoln College of Technology, Business & Management Studies, Cathedral Street, Lincoln LN2 5HQ (0522 30641) *Contact: Roy Sanderson*	F P	F	FM M B E C P S	•	•	•			•
Liverpool University, Eleanor Rathbone Building, Liverpool L69 3BX (051 794 2000) *Contact: P. Stoney*			FM M P S		•	•	•	•	
City of London Polytechnic, 84 Moorgate, London EC2M 6SQ (01 283 1030 ext 324) *Contact: Rosemary Royds*	P		FM M C		•	•			•
London Business School, Sussex Place, Regents Park, London NW1 4SA (01 262 5050) *Contact: C. Gurling*		F P			•		•	•	•
London Institute, 3–396 Oxford Street, London W1R 1FE (01 491 8533) *Contact: R. Owen Roberts*	F P	F P	All	P	•	•	•		
Loughborough University, Loughborough, Leicester LE11 3TU (0509 263171) *Contact: Chris McEvoy*	F P	F P			•	•	•	•	•
Luton College of Higher Education, Dept of Management & Organisational Studies, Putteridge Bury, Hitchin Road, Luton, Beds LU2 8LE (0582 34111) *Contact: R. Wooding*	P		FM M C P S	•	•	•			
The College of Management, Dunchurch, Rugby, Warwicks CV22 6QW (0788 810656) *Contact: Miss F. Edwards*	F P	F	FM M B E C P		•	•		•	
Macclesfield College of Further Education, Business & European Studies, Park Lane, Macclesfield SK11 8LF *Contact: D. Brightmore*	P	P	FM M B E C P S		•			•	
Manchester Business School, Booth Street West, Manchester M15 6PB (061 275 6333) *Contact: F. Chittenden*		P	E	F P	•	•	•	•	•

	1	2	3	4	5	6	7	8	9
Manchester Polytechnic, Dept of Management, Aytoun Street, Manchester M1 3GH (061 228 6171 ext 2462) *Contact: Richard Thorpe*				F P	•	•	•		
Manchester Polytechnic, Centre for Education Development, Shepherds House, Elizabeth Gaskell Site, Hathersage Road, Manchester M13 0JA (061 225 9054) *Contact: Miss Hollinshead*			M P S			•	•	•	•
Merseyside Education Training Enterprise Ltd, 6 Salisbury Street, Liverpool L3 8DR (051 207 2281) *Contact: Michael Ainscow*	F P	F	All	P	•	•	•	•	•
Middlesex Polytechnic, Business School Dept, The Burroughs, Hendon, Middx NW4 4BT (01 202 6545) *Contact: The Dean*						•	•		
Mid-Gloucester Technical College, Stratford Road, Stroud, Glos (04536 3424) *Contact: John Edwards*	P		F M M B			•	•	•	•
Mid-Kent College of Further Education, Horsted, Maidstone Road, Chatham, Kent ME5 9UQ (0634 44470) *Contact: Colin Barlie*	F P	F P			•	•	•	•	•
Milton Keynes Business Venture, Level 3, Civic Offices, 1 Saxon Gate West, Central Milton Keynes MK9 3JH (0908 660044) *Contact: John Carpenter*			F M M B C P		•	•		•	•
Nene College, Management Centre, Moulton Park, Northampton NN2 7AL (0604 719531) *Contact: Dr Salvard*	F	F	F M M B E C P S		•	•	•		
Newcastle Upon Tyne Unviersity, Newcastle Upon Tyne NE1 7RU (091 232 8511) *Contact: Steven Johnson*							•		
New Enterprise Development, 15 Park House, 140 Battersea Park Road, London SW11 4NB (01 627 4991)	P	F	F M M B P S		•	•	•		•
Newcastle Upon Tyne Polytechnic, Manor House, Coach Lane Campus, Newcastle Upon Tyne NE7 7XA (091 266 4878 or 091 235 8189) *Contact: Geoff Parkinson*	P		F M M B C P S	F	•	•		•	•

	1	2	3	4	5	6	7	8	9
Northbrook College of Design & Technology, Littlehampton Road, Goring By Sea, Worthing (0903 830057) *Contact: Derek Haynes*	P	P	All	FP	•	•	•	•	•
North Cheshire College, Business Management & TV Studies, Winwick Road, Warrington, Cheshire (0925 37311) *Contact: A. Conrad*	F	P	FM MB EC PS		•	•	•	•	
NE London Polytechnic, Duncan House, High Street, Stratford, London E15 2JB (01 590 7722 ext 3328) *Contact: Derek Mottershead*	FP	F	FM MB		•	•	•	•	•
Polytechnic of North London, Dept of Business, 2/16 Eden Grove, London N7 8DB (01 607 2789)				•	•	•	•	•	•
North Nottinghamshire College of Further Education, Carlton Road, Worksop, Nottinghamshire S81 7HP (0909 473561) *Contact: J. G. Wilson*	FP	FP	All	FP	•	•	•	•	•
North West Regional Management Centre, Woodlands, Southport Road, Chorley, Lancs PP7 1QR (02572 66942/66833) *Contact: Anne Sheppard*					•				
North Tyneside College of Further Education, Embleton Avenue, Wallsend, Tyne & Wear NE28 9NL (091 626 4081) *Contact: Norman Moore*	FP		MB C		•			•	
Northumberland College of Arts and Technology, Open Learning Unit, College Road, Ashington, Northumberland (0670 856666/811516) *Contact: Peter Dwyer*	P	P	FM MB CP		•	•		•	•
Norwich City College of Further & Higher Education, Management Centre, Ivory House, All Saints Green, Norwich NR1 3NB (0603 28619) *Contact: Rad Spassitch*	P	P	FM MB EC PS	•	•	•	•	•	
University of Nottingham, Economics Dept, Nottingham NG7 2RD (0602 484848) *Contact: Dr M. Binks*							•		•
Oldham, Business & Management, Rochdale Road, Oldham OL9 6AA (061 624 5214) *Contact: B. Kay*	FP		FM MB CP S		•	•		•	

	1	2	3	4	5	6	7	8	9
Open University, Open Business School, Walton Hall, Milton Keynes MK7 6AA (0908 653292) *Contact: Colin Gray*	F P	F P	FM MB CP S			•	•		•
Oxford College of Further Education, Cricket Road, Oxford OX4 3DN (0865 716171) *Contact: David Haywood*	P	F P	All		•	•	•	•	•
Oxford Polytechnic, Lady Spencer Churchill College, Wheatley, Oxford OX9 1XD (08677 819940) *Contact: Dr D. Lawton*	F	F		F P			•	•	
Park Lane Colelge of Further Education, Park Lane, Leeds LS3 1AA (0532 443011) *Contact: Paul Staniland*	P				•				
Peterborough Regional College, Hightrees Management Centre, Park Crescent, Peterborough, Northants (0733 67366) *Contact: Roger Litawski*	P					•	•		•
Plymouth Business School, Plymouth Polytechnic, Drake Circus, Plymouth, Devon PL4 8AA (0752 264655) *Contact: D. Blackler*	F P	F P	FM MB S	•	•	•	•	•	•
Portsmouth College of Art & Design & Further Education, Winston Churchill Avenue, Portsmouth PO1 2DJ (0705 826435) *Contact: Mel Parker*	P	P	FM MB CP	•	•	•		•	•
Portsmouth Polytechnic, Business School, Locksway Road, Milton, Portsmouth (0705 735241) *Contact: Dr A. Hankinson*	P		All	F	•	•	•	•	•
Preston Polytechnic, Heatley Street, Preston PR1 2TQ (0772 22141) *Contact: Nigel Hall*	P	P				•	•		
Quantum Business Services Ltd, New Caledonia Mills, Shelton New Road, Shelton, Stoke on Trent ST1 4PQ (0782 202542 or Freefone Quantum)	P	P	All		•	•	•	•	•
Queen Mary College, London University, Mile End Road, London E1 4NS (01 980 4811) *Contact: Prof C. Levicki*		F P	FM MB CP S	•	•	•	•	•	•
Rockingham College of Further Education, West Street, Wath upon Dearne, Rotherham (0709 760310) *Contact: D. H. Davison*	P	P			•	•	•		

	1	2	3	4	5	6	7	8	9
Rother Valley College of Further Education, Doe Quarry Lane, Dinnington, Sheffield S31 7NH (0742 568681) *Contact: L. Wickham*	P		FM M B C		•				
Rural Development Commission, Local RDC office as listed in telephone directory			M P		•	•			•
St Helens College, School of Management, Water Street, St Helens, Merseyside (0744 33766) *Contact: Raymond Murphy*	P		FM M B C P S		•	•		•	•
Salford University, Business Studies Dept, Salford M5 4WT (061 736 5843) *Contact: W. E. Roberts*					•	•	•	•	
Shackleton Associates, Jubilee House, 92 Lincoln Road, Peterborough PE1 2SN (0733 61273) *Contact: K. Shackleton*	P				•	•	•		•
University of Sheffield, School of Mgt Studies, Sheffield S10 2TN (0742 786555) *Contact: Dr E. Jacobs*	F				F P	•	•	•	•	•
Sheffield Polytechnic, Dept of Business, Pond Street, Sheffield S1 1WB (0742 720911) *Contact: Colin Gilligan*			FM M B C P S	F	•	•			•
Silsoe College, Cranfield Institute of Technology, Silsoe, Beds MK45 4DT (0525 60428) *Contact: Dr S. Vyakarnam*	F	F			•	•	•	•	•
Slough College of Higher Education, Wellington Street, Slough, Berks SL1 1YG (0753 34585) *Contact: Ian Webb*			FM M C P S	P	•	•		•	
South Bristol Technical College, Maggs Howe, Queens Road, Bristol BS8 1QX (0272 21680) *Contact: John Lord*	F P		FM M B C P S		•	•	•	•	•
Southampton University, Dept of Accounting, Southampton SO9 5NH (0703 559122) *Contact: Mike Page*					•	•	•	•	
South Kent College of Technology, Dept of Business Studies, Ashford Branch, Jemmett Road, Ashford TN23 2RJ (0233 24513) *Contact: John Holloway*		P	FM B E C P S	M	•	•	•	•	•

	1	2	3	4	5	6	7	8	9
South West London College, Abbots Wood Road, Streatham, London SW16 1AN (01 677 8141) *Contact: Peter Ayling*	F		FM BC P		•	•			
States of Guernsey College of Further Education, Route des Coutanchez, St Peter Port, Guernsey, Channel Islands (0481 27121) *Contact: M. Vance*		P	FM BC P		•	•	•		•
Stockport College of Technology, Wellington Road South, Stockport SK13UQ (061 480 3897) *Contact: H. Bennett*	FP	FP	All	FP	•	•		•	•
The Suffolk College of Higher & Further Education, Rope Walk, Ipswich IP4 1LT (0473 55885) *Contact: N. Hogg*	P	P	FM MB CE PS		•	•	•		•
Sunderland Polytechnic, 1/4 Thornhill Park, Sunderland, Tyne & Wear SR2 7JZ (0783 41231) *Contact: A. C. Halborg*	FP	FP	FM		•	•	•	•	•
University of Surrey, The Research Park Office, PO Box 112, Guildford, Surrey GU2 5XL (0483 579693) *Contact: Dr Malcolm Parry*					•		•		
Teesside Small Business Club Ltd, Unit 8b, Royce Avenue, Cowpen Industrial Estate, Billingham, Cleveland TS28 4BX (0642 370094)					•	•		•	
Teesside Polytechnic, Flatts Lane Centre, Normanby, Middlesbrough, Cleveland (0642 469611) *Contact: Gerald Kirkwood*	P	P			•	•			
Telford College of Arts & Technology, Business & Management Studies, Haybridge Road, Wellington, Telford, Shropshire TE1 1NP (0942 55511) *Contact: Gerald Wallis*	FP	FP	FM MB CP S		•	•	•	•	
Thames Polytechnic, Riverside House, Beresford Street, London SE18 6BU (01 854 2030) *Contact: Roderick Atkin*	FP	FP			•	•	•	•	•
Thurrock Technical College, Management & Business Studies, Woodview, Grays, Essex (0375 71621) *Contact: Howard Hollow*	P	P	FM MB EC PS		•	•	•	•	

	1	2	3	4	5	6	7	8	9
Tile Hill College of Further Education, Tile Hill Lane, Coventry CV4 9SU (0203 461444) *Contact: D. C. Ferris*	P		All		•	•			•
Trent Polytechnic, Business Development Centre, Burton Street, Nottingham NG1 4BU (0602 418248) *Contact: Ms Sue Dickens, Terry Faulkner, Graham Beaver*		F P	All		•	•	•	•	•
URBED Enterprise Development, 3–5 Stamford Street, London SE1 9NT (01 928 9515) *Contact: Andrea Deletant*	F P	F P	FM M B C P S		•	•	•	•	•
Wakefield District College, Management & Business Studies, Whitwood Centre, Four Lane Ends, Whitwood, Castleford, W. Yorks (0977 554571) *Contact: Roger Thornton*		P	FM M B E C P	•	•	•		•	
University of Warwick, Small Business Centre, Coventry CV4 7AL (0203 523741) *Contact: D. R. Greenaway, Ian Watson*	P	F P	FM M B C P S		•	•	•	•	•
Watford College, Dept of Management Studies, Hempstead Road, Watford, Herts WD2 7HT (01 924 1211) *Contact: K. F. Young*			FM M C P	•	•				
Wellingborough College, Westfield Centre, Brickhill Road, Wellingborough, Northants NN8 3JS (0933 440339) *Contact: L. J. Rigby*	P		All	P	•	•			
West Bromwich College of Commerce & Technology, Small Business Unit, Wood Green, Wednesbury, West Midlands (021 471 2081) *Contact: P. T. Wilson*						•			
West Midlands Regional Management Centre, North Staffordshire Polytechnic, College Road, Stoke-On-Trent ST4 2DE (0782 412143) *Contact: Mrs P. Dickenson*			All		•	•	•	•	•
West Nottinghamshire College of Further Education, Derby Road, Mansfield, Notts NG18 5BH (0623 27191) *Contact: Peter Usher*		P			•	•		•	
West Oxfordshire Technical College, Hollaway Road, Witney, Oxon OX8 7EE (0993 3464) *Contact: R. Evans*		P	FM M B C P L	•	•	•			

	1	2	3	4	5	6	7	8	9
West Suffolk College of Further Education, Out Risbygate, Bury St Edmunds, Suffolk (0284 701301) *Contact: Mrs W. Payne*					•				
Wigan College of Technology, The Management Centre, Ashfield House, Wigan Road, Standish WN6 0EQ (0257 424659) *Contact: J. Swift*		F P	FM M B E C P L	•	•	•	•	•	•
Wirral Metropolitan College, Business & Management Dept, Carlett Park, Eastham, Wirral, Merseyside L62 0AY (051 327 4331) *Contact: D. Mitchell*		P	FM M B C P L	•	•	•			
Wolverhampton Polytechnic, Compton Road West, Wolverhampton WV3 9DX (0902 26547) *Contact: Terry Vokes*	P		FM M B C P S	F	•	•	•		•
Women Into Business, Small Business Bureau, 32 Smith Square, London SW1P 3HH (01 222 0330) *Contact: Irene Jeffery*	P		All		•		•		•
Worthing College of Technology, Dept of Business Studies, Littlehampton Road, Goring by Sea, Worthing, West Sussex BN12 6NV (0903 64424) *Contact: Derek Haynes*	P	P	FM M B E C P L	•	•	•	•	•	•
Wye College, Ashford, Kent TN25 5AH (0233 812401) *Contact: J. Nicholson*	F				•	•	•		

NORTHERN IRELAND

	1	2	3	4	5	6	7	8	9
North Down College of Further Education, Castle Park Road, Bangor, N. Ireland BT20 4TF (0247 271254)		P							
Queens University, Belfast BT7 1NN (0232 245133) *Contact: Richard Harrison, David Fleming*			•				•	•	
University of Ulster, Northern Ireland Small Business Institute, Shore Road, Newtownabbey, Co Antrim BT37 0QB (0232 365060) *Contact: Ken O'Neill*	P	F P	All	F P	•	•	•	•	•

REPUBLIC OF IRELAND

	1	2	3	4	5	6	7	8	9
NIHE, Plessey Technology Park, Limerick, Ireland (061 333 644) *Contact: S. J. Pettit*	P	F P			•	•	•	•	•

	1	2	3	4	5	6	7	8	9
Trinity College, Dublin, School of Business Studies, Dublin (01 77 29 41) *Contact: Head of Dept*	F P	F P	B C		•		•	•	
University College, Dublin, The Enterprise Centre, Belfield, Dublin 4 (01 693 244) *Contact: John Murray*	P	P					•	•	•

SCOTLAND

	1	2	3	4	5	6	7	8	9
Aberdeen University, Dept of Chemistry, Aberdeen AB9 2UE (0224 40241) *Contact: Dr L. Glasser*					•	•			
Angus Technical College, Keptie Road, Arbroath DD11 3EA (0241 72056) *Contact: Ms G. MacMillan*	F P		FM B C P S		•	•	•		
Bell College of Technology, Almada Street, Hamilton, Lanarkshire ML3 0JB (0698 283100) *Contact: J. Rennie*	P	P						•	
Borders College of Further Education, Melrose Road, Galashiels TD1 2AP (0896 57755) *Contact: N. H. Williamson*	F P	F P	FM M B C P		•	•	•	•	
Cardonald College, 690 Mosspark Drive, Glasgow G52 3AY (041 883 6151) *Contact: David Baillie*	P		B C P		•	•	•		•
Dumfries & Galloway College of Technology, Heath Hall, Dumfries DG1 3QZ (0387 61261) *Contact: W. Brydson*	P	P	FM B C P S		•	•	•		•
Duncan of Jordanstone College of Art, Room 6016, 13 Perth Road, Dundee (0382 23261) *Contact: Sultan Kermally*	P		FM P S			•			
University of Dundee, Centre for Continuing Education, Nethergate, Dundee DD1 4HN (0382 23181) *Contact: Mrs C. Rottger*			FM M P				•	•	
Dundee College of Further Education, 30 Constitution Road, Dundee (0382 29151) *Contact: J. Pringle*	P					•			
Dundee College of Technology, Bell Street, Dundee (0382 28818) *Contact: V. Mackinlay*	F P	F P	All	F P	•	•	•	•	•

	1	2	3	4	5	6	7	8	9
University of Edinburgh, Dept of Business Studies, William Robertson Building, 50 George Square, Edinburgh EH8 9IY (031 667 1011) *Contact: Ewan Gowrie*		F	M P		•	•	•		
Falkirk College of Technology, Grangemouth Road, Falkirk, Stirlingshire FK2 9AD (0524 24981) *Contact: Ian Morrison*	P		FM MB CP S				•	•	
Glasgow College of Technology, Dept of Management Studies, Cowcaddens Road, Glasgow G4 0BA (041 332 7090) *Contact: Dick Weaver*	FP	FP	FM ME CP		•	•	•	•	•
University of Glasgow, 53/59 South Parks Ave, Glasgow G12 8LF (041 339 8855) *Contact: P. Vale*		FP	All		•	•	•	•	•
Glenrothes & Buckhaven Technical College, Stenton Road, Glenrothes South KY6 2RA (0592 772233) *Contact: David Gardner*	P		All		•	•	•	•	•
Heriot Watt University, Mountbatten Building, 31/35 Grassmarket, Edinburgh EH1 2HT (031 225 6465) *Contact: Parker Nicol, Ray Oakley*	FP	FP						•	•
Inverness College of Further/Higher Education, Longman Road, Inverness IV1 1SA (0463 236681) *Contact: John Hunter*	F	P	FM MB CP S	F					•
Napier Polytechnic of Edinburgh, Redwood House, 16 Spylaw Road, Edinburgh EH10 5BR (031 444 2266) *Contact: Arthur Morrison*	P		FM MB CP S		•	•	•	•	•
Paisley College of Technology, Small Business Centre, High Street, Paisley PA1 2BE (041 887 5948) *Contact: Alan Leyshon*	FP		FM MC PS		•	•	•		
Perth College of Further Education, Crieff Road, Perth PH1 2NX (0738 21171) *Contact: R. J. Carter*	P		FM MB CP	•	•	•			
Queens College, 1 Park Drive, Glasgow G3 6LP (041 334 8141) *Contact: Alan Sangster*	F	F							
Robert Gordons Institute of Technology, Milton, Aberdeen (0224 482211) *Contact: David Scott*	P	P	FM MB CP S	•	•	•	•	•	•

	1	2	3	4	5	6	7	8	9
University of St Andrews, St Andrews, Fife KY16 9AL (0334 76161) *Contact: Peter McKiernan*				•	•	•	•		•
University of Stirling, Scottish Enterprise Foundation, Stirling FK9 4LA (0786 73171) *Contact: Ms C. Harshorn*	P	F			•	•	•	•	•
University of Strathclyde, Small Business Programme, Duncan Building, Rottenrow, Glasgow (041 552 4400) *Contact: Mrs V. Williamson*	FP		FM MB		•	•	•	•	
Queen Margaret College, Business Development Centre, Clerwood Terrace, Edinburgh EH12 8TS (031 330 2546) *Contact: P. Bell*	P		FM MB CP S		•	•	•	•	•
West Lothian College, Bathgate, West Lothian (0506 634300) *Contact: J. Lornie*	P	P	FM MB CP S		•	•			•

WALES

	1	2	3	4	5	6	7	8	9
Aberdare College of Further Education, Cwmdare Road, Aberdare, Mid Glamorgan (0685 873405) *Contact: W. Owen*	FP	FP	FM BC	•					
Barry College of Further Education, Barry, South Glamorgan (0446 733251) *Contact: Miss Perring*	P		MC						
Cardigan College of Further Education, Cardigan, Dyfed SA43 1AB (0239 2032) *Contact: J. Jones*			BC S	•	•	•			
Crosskeys College, Risca Road, Crosskeys, Gwent NP1 72A (0495 270295) *Contact: Adrian Sherman*	P		FM MB CP	•		•			
Ebbw Vale Department of Business Studies, College Road, Ebbw Vale, Gwent NP3 6LE (302083/4) *Contact: T. Reid*		P	FM MC PS			•	•		
Gorseinon College of Further Education, 52 Belgrave Road, Gorseinon, Nr Swansea, West Glam SA4 2RF (0792 892037) *Contact: L. Davies*	FP	FP	MB CS	•	•	•	•	•	•
Gwent College of Higher Education, Allt Yr Yn Avenue, Newport, Gwent (0633 51525) *Contact: M. Cromey-Hawke*	FP	FP	FM MB CP	•	•	•	•	•	•

	1	2	3	4	5	6	7	8	9
Llandrillo Technical College, Llandudno Road, Rhos on Sea, Colwyn Bay, Clwyd (0492 46666) *Contact: Mrs J. Groves*		P	FM M C	•	•	•	•	•	
Merthyr Tydfil Technical College, Ynysfach, Merthyr Tydfil CF48 1AR (0685 3663) *Contact: Ms S. Grant*	P	P	FM M B C P S	•	•	•			
Mid Wales Development, Ladywell House, Newtown, Powys SY16 1JB (0686 626965) *Contact: H. Evans*	P		FM M B C P S		•			•	•
North East Wales Institute of Higher Education, School of Management, Connah's Quay, Deeside, Clwyd (0244 817531) *Contact: Ivan Davies*	F P	F P	FM M B C P S	•		•	•		•
Pembrokeshire Technical College, Jury Lane, Kenton, Haverfordwest SA61 1TG (0437 5247) *Contact: J. Barter-Davies*	P	P	FM B C P S	•	•				
Polytechnic of Wales, South Wales Microsystems Centre, Maes-Y-Eglwys Annex, St Illtyd's Road, Upper Church Village, Mid Glamorgan CF38 1EB (0493 201933/203428) *Contact: Kay Bignall*	P	P	MB C	•	•	•		•	•
Pontypridd Technical College, Ynys Terrace, Rhydyfelin, Pontypridd (0443 400121) *Contact: D. Herbert*	P	P	FM M B E C P	•	•				
Swansea University College, Swansea SA2 8PP (0792 295179) *Contact: C. Jones*							•		
University College of Wales, Penglais, Aberystwyth (0970 623111) *Contact: Prof M. Haines*				•	•	•			
Welsh Development Agency, Treforest Industrial Estate, Pontypridd, Mid Glam CF37 5UT (0443 841777) *Contact: W. Painter*	P	P	FM M B E P S	•	•	•	•	•	•
West Glamorgan Institute of Higher Education, Mount Pleasant, Swansea SA1 63P (0792 201475) *Contact: D. Davidson*	F P	F P	FM M B E C P S	•	•	•	•		
St Davids University College, University of Wales, Lampeter, Dyfed SA48 7ED (0570 422351) *Contact: Dr D. Kirby*	P		All		•	•	•	•	•

OTHER SMALL BUSINESS COURSES

These institutions also run courses for new and small business:

Construction Industry Training Board, Bircham Newton, King's Lynn, Norfolk PE31 6RH (0553 776677) *Contact: D. J. Bishop* They have introduced a three day residential programme for potential and existing proprietors of small firms. It covers: marketing, working with people, safety, estimating, planning and organising and financial management. Course fee £60. They also have a very comprehensive catalogue of training publications and audio-visual aids.

The Hotel and Catering Industry Training Board, Unit 27/ 28, Park Royal Business Centre, 23 Park Royal Road, North Acton, London NW10 7LQ (01 965 0066) They run frequent short courses for people starting up in these industries. They also offer a small business service from regional centres around the country.

Pickup   Professional, industrial and commercial updating - this is a programme designed by the Department of Education and Science to encourage educational institutions to help businessmen and their employees to keep up with the latest technology and skills.

The Pickup scheme is operated in colleges, universities and polytechnics and can take any form – one-to-one tutorials, distance learning, small group work, and form lectures.

Teaching can take place at an education centre, at the workplace or at home – and at different times of the day, week or year. For small firms the scheme can offer individual teaching or can bring together several businesses with the same or similar needs. Pickup provision can cover any facet of general business, or it can be tailored to the needs of a particular industry or employer.

Each course comprises four days full-time tuition for a group of 10 students, spread over a period of six weeks. Courses are not free – they have to cover their costs – and the DES says that owner/managers should expect to pay a realistic price for training. More details of courses and costs are available from the Pickup agents.

Where to go for a Pickup As well as a national centre in London, the Pickup scheme is operated locally by regional agents. The contacts are:

National Pickup: Adult Training Promotions Unit, Department of Education and Science, Elizabeth House, York Road, London SE1 7PH (01 934 0888)

Avon, Cornwall, Devon, Dorset, Gloucestershire, Somerset, Wiltshire: (0272 659075) *Contact: David Roskilly*

Bedfordshire, Cambridgeshire, Essex, Hertfordshire, Norfolk, Suffolk: (0223 341075) *Contact: Tony Haymer*

Berkshire, Buckinghamshire, NW London, Oxfordshire: (0865 60264) *Contact: David Thomas*

Cheshire, Lancashire, Manchester, Merseyside: (02572 75474) *Contact: Heather Hughes Jones*

Cleveland, Cumbria, Durham, Northumberland, Tyne & Wear: (091 281 9415) *Contact: David Carter*

Derbyshire, Leicestershire, Lincolnshire, Northamptonshire, Nottinghamshire: (0602 298298) *Contact: Roy Frost*

East Sussex, Hampshire, Isle of Wight, Kent, Surrey, West Sussex: (0784 39050) *Contact: Don Jarvis*

Hereford, Worcester, Shropshire, Staffordshire, Warwickshire, West Midlands: (0902 714771) *Contact: Paul Tranter*

Humberside, North Yorkshire, South Yorkshire, West Yorkshire: (0532 438634) *Contact: George Ingle*

London: (01 934 9429/9224) *Contact: Celia Jones*

Scotland: (031 244 5426)

Wales: (0443 493696) *Contact: Ian Roffe*

DISTANCE LEARNING

There are now a number of home study kits and books that can help you learn the basics of running a business, if for one reason or another it is not possible for you to attend a college-based course. Home study kits include:

Association of British Correspondence Colleges, 6 Francis Grove, London SW19 4DT They keep a register of correspondence colleges and courses that they teach. Relevant subjects include: Book-keeping, Computer Appreciation, Cost Accountancy, Market Research, Marketing, Sales Management and Salesmanship. (See also Rapid Results College)

Book-keeping, Financial Accounting and Corporate Finance A series of computer assisted learning modules for use on IBM or fully compatible PCs – priced at £50 each. Each module contains about 10 hours of self-paced learning, and is supported by written material. The material was developed by the alumni of a major American Business School to complement its classroom teaching, and has been completely rewritten for the UK environment. Available from Ivy Software (Holdings) Ltd, Freepost, London SW1W 9YZ – Freefone 0800 282 765.

Business Club Business Club is a BBC-TV series, that shows how other small businesses have faced and dealt with a range of problems. This gives a 'live' insight into the proprietors' thoughts as they face each problem and put solutions into effect. For details of transmissions of the Business Club and other business series, write to Education Liaison, BBC, London W1A 1AA.

Computers in Business A Sunday Times video series launched in June 1988. Available from Listerhills Mail Order Ltd, 69 Campus Road, Listerhills Science Park, Bradford BD7 1HR (0274 305403). A series of 40 minute video programmes aimed specifically at people in business and industry, showing how micro-computers can increase efficiency and profits. Starting with word processing, the series covers spreadsheets, accounting systems and graphics at £26 (plus VAT) per programme.

Henley Open Management Education, Greenlands, Henley-On-Thames, Oxon RG9 3AU (049 166552) The Administrative Staff College has launched a series of distance learning programmes, complete with a 'hot line' to your tutor. Subjects covered include: Accounting, Managing People, Information Management, Marketing, Production and Business Strategy. The course pack includes video and audio cassettes as well as books, and fees start from £500.

Henley also have a distance learning MBA (Master Of Business Administration). Students can expect to take between 2 and 4 years to complete it – and it costs £3,600 (loans for fees can often be provided at subsidised rates from UK clearing banks).

Kingston Polytechnic Business School, MBA Programme, BPP House, Aldine Place, 142/144 Uxbridge Road, London W12 8AA (01 740 1111) Together with BPP Holdings, the professional training and independent education company, they launched the first two year open learning MBA in June 1988.

Open University The Open University has diversified into business and management courses through its Open Business School which was launched in October 1983 with 'The Effective Manager' and 'Personnel Selection and Interviewing'. 'Starting Up a Business' and 'Evaluating and Selecting a Business Computer System' are designed particularly for those in the small business sector where releasing a manager for training is not feasible. About 50 hours of study is required for each course, amounting to 5 hours per week over 3 months.

In 1988 the OU, in conjunction with the Cranfield School of Management, plans to launch a major new programme aimed at the managers of established small business, who are planning for growth.

For further information apply to: Associate Student Central Office, Open University, Box 76, Milton Keynes MK7 6AA (0908 74066)

The Rapid Results College, Tuition House, 27/37 St George's Road, London SW19 4DS (01 947 2211) Jointly developed with Midland Bank and the London Enterprise Agency, a new course entitled 'The Business Start-Up Programme' was launched in 1988. This new Open Learning course aims at helping anyone going into business, or are currently in a start-up position. The main features of the programme include:

- Comprehensive and easy to follow material covering all major start-up issues from assessing personal strengths and weaknesses to raising finance, marketing, selling and preparing a detailed business plan
- Expert business counselling support service by telephone and in writing to help participants work through their own business ideas and plans
- Numerous practical activities, case studies, checklists and assignments to assist participants to apply the material to their own business situations.

Fees are £159, and within 48 hours you could be starting the first pieces of coursework.

The Strathclyde Business School This business school has introduced an MBA Masters Degree in Business Administration by Distance Learning Programme. Participants work alone or in small groups at 'on campus' schools on a series of exercises. Students are issued with specially prepared materials including study guides, guided reading programmes and self assessment questionnaires. Students work at their own pace off campus attending the university only for a one week summer school and two weekend courses. The subjects covered in the MBA are of considerable use to potential entrepreneurs. The course takes up to 4 years and costs around £2,800. Further details from Strathclyde University, 130 Rottenrow, Glasgow G4 0GE (041 552 4400)

Training to Use Patents Polyproducts, Newcastle-upon-Tyne Polytechnic, Lipman Building, Sandyford Road, Newcastle-upon-Tyne NE1 8ST (091 2326002) *Contact: J. Stephenson* Nine separate packages using various media such as video cassettes, tape slide, floppy discs, and a students handbook. Covers everything from 'Inventing the Patent' to 'Computer Online Patent Retrieval Systems'. Packages cost from £5. The complete package costs £450.

Warwick University, Distance Learning MBA Office, 66 Banbury Road, Oxford OX2 6PR (0865 310310) They too have a distance learning MBA run in conjunction with Wolsey Hall, Oxford. The time taken for completion is on a par with Henley's programme, listed above. This programme, which costs £4,190, has an optional small business course as a section in Part II of the degree.

Books and Journals

This is a selection of useful reading that will give you a good appreciation of the subject. Other, more specialist reading is given in other sections.

Black Business Enterprise in Britain by Peter Wilson, Runnymede Trust, 37a Gray's Inn Road, London WC1X 8PP. A survey of Afro-Caribbean and Asian Business activity and opportunities. Price £5.

Choosing and Using Professional Advisers by Paul Chaplin. Published by Kogan Page Ltd in 1986. Price £6.95.

Croner's Reference Book for the Self-Employed and Smaller Business and *Croner's Reference Book for Employers* Croner Publications Ltd, 16–50 Coombe Road, New Malden, Surrey KT3 4QL. Price £45.50 and £53.50 respectively, including first year's amendment.

The Daily Telegraph Guide – Working for Yourself Published each year by Kogan Page Ltd. Price £7.95 (including p&p).

The Dictionary of Business Biography Published in 5 volumes at six monthly intervals starting in January 1984. Contains over 1,000 biographies and should prove to be a valuable reference source for students of entrepreneurship. For more details contact: Mary Allan, Butterworth & Co. Ltd, 88 Kingsway, London WC2.

Directory of Management Training Published by Directory of Training Ltd, 5/9 Headstone Road, Harrow, Middx HA1 1PL (01 861 0342) Annual directory of management training provision in the UK. It features over 2,700 classroom based courses and over 1,000 self-study courses.

European Small Business Journal Amber Publications Ltd, 6 Bank Square, Wilmslow, Cheshire SK9 1AN. Published quarterly it provides a forum for views and research in the small business sector. Single copies £13, annual subscription £48.

The Guardian Guide to Running a Small Business Edited by Clive Woodcock, published annually by Kogan Page Ltd. Price £7.95.

In Business Now Launched in October 1983, it is published by the Department of Industry from 11th Floor, Millbank Tower, Millbank, London SW1P 4QU (01 211 6088).

London Business School Small Business Bibliography Published annually by the London Business School, Sussex Place, London NW1 4SA (01 262 5050) Price £30. This contains details of over 5,000 books and articles published on small business topics.

Management Training Directory Published by Alan Armstrong & Associates Ltd, 72–76 Park Road, London NW1 4SH (01 258 3740)

Bi-annual, describes the courses on offer at the major centres of management training in the UK, Europe and the USA. It gives details on courses (both content and cost), the institutions running them, and there is a separate section on conference training centres, which could be useful if you are planning to hold an in-company training programme.

The Pocket Entrepreneur by Colin Barrow, published in 1987 by the Economist and Basil Blackwell, price £13. A review of the terminology of enterprise and a brief history and description of the major organisations in the field, together with a measure of their size and growth, where appropriate.

The Practice of Entrepreneurship by Meredith, Nelson & Neck, published in 1982 by the ILO, 96/98 Marsham Street, London SW1P 4LY. The first third of the book's 196 pages are devoted to analysing the personal characteristics of entrepreneurs, and as such provide enlightening reading. Price £5.70.

Small Business Confidential A subscription magazine launched in August 1983 and published by Stonehart Publications Ltd, 3 Fleet Street, London EC4Y 1AU.

Starting a Business (2nd edition) by Richard Hargreaves, published in 1987 by Heinemann, 10 Upper Grosvenor Street, London W1X 9PA. A good checklist approach to starting up, including some detailed information on eight different types of venture. Price £12.95.

Starting Your Own Business A free publication (1984) from the Small Firms Division of Department of Employment. Phone Freefone Enterprise for details.

Your Business A monthly magazine for enterprise. Available from most newsagents.

Books on Specific Trades or Industries

Buying A Shop by A. S. & J. Price, published in October 1986 by Kogan Page Ltd, 120 Pentonville Road, London N1. Price £5.95 paperback.

Doing Bed and Breakfast by Wollacott and Christmas (2nd edition), published in 1987 by David & Charles, Brunel House, Forde Road, Newton Abbot, Devon TQ12 4PU (0626 61121). Price £4.95.

Financial Control in the Clothing Industry Published in June 1988 by the Chartered Institute of Management Accountants, price £11.95. The book recommends methods of planning, budgeting and forecasting fashion trends.

Innkeeping From the Brewers Society, 42 Portman Square, London W1. Price £4.95. (They also run short courses in pubmanship.)

Managing and Marketing a Small Holding by Michael Allaby, published in 1986 by David and Charles, Brunel House, Forde Road, Newton Abbot, Devon TQ12 4PU (0626 61121). Price £4.95.

Making Money From Home by Christine Brady, published in 1987 by Corgi. Price £3.95.

The Retail Handbook: A practical guide to running a successful small retail business by Ann Foster & Bill Thomas, published in 1981 by McGraw-Hill Book Co, Maidenhead, Berks SL6 2QL (0628 23431).

Running Your Own series, published by Kogan Page Ltd, 120 Pentonville Road, London N1 9JN (01 278 0433). Titles include: *Buying and Renovating Houses for Profit*, K. Ludman & R. D. Buchanan, 1984 *Making a Living as a Rock Musician*, Kim Ludman, 1987 *Running Your Own Antiques Business*, Noel Riley & Godfrey Golzen, 1987 *Running Your Own Boarding Kennels*, Sheila Zabowa, 1985 *Running Your Own Building Business*, Kim Ludman, 1986 *Running Your Own Catering Business*, Ursula Garner & Judy Ridgway, 1984 *Running Your Own Driving School*, Nigel Stacey, 1984 *Running Your Own Hairdressing Salon*, Christine Harvey & Helen Steadman, 1986 *Running Your Own Mail Order Business*, Malcolm Brickman, 1987 *Running Your Own Photographic Business*, John Rose & Linda Hankin, 1985 *Running Your own Pub*, Elven Money, 1985 *Running Your Own Restaurant*, Diane Hughes & Godfrey Golzen, 1985 *Running Your Own Shop*, Roger Cox, 1985 *Running Your Own Small Hotel*, Joy Lennick, 1988 *Running Your Own Typing Service*, Doreen Huntley, 1987 *Running Your Own Wine Bar*, Judy Ridgway, 1984 *Working for Yourself in the Arts & Crafts*, Sara Hosking, 1986 *Writing for a Living*, Ian Linton, 1987.

Small Beginnings By Alan Bollard, published by Intermediate Technology Publications, 9 King Street, London WC2E 8HN in 1984. Explains in some detail the opportunities for new small ventures in the following industries: the brewing industry, the printing industry, the brick industry, the wool textile industry, plastic and other recycling industries, small repair and service garages, small-scale cheese production. Price £12.50.

Starting Up Your Own Business in the Hotel and Catering Industry from the Hotel and Catering Industry Training Board, International House, High Street, Ealing, London W5 5DB (01 579 2400). Published in 1982.

Successful Salon Management by Roger Cliffe-Thomson, published in 1982 by MacMillan Publishers, Houndmills, Basingstoke RG21 2XF (0256 29242) Price £8.95.

Your Own Dress Agency or Nearly New Shop by Julian Maynard, published by Malcolm Stewart Books (London), High Street, Hornsey, London N8 7TS (01 349 2045) Price £4.50.

THE NATIONAL TRAINING INDEX

Founded in 1968, provides comprehensive information and advice on business training courses, correspondence courses, training films and training packages. The Index provides:

- Detailed information (dates, duration, location, cost and syllabus summaries) on more than 12,000 business courses in the UK
- Comprehensive listings of in-company training schemes, course organisers, correspondence courses, training films and packages
- A thorough but easy-to-use classification system which lists all courses and other training aids under 124 different subject headings
- A quarterly information up-date and newsletter
- A unique and confidential assessment of the quality of courses and training films listed in the Index, based on constant reports (more than 10,000 a year) sent in by members
- The Lecturer's Index maintains cards on 9,600 lecturers who have spoken at training courses, external and internal, during the past decade. Advice can also be given to members planning to run their own in-company training programmes on suitable external speakers
- The Conference Location Guide maintains files on hotels and conference centres with facilities for courses and conferences. Members who let them know the location, size and audiovisual requirements of any external course planned, will be supplied promptly with the names and addresses of suitable venues.

Contact: Stuart Macnair, Manager, National Training Index, 3rd Floor, 6 Hanover Street, London W1R 9HH (01 491 1523)

Membership costs, from 1 April 1988, £550 which is probably the cost of sending one person on one of the shorter courses in the Index. The service may be an attractive proposition to a small company which is sending people on external courses for the first time, or considering running its first internal course.

YOUTH OPPORTUNITIES FOR SELF-EMPLOYMENT

Opportunities for Young People to Start Up a Business

There is a growing recognition that young people have been neglected in the major initiatives intended to help people to get a business started. There are signs that a major push is underway to redress this imbalance. As well as the 18 initiatives briefly described below, the Enterprise Allowance Scheme explained in Section 6 is of real use to young entrepreneurs.

Most of the small business courses listed in Section 8 are open to young people, and the Enterprise Agencies in Section 2 can also help.

Business Ideas for Young Unemployed by Dean Juniper, published in 1985 by Kirkfield Publications, 56 Henley Avenue, Dewsbury, West Yorkshire WF12 0LN. Just what it says, plus some guidance on how to get started.

CRAC Publications Hobsons Ltd, Bateman Street, Cambridge CB2 1LZ (0223 314640) *Your Own Business* This book has been written for school leavers, trainees from MSC schemes, A-level leavers and graduates and designed as a 'starter' to give information, ideas, inside knowledge and know-how on organisation and planning of self-employment.

Included in the book are:
■ Personal stories of successful – and unsuccessful – starters
■ Are you the type? – a quiz to test ideas and attitudes
■ The 'idea' – what every business needs
■ Market research
■ Getting the business on the road
■ Advertising
■ Money matters – how to prepare costs and estimates
■ Premises and equipment
■ Co-operatives and franchises

■ Using the professionals – e.g., accountant, solicitor
■ Where next? – books, organisations to help, and addresses
A4 48pp; illustrated paperback. Price £3.95.

Enterprise Scholarships open to University or college students showing outstanding ability or insight into the area of business enterprise. The scholarships are to allow them to develop relevant knowledge and practical skills whilst at college. Details from Diane McGill, Scottish Enterprise Foundation, University of Stirling, Stirling FK9 4LA (0786 73171).

FACE Workface, Market Place, Glastonbury, Somerset BA6 9HL (0458 33917) They offer training places to young people under the Manpower Services Commission's Youth Training Scheme. As well as providing the opportunity to learn a skill, they provide help to those who want to set up in business for themselves. This support and guidance can continue for up to three years after the training period has finished.

Graduate Enterprise Programme A programme to help recent graduates of universities and colleges, to set up their own businesses. An intensive foundation course, continuous counselling, a training allowance and a market research grant all combine to make this an unbeatable package for potential new entrepreneurs.

The programme is run throughout the UK with various start dates between July and September. Contact one of the following for details:

North East: Graduate into Enterprise, 14 Old Elvet, Durham DH1 3HP (091 374 2251/3) *Contact: David Absalom*

North West: Manchester Business School, Booth Street West, Manchester M15 6PD (061 273 8228) *Contact: George Lester*

East: Cranfield School of Management, Cranfield Institute of Technology, Cranfield, Beds MK43 0AL (0234 751122) *Contact: Michelle Kent*

South West: Enterprise Unit, University of Bristol, Wills Memorial Building, Queen's Road, Bristol BS8 1HR (0272 303615) *Contact: Linda Skinner*

West Midlands: Warwick Business School, University of Warwick, Coventry CV4 7AL (0203 523523) *Contact: Shaun de Wolf*

Yorks and Humberside: Dept of Economic & Marketing Studies, Huddersfield Polytechnic, Queen's Gate, Huddersfield HD1 3DH (0484 22288) *Contact: John Day*

London and South East: South East England Consortium for Credit Accumulation and Transfer, Room 320, PCL Management Block, 35 Marylebone Road, London NW1 5LS (01 487 3337) *Contact: Derek Mottershead*

Scotland: Scottish Enterprise Foundation, University of Stirling, Stirling FK9 4LA (0786 73171) *Contact: Wayne Thomas*

Wales: St David's University College, University of Wales, Lampeter, Dyfed SA48 7ED (0570 422351) *Contact: David Kirby*

Graduate Gateway, University of Glasgow, 25 Bute Gardens, Glasgow G12 8RT (041 339 8855) *Contact: John Lewis* A programme to help unemployed graduates to develop small business skills. They work in a 'consultancy' role in a small business for three months, and are certainly better prepared to start their own firm after their experience. A training allowance is paid throughout (Also at Durham University Business School and Bath University, see Section 8).

Headstart, is a national Industrial Society project, which is run in centres all over the country. It is a free 8 week training programme comprising 120 hours of training, for anyone wishing to start their own business. Further information can be obtained from the Industrial Society at Peter Runge House, 3 Carlton House Terrace, London SW1Y 5DG (01 839 4300) *Contact: Diana Elliott*

Live Wire, 60 Grainger Street, Newcastle Upon Tyne NE1 5JG (091 261 5584) A scheme to help young people aged 16–25 to get their own business started. Run all over the UK as a competition with the winners getting good four figure prizes, and everyone getting help and advice. The initiative comes from Shell UK, but it has many other supporters.

National Youth Enterprise Centre, 17–23 Albion Street, Leicester LE1 6GD (0533 471200) Aim to act as a national resource centre for information, publication, training, research and development, and as a forum for association, discussion and joint action in the broad field of the social education of young people.

Their youth opportunities section have produced some publications on how young people can start up a business, a co-operative, or become self-employed. They try to keep abreast of current events so are a useful organisation to contact.

Newcastle Youth Enterprise Centre, 25/27 Low Friar Street, Newcastle-Upon-Tyne NE1 5UL (0632 616009) A private sector venture to help 16–25 year olds to set up and develop their own business in the North East.

Northern Youth Venture Fund (see Youth Business Kit for address) Loans of up to £5,000 are available at around 5% over periods of up to 3 years.

The Prince's Youth Business Trust, 8 Jockey's Field, London WC1R 4TJ (01 430 0521) Helps 18–25 year olds with a viable business idea to get started. Provides grants of up to £1,000, and soft loans of rather more. To get considered you need to present a business plan – but the Trust can help you put one together. Their advisers provide support and encouragement to all recipients for at least a year after the money is put in. The fund has around £15 million at this moment.

Royal Jubilee Trust, 8 Buckingham Street, London WC2 (01 930 9811) *Contact: Richard Shaw*. The Trust operates a scheme to help youngsters raise money to start a business. It can also give grants of up to £1,000 and can appoint people to help them set up.

Young Enterprise Fund ASSET, 21 Green Street, Saltcoats, Ayrshire KA21 5HQ (0294 602515) They are pioneering low-cost loans for young starters in Scotland.

Young Entrepreneurs Fund, Seymour Suite, 65–69 Walton Road, East Mosley, Surrey. Set up by Sir Philip Harris of the Harris Queensway Group, this fund aims at the slightly older 'young' – aged 20–40. They make investments in the £50,000–100,000 range. A proportion of the fund has been set aside for small investments in start-ups.

Youth Business Initiative, 8 Bedford Row, London WC1R 4BU (01 430 0521) Provides training bursaries to young entrepreneurs of between £300 and £1,000 specifically for start-up costs. You need a realistic plan and will have to accept continuing advice.

Youth Business Kit, is a seven pack training programme for those planning to run 'start your own business' courses for young people. From Project North East, 60 Grainger Street, Newcastle-upon-Tyne NE1 1BR.

STARTING UP OVERSEAS

Interest in going overseas to work has been widespread in the UK for a long time. A more recent activity has been for entrepreneurs to both 'emigrate' and set up a business.

The relaxation of exchange controls by the first Thatcher Government has played their part in making this a more viable option. And of course our membership of the EEC and the 1992 changes have made the environment in those countries less hostile.

The risks inherent in starting up a business in a completely new environment are clearly greater. But both the rewards and the incentives can be greater too. Many countries positively discriminate in favour of the incoming entrepreneur, and have programmes of commercial and industrial support – Canada and Australia for example.

Most countries have a near equivalent to the Small Firms Service, and some have very familiar names.

The commercial attaché at the UK Embassy or High Commission of the country you are interested in starting up in may be able to help you. But the organisations listed in this section will be a source of direct help.

AUSTRALIA

New South Wales: Office of Small Business, 5 Belmore Street, Burwood NSW 2134 (02 744 0066) NSW country callers: 008 45 1151

Victoria: Small Business Development Corporation, 100 Exhibition Street, Melbourne, Victoria 3000 (03 655 3300) Victorian country callers: 008 13 6034

Queensland: Small Business Development Corporation, 545 Queen Street, Brisbane, Queensland 4000 (07 834 6789) Queensland country callers: 008 17 7324

Western Australia: Small Business Development Corporation, NZI Securities Building, 553 Hay Street, Perth, Western Australia 6000 (09 325 3388) Western Australia country callers: 008 19 9125

South Australia: Small Business Corporation of South Australia, 74 South Terrace, Adelaide, South Australia 5000 (08 212 5344) South Australian country callers: 008 18 8018

Tasmania: Small Business Advisory Service, Tasmanian Development Authority, 134 Macquarie Street, Hobart, Tasmania 7000 (002 20 6712) Tasmanian country callers: 008 03 0688

Australian Capital Territory: ACT Small Business Bureau, Level 5, ACT Administration Centre, Cnr London Circuit and Constitution Avenue, Canberra City ACT 2601 (062 75 8888)

Northern Territory: Small Business Advisory Services, Department of Industries and Development, Harbour View Plaza, Cnr Bennett and McMinn Streets, Darwin NT 5794 (089 89 4291) Northern Territory country callers: 008 19 3111

BELGIUM

Brussels: Ministère de la Région Bruxelloise, Rue Royale, 2–6, 1000 Bruxelles (02 513 41 10)

Flemish Area: Vlaamse Executieve, Josef II Straat, 30, B1040 Brussels (02 218 12 10) *Contact: G. Geens*

Walloon Area: Ministère de l'Economie Walloone, Boulevard de l'Empereur, 11, 1000 Bruxelles (02 511 72 95)

CANADA

Alberta: Department of Regional & Industrial Expansion, The Cornerpoint Building, Suite 505, 10179–105th Street, Edmonton, Alberta, Canada T5J 3S3

British Columbia: Department of Regional & Industrial Expansion, Bentall Centre, Tower IV, Suite 1101, 1055 Dunsmuir Street, PO Box 49178, Vancouver, British Columbia, Canada V7X 1K8

Manitoba: Department of Regional & Industrial Expansion, 3 Lakeview Square, 4th Floor, 185 Carlton Street, PO Box 981, Winnipeg, Manitoba, Canada R3C 2V2

New Brunswick: Department of Regional & Industrial Expansion, Assumption Place, 770 Main Street, PO Box 1210, Moncton, New Brunswick, Canada E1C 8P9

Newfoundland: Department of Regional & Industrial Expansion, Parsons Building, 90 O'Leary Avenue, PO Box 8950, St John's, Newfoundland, Canada

Northern Territories: As for Saskatchewan

Nova Scotia: Department of Regional & Industrial Expansion, 1496 Lower Water Street, Halifax, Nova Scotia, Canada B2V 4B9

Ontario: Department of Regional & Industrial Expansion, 1 First Canadian Place, Suite 4840, PO Box 98, Toronto, Ontario, Canada M5X 1B1

Prince Edward Island: Department of Regional & Industrial Expansion, Confederation Court, 134 Kent Street, Suite 400, PO Box 1115, Charlottetown, Prince Edward Island, Canada C1A 7M8

Quebec: Department of Regional & Industrial Expansion, Stock Exchange Tower, 800 Victoria Square, Room 3709, PO Box 247, Montreal, Quebec, Canada H4Z 1E8

Saskatchewan: Department of Regional & Industrial Expansion, Beesborough Tower, Suite 814, 601 Spadina Crescent East, Saskatoon, Saskatchewan, Canada S7K 3G8

Small Business Development Corporation NS: 277 Pleasant Street, SU100, Dartmouth, NS, Canada 32Y 4B7

DENMARK

Information on specific investment questions including location of new industries and assistance in establishing contact with local authorities is provided by:

Information Office For Foreign Investment In Denmark: 25 Sondergade, DK-8600 Silkeborg, Denmark (+45 6 82 56 55)

Ministry of Industry: 12 Slotsholmsgade, DK-1216 Copenhagen K, Denmark (+45 1 12 11 97)

The following organisations will be pleased to mail further information:

Danish Bankers Association, 7 Amaliegade, DK-1256 Copenhagen K, Denmark (+45 1 12 02 00)

The Association of State-Authorised Public Accountants, 8 Kronprinsessgade, DK-1306 Copenhagen K, Denmark (+45 1 13 91 91)

Federation of Danish Industries, 18 H C Andersens Boulevard, DK-1596 Copenhagen V, Denmark (+45 1 15 22 33)

FRANCE

Agence Nationale Pour La Création d'Enterprise, 142 Rue du Bac, 75007 Paris, France *Contact: M. Michel Jallas* Central point for all new enterprise activity in France

Délégation à La Petite et Moyenne Industrie, Ministère de la Recherche et de L'Industrie, 13 Rue de Bourgogne, 75700 Paris ((1) 556 45 30) This department deals specifically with industrial as opposed to commercial firms.

For help in setting up businesses (e.g., in the retail trade) in rural areas, etc, enquirers may seek the assistance of their local Chamber of Commerce and Industry, who will intervene on their behalf (especially as regards grants) with the Direction du Commerce Intérieur, 41 Quai Branly, 75007 Paris.

GERMANY

German Chamber of Industry and Commerce, 12/13 Suffolk Street, St James's, London SW1Y 5HG (01 930 7251) *Contact: Thesy Lobitzer*

GREECE

Ministry of National Economy, Department of Private Investment Promotion and Evaluation, Platia Syntagmatos, Athens (324 8556)

Hellenic Organisation of Small and Medium Sized Industries & Handicrafts, 16 Xenias Str, 115 28 Athens, Greece

HOLLAND

Institute of Small and Medium Businesses, Nettogendoylean 49, Werden, Holland

REPUBLIC OF IRELAND

Industrial Development Authority of Ireland (IDA), Wilton Park House, Wilton Place, Dublin 2, Ireland (0001 686633) *Contact: Colm Regan*

ITALY

Confederazione Italiana, Piccola Industria, Via Colonna Antonine 52, 00186, Roma

Ministero Industrie E Commercio, D G Produzione Industriale, Via Vittorio Veneto 33, 00100, Roma

LUXEMBOURG

Ministère de L'Economie et des Classes Moyennes, Luxembourg, La Boîte Postale 97, 2010 Luxembourg Ville *Contact: Claude Lanners*

NETHERLANDS

Central Institute for Medium and Small Sized Businesses, Dalsteindreef 9, 1112 XC Diemen, The Netherlands

Coordinating Foundation for Maintaining Service-Supply Centres for Small Businesses Address as above

Economic Institute for Medium and Small Sized Businesses, Neuhuyskade 94, 2509 LR, The Hague, The Netherlands

NEW ZEALAND

Small Business Agency, PO Box 11043, Wellington, Central Office, 7th Floor, Commerce House, 126 Wakefield Street, Wellington, New Zealand *Contact: Bruce Harris*

SOUTH AFRICA

Small Business Development Corporation Ltd, National Board House, 94 Pritchard Street, PO Box 4300, Johannesburg 2000 (29 2677)

Small Business Information Centre South Africa, PO Box 1880, Potchefstroom, South Africa 2520

UNITED STATES OF AMERICA

Small Business Administration, 1441 L Street NW, Washington DC 20416 (202 653 6565) The fundamental purposes of the Small Business Administration (SBA) are to aid, counsel, assist and protect the interests of small business; ensure that small business concerns receive a fair portion of Government purchases, contracts and subcontracts, as well as of the sale of Government property; make loans to small business concerns, State and local development companies, and the victims of floods or other catastrophies, or of certain types of economic injury; and license, regulate and make loans to small business investment companies.

TRAINING FOR BUSINESS OVERSEAS

These universities and colleges have a specific expertise in the small business field and may fulfil a similar service to their UK equivalents, listed in Section 8.

AUSTRALIA

James Cook University, Department of Commerce, James Cook University of North Queensland, Townsville, Australia Q4811 (010 61 77 81 4425)

The University of Melbourne, Graduate School of Business Administration, Parkville, Victoria 3052, Australia

The University of Newcastle, Rankin Drive, Newcastle, NSW 2308, Australia (049 680401) *Contact: Alan Williams*

Department of Commerce, NSW 2305, Australia (010 61 49 685 741)

BELGIUM

Centre de Technologie et de Gestion des Affaires, Rue de l'Industrie 20, B-1400 Nivelles, Belgique (010 67 21 07 87) *Contact: J. C. Ettinger*

Economic Council of East Flanders Small Business Department, Kouter 4, 9000 Gent, Belgium (091 23 57 83) *Contact: Andre Buyst*

Seminarie Voor Productiviteitsstudie En Onderzock, Ryksuniversiteit Gent, St Pieternieuustraat 49, B9000 Gent, Belgium (010 3291 256 353)

Solvay Business School, Avenue F D Roosevelt, 19, 1050 Brussels, Belgium (010 32 2 384 9602)

State University of Gent, Interfacultair Centrum Managemeant, St Pietersnieuwstraat 49, B-9000 Gent, Belgium (021 16 42 41 61) *Contact: R. Winard*

CANADA

B C Institute of Technology, 3700 Willingdon Avenue, Burnaby BC, Canada V5G 3H2

Queens School of Business, Kinston Ont., Canada K7L 3NG

Saint Mary's University, Department of Management, Halifax, Nova Scotia B3M 3C3

University of Calgary, Centre for New Venture Development, 2500 University Avenue, Calgary Alta., Canada T2N 1N4 *Contact: Carmen Colborne*

University of West Ontario, London Ont., Canada N6A 3K7

DENMARK

Danish Employers' Confederation, Small Business Management School, Oster Alle 54, OK-8400 Ebeltroft, Denmark (06 344000)

Mr I. B. Ginge Hansen, Safirves, OK-3060 Espergaerde, Denmark

The Jutland Technological Institute, 135 Marselia Boulevard, 8000 Arhus C, Denmark (010 45 6 142 400)

FINLAND

Finnish Institute of Leadership Training, Pohjoiskaari 34, 00200, Helsinki 20, Finland

Helsinki School of Economics, Small Business management Programme, Runeberginkatu 14–16, 00100 Helsinki 10, Finland (43131)

Small Business Unit, Raatihuoneenkatu 13, SF 50100 Mikkeli 10, Finland (Mikkeli 368 952)

FRANCE

Groupe Ecole Supérieure de Commerce de Lyon, 23 Av Guy de Collongue, BP 174, 69132 Ecully Cedex, France (010 33 78 33 81 22) *Contact: Vincent Ramies*

INSEAD, Boulevard de Constance, 77305 Fontainebleau Cedex, France (422 48 27) *Contact: Lister Vickery*

GERMANY

Centre for Technological Co-operation, Technical University of Berlin, Strasse des 17. Juni 135, D-1000, Berlin (West) 12

INDIA
Small Industry Extension Training Institute, Yousufguda, Hyderabad 500 045, India

INDONESIA
Institute for Management Development, Mentene Kaya 9, Jakarta Pusat, Indonesia (375 309)

ISRAEL
Mount Carmel International Training Centre for Community Development, 12 David Pinsky Street, Haifa 31060, Israel

ITALY
Ilo International Centre for Advanced Technical and Vocational Training, 201 Via Ventimiglia, 10127 Turin, Italy

ISTUD – Institute Studi Direzionali, Corso Umberto 1, 67, 28049 Stresa, Italy

SDA Bocconi, Via Sarfatti 25, 1 20136 Milano, Italy (010 39 02 935 1280)

Universita di Urbina, Facolta di Economia e Commercio, Passo Palestro 4, Genova, Italy (894139)

MALAYSIA
MEDEC, Mara Institute of Technology, 14th Floor, Shah Alam, Selangar

THE NETHERLANDS
Centre for Management and Industrial Development, Exchange Building, Coolsingel/Meent, Postbox 30042, 3001 DA Rotterdam, Netherlands

Research Institute for Management Science, PO Box 143, 2600 AC Delft, Netherlands

NORWAY
Norwegian Institute of Technology (STI), Small Business Management Training, PO Box 8116, Dep Oslo 1, Norway

Oppland College, Small Business Management Centre, PO Box 1004, Skurva, N 2601 Lillehammer, Norway (062 55600)

Statens Teknologiske Institutt, PO Box 8116 Dep N-Oslo 1, Norway

PHILIPPINES
University of the Philippines, Institute for Small Scale Industries, Quezon City, Philippines

SOUTH AFRICA
Potchefstroom University, Potchefstroom, South Africa 2520

University of Natal, PO Box 375, Pietermaritzburg, South Africa 3200
Contact: Dr M. G. Lymas, Director Small Business Development

University of Orange Free State, Bloemfontein, South Africa 9301
Contact: P. J. Mans, Unit for Small Business Development

SPAIN
Universidad Autonoma de Madrid, Facultad de Ciencias Economicas y Empresariales, Catno Blanco, Madrid 34, Spain

SWEDEN

Linkoping University, Department of Management and Economics, EK1, S-581, Linkoping, Sweden

Swedish Institute of Management, Stockholm School of Economics, PO Box 6501, S113 Stockholm, Sweden (08 235 820)

UMEA University, Department of Business Administration, S0901 87 UMEA, Sweden

SWITZERLAND

University of Geneva, Département d'Economie Commerciale et Industrielles, 2 Rue de Candolle, Comin/Fac SES 1211 Genève 4, Switzerland (20 93 33)

UNITED STATES OF AMERICA

Baylor University, Waco TX, United States 76798

College of Lake County, 19351 West Washington Street, Grayslake, Illinois 60030 (312 223 6601)

Florida Atlantis University, Boca Raton F1, United States 33441

Harvard Business School, Smaller Company Management Programme, Soldiers Field, Boston MA 02163 (617 495 6450)

Kent State College of Business Administration, Kent OH, United States 44242

Kentucky State University, Frankfurt KY, United States

Memphis State Fogelman College of Business & Economics, Memphis TN, United States 38152

Pace University, The Lubin School of Business, One Pace Plaza, New York, NY 10038 (212 285 3000)

San Diego State Management School of Business Administration, San Diego Cal., United States

Suny at Albany, School of Business, Albany NY, United States 12222

University of Akron, Akron OH, United States 44325

University of DC, 929 E Street NW, Washington DC, United States 20004

University of Florida, 4164 NW 38th Street, Gainesville F1, United States 32606

University of Hawaii, Honolulu HW, United States 96822

University of Montana, Missoula Mt, United States 59812

University of North Alabama, Florence AL, United States 35630

University of Notre Dame, College of Business, South Bend, Indiana, United States 46556 (219 239 5235)

University of South Carolina, Small Business Development Centre, College of business Administration, Columbia SC, United States 29208

University of Tulsa, Tulsa Okla, United States 74104

Washburn University, 17th s College, Topeka KS, United States 66621

Wichita State Department of Market and Business Management, Wichita Kan., United States 67208

These may also be of use:

The Association of International Accountants Ltd, 2/10 St John's Street, Bedford (0234 213577/8)

The Insider's Guide to Small Business Resources by Gumpert and Timmons, published in 1982 by Doubleday, Garden City, New York. A guide to more or less everything in the American small business world.

GLOSSARY OF KEY BUSINESS TERMS

This glossary gives a meaning to words that have either been used in the book (unless explained in the context of their use), or that you are likely to meet early on in your business life.

Access time Time between asking a computer for information, and the information being available.

Account(s) Usually annual financial records of a business.

Accrual An accounting concept that insists that income and expenses for the accounting period be included, whether for cash or credit.

Added value The difference between sales revenue and material costs. See also Value added.

Annual report See Audit.

Articles of association Usually a standard and comprehensive set of rules drawn up when a company is formed to show the purpose of the business.

Asset Something owned by the business which has a measurable cost.

Audit A process carried out by an accountant (auditor) on all companies each year, to check the accuracy of financial records. The auditor cannot be the company's own accountant. The result is the annual report.

Authorised capital The share capital of a company authorised by law. It does not have to be taken up. For example, a £1,000 company need only 'issue' two £1 shares. It can issue a further 998 £1 shares without recourse to law. After that sum it has to ask the permission of its shareholders.

Balance sheet A statement of assets owned by a business and the way in which they are financed taken from both liabilities and owner's equity. This report does not indicate the market value of the business.

Bankruptcy Imposed by a court when someone cannot meet his bills. The bankrupt's property is managed by a court-appointed trustee, who must use it to pay off the creditors as fairly as possible.

Basic Beginners' All-purpose Symbolic Instruction Code. The most popular microcomputer language.

BIT A binary digit, usually represented by '0' or '1', or 'off' or 'on'.

Black economy Usually refers to businesses run by the self-employed who illegally avoid tax and National Insurance. There is therefore no official record, and they are collectively referred to as the Black Economy.

Blue chip In gambling, the high chips are usually blue. In business, this refers to high-status companies and their shares. They are usually large companies with a long successful trading history.

Book-keeping The recording of all business transactions in 'journals' in order to provide data for accounting reports.

Book value Usually the figure at which an asset appears in the accounts. This is not necessarily the market value.

Break-even point The volume of production at which revenues exactly match costs. After this point profit is made.

Byte A sequence of eight 'bits', used to represent one character of information. A letter, digit, symbol or punctuation mark.

Capital It has several meanings, but unprefixed it usually means all the assets of the business.

Cash The 'money' assets of a business, which include both cash in hand and cash at the bank.

Cash flow The difference between total cash coming in and going out of a business over a period of time.

Computer program Instructions telling a computer to carry out a specific task.

Costs of goods sold The cost of goods actually sold in any period. It excludes the cost of the goods left unsold, and all overheads except manufacturing.

Current asset Assets normally realised in cash or used up in operations during the year. It includes such items as debtors and stock.

Current liability A liability due for payment in one trading period, usually a year.

Debenture Long-term loan with specific terms on interest, capital repayment and security.

Depreciation A way of measuring the cost of using a fixed asset. A set portion of the asset's cost is treated as an expense each period of its working life.

Direct costs Expenses, such as labour and materials, which vary 'directly' according to the number of items manufactured. Also called variable costs.

Diskette A flexible disc used to store computer data, often called a 'floppy disc'.

Entrepreneur Someone who is skilled at finding new products, making and marketing them, and arranging finance.

Equity The owner's claims against the business, sometimes called the shareholder's funds. This appears as a liability because it belongs to the shareholders and not to the business itself. It is represented by the share capital plus the cumulative retained profits over the business's life. The reward for equity investment is usually a dividend paid on profits made.

Financial ratio The relationship between two money quantities, used to analyse business results.

Financial year A year's trading between dates agreed with the Inland Revenue. Not necessarily the fiscal year, which starts on 5 April.

Firmware Computer instructions stored in a read-only memory (see ROM).

Fixed assets Assets such as land, building, equipment, cars, etc, acquired for long-term use in the business and not for stock in trade. Initially recorded in the balance sheet at cost.

Fixed cost Expenses that do not vary directly with the number of items produced. For example, a car has certain fixed costs, such as tax and insurance, whether it is driven or not.

Floppy disc See Diskette.

Forecast A statement of what is likely to happen in the future, based on careful judgement and analysis.

Funds Financial resources, not necessarily cash.

Gearing The ratio of a business's borrowings to its equity. For example, a 1:1 ratio would exist where a bank offered to match your investment £1 for £1.

Going concern Simply an accounting concept, it assumes in all financial reports that the business will continue to trade indefinitely into the future unless there is specific evidence to the contrary – i.e., it has declared an intention to liquidate. It is not an indication of the current state of health of the business.

Goodwill Value of the name, reputation or intangible assets of a business. It is recorded in the accounts only when it is purchased. Its nature makes it a contentious subject.

Gross Total before deductions. For example, gross profit is the difference between sales income and costs of goods sold. The selling and administrative expenses have yet to be deducted. Then it becomes the net profit.

Hardware The physical parts of a computer.

Income statement See profit and loss account.

Insolvency A situation in which a person or business cannot meet the bills. Differs from bankruptcy, as the insolvent may have assets that can be realised to meet those bills.

Interface Electronic device that links computer hardware together. For example, a printer or VDU to the computer itself.

Know-how agreement This is a promise to disclose information to a third party. If the disclosure is made for them to evaluate the usefulness of the know-how, the agreement is called a secrecy agreement. If the disclosure is made to allow commercial production, it is called a know-how licence.

Learning curve The improvement in the performance of a task as it is repeated and as more is learned about it.

Liabilities The claims against a business, such as loans and equity.

Liquidation It is the legal process of closing down a business and selling off its assets to meet outstanding debts.

Loan capital Finance lent to a business for a specific period of time at either a fixed or varied rate of interest. This interest must be paid irrespective of the performance of the business.

Marginal cost The extra cost incurred in making one more unit of production.

Marketing mix The combination of methods used by a business to market its products. For example, it can vary its price; the type and quantity of advertising; the distribution channels can be altered; finally, the product itself can either be enhanced or reduced in quality.

Market segment A group of buyers who can be identified as being especially interested in a particular variant of the product. For example, a cheap day return ticket for a train is a variant of a rail fare, especially attractive to people who do not have to get to their destination early, perhaps to work.

Market share The ratio of a firm's sales of a product, in a specified market, during a period, to the total sales of that product in the same period in the same market.

Microcomputer A small computer using a microprocessor as its central processing unit.

Microfiche A sheet of photographic film on which a number of microcopy images have been recorded. You need a special viewer to look at the recorded information, which is very efficiently stored.

Microprocessor Electronic circuitry etched onto a silicon chip that can be used to manipulate information.

Modem A device that allows computers (and ancillary equipment) to communicate over telephone wires. The portable version is called an acoustic coupler.

Non-disclosure agreement An agreement which allows you to reveal secret commercial information – for example, about an invention – to a third party, and which prevents them from making use of that information without your agreement.

Opportunity cost The value of a course of action open to you but not taken. For example, keeping cash in an ordinary share account at a building society will attract about 2% less interest than a five year term at the same society. So the opportunity cost of choosing not to tie up your money is 2%.

Overhead This is an expense which cannot be conveniently associated with a unit of production. Administration or selling expenses are usually overheads.

Overtrading Expanding sales and production without enough financial resources – in particular, working capital. The first signs are usually cashflow problems.

Piggy-backing Usually associated with firms that market other firms' products as well as their own, but the term can be used to describe any 'free riding' activity.

Profit The excess of sales revenue over sales cost and expenses during an accounting period. It does not necessarily mean an increase in cash.

Profit and loss account A statement of sales, costs, expenses and profit (or loss) over an accounting period monthly, quarterly or annually. Also known as the income statement.

RAM Random-access memory is the space used for storing computer data as programs. It can be changed as new programs or data are called up.

Reserves The name given to the accumulated and undistributed profits of the business. They belong to the ordinary shareholders. They are not necessarily available in cash, but are usually tied up in other business assets.

Revenue usually from sales. Revenue is recognised in accounting terms when goods have been despatched (or services rendered) and the invoice sent. This means that revenue pounds are not necessarily cash pounds. A source of much confusion and frequent cash flow problems.

ROM Read-only memory.

Schedule 'D' Cases I and II are the Inland Revenue rules that govern tax allowances for self-employed people.

Schedule 'E' Allowances for employed people.

Seasonality A regular event, usually one that causes sales to increase or decrease in an annual cycle. For example, the weather caused by the seasons or events associated with the seasons: Christmas, spring sales, summer holidays, etc.

Secured creditor Someone lending money to a business whose debt is secured by linking a default in its repayment to a fixed asset, such as a freehold building.

Share capital The capital of the business subscribed for by the owners or shareholders (see Equity).

Software A computer term usually associated with programs and related documentation.

Strategy A general method of policy for achieving specified objectives. It describes the essential resources and their amounts, which are to be committed to achieving those objectives (see Tactics).

Synergy A co-operative or combined activity which is more effective or valuable than the sum of their independent activities.

Tactics The method by which resources allocated to a strategic objective are used.

True and fair An accounting concept that states that the business financial reports have been prepared using generally accepted accounting principles.

Turn key Usually refers to a client-commissioned system, accepted only when you can 'turn on a key' and are satisfied with the results, or output.

Value In accounting it has several meanings. For example, the 'value' of a fixed asset is its cost less its cumulative depreciation. A current asset, such as stock, is usually valued at cost or market value, whichever is the lower.

Value added The difference between sales revenue that a firm gets from selling its products (or services), and the cost to it of the materials used in making those products.

Variable costs See Direct Costs.

Variance The difference between actual performance and the forecast (or budget or standard).

Working capital Current assets less current liabilities, which represents the capital used in the day-to-day running of the business.

Working life The economically useful life of a fixed asset. Not necessarily its whole life. For example, technological development may render it obsolete very quickly.

Work in progress Goods in the process of being produced, which are valued at the lower end of manufacturing costs or market value.

GENERAL INDEX

A

abstract(ing) services, 178–80
Accelerated Business Development
    Scheme, 28
accountancy, 21, 250
accountant(s), 251
    and your business plan, 199–200
    associations of, 240–2
    Business Network, 89
Action Resource Centre (ARC), 25, 26
Advertising Association, 180
advertising signs, 261
Advertising Standards Authority, 264
advisers, 20, 21, 23, 31
Advisory, Conciliation and Arbitration
    Service (ACAS), 266–7
agents
    Manufacturers' Association (MAA), 92
    Register of (BAR), 90
    selecting, 190
Alliance of Small Firms and Self-
    employed People, 82
American Entrepreneurs Association, 93
American Inventors Corporation, 138
architects
    architects and surveyors, 262
    Incorporated Association of Royal
    Institute of British, 262
Assistant Registrar of Friendly Societies,
    104
Association of Bankrupts, 240
Association of British Chambers of
    Commerce, 82
Association of British Correspondence
    Colleges, 303
Association of British Factors, 214
Association of Certified Accountants, 240
Association of Collegiate Entrepreneurs,
    83
Association of Computer Clubs (ACC),
    145
Association of District Councils, 73
Association of Independent Businesses,
    83
Association of Innovation Centre
    Executives (AICE), 138
Association of Investment Trust
    Companies, 222
Association of Invoice Factors, 215–16
Association of Professional Computer
    Consultants, 145

B

bank(s)
    as advisers, 195–9
    manager, 12
    merchant, 211–12
    see also clearing banks
Banking Information Service, 240
bankrupts, *see* Association of *and London
    Gazette*

BAR (Agents Register) Ltd, 90
Bath, University of, 139
BBC Data Enquiry Service, 165, 184
BBC Service to Exporters, 185
Beehive Workshops, 74
bill financing, 204–5
black business
    enterprise agencies, 26
book-keeping, 11
    advice on, 21, 37
    choosing a system, 235–9
    computer assisted learning modules,
    303
Brain Exchange, 184
British Coal Enterprise, 30–2
British Direct Marketing Association, 181
British Export Houses Association, 213
British Institute of Management, 181
British Insurance Association, 240
British Insurance and Investment Brokers
    Association, BIIBA, 271
British Knitting and Clothing Export
    Council, 186
British Merchant Banking and Securities
    Houses Association, 211
British Overseas Trade Board (BOTB),
    18, 170, 185
    regional offices, 185
British Safety Council, 151
British Standards Institution, 151
British Steel (Industry) Ltd, 28–30
British Technology Group, 136, 256
building
    Building Centre, 261
    Building Materials Information Service,
    261
    Building Research Establishment, 261
    Federation of Master Builders, 261
    regulations, 259
business, 11
    adviser, 20, 21
    associations, 82–8
    clubs, 282, 303–4
    Clubs, National Forum of, 85
    Co-operation Centre, 90
    education initiative, The 19
    Exchange, 90
    Grant Services, 240 (*see also* grants)
    in the Community (BIC), 26
    Link-Up, 90
    monitors, 166
    objectives, 18
    opportunities, 12, 89, 126
    Opportunity Team, 28
    transfer agents, 79
businesses, new, 89–96
business expansion
    funds, 223–4
    scheme, 208
business plan(ning), 11, 92
    accountants and your, 199–200
    check list for, 196–8
    Initiative, 18, 200, 240
buy-outs, *see* management buy-outs

334

New Zealand, 318
Norway, 320
South Africa, 318
Spain, 320
Sweden, 320
Switzerland, 321
United States of America, 318, 321
stock(s)
  control, 21
  reduce, 18
Stock Exchange, 208
  regional offices of, 242
Stoy Hayward, 147, 245
strategy(ies), competitive, 18
Stubbs Name Matching Service, 161
Surveyors, Royal Institute of Chartered,
  262
  see also architects

T
Task Force, 26
  list of areas of operation, 27
tax, 249, 251–2, 272
  Schedule 'D', 272
  Schedule 'E', 272
  Tax Payers Society, 274
Teaching Company Scheme, 19
technical
  advice, 21
  Indexes Ltd, 152
  Translations International Ltd, 188
technologist(s), 12
technology(ies)
  Appraisal Project, 141
  Exchange Ltd, 141–2
  exploiting high and not so high, 127–52
  financial and advisory services for, 136–
    43
  Greater London Enterprise, 137
  new, 12
  regional centres, 19
Third Market, 208
3i Ventures, 137
  see also Investors in Industry
tourism, 23, 92
tourist boards, 32
trade
  association(s), 150
  credit, 204
Trade Associations, Directory of, 86
Trade Descriptions Act, 264
trade fairs, national, 23
trade marks, 255–6, 258
  Institute of Trade Mark Agents, 257
  Register of, 257
trading laws, 263–6
training, 21
  books and journals, 306–7
  books on specific trades, 307–9

courses on offer, types, 279
directory of courses, 283–301
distance learning, 303–5
for business overseas, 318–21
National Training Index, 309
other small business courses, 302–3
where to find a course, 281
  see also British Coal Enterprise, British
    Steel (Industry) Ltd, Enterprise
    Agencies, Local Enterprise
    Development Unit, Rural
    Development Commission, Scottish
    Development Agency, URBED,
    Welsh Development Agency
Transmission Systems Ltd, 142
Transport, Rural Development Advisers,
  23

U
Unfair Contract Terms Act, 264
Union of Independent Companies, 86
university(ies), 19
  see also pages 281–301
Unlisted Securities Market (USM), 208
Unsolicited Goods and Services Act, 264
Urban Development Corporations, 82
Urban Programme, 17
URBED (Urban and Economic
    Development) Ltd, 32–3, 79

V
Value Added Tax (VAT), 12, 249, 273
venture capital, 208, 225
  British Association, 240
  directory of institutions, 227–34
village shop(s), advice on buying, 23

W
Wales
  Development Agency, 35
  enterprise agencies, 62–3
  small business courses, 300–1
Warwick Business Information Services,
  177
Weights and Measures Acts, 264
Welsh Development Agency (WDA), 35
women
  in Enterprise, 87
  Into Business, 87
Workshops
  establishment of, 32
  managed, 29, 30, 31

Y
Young Entrepreneurs Fund, 314
Youth Business Initiative, 314
youth opportunities for self-employment,
  311–14